Object-Oriented Programming

Object-Oriented Programming

Peter Coad and Jill Nicola

YOURDON PRESS
P T R Prentice Hall Building
Englewood Cliffs, New Jersey 07632

Library of Congress Cataloging-in-Publication Data

Coad, Peter.
  Object-oriented programming/Peter Coad and Jill Nicola.
     p. cm.–(Yourdon Press computing series)
  Includes bibliographical references and index.
  ISBN 0-13-032616-X
  1. Object-oriented programming. I. Nicola, Jill. II. Title.
  III. Series.
  QA76.64.C62 1993   92-33278
  005.1'1–dc20   CIP

Editorial/production supervision: HARRIET TELLEM
Buyer: MARY E. McCARTNEY
Acquisitions editor: PAUL W. BECKER
Editorial assistant: NOREEN REGINA
Photos by: DON ROGERS PHOTOGRAPHY—Austin, Texas USA
The OOA and OOD models in this book were produced using ObjecTool™ from
Object International.

Published by P T R Prentice Hall
Prentice-Hall, Inc.
A Paramount Communications Company
Englewood Cliffs, New Jersey 07632

The publisher offers discounts on this book when ordered in bulk quantities. For more
information, contact:

Corporate Sales Department
PTR Prentice Hall
Englewood Cliffs, NJ 07632

Phone: 201-592-2863
Fax: 201-592-2249

ISBN 0-13-032616-X

Prentice-Hall International (UK) Limited, *London*
Prentice-Hall of Australia Pty. Limited, *Sydney*
Prentice-Hall Canada Inc., *Toronto*
Prentice-Hall Hispanoamerica, S.A., *Mexico*
Prentice-Hall of India Private Limited, *New Delhi*
Prentice-Hall of Japan, Inc., *Tokyo*
Simon & Schuster Asia Pte. Ltd., *Singapore*
Editora Prentice-Hall do Brasil, Ltda., *Rio de Janeiro*

Dedication

By Peter Coad:

To Benjamin Peter Coad,
My brilliant, talented, and tenderhearted one.
I love you.
Dad

By Jill Nicola:

To Mom and Dad.
You listen, you love, you care.
Thank you, my dear friends.

Contents

Preface

A Revolution

OOP—Object-Oriented Programming—is a revolutionary change in programming. Without a doubt, OOP is the most significant single change that has occurred in the software field.

It's more significant than the change from machine language to assembly language. It's more important than the move from assembly language to procedural language. And more valuable than the move from procedural language to package-oriented languages.

Why?

OOP enables programmers to write software that is organized like the problem domain under consideration.

The impact?

Uniformity. With OOP, developers apply one underlying representation from analysis to design to the code itself.

Understandability. With OOP, the code can be organized in classes that correspond to the business domain.

Flexibility. OOP, when applied as part of a uniform underlying representation for software development, is the enabling technology for concurrent development (and this means deliverance at long last from the fallacy of waterfalls and phased development, even on large projects).

Stability. The underlying problem domain is what remains most stable over time (not just functions, not just data). OOP makes it possible to organize code based on that stability.

Reusability. Reuse is so sorely needed. OOP is the enabling technology for reuse. How? By increased understandability so that a reusable component might be considered for reuse. And by inheritance, so that something that is reusable might actually get reused.

A Comprehensive Approach

Most programming books are books on syntax and fairly boring examples (one can get just so excited about another round of stacks, queues, and linked lists).

An object-oriented programming book with just syntax lessons and perhaps a few words about object-oriented design is of little value. Why? Because object-oriented programming is much more than just applying some new language syntax.

An object-oriented programming book—if it is to communicate meaningfully, effectively, and powerfully—*must* help you learn a number of essential strategies and skills.

This OOP book will help you to:

Learn how to "object think." Rather than rely on trial and error, you'll learn how to think effectively with objects. You'll apply OOA and OOD to help you architect a more effective solution for construction with OOP.

Learn with engaging, provocative examples. Rather than use hundreds of terse, isolated code fragments, you'll experience a graduated series of four engaging and extensive examples. At the end of each major example, you'll run the application; this will give you frequent, tangible, working results—along with a sense of accomplishment, satisfaction, and closure.

Learn with examples that show what really happens. Rather than read an idealized solution (often the solution that an author wished he or she could have come up with the first time), you'll get to follow along with the initial steps, false starts, evolving solution, and some surprise observations.

Learn a holistic approach to reuse. Reuse is a fully integrated facet of OOA, OOD, and OOP. You'll reuse and build for reuse all along the way.

Do it—hands on, hands on, hands on. Rather than just read about object-oriented programming, you can learn, hands on. The book includes complete source code on diskette.

Learn both C++ and Smalltalk, with major examples worked out in parallel. The two leading object-oriented programming languages are C++ and Smalltalk. You'll learn how to "object think" and express yourself in both languages. If you already are familiar with one of these languages, then these parallel examples will help you to rapidly learn the other. And, should the need arise, you'll be able to apply what you learn to other object-oriented programming languages (for example, Eiffel, Objective-C, Oberon, or CLOS).

Key Topics

This book, *Object-Oriented Programming*, is the first book of its kind to include all of these much needed features.

Four comprehensive examples. Chapters 1 to 4 present four major examples:

- The Count
- Vending Machine
- Sales, Sales, Sales
- Go with the Flow

You'll apply OOA, OOD, and OOP, learning effective "object think" and vital language syntax along the way.

And more. Appendix A presents concise language summaries for Smalltalk and C++. Appendix B is a concise summary of OOA and OOD notation. And Appendix C presents the memorable and practical principles applied throughout the book.

The Intended Audience and Some Prerequisites

The book is written for software engineering and data processing professionals with experience in one or more programming languages.

Programmers will read it to learn how to become really effective in an OOPL. Designers will read it for insights on better design architectures and how such things as GUI libraries can be used most effectively. Analysts will read it to see firsthand how OOA results fit right in the midst of the OOD results, and how the OOA and OOD classes are directly implemented as classes in OOP.

More and more, team members work together through OOA, OOD, and OOP. Each member has a primary expertise—analyst, designer, programmer. And all members work together in all three areas. A singular, uniform, underlying representation makes this possible. And this book shows how.

The book assumes no prior knowledge of Smalltalk or C++.

But to understand the C++ examples, you'll need a reading knowledge of C. If you are not yet familiar with C, we suggest that you skip the C++ examples on your first reading of this book. You'll still benefit greatly from the OOA, OOD, and Smalltalk examples. Then you might want to find a short primer on C++, written for someone with no background in C, study its examples, and then come back and explore the C++ sections.

Why C++ and Smalltalk?

There are many different OOPLs. Currently, the most widely used ones are C++ and Smalltalk. Others include Objective-C, Eiffel, Actor, and CLOS.

Through practical experience and observation, we've seen that once a person learns how to express "object think" in one OOPL, he is ready to do the same with others. At that point, it's mostly a shift in syntax.

So the key in choosing a first OOPL has more to do with how well it forces you, or at least prods you along, to think in terms of objects.

It is our opinion, in teaching "object think," that the superior vehicle for this first-time exposure is Smalltalk (or its close derivatives, Objective-C and Actor).

There are variations within each OOPL product, notably in each class library and environment.

This book uses Objectworks for its Smalltalk examples. We chose Objectworks because of its well-partitioned and loosely coupled approach to human interaction. This separation of concerns is essential for increasing the likelihood of reuse.

There is no standard for Smalltalk syntax or its core classes. So there are some variations from one Smalltalk product to the next. However, the majority of the lessons in this book apply to other dialects of Smalltalk, too (notably Digitalk's Smalltalk/V).

This book uses Borland C++ for its C++ examples. Since C++ is a standardized language, the C++ code applies to other C++ products as well, including those from AT&T/USL, Centerline, Microsoft, and Symantec.

This Book—the Third in a Series

Object-Oriented Programming is the third book in a series on object-oriented development.

The first book, *Object-Oriented Analysis*, second edition (by Peter Coad and Edward Yourdon), presents how to architect an effective object-oriented model within a particular business domain.

The second book, *Object-Oriented Design* (also by Peter Coad and Edward Yourdon), presents how to architect an effective design, including human interaction, task management, and data management.

This book, *Object-Oriented Programming*, presents how to "object think" and program with the two leading object-oriented programming languages—C++ and Smalltalk.

Each book in the series is designed to stand on its own. You can read them in any particular order. In teaching and consulting, we most often teach OOA, then OOD, establishing effective mental models; then OOP, how to express "object think" within the leading languages.

The Diskette That Comes with This Book

The diskette that comes with this book contains complete C++ and Smalltalk source code for all four major examples.

It's formatted for PCs.

For Mac and Unix, just use the utility software on your machine to read the diskette. And you're ready to go. It's that simple.

Multisensory Engagement Is a Must!

Your active, multisensory engagement is a must for gaining effective "object think" skills.

Multisensory engagement means much more than just casually reading this book on a Sunday afternoon. Reading is a start. But it won't be enough to get you to flip into effective "object think."

Please, dear reader, do more.

At a minimum, use an index card or an opaque ruler to pace your eyes while you read. When you come up to a model or some code, keep it covered. And work it out for yourself!

Get more involved. Work out the models with paper and pencil. Stand up and act out the scenarios. Really!

When you get to the code, you need to work it out. How could you expect to learn a programming language and way of thinking by any other means?

Begin by loading in the files from diskette. Then browse the code, spending some time just "reading the literature."

Then write some pieces yourself. Make some changes. Explore. Play. Get fully engaged. And learn.

The end result: accelerated mastery of "object think."

Enjoy!

On-Going Support

Peter writes a continuing series of special reports called The Coad Letter™. As a reader of this book, you can get a free subscription.

Also, you may want to get a copy of The Object Game™, a great way to help others get started with "object think" right away. It includes a video, game boards, game pieces, whistles, and game ball!

Just send in the attached reply card. Or call or write:

Object International, Inc.
7301 Burnet Road, Suite 102-259
Austin, TX 78757-1022 USA
1-800-OOA-2-OOP (1-800-662-2667)
1-512-795-0202 or fax 1-512-795-0332
object@acm.org

Peter Coad and Jill Nicola
Object International, Inc.
Austin, Texas USA

Acknowledgments

We especially thank these colleagues and friends for helping us make this book possible:

John Kolts at Object International, Inc... for sharing his ideas and technical savvy, working diligently with us on this book.

The book reviewers... for giving their time and talents toward making this a better book. This book is *far* better because of their advice. (Occasionally, we had to agree to disagree; a few of the footnotes document such matters. As authors, we take full responsibility for the final results.) We sincerely thank:

Adele Goldberg and *Glenn Krasner* at ParcPlace Systems

Bjarne Stroustrup and *Peter Juhl* at AT&T Bell Telephone Laboratories

Mark Mayfield and *Teri Roberts* at Object International

Martin Rösch at Rösch Consulting

Ben Stivers and *Scott Pruitt* at Harris Data

Mats Weidmar at Enea Data

The OOP training event partcipants... for allowing us the privilege of working and leaning together

The team at Prentice Hall... for encouraging us and doing superb work. We especially thank *Paul Becker* and *Harriet Tellem*.

The team at Morgan-Cain & Associates... and especially *Karen Comstock,* for skillfully preparing our work for publication.

And finally, thanks to *Dale Carmichael* at Hill Elementary School... for teaching us to introduce each concept "just in time"—right at the moment one can apply it successfully.

So much to be thankful for!

Peter Coad and Jill Nicola
Object International, Inc.
Austin, Texas USA

Introduction

This book will help you to effectively "object think" through a series of four comprehensive examples.

These examples will help you to gradually and gently flip your system-building mind-set into an object-oriented perspective.

The book won't jump up and say, "Here it is. Think about this way. It's the obvious choice." Instead, it will lead you through a discovery process, so you can feel the thrills of making your own discoveries.

In fact—and be warned!—not every path this book follows leads directly to object nirvana. This is intentional. Just keep reading. Every path does have its purpose. And, at times, the book will explore false paths with you so that you can experience firsthand the "aha" sensation, the amazing elegance, of a properly conceived object-oriented architecture. This experience is vital to embracing, with thorough understanding, effective "object think" principles.

There is a destination. And you'll get there, example by example. It all begins with a very simple first example. Even with such a simple example, you'll get to explore different paths along the way.

Don't let the simplicity of an example fool you. You need to think carefully, each step of the way.

With each example, you'll begin with an OOA model. You'll make OOD additions along the way. From those results, you'll plan and begin constructing Smalltalk and C++ applications. And then you'll continue with more OOA, OOD, and OOP—until you complete the applications.

By doing this, you'll go through the discovery process of developing your object-oriented architecture in a flexible medium—one you can use to "talk it through" with problem domain experts—before the expense, effort, and emotional commitment of writing code. Even on simple problems, you'll see that such up-front concise thinking and accurate conceptualizing is at the very core of effective object-oriented development, and for all reuse, be it OOA, OOD, or OOP.

Each example comes from everyday life. This is by design. First, examples should be interesting—and fun (this means no stack and queue examples, please). Second, such examples are ones in which you already have some domain expertise (this means no lengthy problem definition statements). Third, such examples are ones that, when you see them in real life, will remind you of the corresponding "object think" lessons in this book!

Let the games begin!

1

The Count

In this chapter, you'll experience:

OOA and OOD
- Applying practical OOA and OOD notations and strategies
- Planning and doing concurrent development
- Thinking about what an object knows and does—in the first person
- Fitting an OOD with available class libraries
- Architecting for reuse
- Applying the model-view pattern

OOP (Smalltalk)
- Adding a class
- Implementing generalization-specialization with superclass-subclass
- Implementing attributes with instance variables
- Implementing services with methods
- Defining methods
- Sending messages
- Creating objects
- Working with human interaction classes: button and text view
- Applying the broadcast mechanism between model and view classes
- Building a display box class
- Building and reusing a container class

OOP (C++)
- Declaring a class
- Defining member functions
- Implementing generalization-specialization with base class and derived class
- Implementing attributes with data members
- Implementing services with member functions

- Controlling access: public, protected, private
- Using templates
- Creating objects
- Outputting to the console using the insertion operator
- Applying platform-independent human interaction
- Building components for console interaction
- Building a container class
- Using templates to architect reusable human interaction classes
- Using a standard library class: date

You'll learn and apply these techniques right when you need them to solve real problems. Get ready for some fun!

GETTING STARTED WITH SOME OOA

Here's what the counter customer (one from a counter culture...) has to say:

> Dear System Builder,
>
> I love to count. Build me a system to help me with that counting.
>
> I want to know how much I've counted. And I want to increment and decrement the counter.
>
> I had a bright red plastic counter when I was growing up. It looked something like this:

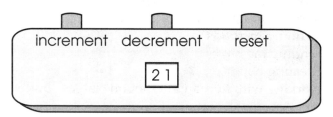

> It had an increment button, a decrement button, and, oh yes, a reset button. I could see the amount along the side of this little device.
>
> I love to count lots of things.
>
> Regards,
>
> The Count

Some OOA

So where should you begin?

Perhaps with a counter. It seems like it might be central to this problem domain.

So you could begin by building an OOA model[1] of a counter.

But before you start an OOA model, consider more carefully the name "counter" and its implications.

The principle that applies here is the "I'm alive!" principle:

> *The "I'm alive!" principle.* Objects can be better understood by thinking about them and talking about them in the first person—"I know my own _____ and I can _____ myself."

Consider these words. "I'm a counter. I know my own value. And I know what to do with that value—increment, decrement, reset. Tell me increment, decrement, or reset, and I'll do it."

But wait. Something is not right with these statements. They fail to pass the "read it again, Sam" principle.

> *The "read it again, Sam" principle.* Read your model aloud. Do your words make sense? Do they really? If what you say doesn't make sense, don't blame it on object-oriented thinking (a lame excuse, indeed!). Instead, revise the model to better reflect what you want them to say.

Read the preceding "first person" description of a counter. It doesn't quite ring true for the "I'm alive" principle. What's wrong?

A counter is something that works on a value. It works on a value. This implies that a counter itself is not an object, but rather a manager. So a more precise personification of counters is "I'm a value manager." Ugh! Barf!

This makes a counter a manager, and in "object think," managers are bad (apology extended to managers everywhere). Why? Because the "manager–managed one" pattern smacks of functional decomposition, which is not a principle for organizing classes and responsibilities effectively.

Not that behavior across a collection is bad; it's necessary in human organizations, too. But managers tend to do too much—more than just behavior across a collection—and grab onto work that is better encapsulated and done by a managed one.

This leads up to the "-er-er" principle:

---

[1]OOA establishes the problem domain classes. It specifies what each object in each class needs to know and do. And it specifies object interactions. All in one model.

OOA results fit right in the midst of OOD.

OOD adds design considerations to the OOA results. Mainly, OOD focuses on human interaction, data management, and task management classes. It includes additional detail on what each object in each class needs to know and do. And it specifies additional object interactions. All in one model.

The "-er-er" principle. Challenge any class name that ends in "-er." If it has no parts, change the name of the class to what each object is managing. If it has parts, put as much work in the parts that the parts know enough to do themselves.

Manager objects are just a part of intermediate object think.

The "amount of object think" principle.

Low	Functions—applying functional decomposition rather than an object-oriented partitioning across much of a system
Medium	Managers and data encapsulators—putting all the work in the manager, leaving its subordinates with very little to do
High	Objects at work—putting each action in the object that knows enough to directly carry it out

More advanced "object think" takes better advantage of the problem domain partitioning, using it to divide up the responsibilities of the system under consideration.

So what increments or decrements itself? A counter? Or a count? How about a count?

Better yet: say it in the first person. "I increment and decrement myself. Who am I?"

A count (Figure 1–1).

Figure 1–1: A count.

This symbol represents a class and one or more objects in that class.

Terminology

An *object* is a person, place, or thing. In object-oriented development, an object represents what a system needs to *know* and *do* about an actual person, place, or thing.

A *class* is a grouping of objects together, based on common characteristics. In object-oriented development, a class defines those things that each of its objects knows and does.

Notation

The symbol in the preceding figure is called a "class-&-object" symbol. It represents a class and one or more objects in that class. In

OOP, a class that may have corresponding objects is called a "concrete" class.

The heavy, inner rounded rectangle represents the class. The lighter, outer rounded rectangle represents one or more objects in that class.

In the models in this book, names that refer to classes begin with a capital letter; other names don't. Initial capital letters offset words within a name.

In this chapter, you'll learn OOA and OOD notation all along the way, right when you need it. (In addition, an appendix describes all the notation.)

Some principles behind effective notations

Effective object-oriented notations and strategies must be built on these guiding principles:

The "continuum of representation" principle. Use a single underlying representation, from problem domain to OOA to OOD to OOP.

The "one model" principle. Use a single model for classes, objects, and other constructs—across OOA, OOD, and OOP. (Multiple model approaches have floundered ever since first introduced in the 1970s.)

The "simplicity, brevity, and clarity" principle. OOA, OOD, and OOP notations and strategies find strength in simplicity, brevity, and clarity. What's needed is just enough notation (1) to communicate well and (2) to accelerate frequent, tangible results.

The comprehensive examples in this book show just how effective these OOA, OOD, and OOP notations and strategies really are.

Continue with count

"I can increment, decrement, and reset myself." A *service* describes something that an object does (Figure 1–2).

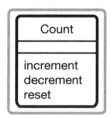

Figure 1–2: A count—"I do things."

"I know my value. And I know my reset value." An *attribute* represents something that an object knows (Figure 1–3).

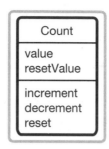

Figure 1–3: A count—"I know things and do things."

Note that simple "get value" and "set value" services are not normally shown in a model; every object with attribute values needs these basic services; and attribute constraints capture any special needs.

About the letters from The Count

You'll soon discover that this chapter contains more letters from "The Count." These letters teach an approach for thinking through the potential specializations of a single class, the count class. And this discipline is one that you can apply even in the very likely absence of such letters.

Step by step, these letters from The Count explore the potential specializations, working from ones that are simpler and easier understood to ones that are more and more complex. This is exactly the strategy to apply.

The principle illustrated by the "letters from The Count" is:

> *The "simpler specializations first" principle.* For a class, systematically explore potential specializations, from ones that are simpler and easier understood to ones that are more complex.

Each and every class that you define may be scrutinized in this fashion.

More OOA

So you're up to date with the latest demands from your client. But just then, you get another communique from your beloved client:

> Dear System Builder,
> I forgot to tell you.
> I also like to count in hexadecimal (base 16).
> Regards,
> The Count

So now what do you do?

You could just go ahead and add a specialization class (Figure 1–4). Why not?

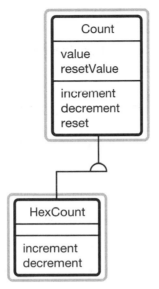

Figure 1–4: Adding a specialization class for hexadecimal counts.

More notation

Look at the line with semicircle, drawn between the classes (the heavy rounded rectangles). This notation represents generalization–specialization. It's called a *gen–spec structure.*

A gen–spec structure portrays one or more generalization classes and one or more specialization classes. Here, count is the generalization class and hex count is the specialization class.

You can check a generalization-specialization for reasonableness by applying the "is a kind of test." Here it is:

<specialization> is a kind of <generalization>

Here, a hex count is a kind of count. All is well.

A gen–spec structure indicates a class hierarchy. And inheritance. Here, hex count inherits the attributes and services from count. And it extends whatever is defined for increment and decrement.

Specialize count

Why not just go ahead and add a specialization? Because if the conceptualization is not sound, then this quick fix will come back to haunt you … as an obstacle in the system under consideration, and as an obstacle to future reuse, too.

But it can even get messier than that.

What if The Count wants to count in base 5? 24? 56? Must you specialize forever and ever?

The "perpetual employment" principle. Adding a class with endless specializations is not effective, but it can keep you perpetually employed.

When you find yourself creating abundant specializations, it's time to stop. Get quiet.

And play a game: what's the same? what's different?

What's the same?

> I'm a count.
>> I know my own value.
>> I know how to increment, decrement, and reset myself.

What's different? Ask this question in these three ways:

- How am I different in what I know? Such differences point to generalization–specialization.
- How am I different in what I do? Such differences also imply generalization–specialization.
- How am I different in how my values are presented? These differences are just an added presentation service; an additional specialization is not needed for this.

For hex counts versus other counts:

- What I know—no difference.
- What I do—no difference.
- How I present my values—this is the only difference!

Thus, you can simplify the OOA model as shown in Figure 1–5.

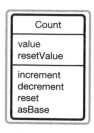

Figure 1–5: Using services (rather than abundant specializations) to express presentation differences.

What you just went through can be summarized in a principle. Here, you've used it to curb the number of specializations that you really need in the OOA model.

The "what's the same; what's different" principle. For two or more specialization classes, ask what's the same? what's different? For differences in presentation, use a service. For differences in attributes and services, apply generalization-specialization.

This same principle may be applied again. This time consider what's the same and what's different about counts. What's the same is the ability to increment, decrement, and reset, plus knowing a value and a reset value. What's different is that the ability to do "asBase" applies only to numbers. Hence, it's a service that applies only to objects of the number count and its potential specializations—integer count, real count, complex count.

Here, for simplicity's sake in this initial example, consider just count and integer count.

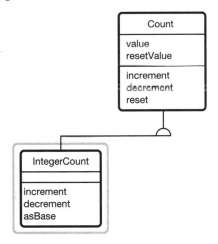

Figure 1–6: Adding the integer count class.

A bit more notation

In this OOA model, count is shown as a "class" symbol. It represents a class that has no objects; only its specializations (or their specializations) may have objects. In OOP, a class that has no objects is called an *abstract* class.

Continue with integer count

Here, the "asBase" service applies only to integer counts. So it appears in the specialization class, and not in the generalization class.

The count class defines two attributes (value and reset value) and one service (reset). However, it cannot specify the details of two other services (increment and decrement). What it can do is establish that its specialization classes, both now and in the future, must specify how to do the "increment" and "decrement" services. This establishes a convention that the specialization classes must adhere to.

The "do as I say, not as I do" principle. Use a generalization class to establish a convention that its specializations, both now and in the future, must follow, even when the generalization does no more than define the convention itself.

Following the convention defined in the generalization, the specialization "integer count" must define two services:

increment
value = value + 1
decrement
value = value - 1

A bit more OOA

Oh no. Not again.

Dear System Builder,
I forgot to tell you.
I also like to count in many bases, especially base 4, base 8, and base 16.
Regards,
The Count

What a relief. You beat him to the punch this time. No changes needed. No problems.

Putting Together a Plan

Plan? What plan? Why not just start cranking out the code? Code it up; it'll be right, because my people are good; just test it at the end.
Ugh!

The "don't touch the whiskey" principle. Don't rapidly respond to management's "WHISKEY" cry: "Why in the H— Isn't Someone 'Koding' Everything Yet?"

Take the time you need to architect

You do need to take the time—really take the time—to properly architect your system.

If you begin coding with the very first architecture that comes to mind, you'll waste a lot of time thrashing around in code.

And without a clear understanding of OOP principles, you'll be much more likely to end up with a hacked-up and brittle compromise. It's worth the time and effort to come up with a conceptually sound approach, better supporting future reuse.

The "no big bang" principle. Never, never, never write all the code at once. No big bang event will suddenly make it work correctly.

Planning and good politics

Apply these principles for better political (sociological) results:

The "good politics" principle. Implement capabilities beginning with the ones that are most valued by the client, followed by lesser capabilities, in descending order.

The "success breeds success" principle. Implement capabilities that are easier. Demonstrate success. Then build on that experience to help you with more challenging capabilities.

The "tiny step" principle. Choose a very tiny first step. Get it working. Then add more very tiny steps.

The "strut your stuff" principle. Implement a rudimentary version of the human interaction class(es) early, so others can appreciate what you are accomplishing.

Concurrent development—the "baseball" model

So far you've worked through some OOA.

You've not yet done any OOD.

But even with just some initial OOA results, you can accept those as a start at OOD classes. And go ahead and build them with OOP.

Why now? Why not just do all the OOA, all the OOD, and then all the OOP. And boldly proclaim "waterfall process forever."

Barf!

Why add that risk? Why wait to explore how it really works? Why wait to check out your core classes in minute detail? Why wait to verify your assumptions? Why wait so long before demonstrating even a modest tangible result (working software! not piles of paper).

Concurrent development is the way to go.

Consider the following three principles:

The "concurrent development" principle. Apply a concurrent activity development process: with your team, concurrently apply OOA, OOD, and OOP. Why? To improve your understanding of what is needed. To reduce risk. To deliver frequent, tangible results. To get working products to the international marketplace sooner. (See Figure 1–7.)

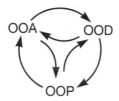

Figure 1–7: Concurrent development—the "baseball" model.

The "smaller is better" principle. Put together a small team of up to 12 participants. Include people with special ability—in problem domain knowledge, in OOA, in OOD (human interaction, task management, data management), and in OOP. With larger projects, put together a number of loosely coupled teams.

The "I do it all; I'm the best at ..." principle. As a team member, you may have special ability in the problem domain, in OOA, in OOD, or in OOP. Get busy doing what you do best. And contribute in each of the other areas, too.

If you can apply these principles in your organization, take bold, visible action. But if political pressures make this a hard thing to do, take quiet action anyway. You and your clients need the benefits.

In light of these principles, do some planning for the upcoming Smalltalk and C++ construction.

But how do you proceed?

OOD consists of four major components:

- *The problem domain component.* OOA results fit right here and are extended during OOD.
- *The human interaction component.* OOD classes for supporting human interaction go here.
- *The data management component.* OOD classes for supporting data management go here.
- *The task management component.* OOD classes for supporting task management go here.

Even as a team with just one team member, you can still apply the concurrent development principle, using something like this:

> Do some OOA.
>> Move those classes into the problem domain component.
>
> Do some OOD: problem domain component design.
>> Add design attributes, services, and classes that are needed to practically implement the OOA results.

Do some OOP: build it.
Do some OOD: human interaction design.
Do some OOP: build it.
Do some OOD: task management design.
Do some OOP: build it.
Do some OOD: data management design.
Do some OOP: build it.

Repeat OOA, OOD, and OOP as needed, again and again.

For this first pass, with the OOA for count and integer count, bring those classes into the problem domain component. Add the design detail. Program the classes. And then run and demonstrate that the code works.

Then add the classes and interaction mechanisms for human interaction.

For later passes, add one specialization class each time, gradually building from simpler specializations to more complex ones. And take that class from OOA to the problem domain component to code, and then its human interaction component to code. (Chapter 3 takes an example through the data management component, too.)

OOP—PROBLEM DOMAIN COMPONENT: SMALLTALK

Some Notes

Which Smalltalk?

At present, Smalltalk lacks a language standard and a class library standard. So there are some differences among various Smalltalk products.

Perhaps the biggest difference is the support for human–computer interaction. Smalltalk products use different overall architectures to support human–computer interaction. It's helpful if it supports keeping the problem domain classes and the human–computer interaction classes distinct and loosely coupled.

This book uses Objectworks\Smalltalk.

Yet you can apply the lessons from this book, and much of the Smalltalk code, within any Smalltalk product.

Terminology

Smalltalk uses "superclasses" and "subclasses" to implement generalization classes and specialization classes.

Smalltalk uses "variables" and "methods" to implement attributes and services.

Also note: by convention, names that refer to classes or categories of classes begin with a capital letter; other names don't. And initial capital letters offset words within a name.

The Count Class

You want to define a Smalltalk class for count. Where do you begin?

Smalltalk comes with many predefined classes, ready for you to reuse. The classes are organized in one overall hierarchy. At the root of the hierarchy is a single class, called the object class (Figure 1–8).

Figure 1–8: The root class is called the "object" class.

In Smalltalk, one very important specialization of the root class is called the model class (Figure 1–9). All problem domain classes—the OOA results, further expanded during OOD—are specializations of this class.

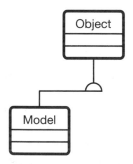

Figure 1–9: The model class is the root of all problem domain classes.

But why use a model class?

First, the model class provides a sharp distinction between classes that are from a problem domain and those classes that support human interaction, task management, and data management. The impact? Increased reuse. Why? Because the problem domain classes will apply again and again in future systems, no matter what choices you make next time for human interaction, task management, or data management. The model class is an important key to reuse in the large, across OOA results, OOD results, and code.

Second, the model class defines a broadcasting mechanism that all its specializations inherit.[2] The impact? The model classes remain loosely coupled with the other classes needed during design. And that means that alternative design choices can be made—both now and in the future—and plugged into the system without reworking all the problem domain classes.

"Count" is a problem domain class. And it's not a specialization of some other problem domain class. So make it a direct specialization of the model class (Figure 1–10).

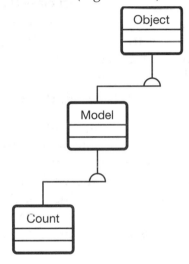

Figure 1–10: Define the count class as a specialization of the model class.

In addition to organizing classes in a single overall hierarchy, Smalltalk provides a class category mechanism, so that classes can be grouped according to a common class category or purpose, regardless of where those classes might appear in the hierarchy.

Add this class to the Smalltalk hierarchy. And place it in an overall class category, one for classes in this problem domain.

(The point-and-click steps for doing this are included with the documentation that comes with Smalltalk.)

---

[2]Actually, the root ("object") class defines a more general broadcasting mechanism that all of its specializations—including model—inherit. The model class specializes this capability, adding additional dependency mechanisms.

Add a class and its instance variables

You'll see this class template:

```
NameOfSuperclass subclass: #NameOfClass
    instanceVariableNames: 'instVarName1 instVarName2'
    classVariableNames: 'ClassVarName1 ClassVarName2'
    poolDictionaries: ''
    category: 'Counts'
```

It's time to fill the template in. Work it out, line-by-line.

```
NameOfSuperclass subclass: #NameOfClass
```

Smalltalk uses the terms superclass–subclass rather than generalization class–specialization class.

The underlying principle is still generalization–specialization.

Without that principle, calamity results. Novice programmers see a single variable like altitude for the class mountain. And they want to reuse it. So they subclass from mountain down to aircraft. That may save a line or two of code, but who is going to understand it? Or extend it during reuse? Ugh!

Other novice programmers see a couple of common lines of code, and then leap to factor out that code into a new superclass. That saves a few lines of code, but how likely is that factoring going to apply when the code needs to be reused? And who will really understand the name of the class with the "factored out" code?

Many inheritance pitfalls melt away, once you insist upon thinking about superclass–subclass as generalization class–specialization class.

Generalization–specialization produces more understandable class hierarchies. It also produces class hierarchies that are more stable over time.

Define count as a specialization of model:

```
Model subclass: #Count
```

An attribute is implemented as an *instance variable* (or at times, several instance variables) in Smalltalk. Instance variables are what an object knows.

In this example, the count class needs two instance variables. Put them into the template.

```
Model subclass: #Count
    instanceVariableNames: 'value resetValue'
```

Smalltalk also uses *class variables*. The values of class variables are shared by all objects in a class. Abundant global variables for use within a class? No way. That's no way to "object think." The same holds for pool dictionaries.[3]

And so the filled-in template for count looks like this:

```
Model subclass: #Count
    instanceVariableNames: 'value resetValue'
    classVariableNames: ''
    poolDictionaries: ''
    category: 'Counts'
```

Add this count class to the class library.

About methods

OOA and OOD services are defined in Smalltalk with some number of methods. Methods are what each object does.

A method is a member function defined within a class. Methods determine how an object responds to a message. When you send an object a message, it looks for a method with the same name. It executes that method and returns the result from the method to the message sender.

About method categories

In Smalltalk, methods are grouped together into functional groupings, called *method categories* or *protocols*.

The most common method categories for *class* methods are the following:

- *class initialization*
  methods to initialize class variables or create special objects in this class
- *demo*
  methods that demonstrate the capabilities defined for the objects in this class
- *instance creation*
  create a new object and return it to the sender

The most common method categories for *instance* methods are the following:

---

[3]There are limited occasions where a class variable may be useful. You'll see just one used in this book—in Chapter 3.

- *accessing*
  set or retrieve one of my attributes, held by an instance variable
- *adding*
  add an object to me (I'm a collection)
- *comparing*
  compare myself with an object that is an argument in the message I've just received
- *connecting*
  set or retrieve one of my connections to another object, held by an instance variable
- *converting*
  transform myself into an object of another class
- *copying*
  make a copy of myself
- *displaying*
  display myself on a displayable medium
- *enumerating*
  perform an element-by-element operation on my elements
- *error handling*
  raise an exception
- *initialize-release*
  initialize myself or release one of my dependency connections
- *menu messages*
  perform a menu operation
- *printing*
  provide a printable representation of myself
- *private*
  methods that are visible only to objects of this class
- *testing*
  apply a test to myself and return a Boolean object

In published form, methods like:

```
value
    "Return my value."

    ^ value
```

often are preceded by the class name and method category:

```
Count methodsFor: 'accessing'
```

```
value
    "Return my value."

    ^ value
```

The first line adds some information that is maintained by the environment itself. Such a first line is included for convenient reading; it's not part of the actual method code.

Add accessing methods

Every object of the count class has its own values for the instance variables. Only an object can read and assign values for its own instance variables.

If you want to allow other objects to read or assign values to these instance variables, then you need to include *access methods*. Most Smalltalk classes include access methods.

Add an accessing method category (protocol).

Add an accessing method to "get" the count's value.

```
Count methodsFor: 'accessing'
```

```
value
    "Return my value."

    ^ value
```

In Smalltalk, a pair of double quotes marks off a comment.

Use comments to guide future readers (including yourself) through the code. *Far* more important than comments is *readable code*.

With an OOPL, you get far more syntax for capturing problem domain semantics. But it's up to you to choose names and use the syntax effectively.

Write readable code. Make the code itself read like a story. Let the code itself more fully document the system.

Now consider the statement:

```
    ^ value
```

The caret (^) marks a return point from a method. The object that follows the caret is returned to the sender.

Next, go ahead and tell the environment to accept the method.

Most "get" methods have a companion "set" method. The "set" method sets the value of an instance variable to the value of the parameter passed to the method.

```
Count methodsFor: 'accessing'
```

value: aValue
   "Set my value to aValue."

   value := aValue

The colon ":" in the method name "value:" indicates that something else follows—a parameter.

The ":=" is read as "gets" (or "gets assigned the result of" or "holds").

The ":=" *must* be preceded by a space.

Also, note that no return value is specified in this method definition. When this happens, the object itself—the one which is executing the method—is returned.

Next, add methods to get and set the instance variable, "resetValue."

```
Count methodsFor: 'accessing'
```

resetValue
   "Return my resetValue."

   ^ resetValue

resetValue: aValue
   "Set my resetValue to aValue."

   resetValue := aValue

Most often, go ahead and define both the "get" and "set" accessors for each instance variable. And this is customary Smalltalk style. The only time you wouldn't do this is when you want to limit access to an instance variable.

Add counting methods

Now you are ready to add methods for the count's services—increment, decrement, reset.

```
Count methodsFor: 'counting'
```

increment
   "Increment my value.
   Subclasses must implement this."

decrement
   "Decrement my value.
   Subclasses must implement this."

reset
```
    "Restore my value to its original state."

    value := resetValue
```

Congratulations! You defined your first class in Smalltalk.

Look at those three methods for counting.

Increment and decrement *are not* defined here. Why? Because "increment" and "decrement" vary for each kind of count, for each subclass (specialization class).[4]

Reset *is* defined here. Why? Because its algorithm applies to the generalization and to all potential specializations.

Whenever a class has one or more methods that are undefined, it is an abstract class (a class that won't have corresponding objects). Normally, an abstract class does not have objects; you have to look to its specialization classes and find concrete classes, those that have objects.

However, even though it is an abstract class, in Smalltalk you can check it out by creating an object with the following statements:

```
    | aCount |
    aCount := Count new.
    aCount value: 12
```

Try it out. Select the statements. Evaluate it.

You should see this:

aCount

meaning, it's an object of the count class.[5]

Congratulations! You created your first object in Smalltalk.

Take a look at the code.

Begin with:

```
    | aCount |
```

Vertical bars mark out *temporary* (local) *variable(s)*. Most temporary variables are normally defined at the beginning of a method.

By convention, a temporary variable begins with a lowercase letter.[6]

Next, consider the statements

---

[4]A later chapter explains a way to write such requirements on a subclass (specialization class) into the code itself.

[5]Later, you may want to use an inspector to check it out in detail.

[6]By convention, names with local scope begin with a lowercase letter; names with global scope begin with an uppercase letter.

```
aCount := Count new.
aCount value: 12
```

In Smalltalk, statements usually follow this format:

```
<object or class> <message>⁷
```

An assignment statement follows this format:

```
<variable> := <object or class> <message>
```

The statement:

```
aCount := Count new
```

is read aloud as

```
"aCount gets Count new."
```

The message "new" is sent to the count class, to create a new object in the class. A class knows how to create new objects in that class. Each class inherits this behavior from the root class (called the object class).

The inherited "new" method knows how to create a new object, but it does not know how to initialize a new object.

In this example, here is what happens:

> The message "new" is sent to the count class.
>
> The count class returns an object.
>
> And aCount is the variable that holds (points to) that new object.

You can read this statement

```
aCount value: 12
```

aloud as

```
"aCount value colon 12"
```

or, when reading code rapidly to a colleague, you might read it aloud just as

```
"aCount value 12"
```

Here is what happens:

> "I'm an object, held by a variable called 'aCount.'"
>> "Someone sends me the message "value: 12."
>>
>> "I do the work."
>>
>> "I return the result to the sender."

⁷ In Smalltalk, a class is also an object. So this could be written just as `<object>` `<message>`.

The period at the end of each statement is a statement separator, not a statement terminator.

And so

```
| aCount |
aCount := Count new
```

needs no period at the end of the one statement. And that's why the first statement in

```
| aCount |
aCount := Count new.
aCount value: 12
```

needs a period, in order to separate the two statements.

The Integer Count Class

Before reading ahead, go off on your own and define the integer count class. Here are a few tips:

1. Integer count inherits (from count) the instance variable "value." Don't define another one.
2. Integer count inherits (from count) the methods "increment," "decrement," and "reset." Don't name the method in the subclass unless its needs to define, extend, or otherwise change an inherited method.
3. Use standard method categories. When you need other categories, be consistent with whatever message categories are used by its superclasses (generalization classes).

Go do it!

Here's the first pass for integer count:

Add a class and its instance variables

```
Count subclass: #IntegerCount
   instanceVariableNames: ''
   classVariableNames: ''
   poolDictionaries: ''
   category: 'Counts'
```

Add counting methods

```
IntegerCount methodsFor: 'counting'
```

decrement
```
   "Decrement myself."

   value := value - 1
```

```
increment
   "Increment myself."

   value := value + 1
```

Add converting methods

IntegerCount methodsFor: 'converting'

asBase: aBase
```
   "Return a string representing my value
   in the number base, aBase."

   ^value printStringRadix: aBase
```

Run the code

Congratulations! You defined your first concrete class (a class that may have corresponding objects) in Smalltalk.

So what are you waiting for? Try it out.

```
| aCount |
aCount := IntegerCount new.
aCount increment
```

Oh-oh. Something happened. A window popped up to report a problem. For now, just close that window.

Your increment method didn't work. How come? Consider the increment method.

```
increment
   "Increment myself."

   value := value + 1
```

What if "value" is not a number? Hmm. What happens then? The code breaks!

In Smalltalk, uninitialized variables contain the value "nil," which simply means that the variable is undefined.

It's good practice to extend the inherited "new" method so that it not only creates a new object, but also tells that object to initialize itself. And that's exactly what is needed here.

Adding More to the Count and Integer Count Classes

Add object creation

A class knows how to create new objects in that class.

Each class inherits this behavior from the root class (called the object class).

The inherited "new" method knows how to create a new object, but it does not know the particulars of how to initialize a new object.

Each class should have a method to extend the "new" method to satisfy its own initialization needs.

What should the integer count's specialized "new" method do? Simply this:

> Create a new object in the class (an inherited capability).
>
> Initialize a new integer count's value (an extended capability).

The "new" method is a class method (in contrast with most methods, which are instance methods).

Add this class method:

```
Count class methodsFor: 'instance-creation'

new
    "Create a new one of me and initialize it."

    | aCount |
    aCount := super new.
    aCount initialize.
    ^aCount
```

The first statement:

```
aCount := super new.
```

uses a special Smalltalk variable, called "super." This is one of two special Smalltalk variables. The other one is the "self" variable.

What purpose do "super" and "self" serve?

The "self" variable holds the object under consideration. Using "self," an object can send a message to itself.

When "super" is used instead of "self," an object executes its inherited method rather than its own extension of that method.

So the first statement

```
aCount := super new.
```

means execute my inherited method for "new."

The second statement:

```
aCount initialize.
```

tells the new object to initialize itself.

And the third statement:

```
^aCount
```

tells it to return itself to the sender.

A more compact way to write this method is:

```
new
    "Create a new one of me and initialize it."

    ^(super new) initialize
```

and is most often just written as

```
new
    "Create a new one of me and initialize it."

    ^super new initialize
```

Notice that statements are evaluated from left to right, with precedence given to that which is in parentheses.

But wait! Now integer count needs an initialize method.

But there is no "initialize" method yet. The "initialize" message is sent to the new count object. An instance method called "initialize" is needed.

Add initialization

Add an initialize method to both count and integer count; put it in the *instance* method category "initialize–release."

```
Count methodsFor: 'initialize-release'

initialize
    "Initialize my value to the reset value."

    self reset

IntegerCount methodsFor: 'initialize-release'

initialize
    resetValue := 0.
    super initialize
```

Run the Code

You can write directly to the system transcript window by sending it a "show:" message with a string argument. For example:

```
Transcript show: 'Releasing item:   '
```

The message "cr" adds a carriage return.

```
Transcript cr.
Transcript show: 'Releasing item:   '
```

Here's how to show a number.

```
Transcript show: (15 printString)
```

The expression:

```
(15 printString)
```

returns a string. Every object in Smalltalk understands the message "printString" and responds by returning a string describing itself. In this case, the number 15 gets the message, does its work, and returns a string.

Now test your integer count, using the transcript window.

```
| aCount |
aCount := IntegerCount new.
aCount value: 10.
Transcript cr.
Transcript show: 'Current value:  '.
Transcript show: aCount value printString.

aCount increment.
aCount increment.
Transcript cr.
Transcript show: 'Current value:  '.
Transcript show: aCount value printString.

aCount decrement.
Transcript cr.
Transcript show: 'Current value:  '.
Transcript show: aCount value  printString.

aCount reset.
Transcript cr.
Transcript show: 'Current value:  '.
Transcript show: aCount value  printString.
```

This is what you'll see on the transcript window.

```
Current value:  10
Current value:  12
Current value:  11
Current value:  0
```

Way to go!

OOP—PROBLEM DOMAIN COMPONENT: C++

Some Notes

Which C++?

This book uses AT&T C++, version 3.0.

C++ is a standardized language. This book restricts itself to platform-independent human interaction, so its examples are vendor independent and platform independent.

You can compile and run the examples in this book with any C++ compiler that complies with AT&T C++, version 3.0.

The examples in this book were developed using Borland C++.

Terminology

C++ uses "base" classes and "derived" classes to implement generalization classes and specialization classes.

C++ uses "variables" (also called data members) to implement attributes.

C++ uses "member functions" to implement services.[8]

C++ uses the term "member" when describing both data members and member functions.

By convention (although it varies somewhat), class names begin with a capital letter; other names don't. And initial capital letters and underscores offset words in a class name; and underscores alone offset words in other names.

In C++, you first *declare* a class and then *define* the member functions for that class.

Next, consider accessibility.

Members are declared with specific accessibility—public, protected, private.

Any function can access a *public* member.

Only the member functions of the class and its derived classes can access a *protected* member.

Only member functions of the class can access a *private* member.

A derived class inherits all members, even those that are declared private.

Next, consider strong typing.

---

[8]Member functions are those functions that are defined within the scope of a class; ordinary functions are defined at file scope. A member function has full access privileges to all the members in the class it is in; an ordinary function may access just the public members of a class.

C++ is a strongly typed language.

Compilers for strongly typed languages check and demand that all initializations and assignment statements comply with the type rules at compile time.

And this is something that will affect how you declare variables, especially in a base class and its derived classes.

About templates

Consider count and integer count (Figure 1–11).

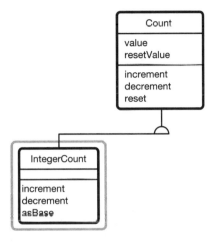

Figure 1–11: Count and integer count.

In C++, you must declare the type for each variable.

What is the type for the variable "value"? And what is the type for "reset value"?

In this example, the base class "count" includes a value and a reset value. These variables are place holders, without a specific type. Only a derived class knows what type really applies.

The solution? One solution is to only define such variables in the derived class(es). Then the base class won't need to declare a type for that variable. But taking this approach means that the code won't explicitly communicate what all of its specialization classes, both now and in the future, must define for itself; moreover, the generalization–specialization in a model won't get explicitly expressed in the code itself.

Before C++ version 3.0, that was the only choice.

With version 3.0, some new syntax came on the scene. Some syntax that addresses this very problem.

This new syntax is used to define a "template." A template allows you to indicate the types that you need for different objects of a class.

In a template, you can declare data members with the type "Some_Type." And you can declare member functions that return a value of type "Some_Type."

This added syntax captures more of the generalization–specialization in the code itself. And that makes it a significant improvement.

How to declare a class with a template

To declare "My_Class" as a base class, using a template, follow this pattern:

```
template<class Some_Type>
class My_Class {
public:

    // Constructors/destructors
    My_Class() { }
    ~My_Class() { }

    // Implementors
    virtual void my_member_function();

    // Accessors
    Some_Type member_function_without_a_specific_type_yet();

protected:

    // Data members
    Some_Type variable_without_a_specific_type_yet;

};
```

The public section consists of constructors–destructors, accessors, and member functions.

A constructor member function initializes objects; a constructor member function is called when an object is created. A destructor member function de-initializes an object; destructor member functions may be called explicitly (in a source code statement) or implicitly (whenever an object goes out of scope).

The implementors are the member functions that implement the OOA/OOD services.

The accessors are member functions that provide "get value" and "set value" access to private data members.

About pure virtual member functions

To declare a member function that must be defined in each derived class that is a concrete class (a class that may have objects), use this syntax:[9]

```
virtual void my_member_function() = 0;
```

A "virtual" member function is one that has dynamic binding. Dynamic binding is the ability to resolve function calls at run time. This means that the exact function call—the one needed by a particular object—finally is known at run time.[10]

"Void" indicates that no return value is expected from the function. (In effect, this makes the member function act like what Pascal and Ada call a procedure).

The syntax "= 0" indicates that every concrete derived class must define its own version of that member function. (A bit obscure, perhaps, but that *is* the syntax.) Virtual member functions initialized to zero are called "pure virtual member functions."

The syntax that makes a class an abstract class

A class is an abstract class when it has one or more pure virtual member functions. Otherwise, the class is a concrete class.

Declare the Count Class and the Integer Count Class

Declare the count class, using a template

Declare the count class, using a template:

```
template<class Count_Type>
class Count {
public:

    // Constructors/destructors
    Count() { }
    virtual ~Count() { }
```

---

[9]You could implement a service without using the virtual member function mechanism. And put in a comment that specializations must implement it. But it's better to put this in the code itself, rather than just in a comment.

[10]A "virtual" member function mechanism means dynamic binding. But even when a virtual member function is declared, if a compiler can determine the kind of object it is dealing with, then it will probably just go ahead and use static binding.

When you create a class with a virtual member function, you should make the destructor for that class virtual, too. You'll see why in a later chapter.

```
// Implementors
virtual void increment() = 0;
virtual void decrement() = 0;
void reset(){ value = reset_value; }

// Accessors
Count_Type get_value() { return value; }
void set_value(Count_Type new_value) { value =
        new_value; }

Count_Type get_reset_value() { return reset_value; }
void set_reset_value(Count_Type new_value) { value =
        new_value; }

protected:

// Data members
Count_Type value;
Count_Type reset_value;
};
```

Declare the integer count class, derived from another class

Now for an example of declaring a derived (specialization) class, derived from a class declared with a template:

```
class Integer_Count : public Count<int> {
public:

// Constructors/destructors
Integer_Count() { reset_value = 0; reset(); }
Integer_Count(int new_value)
    { reset_value = 0; value = new_value; }
~Integer_Count() { }

// Implementors
void increment();
void decrement();
char* asBase(int number_base);
};
```

Congratulations! You declared your first concrete class (a class that may have corresponding objects) in C++.[11]
The syntax:

```
class Integer_Count: public Count<int>
```

[11]Increment and decrement are better known in C++ as "++" and "--," respectively. With operator overloading, you can use "++" and "--" for counts, too. A subsequent chapter presents operator overloading.

declares the integer count class as a derived class of the count class, parameterized over the integer type. Integer count inherits all members from the parameterized count class.

The constructor and destructor member functions are the same as the class name and a "~" immediately preceding a class name, respectively.[12]

Here, the constructor and destructor member functions are defined "inline." The alternative? Declare them here and then define them separately, in a class definition.

Note that you can declare more than one constructor per class. And also note: you are allowed to declare only one destructor per class.

About inline member functions

When a member function is especially short, you might choose to declare it as an "inline" member function.[13] For inline member functions, the compiler will insert the inline code in each place that the member function is called; it saves a few microseconds by getting rid of the member function call; it adds a few more bytes to the compiled code.

Using an inline member function is a time versus size trade-off. There is no free ride. If the member function is going to be invoked many times, and time is more important than size, then you may choose to use an "inline" member function.

However, until you build some code and profile it, you really don't know whether such effort will pay any dividends at all. Rather than optimize everything in sight, you exercise better engineering judgment when you build some, measure it, and then optimize it to meet a measurable performance goal.

To define an inline member function, place the code for the member function in curly braces, immediately following the member function declaration. For example:

```
void set_value(int new_value) { value = new_value; }
```

The constructor and destructor member functions for integer count are also defined inline.

```
Integer_Count() { reset_value = 0; reset(); }
Integer_Count(int new_value){reset_value = 0;
   value = new_value; }
~Integer_Count() { }
```

---

[12]The "~," C's complement operator, is meant to suggest that a complement of a constructor is a destructor.

[13]If a compiler considers an inline member function to be too long or too complex, it will generate member function calls rather than inline code.

About creating and initializing an object

Suppose the count and integer count class definitions are in a file called "count.h." You can create a new integer count object in a number of ways. You can create a new object without even explicitly using a constructor. Just do this:

```
#include "count.h"

int main ()
{
    Integer_Count first_count;     // Create an integer count
                                   // object.

return 0;
}
```

Congratulations! You created your first object in C++.

Or you can create an integer count and initialize it by explicitly calling the constructor "integer count."

```
#include "count.h"

int main ()
{
    // Create an initialized integer count object with
    // default value = 0.
    Integer_Count first_count = Integer_Count();

    // Integer_Count first_count(); Whoops! This just
    // declares a member function.

return 0;
}
```

Or you can create an integer count and initialize it with some other value, using this constructor:

```
#include "count.h"

int main ()
{
    // Create an intialized integer count object with
    // default value = 4.
    Integer_Count first_count = Integer_Count(4);

    // The most common way
    Integer_Count second_count(4);

return 0;
}
```

Or you can create an integer count and then, in a separate statement, set its value using the "set value" accessor:

```
#include "count.h"

int main ()
{
   Integer_Count first_count;   // Create an integer count
                                // object.
   first_count.set_value(12);   // Set its value to 12.

return 0;
}
```

Define the Member Functions

This is how to define the member functions for integer count:

```
// Integer_Count member functions
void Integer_Count::increment()
{
   value++;
}

void Integer_Count::decrement()
{
   value--;
}

char* Integer_Count::asBase(int new_base)
{
   char answer_string[80];
   char partial_answer_string[80];
   char remainder_string[10];
   int quotient;
   int remainder;

   remainder = value % new_base;
   quotient = value / new_base;
   itoa(remainder, remainder_string, new_base);
   strcpy(answer_string, remainder_string);
   while (quotient != 0)
   {
      remainder = quotient % new_base;
      quotient = quotient / new_base;
      itoa(remainder, remainder_string, new_base);
      strcpy(partial_answer_string, remainder_string);
      strcat(partial_answer_string, answer_string);
      strcpy(answer_string, partial_answer_string);
   }

   return answer_string;
}
```

Whenever you need to refer to an accessible class member outside the scope of the class declaration itself, you must use the class name followed by the scope resolution operator "::" followed by the member name. For example,

```
My_Class::my_member_function
```

Run the Code

Now go ahead and try out the integer count code.

Use this main program to create and test some integer count objects:

```cpp
#include <iostream.h>
#include "count.h"

int main ()
{
  // Create an integer count object with an initial value
  // of 5.
  Integer_Count intcount(5);

  // Get its value. And display it.
  cout << endl << "INTEGER Demo" << endl << endl;
  cout << "Current value:   " << intcount.get_value()
          << endl;

  // Tell it to increment itself twice.
  intcount.increment();
  intcount.increment();

  cout << "Current value:   " << intcount.get_value()
          << endl;

  // Tell it to decrement itself three times.
  intcount.decrement();
  intcount.decrement();
  intcount.decrement();

  cout << "Current value:   " << intcount.get_value()
          << endl;

  // Tell it to reset itself.
  intcount.reset();

  cout << "Current value:   " << intcount.get_value()
          << endl;

  cout << endl << "Happy trails." << endl;
```

```
    return 0;
}
```

Note the syntax for invoking a member function, when you are accessing it from outside of its class through a class object:

```
<object>.<member function name> (<arguments>);
```

Try it out, you'll see this on your console:

INTEGER Demo

Current value: 5
Current value: 7
Current value: 4
Current value: 0

Happy trails.

OOD—HUMAN INTERACTION COMPONENT

Design a Layout

Now you are ready to begin designing the human interface of the value window. What should it look like?

Rather than go off in a corner and make your decision, go over and ask the person who is going to use the system.

Remember the picture from The Count (Figure 1–12)? Use it as a starting point:

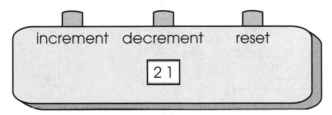

Figure 1–12: What the customer sketched out.

Build an interface that looks something like this familiar interface.

Design a Human Interaction Component

You've defined and built the count and integer count classes. You've created an object and told it to increment, decrement, and reset itself.

So far, the classes that you've worked on are those found in OOA and extended during OOD. These classes fit into the overall design in what's called the problem domain component.

But what about the human interaction classes? These are the classes that form the human interaction component.

To identify the human interaction classes, apply the "OOA on OOD" principle:

> **The "OOA on OOD" principle.** To design an OOD human interaction component, task management component, or data management component, apply OOA strategies upon the respective specialized design area.

To display results in a windowing system, you need to use a window. But what kind of window should you use? You could use a count window. And that would be good for all counts.

But by applying another principle, you can increase the likelihood of reuse:

> **The "name a window by what it holds" principle.** Name a window by what it holds, rather than by a project-specific, limiting name.

In this case, if you name the window for what it contains—a value— you'll name the class in a way that is more likely to be reused in the future.

It's a "value window."

Add a value window class (Figure 1–13). Put it in the human interaction component. Label the problem domain component as "PDC." And label the human interaction component as "HIC."

Human interaction classes are together with, yet distinctly independent of, the problem domain component classes. This separation of concerns increases the likelihood of reuse for OOA, OOD, and OOP results.

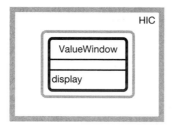
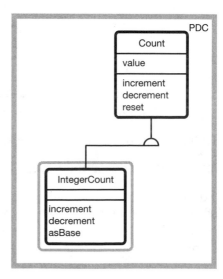

Figure 1–13: Adding the value window class.

Notation

A numbered box indicates a *design component*. The four OOD components are the problem domain component, the human interaction component, the task management component, and the data management component.

These design components support this principle:

The "separation of concerns" principle. Keep problem domain classes, human interaction classes, task management classes, and data management classes distinct. Why? To facilitate change and reuse, by making it easier to add or change classes in one component without severely impacting the others.

Find, show, change

What details do you need to support the human interaction?

The "I find. I show. I change." principle. For each human interaction object, define what it takes to do this: "I *find* the information that I need to find; I *show* the information that I need to show; and I *change* the information that I need to change."

Apply this principle to the value window for the count.
As a value window:

"I *find* the information I need by asking a count object for its value."

"I *show* the value."

"I *change* the count's value in response to someone's actions."

A value window might "show" its value in many ways—text or graphics, color or gray scale, visual or audio.

To begin with, use the simplest approach: text. Then consider something more sophisticated.

Why? First, establish the loose coupling between a value window and a count. Then increase the human interaction capability.

Putting this into a concise principle:

The "communication then presentation" principle. Design how human interaction objects communicate with problem domain objects. Then incrementally refine the presentation of the results.

Once you get the communication established, then you can change the localized "I show" presentation service.

Add object interactions

Act out the object interactions. Write up a scenario script, capturing the dynamics. And then add the scenario script and the corresponding message interaction to the design itself.

> I'm an integer count.
>> I receive an increment message.
>> I increment myself.
>> I announce that my value changed (message A1).

> I'm a value window.
>> I receive an update message, telling me that my count's value changed.
>> I ask my count for its new value.
>> I display the new value (message A2).

The count announces that its value changed, telling all objects that depend on it (in this case, the only dependent object is the value window).

When the value window gets this announcement, it updates itself by getting the new value and displaying it.

Why use this broadcast and receiver handshaking? Here's why.

First, it supports a crisp distinction between problem domain classes and human interaction classes. And this increases the likelihood of reuse of both.

Second, such mechanisms are already designed and built, ready for you to inherit and reuse. The classes are called model and view (in a Smalltalk architecture) or subject and view (in C++ InterViews, as described in [Linton]).

Add these object interactions (Figure 1–14) and the scenario script to your design.

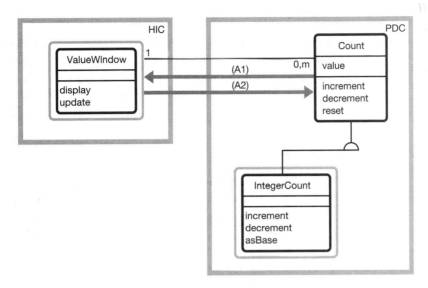

Figure 1–14: A value window and an integer count interact.

More notation

A solid line between value window and count is called an *object connection*. It's an association, a mapping, between objects. In this example, the object connection shows that a value window knows about one object of some specialization of count, and that an object of some specialization of the count knows about zero up to some number of value window objects.

A shaded (or dashed) arrow is a *message*. A message has an optional label. The label may consist of a scenario letter and message number (e.g., A1). Alternately, it may consist of a name or description. A message portrays an interaction from one object to another, and back again. (It may also show interaction with a class; in this case, the arrow's end point(s) go all the way to the inner rounded rectangle of the class-&-object symbol.) In this example, an integer count object sends a "value changed" message to its corresponding value window. The value window sends an "access" (or "get value") message to its corresponding integer count object to get the change.[14] Then the value window displays the change.

---

[14]All classes with objects need a create service. And all objects (with attributes, connections, or both) need access, connect, and release services. Rather than put these four names on nearly every symbol, OOA/OOD treats them as inherited, not written on the model itself.

What the integer count class inherits

The integer count class inherits the "value" attribute and the "increment, decrement, and reset" services. The integer count also inherits the ability to know about a corresponding value window (represented by the object connection). And because it inherits services, integer count messaging includes that messaging defined for count.

Add human interaction classes

Begin by identifying the additional human interaction pieces that are needed to provide the interface. And then add the corresponding classes to the human interaction component of the OOA/OOD model.

One added part is a button with a label; it can be pushed; it needs to display its label.

Another added part is a display box; it needs to display a value.

Add these to the human interaction component (Figure 1–15).

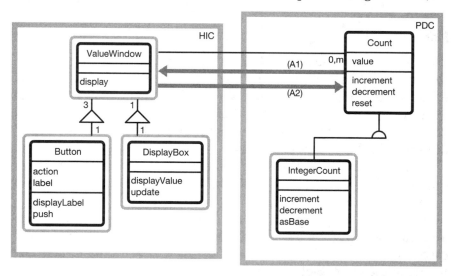

Figure 1–15: Adding human interaction pieces to the value window.

A bit more notation

The line with a triangle on it is called a *whole-part structure*. The triangle points to the "whole."

Whole-part is one of three basic methods of organization that people use. (The other two are "objects and attributes" and "classes and distinguishing between them" [Britannica]). Whole-part takes on three basic forms: assembly-parts, container-contents, and collection-members.

A whole-part structure is a mapping between objects, just like an object connection. But it's much stronger in meaning.

In this example, whole-part structure illustrates that a value window contains three buttons and one display box. It also indicates that each button is part of one and just one value window, and that each display box is part of one and just one value window.

Continue with human interaction

Act out the scenario for the increment button.

> I'm an increment button.
>> I get pushed.
>> I send a message to ??? to increment.
>>> Help! I don't know to whom to send this message!

Something is not right here. The button doesn't know to whom to send a message.

What can you do about it? How about send a message to the value window?

> I'm an increment button.
>> I'm pushed.
>> I send an increment message to my value window.
>>> (Warning: value windows do not...and should not...know how to increment.)
> I'm a value window.
>> I send an increment message to an integer count.
> I'm an integer count.
>> I increment myself.

A value window doesn't need to know how to increment. The value window is just getting in the way. Instead, a button could communicate directly with its corresponding integer count.

This begs for another principle:

The "throw out the middle man" principle. Throw out objects that do nothing more than take a request and pass it on to another object.

Who's the middle man in this case? It's value window.
Get rid of him (Figure 1–16).
And then put in new connections.
A button needs to know about its corresponding count. A button sends a message to its count.

A display box needs to know about its corresponding count.

A count needs to know about its corresponding display box. A count sends a message to a display box.

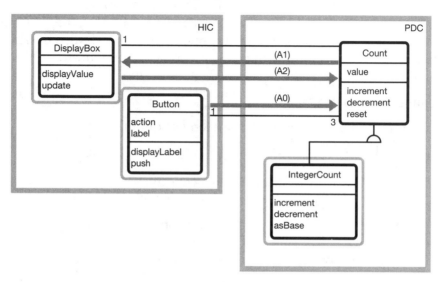

Figure 1–16: Eliminate the middle man between a human interaction object and a problem domain object.

You need one more thing.

You need something to hold the display box and the button. And actually lay them out within a window.

What you need is a visual container. Most graphical user interface (GUI) class libraries include such classes, ready for you to use.

A visual container object is an entirely visual component.

> I'm a visual container.
> I know how to lay out visual components in a window.
> I know how to wrap visual components in a way that
> supports one or more GUI interface conventions.
> I don't need to know about or interact with a model.

You can call the visual container for this example something like a "count view" container. It's a container. It contains some number of count views.

Add the count view container class to the OOA/OOD model (Figure 1–17).

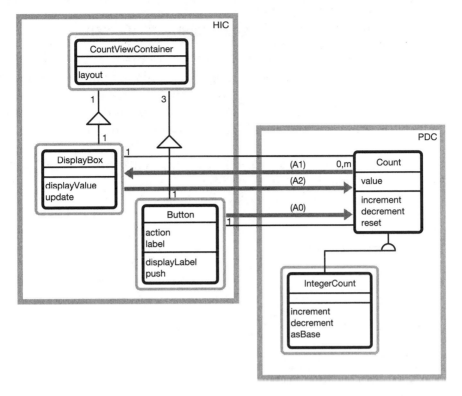

Figure 1–17: Adding a visual container.

Take this model and check it out one more time—with its corresponding scenario script.

> I'm a button.
>> My label is "increment."
>> I display my label.
>> At some point later...I'm pushed.
>> I know about an integer count. I send it an increment message.
> I'm an integer count.
>> I just got a message to increment.
>> I increment myself.
>> I know about my dependents.
>> I send messages, broadcasting an announcement to my dependents that I've changed.
> I'm a display box.
>> I receive a message, announcing that a change that I'm interested in has occurred.
>> I know about an integer count. I send it a message to get its value.
>> I display the value.

Supporting the Interaction between
Problem Domain Objects and Human Interaction Objects

The interaction between the problem domain objects and the human interaction objects is something that occurs again and again.

Wouldn't it be nice if you could just inherit such capabilities?

Many GUI class libraries now contain classes that support the reusable interaction pattern between a problem domain object and a window that views it.

In Smalltalk, this pattern is expressed with the "model" and "view" classes (Figure 1–18).

The overall architecture looks like this:

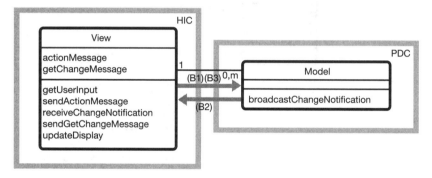

Figure 1–18: Interaction defined in the model and view classes.

To understand the interaction between model and view objects (more precisely, between objects of classes that are specializations of model and view), consider the following scenario script.

This scenario script shows the dynamic interaction between a view and a model:

> I'm a view.
>> I get an input.
>> I send an action message to my corresponding model.
> I'm a model.
>> I do the action that someone tells me to do.
>>> (The action method is defined in a specialization of
>>> the model class.)
>> When I have a change that needs to be broadcast, I
>>> broadcast a change notification to my dependents.
> I'm a view.
>> I get a change notification.
>> I send a message to get the change that I need.
> I'm a model.

> I get the change and return the result to the sender.
> (The "get change" method is defined in
> > a specialization of the model class.)
>
> I'm a view.
> > I update my display.

Actually, Smalltalk uses three classes: model, view, and controller. The two key classes are model and view; the controller class just takes care of getting user input.

InterViews, a C++ GUI class library, uses two classes: subject and view. A subject has a list of views that it sends notifications to; each view knows about a subject.

About the Human Interaction Component and Available Class Libraries

Effective OOD using GUI class libraries

Effective OOD results for an application hold true no matter which GUI class library you might select at a particular time. Why?

First, all GUI class libraries offer many similar classes, including buttons, lists, input boxes, text windows, and the like. So there is no need to commit to just one vendor's GUI classes.

Second, all GUI class libraries change. So even if you have just one favorite GUI class library, it will change over time.

Third, new GUI class libraries are coming out almost daily. So you might choose certain GUI classes today, and yet need to move to better choices in the not too distant future.

Fourth, you may need to support multiple GUI interfaces on one or more platforms. You may need to work with different GUI class libraries. Or you may find an acceptable platform-independent GUI class library; even then, you may eventually need to switch to a different platform-independent GUI class library.

So, it makes good sense to keep your overall OOD results independent of a particular GUI class library. The design is then more resilient to change. And it provides a basis for more gracefully accommodating GUI class library changes.

Selecting GUI classes

With GUI libraries, look for those classes that best match the classes in your OOD. The primary matching criterion is finding a class with the same purpose or objective as the one in your OOD.

Here's the strategy.

First, look for an exact match. You can create a new object in that class and use it directly.

Second, look for its generalization. You can add a specialization class, inheriting the capabilities from the generalization, and add to it.

But what if you cannot find an exact match or an applicable generalization? What then?

Two additional options exist. Neither option is ideal.

These additional options require you to violate the principle of generalization–specialization. This impedes code understandability. And it decreases the reuse potential for the classes involved. But it does allow you to reuse some of the code that is in the GUI class library. Hence, it's a trade-off between "kludged" reuse this time versus better understandability and increased likelihood of reuse next time. And for the system that you are building, you'll need to pick the lesser of two evils.

Third, look for a class that does *part* of what you need, even though generalization–specialization does not apply. You can inherit that capability and add what you do need.

Fourth, look for something that does *more* than you need. You can inherit its capabilities, override what you don't need, add what you do need. (This implies that a previous designer could have applied generalization–specialization a bit more than he did.)

Otherwise, build your own.

Putting the strategy into a principle:

The "selecting GUI classes" principle. For each OOD human interaction class, look in the available GUI class libraries—and consider the purpose of each class. Go for (1) an exact match, (2) a generalization you can specialize, (3) a part of what you need, or (4) something more than what you need.

OOD—HUMAN INTERACTION COMPONENT: SMALLTALK

The Smalltalk Classes

Finding classes to reuse

Admittedly, to reuse any class library, you need to know what's generally there—and have some sort of browsing capability so you can find a class that might suit your needs.

You don't need to master every aspect of a class library before you can reuse one of its classes. But you do need to spend some time browsing through a class library, to get a feel for how it is organized. Then you'll have some idea where to look when you're looking for classes that you might reuse.

Some platform-independent GUI classes

Consider Smalltalk. The class library comes with a variety of GUI classes, ready for you to use. Moreover, these GUI classes are platform independent. This means that you'll be able to run the same source code from this book on a variety of platforms—and have a GUI interface, too. (Over time, more sophisticated GUI class libraries will support platform-specific look-and-feel. By keeping your OOD results independent of a specific GUI class library, you'll be able to readily incorporate those capabilities, too.)

The button class

Begin with the button class.

Does it have an exact match in the GUI class library? Yes.

The button class corresponds to a Smalltalk class called "labeled Boolean view." Yes, that's a rather strange name. But this class does serve the same purpose as the button class.

"Labeled Boolean view" is a subclass (specialization class) of "Boolean widget view," which in turn is a subclass (specialization class) of "view."

So "labeled Boolean view" inherits the capabilities that all views have, as described earlier in this chapter.

The display box class

Next, consider the display box class.

Does it have an exact match? No. Does it have a corresponding generalization class? No. Does a class exist that does just part of what you need? No. Does a class exist that does more than you need? Yes.

The "text view" class achieves the same purpose—and a bit more. The text view class displays text and a cursor, and allows someone to type in a new value. The "text view" class fits into the class hierarchy like so:

Object
   VisualComponent
    VisualPart
       DependentPart
        View
           AutoScrollingView
            ComposedTextView
             TextView

Whew!

But wait. Text view is a class that does more than you need. Ugh! This is an example of the need for more generalization–specialization.

Something like "text view" subclassing (specializing) into "changeable text view" would have been easier to understand *and* easier to reuse. (Well, no human designer or design is perfect. And it's okay! Besides, such things make interesting teaching points.)

Use the text view class. Add a subclass (although it's not really a specialization) called display box. Override the unwanted capabilities.

The count view container class

Now consider the count view container class.

Does it have an exact match? No. Does it have a corresponding generalization class? Yes.

The composite part class is the generalization class needed here. It's a subclass (specialization class) of the visual part class, which is a subclass (specialization class) of the visual component class.

So you can add a count view container class, subclassing (specializing) from the composite part class.

Fitting the OOD classes within the Smalltalk hierarchy

The OOD remains the same. Figure 1–19 is a graphical portrayal of how the OOD human interaction classes fit into the classes in the Smalltalk hierarchy.

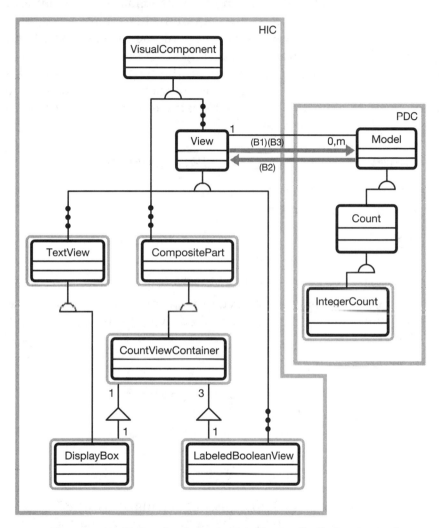

Figure 1–19: Fitting the design within the Smalltalk class hierarchy.

Notation and notes

The ellipsis (triple dot) marking indicates that some of the intervening classes are collapsed, hidden on a particular diagram.

The superclass (specialization class) of visual component and model classes is the object class, the root of the hierarchy.

The interactions between the human interaction component and the problem domain component are shown between the model class and the view class, rather than lower in the respective class hierarchies. Why? Because that's where the interaction mechanisms are implemented in a Smalltalk architecture; the interaction mechanisms are inherited by the subclasses.

OOP—HUMAN INTERACTION COMPONENT: SMALLTALK

Adding Human Interaction Support to the Problem Domain Component

Begin with the classes in the problem domain component. When a count modifies its value:

I need to broadcast that I've changed.

Most of this capability is inherited from the model class. All you need to add is a single line to the accessor method that puts in a new value. Here it is:

```
value: aValue
"Set my value to aValue.
Notify my dependents I changed my value."

    value := aValue.
    self changed: #value
```

The new statement is

```
self changed: #value
```

It means "I send myself the message "changed: #value."

The "changed:" method is inherited. It includes the code that's needed to broadcast a change notice to various dependents.

Next, check this class and its specializations. Wherever value is set with

```
value :=
```

replace it with

```
"self value:"
```

so that each value change gets broadcast.

And so, for count, you need to change its "reset" method:

```
Count methodsFor: 'accessing'
```

reset
```
"Restore my value to its original state."

self value: resetValue
```

For integer count, you need to change the specific increment, decrement, and reset methods:

```
IntegerCount methodsFor: 'counting'
```

increment
```
"Increment my value ."

self value: value + 1
```

decrement
```
"Decrement my value ."

self value: value - 1
```

The Count View Container Class

The count view container class creates an object that holds one display box and three buttons.

Add a class and its instance variables

The count view container class is a subclass (specialization class) of composite part:

```
CompositePart subclass: #CountViewContainer
    instanceVariableNames: ''
    classVariableNames: ''
    poolDictionaries: ''
    category: 'Count Views'
```

Add a view layout method

Add a method which builds a display box and buttons on a count object.

```
CountViewContainer methodsFor: 'view layout'
```

buildViewsOn: aCount
```
    self addDisplayBoxOn: aCount.
    self addIncrementButtonOn: aCount.
    self addDecrementButtonOn: aCount.
    self addResetButtonOn: aCount
```

Add a view opening method

A count view container can't appear on a computer screen all by itself. A count view container needs to be inside a window. And that is exactly what this next method takes care of:

```
CountViewContainer methodsFor: 'view opening'

openOn: aCount labeled: aLabel
  | win |
  self buildViewsOn: aCount.
  win := ScheduledWindow new.
  win component: self.
  win label: aLabel.
  win minimumSize: 200 @ 66.
  win open
```

What does a count view container do with its openOn: method? Here it goes:

> I'm a count view container.
>
>> I build all the views for the count inside the view container:
>>
>> ```
>> self buildViewsOn: aCount.
>> ```
>>
>> Then I create a window:
>>
>> ```
>> window := ScheduledWindow new.
>> ```
>>
>> Then I place myself inside the window:
>>
>> ```
>> window component: self.
>> ```
>>
>> I define the window's label and minimum width (200 pixels) and height (66 pixels).
>>
>> ```
>> window label: aLabel.
>> window minimumSize: 200 @ 66.
>> ```
>>
>> I open the window:
>>
>> ```
>> window open
>> ```

About the Text View Class

Views are created *on* a model.
A method name that creates or initializes a view often has

```
on: <model object>
```

as part of its name.

Most often, these methods are class methods. And such a class method usually creates the view *and* connects that view to its model.

For example, consider the text view class. One of its methods creates a new text view, specifies its corresponding model, and then establishes the line of communication between that view and that model. The class method is called:

```
on: aspect: change: menu: initialSelection:
```

Once the class method creates a new text view object, it sends that text view object a message, telling it:

```
on: aspect: change: menu: initialSelection:
```

Here's the class method.[15] Be sure to read the comments:

```
TextView class methodsFor: 'instance creation'

on: anObject aspect: aspectMsg change: changeMsg
     menu: menuMsg initialSelection: sel

   "Create a 'pluggable' (see class comment) textView
         viewing anObject.

   aspectMsg is sent to read the current text value
         in the model. It is also used as the changed:
         parameter for this view.

   changeMsg is sent to inform anObject of new text
         for the model.

   menuMsg is sent to read the operate button menu
         for this view.

   initialSelection (if not nil) is a string that will
         be searched for, and then highlighted if found
         initially."

   | aTextView |
   aTextView := self new.
   aTextView initialSelection: sel.
   aTextView on: anObject aspect: aspectMsg change:
         changeMsg menu: menuMsg.
   ^aTextView
```

Notice that, for the class, the aspectMsg is the message sent to read the current text value in the model.

---

[15]From ObjectWorks\Smalltalk, Version 4.1. Used with permission from ParcPlace Systems.

What about the instance method, the one with the same name?

```
TextView methodsFor: 'private'

on: anObject aspect: aspectMessage change: changeMessage
       menu: menuMessage
    partMsg := aspectMessage.
    acceptMsg := changeMessage.
    menuMsg := menuMessage.
    self model: anObject
```

Here, the instance method takes the aspectMsg and stores it in a variable called partMsg.

"partMsg" means "this is the part of the model I display."

"acceptMsg" means that it is the message that is sent after a person using the system "accepts" the text (by pressing a return key, an enter key, or whatever else might be used).

The Display Box Class

Add a class and its instance variables

The display box class is a subclass (specialization class) of the text view class.

```
TextView subclass: #DisplayBox

    instanceVariableNames: ''
    classVariableNames: ''
    poolDictionaries: ''
    category: 'Count Views'
```

Override a method that you don't need

Text view has some capabilities that just are not needed by display box.

What does this mean?

The design could have been better.

The design puts too much responsibility into the text view class. With generalization–specialization, it could have used at least two classes, perhaps something like a text view class *and* a text view with input class.

What do you do when this happens? Mutter about the designer? No way!

The "discuss the design, not the designer" principle. Discuss the design and how to make it better. Don't tear down the designer; all of us make mistakes; unkind words are of no profit.

So what can you do?

One approach is to cut and paste code from a text view class into a new class. This is "cut and paste" reuse; it duplicates code (and increases the testing and maintenance burden).

Another approach is to inherit from text view and then override unwanted methods. This is inheritance-based reuse. And no code is needlessly duplicated.

How do you do it?

In Smalltalk, a subclass inherits everything in the superclass. As long as a class architect adheres to generalization–specialization, that makes good sense.

But at times, one must subclass and use just part of its superclass, even though it's a violation of generalization-specialization. Smalltalk provides no special syntax for this eventuality.

So what happens?

In Smalltalk, you can override unwanted methods by naming the method, not using any of its inherited capability, and including a statement to return the object to the sender:

```
^self
```

In this way, you turn the method into a "no-op."

Also in Smalltalk, you cannot override unwanted variables. At best, you can just ignore them.

For text view, you need to override one unwanted method—the one that displays an insertion point and allows someone to type in some text:

```
DisplayBox methodsFor: 'selection'
```

displayInsertionPointFor: aCharacterBlock **on:**
        aGraphicsContext
    "Override this method so I will not display a cursor,
            and a user cannot type inside of me."

```
^self
```

Add a model access method

You need to add a method to display box.

The method needs to send a "get change" message to the corresponding object of a class that is a specialization of model.

Most of this capability is inherited.

You just need to send the model the message

```
perform: partMsg
```

where partMsg is a variable inherited from the text view class. The partMsg variable contains the message that needs to be sent. When you create a display box you need to set this variable so the display box knows that the message it is to send is "value."

Here's the method that enables a display box to get the content it needs from its corresponding model object:

```
DisplayBox methodsFor: 'model access'
```

getContents
```
    "Ask the model to perform the partMsg and convert the
        result to a String."

^(model perform: partMsg) printString
```

This method gets the value from the model. Then it converts the result into a string.

Note that the method category (protocol) is "model access." Sometimes a method is added just to support model-view interaction. That's what is happening here. The applicable protocol is this one:

- *model access*
  (as a view object) get or set the model on which I am dependent

Add a "make a display box" method

One thing that the count view container does is create a display box.

```
CountViewContainer methodsFor: 'private'
```

makeDisplayBoxOn: aCount
```
    "Make a display box to display aCount's value. The display
    box will update when aCount sends a change message with
    the symbol, #value."
    | itemView |
    itemView := DisplayBox
            on: aCount
            aspect: #value
            change: nil
            menu: nil.

    ^itemView
```

The method
```
on: aspect: change: menu:
```

is inherited from the text view class.

Consider the message sent to the display box class.

The display box is a view *on* a count. This makes a count the model that corresponds to the display box.

Note that part of the message sent to the display box class is

```
aspect: #value
```

The number sign (#) is used in Smalltalk to mark out certain literals. In this case, it immediately precedes something that is being declared as a unique name, called a symbol.

This part of the message supplies the message name that the display box view sends to its corresponding model, "aCount." (Whatever a count responds with is what the display box will use for display.)

In addition, this part of the message is also the change name that the display box looks for whenever a count broadcasts a change. In this way, a display box is notified that a change has occurred *and* what kind of change it was.[16]

The display box cannot receive inputs. So it doesn't ever send a change message to a count. Hence, part of the message sent to the display box class is

```
change: nil
```

The Count View Container Class (cont.)

Add a method to make a button

A count container view also needs to make some buttons.

CountViewContainer methodsFor: 'private'

makeButton: buttonLabel **on:** aCount **for:** action
    "Make a button to send a message to aCount to perform
        an action."

    | buttonView buttonAdaptor |
    buttonAdaptor := (PluggableAdaptor on: aCount)
            performAction: action.
    buttonView := LabeledBooleanView new.
    buttonView model: buttonAdaptor.
    buttonView label: buttonLabel.
    buttonView beTrigger.
    buttonView controller beTriggerOnUp.
    ^buttonView

---

[16]A better approach? Use a different notification name. Then a model could choose different granularities of change notification.

In Smalltalk, a button is implemented in a way that's a bit different than the way other views are implemented. A button requires a "supporting object" to talk to its model. And only buttons need this kind of help.

Why? To keep buttons themselves easier to use … and to hide some of the details that are needed for the many different kinds of buttons.

There are many kinds of buttons—radio buttons, check boxes, switches, toggles, triggers. When pushed, each kind of button has its own unique behavior visually; for example, an action button flashes, while a check box adds or removes its check mark. Each kind of button works in slightly different ways.

The "supporting object" is called a pluggable adaptor.

A pluggable adaptor can store some arbitrary number of Smalltalk statements. When a button is pushed, it tells the pluggable adaptor to execute its statements.

So the statement

```
buttonAdaptor := (PluggableAdaptor on: aCount)
        performAction: action.
```

sends a message to the pluggable adaptor class. That class creates an object that stores a statement to send the action message to a model object, a count. Then, when the pluggable adaptor executes the statement, it sends the action message to a count.

Different kinds of buttons

What kind of button do you need here?

The count view container creates labeled trigger buttons. It does this with the statements

```
buttonView label: buttonLabel.
buttonView beTrigger.
```

How the button works is defined with this statement:

```
buttonView controller beTriggerOnUp.
```

Note the "controller." It's something that you'll investigate in detail in Chapter 2. For now, just think of the above statement as one that's needed to define the button.

Add view creation methods

The count view container's methods for building its views follow this very simple pattern:

> I'm a count view container.
>
>> I create the view.
>>
>> I build a constraint frame to bound the view's size and location.
>>
>> I put the view inside of me, using the constraint frame's area.

The following method builds an increment button:

```
CountViewContainer methodsFor: 'view creation'

addIncrementButtonOn: aCount
    | button buttonArea |
    button := self makeButton: 'increment'
            on: aCount
            for: #increment.
    buttonArea := self constraintFrame: 0 @ 0
            corner: 1/3 @ (1/3).
    self addView: button in: buttonArea
```

An increment button is a view *on* a count. The increment button label is "increment." And when the increment button is pushed, its pluggable adaptor sends the message "increment" to a count.

In the "addIncrementButtonOn:" method, the statement

```
    buttonArea := self constraintFrame: 0 @ 0
            corner: 1/3 @ (1/3).
```

sets up something called a constraint frame.

A constraint frame determines the relative size and location of a view inside a view container. Constraint frames are specified using fractions, indicating proportions rather than absolute size.

For example, a constraint frame that extends from 0 @ 0 to 1/3 @ (1/3) spans the upper-left corner of a container view (1/3 of the horizontal span, 1/3 of the vertical span). See Figure 1–20.

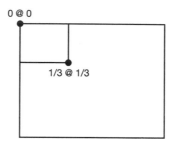

Figure 1–20: Constraint frame 0 @ 0 corner: 1/3 @ (1/3).

The "constraintFrame: corner:" method actually looks like this:

```
CountViewContainer methodsFor: 'private'

constraintFrame: originConstraints corner:
    cornerConstraints

    ^LayoutFrame originFractions: originConstraints
             cornerFractions: cornerConstraints
```

In the "addIncrementButtonOn:" method, the statement

```
self addView: button in: buttonArea
```

adds a view to the count view container.

Next, look at the "addView:" method:

```
CountViewContainer methodsFor: 'private'

addView: view in: area
    | wrapper |
    wrapper := BorderedWrapper on: view in: area.
    self addWrapper: wrapper
```

Most views are added to view containers using something called wrappers. Wrappers are used to add special decorations to the view.

> I'm a count view container.
> I place this view in a wrapper with a border.

The methods that add and arrange the buttons and the display box in the count view container follow this same pattern.

```
CountViewContainer methodsFor: 'view creation'

addIncrementButtonOn: aCount
    | button buttonArea |
```

```
button := self makeButton: 'increment'
        on: aCount
        for: #increment.
buttonArea := self constraintFrame: 0 @ 0
        corner: 1/3 @ (1/3).
self addView: button in: buttonArea
```

addDecrementButtonOn: aCount
```
| button buttonArea |
button := self makeButton: 'decrement'
        on: aCount
        for: #decrement.
buttonArea := self constraintFrame: 1/3 @ 0
        corner: 2/3 @ (1/3).
self addView: button in: buttonArea
```

addResetButtonOn: aCount
```
| button buttonArea |
button := self makeButton: 'reset'
        on: aCount
        for: #reset.
buttonArea := self constraintFrame: 2/3 @ 0
        corner: 1 @ (1/3).
self addView: button in: buttonArea
```

addDisplayBoxOn: aCount
```
| itemView itemArea |
itemView := self makeDisplayBoxOn: aCount.
itemArea := self constraintFrame: 1/3 @ (1/2)
        corner: 2/3 @ 1.
self addView: itemView in: itemArea
```

Run the Code

In a Smalltalk workspace, try out the integer count code by typing and evaluating the following:

```
| anIntegerCount |

anIntegerCount := IntegerCount new.
CountViewContainer new openOn: anIntegerCount labeled:
        '...integers...'
```

Your count view should appear on the screen, looking something like Figure 1–21.

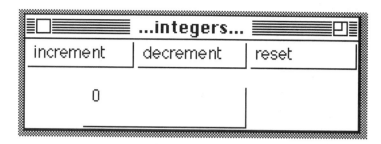

Figure 1–21: An integer count.

The window is labeled "…integers…". Inside the window is the count view container. And inside the count view container are the three buttons and a display box.

Try it out!

Congratulations! You've just completed your first Smalltalk application.

Way to go!

OOD—HUMAN INTERACTION COMPONENT: C++

A Simple, Platform-Independent Approach

A C++ product often includes its own class library support for a single GUI on a single platform. Platform-independent GUI tools are beginning to appear in the marketplace.

There are many fine C++ GUI libraries; which one you might choose depends on your version of C++ and what type of machine you're using.

This book chooses platform independence over a single GUI class library and platform. This means that you'll see GUI interfaces in the Smalltalk sections, and somewhat simpler interfaces in the C++ sections.

But that's not so bad. Suppose that The Big Cheese wants to see something right away. For the first pass, you don't need to show him the whole application. You do need just enough to demonstrate that the application works.

You can build a simple (and platform-independent) human interaction component just by reading from and writing to the console. And this makes good sense, demonstrating early results. Then you can replace your simple human interaction classes with GUI classes.

Where to begin

Begin with the OOD results from earlier in this chapter. The same OOD applies (Figure 1–22).

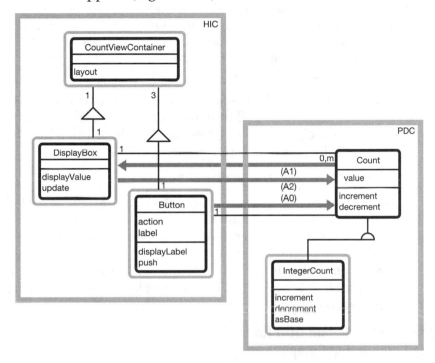

Figure 1–22:   The same overall OOD result applies here, too.

Fitting the design within human interaction constraints

What do you do when a GUI class library is not available? Or when one is not easy to drop into place? And a deadline is close at hand?

Take the same overall OOD and fit the design within your constraints.

Plan the human interaction as just a simple menuing system. It's standard C++ all the way. No GUIs. And no support for something like the model-view.

What should you do with the design? Should you smash all the human interface classes into one big monster class? Should you combine the problem domain and human interaction components into an inseparable pile of spaghetti code?

Or is there another way? One that will preserve the design. One that will keep the code simpler now. And one that will be much more resilient to additions and changes in the future.

Yes, there is a better way. And this is the principle to apply:

The "conservation of architecture" principle. Whenever possible, preserve the shape of the OOD architecture when programming it in an OOPL. Even if some of the classes have very few responsibilities, you'll benefit—the same class architecture will still apply when you add or change capabilities in the future.

So endeavor to keep the same overall OOD architecture—one that you can adapt to a variety of human interaction possibilities.

The *display box* class. "As an object in this class, I need to display the current value." It might look something like this:

The current value: <value>

The *button* class. "As an object in this class, I know my label. And I know how to display my label."

To remain platform independent, stick to working with a console. No buttons. Yes, a *console menu.*

The *count view container* class. "As an object of this class, I'm responsible for doing that which is needed to glue together my parts so I can achieve the desired human interaction results."

Platform-Independent OOD for the C++ Human Interaction Component

The console menu

Use a single menu, one that begins like:

1. Increment
2. Decrement
3. Reset

follows with a prompt string:

Make a selection:

and concludes with this:

4. Quit

To do this, the console menu class looks something like Figure 1–23.

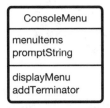

Figure 1–23: The console menu class.

A console menu gets a selection—and remembers it (Figure 1–24).

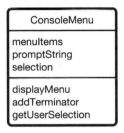

Figure 1–24: "As a console menu, I get and I remember a selection."

And it executes a selection by sending a message to its corresponding integer count.

But which message does it send? C++ is a strongly typed language. So you need to specifically put in the message and what types are involved. And so the OOD looks like Figure 1–25.

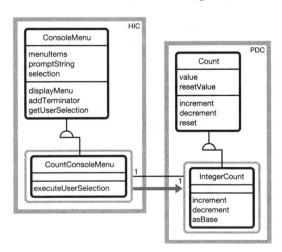

Figure 1–25: "As a count console menu, I communicate directly with my integer count."

The console display box

"I'm a console display box, I display some sort of label." For example:

Current value:

"I also display the actual value that I get from some object."

Current value: 25

Here, you need a console display box, one that knows its label string and displays it.

You also need a count console display box, one that gets its display value from an integer count (Figure 1–26) and then displays it.

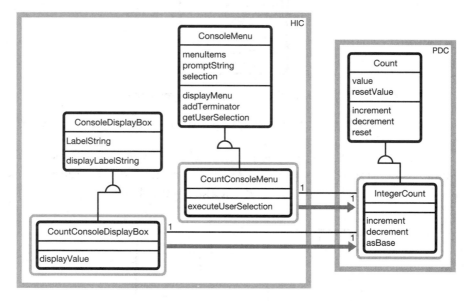

Figure 1–26: "As a count console display box, I communicate directly with my integer count."

The count view container

Putting in the new count view container, the platform-independent C++ OOA/OOD model now looks like Figure 1–27.

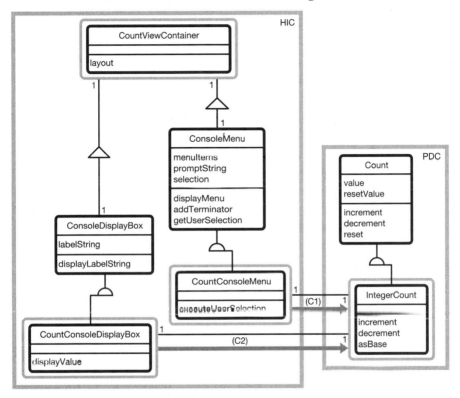

Figure 1–27: Platform-independent C++ OOD for this example.

What does the count view container do?

> I'm a count view container.
>> I create a console menu and a console display box.
>> Then I do the following:
>>> Do until finished:
>>>> tell the menu to get a selection
>>>> execute the selection
>>>> tell the display box to display a value

Note that this OOD is still very much like the one you saw earlier in this chapter. Most of the differences go away *if* something like C++ InterViews and some GUI classes are available for the platform(s) you are interested in.

OOP—HUMAN INTERACTION COMPONENT: C++

The overall plan

Build the components, then the container:

> console menu
> count console menu
> display box
> count display box
> count view container

For each class: declare it, then define it.

The Console Menu Class

Declare the class

Walk through the basics of what an object of the console menu class needs to know and do:

I'm a console menu.

- I know my menu, an array of labels:

```
char* menu_items[MAX_CONSOLE_MENU_SIZE];
```

- I know my prompt string:

```
char* prompt_string;
```

- I know my selection:

```
int selection;
```

- I know the number of labels that I have:

```
int menu_size;
```

Take a first pass at the console menu class declaration:

```
const MAX_CONSOLE_MENU_SIZE = 10;

class Console_Menu {
public:

    // Constructors/destructors
    Console_Menu() { menu_size = 0; }
    ~Console_Menu() { }

    // Accessors
    int get_selection() { return selection; }
```

```
protected:

    // Data members
    char* menu_items[MAX_CONSOLE_MENU_SIZE];
    char* prompt_string;
    int menu_size;
    int selection;
};
```

Note that this code puts the data members in the *protected* section. This makes them visible to derived classes; the count console menu class needs access to them.

Also note the "*" syntax: Read an "*" which immediately follows a type name as "pointer." In this example, the code includes two pointers to characters (more commonly known as "char stars," with the "ch" pronounced as "ch" not "k").

What other members do you need?

As a console menu,

- I need to build myself.
- I know how to add a menu prompt,
  a menu item, and a terminator.

```
    void add_prompt(char* menu_prompt);
    void add_item(char* new_item);
    void add_terminator(char* quit_label);
```

- I know how to display myself and get the user's selection.

```
    void display_menu();
    int get_user_selection();
```

- Plus, I know how to check for a valid selection.

```
    Boolean validate_selection(int selection);
```

Add these member functions to the console menu class declaration:

```
const MAX_CONSOLE_MENU_SIZE = 10;

class Console_Menu {
public:

    // Constructors/destructors
    Console_Menu() { menu_size = 0; }
    ~Console_Menu() { }

    // Implementors
    void add_item(char* new_item);
    void add_terminator(char* quit_label);
    void add_prompt(char* menu_prompt);
```

```
void display_menu();
int get_user_selection();

// Accessors
int get_selection() { return selection; }
```

protected:

```
Boolean validate_selection(int selection);

// Data members
char* menu_items[MAX_CONSOLE_MENU_SIZE];
char* prompt_string;
int menu_size;
int selection;
};
```

Define the add member functions

Write the member function to add a menu item.[17]

```
void Console_Menu::add_item(char* new_item)
{
    // Add new_item to the menu.
    char* menu_item;
    char* item_string = new char[25];

    sprintf(item_string, "%i. %s", menu_size+1, new_item);
    menu_item = new char[strlen(item_string) + 1];
    strcpy(menu_item, item_string);
    menu_items[menu_size++] = menu_item;
    delete[] item_string;
}
```

Note the console menu array. It's a data member for console menu; it can be used in any console menu member function.

The "sprintf" function with the formatting directives creates a new string from an integer number and string. For example, to put "1. Increment" into a menu item

```
sprintf(menu_item, "%i. %s", 1, "Increment");
```

---

[17]In C++, you can use its class facility to build your own versions of basic data types. In the next chapter, you will learn about a string class, and how to use a string object in place of char*.

Classes which can be reused frequently, such as the string class, are placed within class libraries. For a thorough discussion on how to use C++ to build effective class library classes see [Stroustrup, 1991].

Next, define the member function to add a terminator string to the menu array.

```
void Console_Menu::add_terminator(char* quit_label)
{
   this->add_item(quit_label);
}
```

Note the special syntax for describing a member. The statement

```
this->add_item(quit_label);
```

says "add a menu item (with this label) to this one." *Think* about such a statement this way: "I tell myself to add a menu item (with this label)."[18]

Write the member function to add a prompt to the console menu.

```
void Console_Menu::add_prompt(char* new_prompt)
{
   prompt_string = new_prompt;
}
```

Define the display member functions

Write the member function so a console menu can display itself.

```
void Console_Menu::display_menu()
{
   cout << endl;
   for (int i = 0; i < menu_size; i++)
      cout << menu_items[i] << endl;
   cout << endl << prompt_string;
}
```

This member function displays the labels in the menu array on the console. "cout" is the standard output stream in C++. The insertion operator, "<<", inserts data into the stream, which then appears on the console. The statement

```
cout << endl;
```

inserts a new line.

Define the select member functions

Write out what the console menu needs to do.

[18]The "this->" syntax is not required C++ syntax. And over time, you may choose to drop it. So why use it now? We've found that to help people go beyond C++ "as just a better C" ... and move into "object think" ... that thinking about what an object does is a key ingredient. The "this->" syntax supports that notion; without it, the code reads just like any other list of regular old function calls. For this reason, this book includes the optional "this->" syntax.

I'm a console menu. Here's what I do to get a selection:
  get selection
    repeat
      display my menu
      read the selection
      validate the selection
    until I get a valid selection
    if quit selected, return zero
    return selection

Start with the "validate selection" member function. What's a valid selection? Any selection that's between 1 and the menu size.

```
Boolean Console_Menu::validate_selection(int selection)
{
    if ((selection <= menu_size) && (selection > 0))
        return true;
    else
        return false;
}
```

Now define the get user selection member function.

```
int Console_Menu::get_user_selection()
{
    int choice, quit_choice = menu_size;
    char choice_char;
    Boolean valid_selection = false;

    while (!valid_selection)
    {
        this->display_menu();
        // Read the first character; ignore the rest.
        cin.get(choice_char);
        cin.ignore(100, '\n';
        // Convert the character to an integer.
        if (!isdigit(choice_char))
            choice = 0;
        else
            choice = atoi(&choice_char);
        // Check if the choice is valid.
        if (!this->validate_selection(choice))
            cout << "Invalid choice, try again." << endl;
        else
            valid_selection = true;
    {
    // Set the selection and return it.
    if (choice == quit_choice)
        selection = 0;
```

```
    else
       selection = choice;
    return selection;
}
```

Note the "preceding &" syntax. Read an "&" which immediately precedes a variable name as "the address of."

Run the code

Try out a console menu.

```
int main()
{
   cout << endl << "CONSOLE Menu" << endl;

   int selection;
   Console_Menu menu;

   menu.add_item("Increment");
   menu.add_item("Decrement");
   menu.add_item("Reset");

   men.add_terminator("Quit");

   menu.add_prompt
        ("Make a selection:  ");

   selection = menu.get_user_selection();
   while (selection != 0)
      selection = menu.get_user_selection();
   cout << endl << "Happy trails." << endl;

   return 0;
}
```

Now, run your demo. On your screen you see:

INTEGER COUNT Menu

1. Increment
2. Decrement
3. Reset
4. Quit

Make a selection: 4

Happy trails.

The Count Console Menu Class

Declare the class

Now it's time to build a menu that does something once it gets a selection—a count console menu.

I'm a count console menu.
- I know and do some things beyond what a console menu knows and does.
- I know my count.

```
Integer_Count* count;
```

- I know how to make my menu items for myself.

```
void make_items(Integer_Count& new_count);
```

- And I know how to execute a selection.

```
void execute_selection();
```

Declare the count console menu class:

```
class Count_Console_Menu : public Console_Menu {
public:

    // Constructors/destructors
    Count_Console_Menu() { }
    ~Count_Console_Menu() { }

    // Implementors
    void execute_selection();
    void make_items(Integer_Count& new_count);

    // Accessors
    Integer_Count& get_count() { return *count;}
    void set_count(Integer_Count& new_count)
            { count = &new_count; }

private:

    // Data members
    Integer_Count* count;
};
```

Note that a count console menu remembers its integer count by keeping a pointer to it. This statement:

```
Integer_Count* count;
```

declares "count" as a pointer to an integer count.

The accessor to set the value of the count expects a reference to an integer count object. A reference to an object is very much like a pointer to an object. They both contain the address of the object assigned to them. To get the object assigned to a pointer, you must explicitly dereference the pointer. A reference, however, is implicitly dereferenced for you. This means you can use a reference to an object the same way you use the object it refers to. This statement:

```
void set_count(Integer_Count& new_count)
```

declares that "new_count" is a reference to an integer count. This means "new_count" is passed by reference (not by value).[19]

Note that an "&" that immediately follows a type name is read as a "reference to" an object of that type.

The accessor also sets the count data member to the address of the object which is passed by reference:

```
{ count = &new_count; }
```

The accessor to get the count object uses the dereference operator, *, to return the object pointed at by the count pointer:

```
Integer_Count& get_count() { return *count; }
```

Read an "*" which immediately precedes a variable as "that which is pointed to by the _____ pointer."

Define the member functions

Define the make items member function.

```
void Count_Console_Menu::make_items(Integer_Count&
        new_count)
{
    this->add_item("Increment");
    this->add_item("Decrement");
    this->add_item("Reset");
    count = &new_count;
}
```

Define the execute selection member function.

```
void Count_Console_Menu::execute_selection()
{
    switch (selection)
        {
        case 1:
```

---

[19]"Pass by reference" means that only the location value, or memory address, of a variable is passed as an argument into a function. This is sometimes referred to as a variable's lvalue (pronounced "ell-value"). Changes made to that lvalue will remain in effect even after the function terminates.

"Pass by value" means that a copy of a variable is passed as an argument into its function. Any changes that a function makes to it remain in effect only during the current invocation of that function.

```
                count->increment();
                break;
            case 2:
                count->decrement();
                break;
            case 3:
                count->reset();
                break;
            };
    }
```

Run the code

Try out a count console menu.

```
int main()
{
    cout << endl << "INTEGER COUNT Menu" << endl;

    Count_Console_Menu menu;
    Integer_Count an_integer_count(10);

    cout << endl;
    cout << "Starting count: " << an_integer_count.get_value();
    cout << endl;

    // Make the console menu on the integer count.
    menu.make_items(an_integer_count);
    menu.add_terminator("Quit");
    menu.add_prompt("Make a selection:   ");

    menu.get_user_selection();
    menu.execute_selection();

    cout << endl;
    cout << "Ending count:   " << an_integer_count.get_value();

    cout << endl << endl << "Happy trails." <<endl;

    return 0;
}
```

And on your screen you see something like this:

INTEGER COUNT Menu

Starting count: 10

1. Increment
2. Decrement
3. Reset
4. Quit

Make a selection: 1

Ending count: 11

Happy trails.

Congratulations on your first working human interaction component in C++.

But don't stop now. It's time for you to build a console display box.

The Console Display Box Class

Declare the class

Declare a label string—and a member function to display it.

```
char* label_string;
void display_label_string();
```

It's a very simple display box. Declare it.

```
class Console_Display_Box {
public:

    // Constructors/destructors
    Console_Display_Box() { label_string = ""; }
    ~Console_Display_Box() { }

    // Accessors
    char* get_label_string() { return label_string; }
    void set_label_string(char* a_string)
            { label_string = a_string; }

protected:

    void display_label_string();

private:

    // Data members
    char* label_string;
};
```

Define the member functions

Define the "display label string" member function.

```
void Console_Display_Box::display_label_string()
{
    cout << endl << label_string;

}
```

The Count Console Display Box Class

Declare the class

Now it's time to build a console display box that knows about its count —a count console display box.

"I'm a count console display box.
I know and do some things beyond what
a console display box knows and does."
"I know my count."

```
Integer_Count* count;
```

"I know how to display my value."

```
void display_value();
```

Declare the class.

```
class Count_Console_Display_Box : public
        Console_Display_Box {
public:

    // Constructors/destructors
    Count_Console_Display_Box() { }
    ~Count_Console_Display_Box() { }

    // Implementors
    void display_value();

    // Accessors
    Integer_Count& get_count() { return *count; }
    void set_count(Integer_Count& new_count)
            { count = &new_count; }
private:

    // Data members
    Integer_Count* count;
};
```

Define the member functions

Define the "display value" member function.

```
void Count_Console_Display_Box::display_value()
{
    this->display_label_string();
    cout << count->get_value()
        << endl;
}
```

Run the code

Try out a count console display box, using it to display the value.

```
int main()
{
    cout << endl << "INTEGER COUNT Menu" << endl;

    Count_Console_Menu menu;
    Count_Console_Display_Box display_box;
    Integer_Count an_integer_count(10);

    display_box.set_label_string("Current value:  ");
    display_box.set_count(an_integer_count);

    menu.make_items(an_integer_count);
    menu.add_terminator("Quit");
    menu.add_prompt("Make a selection:  ");

    display_box.display_value();
    menu.get_user_selection();
    menu.execute_selection();
    display_box.display_value();

    cout << endl << "Happy trails." << endl;

    return 0;
}
```

On the console, you should see something like this:

INTEGER COUNT Menu

Current value: 10

1. Increment
2. Decrement
3. Reset
4. Quit

Make a selection: 4

Happy trails.

The Count View Container Class

Declare the class

You've built the console menus and display boxes that interact with the integer count. Now build their container, the count view container.

I'm a count view container.

Given an initial value:
I create an integer count.
I create its views.
I present those views on a console.

Declare the count view container class:

```
class Count_View_Container {
public:

    // Constructors/destructors
    Count_View_Container () { }
    ~Count_View_Container () { }

    // Implementors
    void display_count_views(int initial_value);
};
```

Define the member functions

Finally, yes finally, all the pieces of the human interaction play together:

```
void Count_View_Container::display_count_views
        (int initial_value)
{
    // Create and initialize an integer count.
    Integer_Count an_integer_count(initial_value);

    // Create a console menu and a display box.
    Count_Console_Menu menu;
    Count_Display_Box display_box;

    // Customize the menu for the integer count.
    menu.make_items(an_integer_count);
    menu.add_terminator("Quit");
    menu.add_prompt("Make a selection:  ");

    // Customize the display box for the integer count.
    display_box.set_count(an_integer_count);
    display_box.set_label_string("Current value:  " );

    // Display the count views.
    display_box.display_value();

    while (menu.get_user_selection()!= 0)
        {
        menu.execute_selection();
        display_box.display_value();
        }
}
```

The count view container creates and customizes a count console menu and a console display box for an integer count. The count view container determines the presentation order. The count view container applies a user-driven event loop.

Run the Code

Try out the full integer count code.

```
int main()
{
    // Create a count view container.
    Count_View_Container my_count_view_container;

    cout << endl << "INTEGER COUNT Demo" << endl << endl;

    my_count_view_container.display_count_views(10);

    cout << endl << "Happy trails." << endl;

    return 0;
}
```

On the console, you should see something like you did before. This time, you did it with a count view container.

Congratulations!

ASCII COUNT

Just when you think that you are safe, and that the OOA, OOD, and OOP work is in good shape, guess who you hear from?

> Dear System Builder,
>
> Thanks for walking through that OOA model with me last week.
>
> You really got me thinking.
>
> I want to count characters, too. For example, if the count is 'a' and I increment, the value should be 'b.'
>
> Regards,
> The Count

Now what?

You need a new kind of count, a character count. At this point, you might just add one for ASCII characters. After all, they correspond to a contiguous integer sequence.

You can even build it as a wraparound counter, too.

(But wait! What about other character systems, ones that don't follow a contiguous integer sequence? No problem. You'll need another specialization of the count class to cover that one. And it's covered later in this chapter.)

Apply the "what's the same; what's different" principle:

What's the same: the value and reset value attributes; the reset service

What's different: the increment and decrement services (the algorithms are different)

The services are different. So you need to add a new problem-domain-based specialization class, modeling those differences.

Just add an ASCII count class to the ongoing model (Figure 1–28).

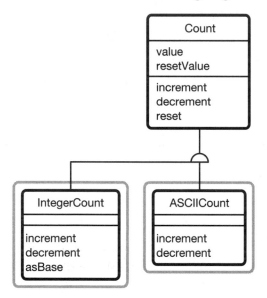

Figure 1–28: Adding an ASCII count class.

No additional attributes or services are needed to support the OOD.

ASCII COUNT: SMALLTALK

Programming the Problem Domain Component

In Smalltalk, individual ASCII characters are objects.

You can create a literal character by typing a "$" followed by one letter. So, "$z" is the character "z." You can also create a character by sending a "value:" message to the character class.

```
Character value: 97
```

This statement creates a character whose ASCII value is 97, displayed as "$a."

Going in the other direction, you can find out the ASCII value of any character by sending it an "asInteger" message.

Try it yourself. Program the initialize, increment, and decrement methods (with increment and decrement wraparounds).

Add a class and its instance variables

Add the ASCII count class.

```
Model subclass: #ASCIICount
    instanceVariableNames: ''
    classVariableNames: ''
    poolDictionaries: ''
    category: 'Counts'
```

Add initialization

ASCIICount methodsFor: 'initialize-release'

initialize
```
    resetValue := $a.
    super initialize
```

ASCIICount methodsFor: 'counting'

Add counting methods

increment
```
    "Set my value to the character with the next ASCII
          value. Check for invalid values and use
          wraparound when the value becomes unprintable."

    | newAsciiValue |
    newAsciiValue := value asInteger > 125
          ifTrue: [33]
          ifFalse: [value asInteger + 1].
    ^self value: (Character value: newAsciiValue)
```

decrement
```
    "Set my value to the character with the previous ASCII
          value. Check for invalid values and use
          wraparound when the value becomes unprintable."

    | newAsciiValue |
    newAsciiValue := value asInteger < 33
          ifTrue: [126]
          ifFalse: [value asInteger - 1].
    ^self value: (Character value: newAsciiValue)
```

Programming the Human Interaction Component

No changes are needed! Use it as is.

Run the Code

Try it out. Create an ASCII count. And create a corresponding count view container (Figure 1–29).

```
CountViewContainer new openOn: ASCIICount new labeled:
    '...ASCII...'
```

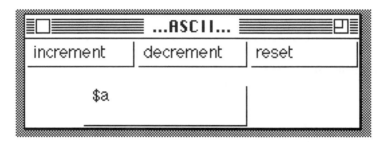

Figure 1–29: An ASCII count.

A Big Point

You just added a new problem domain specialization class.
You left the human interaction component untouched.
And it worked!
The separation of concerns between the human interaction component and the problem domain component—along with inherited mechanisms to keep them loosely coupled—is profound. For effective architecting. For resiliency to change. For increased reuse.

ASCII COUNT: C++

Programming the Problem Domain Component

In C++, characters are represented by integer codes.
This means you can treat characters like integers and perform basic arithmetic operations on them. For example, you can write

```
character = character + 2
```

The integer representation of characters makes it easy to increment and decrement characters. By including the "<ctype.h>" header file, you can use the "toascii" library function. That function translates integer codes into ASCII values.

Declare the class

Try writing out the class declaration yourself. Use the C++ code that you worked out earlier in this chapter as a guide. Make it a wraparound counter while you're at it.

Put the class declaration in a header file:

```
const MIN_ASCII_VALUE = 32;
const MAX_ASCII_VALUE = 126;
class ASCII_Count : public Count<char> {

public:

  // Constructors/destructors
  ASCII_Count() { reset_value = 'a'; reset(); }
  ASCII_Count(char new_char) { reset_value = 'a';
        value = new_char; }
  ~ASCII_Count() { }

  // Implementors
  void increment();
  void decrement();
};
```

Note that the ASCII count class has two constructors.

The first constructor: "As an ASCII count, I set my reset value to the character 'a'; then I set my value to the reset value."

The second constructor: "As an ASCII count, I set my reset value to the character 'a'; then I set my value to the value passed to me as an argument."

Define the member functions

Next, try defining the member functions yourself. Just do it.
Put the definitions in a source file.

```
#include <ctype.h>
#include "count.h"

void ASCII_Count::increment()
{
  value++;

  // Handle wraparound
  if (toascii(value) > MAX_ASCII_VALUE)
    value = (char) MIN_ASCII_VALUE;
}

void ASCII_Count::decrement()
{
```

```
value--;

// Handle wraparound
if (toascii(value) < MIN_ASCII_VALUE)
   value = (char) MAX_ASCII_VALUE;
}
```

Programming the Human Interaction Component

With your first human interaction classes in C++, you created a count console menu and a count console display box.

So what now?

Should you jump in and build an ASCII count console menu and an ASCII count console display box?

Before you do, spend a few minutes playing the "what's the same; what's different" game.

What's the same for an integer count console menu and an ASCII count console menu? They have the same labels:

> Increment
> Decrement
> Reset

They send the same messages:

```
count->increment();
count->decrement();
count->reset();
```

What's different? They interact with different types of counts:

```
Integer_Count* count;
ASCII_Count* count;
```

In C++, what do you do when classes are structurally the same (isomorphic) but differ only in the types of their data members?

You parameterize them using templates!

Parameterizing the Human Interaction Classes

You want to make the "count console menu" class so it works for all types of counts, not just integer counts.

In other words, you want to parameterize the class over the type of count.

It's easy.

Parameterize the Count Console Menu Class

Declare the class

Declare the class, this time replacing the previous type declarations with "Count_Type."

```
template<class Count_Type>
class Count_Console_Menu : public Console_Menu {
public:

  // Constructors/destructors
  Count_Console_Menu() { }
  ~Count_Console_Menu() { }

  // Implementors
  void execute_selection();
  void make_items(Count_Type& a_count);

  // Accessors
  Count_Type& get_count() { return *count; }
  void set_count(Count_Type& a_count)
        { count = &a_count; }

private:

  // Data members
  Count_Type* count;
};
```

Define the member functions

Define the affected class member functions, replacing the previous type declaractions with "Count_Type."

But—and this is an important "but"—the definitions of parameterized member functions must be put in the header file with the class declarations.[20]

```
template<class Count_Type>
void Count_Console_Menu<Count_Type>
        ::make_items(Count_Type& a_count)
{
  this->add_item("Increment");
  this->add_item("Decrement");
  this->add_item("Reset");
  count = &a_count;
}

template<class Count_Type>
void Count_Console_Menu<Count_Type>::execute_selection()
{
  switch (selection) {
    case 1:
      count->increment();
      break;
```

[20]The compiler must see the actual definition of a template function, not just its prototype, to instantiate it.

```
      case 2:
        count->decrement();
        break;
      case 3:
        count->reset();
        break;
    };
  }
```

Parameterize the Count Console Display Box Class

Declare the class

Do the same for the count console display box class. First, declare it:

```
template<class Count_Type>
class Count_Console_Display_Box : public
      Console_Display_Box {
public:

  // Constructors/destructors
  Count_Console_Display_Box() { }
  ~Count_Console_Display_Box() { }

  // Implementors
  void display_value();

  // Accessors
  Count_Type& get_count() { return *count; }
  void set_count(Count_Type& a_count) { count = &a_count; }

private:

  // Data members
  Count_Type* count;
};
```

Define the member functions

Second, define its parameterized member function:

```
template<class Count_Type>
void Count_Console_Display_Box<Count_Type>
      ::display_value()
{
  cout << this->get_label_string()
    << count->get_value()
    << endl;
}
```

Parameterize the Count View Container Class

How about the count view container class for integer counts? Does it need to be parameterized?

Yes. The member function "display count views" creates an *integer count* and initializes it with an *integer* ("initial value").

Oh-oh. Two types. So "display count views" needs to be parameterized over two types. This is a practical example of something called "multiple parameterization."

You can do it. Really!

Here's how.

Declare the class

Declare the class with two parameterized types:

```
template<class Count_Type, class Value_Type>
class Count_View_Container {
public:

  // Constructors/destructors
  Count_View_Container () { }
  ~Count_View_Container () { }

  // Implementors
  void display_count_views(Value_Type initial_value);
};
```

Define the member functions

Define its parameterized member function:

```
template<class Count_Type, class Value_Type>
void Count_View_Container<Count_Type, Value_Type>
    ::display_count_views(Value_Type initial_value)
{
  // Create and initialize the count.
  Count_Type count(initial_value);

  // Create the console menu and display box.
  Count_Console_Menu<Count_Type> menu;
  Count_Console_Display_Box<Count_Type> display_box;

  // Customize the menu for the count.
  menu.make_items(count);
  menu.add_terminator("Quit");
  menu.add_prompt("Make a selection:  ");
```

```
// Customize the display box for the count.
display_box.set_count(count);
display_box.set_label_string("Current value:   " );

// Display the count views.
display_box.display_value();
while (menu.get_user_selection() != 0)
    {
    menu.execute_selection();
    display_box.display_value();
    }
}
```

Run the Code

Try out your new human interaction class—the one that now works for an integer count and for an ASCII count.

```
int main()
{
// Create views for various types of counts.
Count_View_Container <Integer_Count, int>
            integer_count_container;

Count_View_Container<ASCII_Count, char>
            ascii_count_container;

// Demo the various types of counts.
cout << endl << "INTEGER Demo" << endl << endl;
integer_count_container.display_count_views(10);

cout << endl << "ASCII demo" << endl;
ascii_count_container.display_count_views ('k');

cout << endl << "Happy trails." << endl;

return 0;
}
```

On the console, you'll see something like this (the integer demo):

INTEGER Demo

Current value: 10

1. Increment
2. Decrement
3. Reset
4. Quit

Make a selection:

Then (after you quit the integer demo) the ASCII demo:

ASCII Demo

Current value: k

1. Increment
2. Decrement
3. Reset
4. Quit

Make a selection: 4

Happy trails.

DATE COUNT

Guess who you hear from again?

Dear System Builder,

You might consider this a change in requirements. But...I really want to increment and decrement calendar dates, too.

Just thought you'd like to know.

Regards,

The Count.

No problem.

With OOA and OOD, you build models that are resilient to change. And this is essential. Why? Because the world continually changes, and that change must be accommodated. And because increased resiliency to change increases the likelihood of reuse.

All you need to do is add another specialization of the count class! Apply the "what's the same; what's different" principle:

What's the same: the value and reset value attributes; the reset service

What's different: the increment and decrement services (the algorithms are different)

Add a new problem-domain-based specialization class (Figure 1–30).

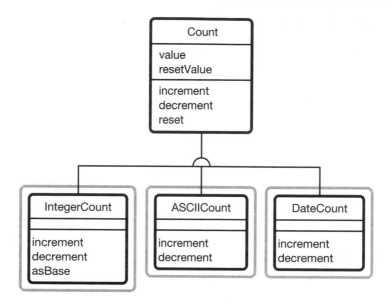

Figure 1–30: Adding a date count.

Notice just how little effort it took to add another kind of count. All you need to do is add another specialization class.

Why so little effort? Simply this: you organized your classes using generalization–specialization. When you do this, you increase the reuse and extensibility of your results—here, for your OOA results.

DATE COUNT: SMALLTALK

Programming the Problem Domain Component

Guess what. In Smalltalk, dates are objects.

You can get today's date by sending the message "today" to the date class.

You can go backward in time with the "subtractDays: " message. And you can go into the future with the "addDays:" message.

Add a class and its instance variables

Add the date count class.

```
Model subclass: #DateCount
   instanceVariableNames: ''
   classVariableNames: ''
   poolDictionaries: ''
   category: 'Counts'
```

Add initialization

DateCount methodsFor: 'initialize-release'

initialize
```
    resetValue := Date today.
    super initialize
```

Add counting methods

Try building the initialize, increment, and decrement methods yourself.

DateCount methodsFor: 'counting'

increment
```
    "Increment my value to the next date."

    ^self value: (value addDays: 1)
```

decrement
```
    "Decrement my value to the preceding date."

    ^self value: (value subtractDays: 1)
```

Programming the Human Interaction Component

No changes are needed! Use it as is.

Run the Code

Try out the date count code with something like the following:

```
CountViewContainer new openOn: DateCount new labeled:
'...dates...'
```

You should see something like this (Figure 1–31):

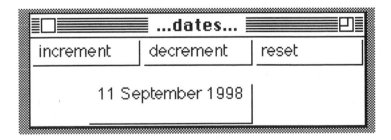

Figure 1–31: The date count.

DATE COUNT: C++

Programming the Problem Domain Component

Dates? There's no date type in the C++ language. However, most C++ class libraries do have a date class.

But don't fret if you can't find one. There's a date class on the source diskette provided with this book.

Here's what its declaration looks like.

```
class Date {
public:

   // Constructors/destructors
   Date();
   Date(int day, int month, int year);
   ~Date() { }

   // Implementors
   void set_date(int day, int month, int year);
   char* print_string();

   // Operators
   Date operator++();          // prefix increment
   Date operator++(int);       // postfix increment

   Date operator--();          // prefix decrement
   Date operator--(int);       // postfix decrement

   friend ostream& operator<< (ostream& os, Date& aDate);

private:
   time_t calendar_time;
   static long seconds_per_day;
};
```

You can create a date for today.

```
Date today;
```

Or, you can create a specific date.

```
Date some_birthday(11,9,98);
```

You can also increment, decrement, and print out dates.

```
Date today;
cout << today;
today++;
today++;
cout << today;
```

```
--today;
cout << today;
```

Declare the class

Now put together the date count class, yourself.

Derive the class from the count class. In the class declaration, declare the constructors and destructors, the accessors, and the member functions (increment, decrement, and reset).

Put the date count class declaration in the file with the count and integer count class declarations. Put the member functions in a separate source file.

Here it is:

```
class Date_Count : public Count<Date> {
public:

    // Constructors/destructors
    Date_Count() { this->reset(); }
    Date_Count(Date& new_date) { reset_value = new_date;
            this->reset(); }

    ~Date_Count() { }

    // Implementors
    void increment();
    void decrement();
};
```

Define the member functions

And so here is the code for the member functions:

```
void Date_Count::increment()
{
    value++;
}

void Date_Count::decrement()
{
    value--;
}
```

Programming the Human Interaction Component

Hmm.

There's a slight problem with the parameterized human interface.

The problem is in the "display value" member function for count console display box:

```
template<class Count_Type>
void Count_Console_Display_Box<Count_Type>
        ::display_value()
{
   cout
      << this->get_label_string()
      << count->get_value()
      << endl;
}
```

In the past examples, an object could just go ahead and directly output the result of the "get value" member function right onto the console.

But no more. A date count value needs special formatting.

What went wrong with the count display box design? Just this: the design and the code assumed too much about the internal details of the count object; that is, it assumed that a count's value is directly displayable—but that's not always true. Tsk, tsk, tsk.

There's a better way. Make the count display box ask its count for its *display* value.

```
count->get_display_value()
```

Note that this puts a service into a problem domain class to support a human interaction class. This is fine. It's part of providing the loose coupling between the problem domain component and the human interaction component.

Do it.

Change the count console display box member function:

```
template<class Count_Type>
void Count_Console_Display_Box<Count_Type>
        ::display_value()
{
   cout
      << this->get_label_string()
      << count->get_display_value()
      << endl;
}
```

Add the "get display value" member function to the count class, ready for use by all its specializations.

```
Count_Type get_display_value() { return value; }
```

Then specialize this member function in the date count class.

First, add the declaration:

```
char* get_display_value();
```

Then, add its definition:

```
char* Date_Count::get_display_value()
{
    return value.print_string();
}
```

Run the Code

Finally, add the date count to your demo program.
Put in a line to create a count view container for a date count.

```
Count_View_Container<Date_Count, Date>
        date_count_container;
```

Insert lines to display the human interaction component.

```
cout << endl << "DATE Demo" << endl << endl;
date_count_container.display_count_views(Date());
```

And on your console, you'll see something like the following as a part of your demo:

DATE Demo

Current value: Fri Sep 11, 1998

1. Increment
2. Decrement
3. Reset
4. Quit

Make a selection: 4

Happy trails.

SEQUENCE COUNT

Guess who contacts you. Again.

> Dear System Builder,
>
> I'd like to count crayons, too. By color. From white...all the way to black. If I increment a color from white, and increment 2 times, I expect that the value might be beige.
>
> Got it?

Regards,

The Count

P.S. I need this for 128 colors. Or even 256 colors.

"Another count, another specialization" is almost becoming a habit by now.

Yet hacking in a specialization without proper conceptualization may lay the groundwork for problems in the future.

Explore the possibilities a bit further.

Suppose that you are an object of the color count class (Figure 1–32). Your value is 'red.' And someone sends you the message "increment." What do you do? What do you need to know?

Think about this for a bit. Really. Then continue reading.

> I'm a color count.
>> I know my color sequence.
>> I know my current position in my color sequence.

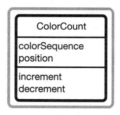

Figure 1–32: "As a color count, I know my color sequence and my position."

This works for any number of colors.

But look at this a bit more. And apply another principle.

The "strip search" principle. Take a compound name and strip out each partial name. Examine each partial name, and see if it might be (1) the name for another class, one that you need, or (2) something that is unnecessarily limiting.

Apply the strip search principle to the name "color sequence." Strip the words apart: color and sequence. Is color the name of another class that you need? No. Is it a word that unnecessarily limits the sequence to being just a color sequence? *Yes.* A color sequence is really just a certain kind of sequence.

Also apply the strip search principle to the name color count. The words are color and count. Is the word "color" another class? No. Is it a word that needlessly limits this special kind of count? *Yes.*

This kind of count is a sequence count (Figure 1–33).

I'm a sequence count.
 I know my sequence.
 I know my current position in my sequence.

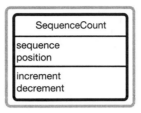

Figure 1–33: "As a sequence count, I know my sequence and my position."

You can apply a sequence count class to many kinds of sequences:

8, 24, 256 colors
An arbitrary character sequence
A non-ASCII character sequence
The cards in a deck
The 131 flavors of ice cream
The room numbers in a hotel

Add the new specialization class: sequence count (Figure 1–34).

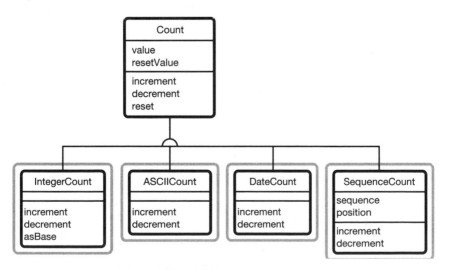

Figure 1–34: Adding a sequence count.

Do you need to add specializations for each kind of sequence count? Only if you want to define a specific sequence one time and then instantiate it many times. In that case, you'd go ahead and add a specific specialization of the sequence count class.

SEQUENCE COUNT: SMALLTALK

Programming the Problem Domain Component

Add a class and its instance variables

Add the sequence count class. Include two instance variables—sequence and position.

```
Count subclass: #SequenceCount
    instanceVariableNames: 'sequence position '
    classVariableNames: ''
    poolDictionaries: ''
    category: 'Counts'
```

Add initialization

When a sequence count is first created, it needs an empty sequence. In Smalltalk, the sequence can be initialized as an object of the ordered collection class.

As long as the sequence is empty, no reset value is known. And increment and decrement just do nothing if the sequence is empty.

SequenceCount methodsFor: 'initialize-release'

initialize
```
    "Initialize the sequence and the sequence pointer.
    I can't initialize my resetValue because the sequence is
    empty."

    position := 1.
    sequence := OrderedCollection new.
    super initialize
```

initializeResetValue
```
    sequence isEmpty ifTrue: [^nil].
    resetValue := sequence first.
    self reset
```

Add counting methods

SequenceCount methodsFor: *'counting'*

increment
"If my sequence is empty, don't do anything.
Otherwise, advance my index pointer.
Don't go past the last item in the sequence."

sequence isEmpty ifTrue: [^self].
position := position + 1 min: sequence size.
self value: (sequence at: position)

decrement
"If my sequence is empty, don't do anything.
Otherwise, back up my index pointer.
Don't go past the first item in the sequence."

sequence isEmpty ifTrue: [^self].
position := position - 1 max: 1.
self value: (sequence at: position)

reset
"Reset my index pointer, then perform my generalization's
reset method."

position := 1.
super reset

Add an attribute accessor

Add a method to access (in this case, set) the sequence itself.

SequenceCount methodsFor: *'sequence accessing'*

setSequence: aCollection
"Set my sequence to aCollection.
Now I can initialize my resetValue."
sequence := aCollection.
self initializeResetValue

Programming the Human Interaction Component

No changes are needed! Use it as is. How sweet it is.

Run the Code

Try out the sequence count code, using something like the following (Figure 1–35):

```
| sequenceCount |
sequenceCount := SequenceCount new.
sequenceCount setSequence: ColorValue constantNames.
CountViewContainer new openOn: sequenceCount labeled:
        '...sequences...'
```

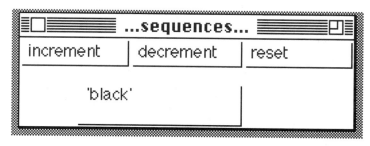

Figure 1–35: A sequence count for a color sequence.

SEQUENCE COUNT: C++

Programming the Problem Domain Component

Build a sequence count that works for sequences of strings. For now, just use a "char star" array (an array of pointers to characters).

```
char* sequence[MAX_SEQUENCE_SIZE];
```

Declare the class

```
class Sequence_Count : public Count<char*> {
public:

// Constructors/destructors
Sequence_Count() { position = -1; }
Sequence_Count(char* new_sequence[]);
Sequence_Count(char* new_sequence[], int sequence_size);
~Sequence_Count() { }

// Implementors
void increment();
void decrement();
void reset();
```

```
    // Accessors
    char** get_sequence() { return sequence; }
    void set_sequence(char* new_sequence[]);

    // Supporting member functions
    void initialize_reset_value();

  private:

    // Data members
    char* sequence[MAX_SEQUENCE_SIZE];
    int position;
  };
```

Note that the constructors and the "set sequence" members aren't defined inline. They're a bit complex for inline definition.

Also note that a new supporting is added here—"initialize reset value." You can use it to initialize the reset value whenever a sequence in a sequence count changes.

Define the member functions

Define the constructors so that they initialize the sequence array as an array of strings:

```
Sequence_Count::Sequence_Count(char* new_sequence[], int
      new_size)
{
   for (int i = 0; i < new_size; i++)
     sequence[i] = new_sequence[i];
   position = 0;
   this->initialize_reset_value();
}

Sequence_Count::Sequence_Count(char* new_sequence[])
{
   this->set_sequence(new_sequence);
}
```

Define the "set sequence" accessor:

```
void Sequence_Count::set_sequence(char* new_sequence[])
{
   for (int i = 0; i < MAX_SEQUENCE_SIZE; i++)
     sequence[i] = new_sequence[i];
   position = 0;
   this->initialize_reset_value();
}
```

Define the "initialize reset value" supporting member function:

```cpp
void Sequence_Count::initialize_reset_value()
{
   if (position >= 0)
      {
      reset_value = sequence[0];
      this->reset();
      }
}
```

Finally, define how a sequence count increments, decrements, and resets itself:

```cpp
void Sequence_Count::increment()
{
   // If the position is in bounds, increment the position
   // and assign the value.
   if ((position >= 0) && (position < (MAX_SEQUENCE_SIZE -
         1)))
      value = sequence[++position];
   else
      this->reset();
}

void Sequence_Count::decrement()
{
   // If the position is in bounds, decrement the position
   // and assign the value.
   if (position >= 1)
      value = sequence[--position];
}

void Sequence_Count::reset()
{
   // Reset the position and value.
   // (Arrays in C++ begin with location 0.)
   position = 0;
   value = sequence[position];
}
```

Programming the Human Interaction Component

No changes are needed! Use it as is. How sweet it is!

Run the Code

To the demo, add a line to create a count view container for a sequence count:

```
Count_View_Container<Sequence_Count, char**>
    sequence_count_container;
```

Add the lines to display the human interaction component and establish an initial sequence:

```
cout << endl << "SEQUENCE Demo" << endl << endl;
char* color_sequence[MAX_SEQUENCE_SIZE] =
    { "white", "yellow", "orange", "red", "green",
        "blue", "violet", "black" };
sequence_count_container.display_count_containers
        (color_sequence);
```

On the console, you should see something like this:

SEQUENCE Demo

Current value: white

1. Increment
2. Decrement
3. Reset
4. Quit

Make a selection: 4

Happy trails.

SUMMARY

In this chapter, you learned and applied:

OOA and OOD
- Applying practical OOA and OOD notations and strategies
- Planning and doing concurrent development
- Thinking about what an object knows and does—in the first person
- Fitting an OOD with available class libraries
- Architecting for reuse
- Applying the model-view pattern

OOP (Smalltalk)
- Adding a class
- Implementing generalization-specialization with superclass-subclass
- Implementing attributes with instance variables
- Implementing services with methods
- Defining methods
- Sending messages
- Creating objects
- Working with human interaction classes: button and text view
- Applying the broadcast mechanism between model and view classes
- Building a display box class
- Building and reusing a container class

OOP (C++)
- Declaring a class
- Defining member functions
- Implementing generalization-specialization with base class and derived class
- Implementing attributes with data members
- Implementing services with member functions
- Controlling access: public, protected, private
- Using templates
- Creating objects
- Outputting to the console using the insertion operator

- Applying platform-independent human interaction
- Building components for console interaction
- Building a container class
- Using templates to architect reusable human interaction classes
- Using a standard library class: date

You also learned and applied these principles:

The "I'm alive!" principle. Objects can be better understood by thinking about them and talking about them in the first person—"I know my own _____ and I can _____ myself."

The "read it again, Sam" principle. Read your model aloud. Do your words make sense? Do they really? If what you say doesn't make sense, don't blame it on object-oriented thinking (a lame excuse, indeed!). Instead, revise the model to better reflect what you want them to say.

The "-er-er" principle. Challenge any class name that ends in "-er." If it has no parts, change the name of the class to what each object is managing. If it has parts, put as much work in the parts that the parts know enough to do themselves.

The "amount of object think" principle.
Low   Functions—applying functional decomposition rather than an object-oriented partitioning across much of a system
Medium   Managers and data encapsulators—putting all the work in the manager, leaving its subordinates with very little to do
High   Objects at work—putting each action in the object that knows enough to directly carry it out

The "continuum of representation" principle. Use a single underlying representation, from problem domain to OOA to OOD to OOP.

The "one model" principle. Use a single model for classes, objects, and other constructs—across OOA, OOD, and OOP. (Multiple model approaches have floundered ever since first introduced in the 1970s.)

The "simplicity, brevity, and clarity" principle. OOA, OOD, and OOP notations and strategies find strength in simplicity, brevity, and clarity. What's needed is just enough notation (1) to communicate well and (2) to accelerate frequent, tangible results.

The "simpler specializations first" principle. For a class, systematically explore potential specializations, from ones that are simpler and easier understood to ones that are more complex.

The "perpetual employment" principle. Adding a class with endless specializations is not effective, but it can keep you perpetually employed.

The "what's the same; what's different" principle. For two or more specialization classes, ask what's the same? what's different? For differences in presentation, use a service. For differences in attributes and services, apply generalization-specialization.

The "do as I say, not as I do" principle. Use a generalization class to establish a convention that its specializations, both now and in the future, must follow, even when the generalization does no more than define the convention itself.

The "don't touch the whiskey" principle. Don't rapidly respond to management's "WHISKEY" cry: "Why in the H— Isn't Someone 'Koding' Everything Yet?"

The "no big bang" principle. Never, never, never write all the code at once. No big bang event will suddenly make it work correctly.

The "good politics" principle. Implement capabilities beginning with the ones that are most valued by the client, followed by lesser capabilities, in descending order.

The "success breeds success" principle. Implement capabilities that are easier. Demonstrate success. Then build on that experience to help you with more challenging capabilities.

The "tiny step" principle. Choose a very tiny first step. Get it working. Then add more very tiny steps.

The "strut your stuff" principle. Implement a rudimentary version of the human interaction class(es) early, so others can appreciate what you are accomplishing.

The "concurrent development" principle. Apply a concurrent activity development process: with your team, concurrently apply OOA, OOD, and OOP. Why? To improve your understanding of what is needed. To reduce risk. To deliver frequent, tangible results. To get working products to the international marketplace sooner.

The "smaller is better" principle. Put together a small team of up to 12 participants. Include people with special ability—in problem domain knowledge, in OOA, in OOD (human interaction, task management, data management), and in OOP. With larger projects, put together a number of loosely coupled teams.

The "I do it all; I'm the best at ..." principle. As a team member, you may have special ability in the problem domain, in OOA, in OOD, or in OOP. Get busy doing what you do best. And contribute in each of the other areas, too.

The "OOA on OOD" principle. To design an OOD human interaction component, task management component, or data management component, apply OOA strategies upon the respective specialized design area.

The "name a window by what it holds" principle. Name a window by what it holds, rather than by a project-specific, limiting name.

The "separation of concerns" principle. Keep problem domain classes, human interaction classes, task management classes, and data management classes distinct. Why? To facilitate change and reuse, by making it easier to add or change classes in one component without severely impacting the others.

The "I find. I show. I change." principle. For each human interaction object, define what it takes to do this: "I *find* the information that I need to find; I *show* the information that I need to show; and I *change* the information that I need to change."

The "communication then presentation" principle. Design how human interaction objects communicate with problem domain objects. Then incrementally refine the presentation of the results.

The "throw out the middle man" principle. Throw out objects that do nothing more than take a request and pass it on to another object.

The "selecting GUI classes" principle. For each OOD human interaction class, look in the available GUI class libraries—and consider the purpose of each class. Go for (1) an exact match, (2) a generalization you can specialize, (3) a part of what you need, or (4) something more than what you need.

The "discuss the design, not the designer" principle. Discuss the design and how to make it better. Don't tear down the designer; all of us make mistakes; unkind words are of no profit.

The "conservation of architecture" principle. Whenever possible, preserve the shape of the OOD architecture when programming it in an OOPL. Even if some of the classes have very few responsibilities, you'll benefit—the same class architecture will still apply when you add or change capabilities in the future.

The "strip search" principle. Take a compound name and strip out each partial name. Examine each partial name, and see if it might be (1) the name for another class, one that you need, or (2) something that is unnecessarily limiting.

2

The Vending Machine

By now, you have probably gotten the idea that a disarmingly simple example can have many profound lessons.

The example this time? A vending machine.

You'll experience:

OOA and OOD
- Finding more effective class names
- Acting out key scenario scripts
- Architecting for reuse
- Designing whole-part structures and object connections
- Applying the model-view-controller pattern
- Planning and doing concurrent development

OOP (Smalltalk)
- Implementing whole-part structures and object connections
- Using ordered collections
    - adding/removing elements
    - iterating over all elements
- Implementing a thread of execution
    - writing out the thread
    - finding supporting methods
    - working backwards through the scenario
- Testing object identity: equality vs. equivalence
- Printing an object on the transcript window
    - the default approach
    - how to specialize
- Using the cascade operator to send multiple messages
- Writing conditional tests with boolean and block objects
- Repeating statements with conditional loops
    - while loop
    - times repeat

- Building a reusable container class
  creating buttons
  creating display boxes
  opening a window with a label and a size
- Adding the controller to the model-view-controller pattern
OOP (C++)
- Class libraries: object-oriented versions of basic types
- Replacing char* variables with string objects
- Using reference variables for pass-by-reference function calls
- Declaring a class with a forward reference
- Implementing whole-part structures and object connections
- Resolving order of declaration conflicts
  using pointers and references, not objects
  accessing after definition, not declaration
- Writing member functions
  using the "this" pointer
  using the class member access operator
  accessing data members and invoking member functions
- Overloading operators—equality insertion
- Refining the human interaction classes, using string objects
- Using display flags to build multi-purpose human-
  interaction classes

Let the games begin ...

SOME OOA

It all begins one day with a memo from The Big Cheese.

> Dear Troops:
>
> Effective today, I want you to build me a new vending machine system.
>
> It'll be kind of like the one I grew up with—it's a machine with columns of cans in it. Put in some coins. Make a selection. And out comes a Coca-Cola. A Pepsi. Or that Jolt you young people like to drink.
>
> Simple, right?
>
> Of course, we'll want to use this system on all our vending machines. But that object dust you use makes reuse a snap, right? Ha! I'll believe it when I see it.
>
> Go get 'em.

Sincerely yours,

The Big Cheese

Begin with some OOA. This time, you'll apply an OOA strategy that emphasizes class name refinement and scenario scripts.

Getting Some Initial Classes

Hurry. You've got to rush out a quick solution to The Big Cheese.

Sketch out a plan. Do some OOA and OOD this afternoon. Find some initial classes. Refine them tonight. And start coding in the morning (but not too early, though; even The Big Cheese needs to face that reality).

Take a look at the boss's vending machine (Figure 2–1).

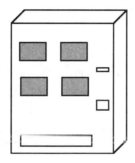

Figure 2–1: The boss's vending machine.

Using the boss's vocabulary, what are the core classes? How about column, can, and cash device (Figure 2–2)?

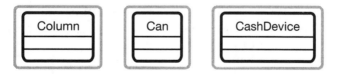

Figure 2–2: A first cut at the core classes.

Do you need a vending machine class? Probably not. Why? The entire OOA model describes what a vending machine is all about; the OOA model describes what the system needs to know and do, partitioned and presented using problem domain classes.

When would you need a vending machine class? Only when you need to capture something the system needs to know or do which doesn't otherwise fit into other problem domain classes. Examples: the vending machine's manufacturer, model number, and serial number; the vending machine's behavior across a collection of columns.

A column may hold some number of cans. It's a container. Its content is zero or some number of cans.

A can is held in a specific column.

Add a whole-part structure to the OOA model (Figure 2–3).

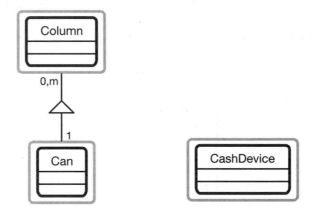

Figure 2–3: A column and its cans.

Have you chosen effective class names?

Who cares?

After all, if the boss wants a can vending machine, you could just give him a can vending machine. Just go ahead and design the human interaction and code it up.

Oh yeah?

With this attitude, reuse of OOA, OOD, and OOP results is very unlikely.

It *is* worth the time and effort to get the class names right. The primary principle is:

The "pay up" principle. Pay me now. Or pay much, much more later.

And it comes along with a number of supporting principles:

The "haste makes waste" principle. Haste makes waste, even with objects.

The "hacker's paradise" principle. No matter what the language, the universal cry for hackers is "I just code it up." Systems built this way are truly a hacker's paradise.

The "change, change, change, change, change" principle. Use a simple set of pictures to architect a system. Use a medium that you can inexpensively change again and again, encouraging and supporting creativity and innovation. Simple, flexible notation is essential.

The "emotionally attached" principle. Architect with OOA and OOD. Look for innovative ideas and apply them early in your work (while the project is young and your emotional investment in a particular solution is not as great). A warning sign? Rejecting new ideas with the words "after all, I've already built this much and it runs just fine." Such emotional attachment can be very counterproductive to finding new, breakthrough ideas on how to best architect a system.

The "perpetual employment" principle. Years ago, assembly language programmers learned that obscure coding resulted in perpetual employment. By shortcutting past OOA and OOD, you can do the same; the code will be so obscure and so brittle that you'll be sorely needed, forevermore.

The "Frankenstein" principle. Be careful what you hack up one night in the lab; the result may follow you for years to come.

By spending a little time up front getting the conceptualization right, you can develop an architecture that will remain stable across a family of systems. Here, this includes the Big Cheese's can machine, simpler ones (ones that dispense cans at no cost) and more complex ones (ones that work with UPCs, Universal Product Codes).

Without investing the time and effort to discover a reasonable conceptualization, you have little hope for reuse in-the-large.

With it, you've taken a very significant step toward future reuse of analysis, design, and code.

It's worthwhile to expand the vending machine OOA model so that it can graciously accommodate change during the construction of this system. You'll also position the results for better competitive advantage should you choose to build a family of systems.

Are you thinking about just one kind of human interface?

Are the class names you've selected just too narrow in scope because you're familiar with what the human interface normally looks like?

One principle is key here.

The "variety pack" principle. Consider a series of human interaction alternatives, from simple to futuristic. If you are already familiar with just one or two approaches, work through a family of possibilities.

Especially if you are familiar with just one human interface for the system under consideration, watch out. You might pick classes that mimic that one presentation and interaction style.

The variety pack principle is another key for developing an overall architecture that is more resilient to change and more likely to be reused.

Consider a wide variety of possibilities for human interfaces. Think of some options that are a bit on the wild side. Make sure that the class names you have chosen apply across a family of potential systems.

To begin with, consider a variety of vending machines in use today (built by your company or by competitors). Get out and take a look at what vending machines are available (Figure 2–4).

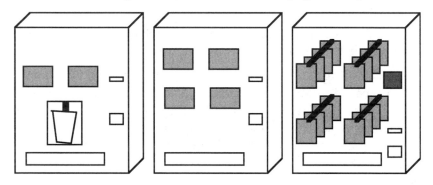

Figure 2–4: Some present-day vending machines.

What might scenarios be for an advanced system?

Future 1. I ask for an individual item I see at some position in a rack. Based on the individual item's UPC and the package expiration date (captured electronically when the item is put into the rack), the price is looked up and displayed. I see the price for that item, displayed in several currencies. I put cash in. I get the item that is dispensed to me. I get change (if any) in the currency that I first entered into the machine.

Future 2. I scroll through a list of items that are available. I ask for one. I read the item name, brand, photo, and sales pitch presented on the screen. An aroma generator gives me a sniff of the item itself, enticing me to make a purchase ("just smell that aroma of fresh-baked cookies"). I put in my credit card. I get the item that is dispensed to me.

All three class names—column, can, and cash device—seem too restrictive. They just don't apply across a family of systems. But how can you improve these names?

When and how to generalize a class name

Are the class names too specific? Are they going to impede reuse by assuming a focus that's needlessly narrow?

It's worth some time and effort to look carefully at each class name.

The "it's my name; generalize it" principle. Take all or part of a class name. Generalize it into a new name. If both names imply identical system responsibilities, then just use the more general name (encourage wider reuse). However, if the names imply different system responsibilities, use both classes in your model (increase the problem domain partitioning of system responsibilities).

Column. Generalize for a better fit. A column holds some number of items. And it dispenses whatever item is "dispensable."

A column is a holder. It also is a dispenser.

A column is a certain kind of dispensing holder. Each dispensing holder holds items. And each dispensing holder knows how to "dispense."

Both class names imply the same responsibilities. So to encourage reuse in a wide number of applications, use "dispensing holder" for the class name.

Can. Generalize for a better fit. A can is an item. An item has a name and price (plus perhaps a description, a serving size, and the like). The same things that apply to "can" apply to "item." Nothing additional is needed for a "can." So use the more generally applicable name here: item.[1]

Cash device. Generalize to point to the future. A cash device is a specialization of a money device. A money device might specialize into different kinds of money devices, for example, cash device and electronic funds device. A cash device gets cash; it knows the amount

---

[1] This OOA model could be expanded a bit further by including both item and product. Then an item has attributes like its own expiration date and manufacturing plant location; a product has attributes like a standard name and standard price. This is an application of an object pattern called "item–item description"; see the article [Coad-1] for more details. The outcome is much the same for this example.

collected. An electronic funds device might get an authorization or approval.

Cash device is what is needed now. A money device class might be useful in the future, in building a system with expanded system scope.

Revise the OOA model in a simple but significant way—with new class names (Figure 2–5).

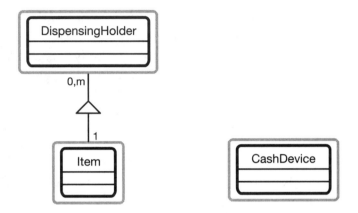

Figure 2–5: Using more effective class names.

A dispensing holder may contain some number of items. And an item is contained in a dispensing holder. Figure 2–6 shows what the whole-part structure in the OOA model represents.

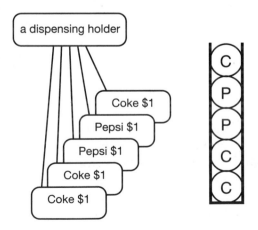

Figure 2–6: A dispensing holder and its items.

Acting Out Interactions

Acting out human interactions

Begin with a vital principle:

The "service with a smile" principle. As an object, I know things and I do things, all for the direct or indirect benefit of someone who uses the system.

What things do these objects need to do to support a person—a person working effectively as a part of this overall system under consideration?

> I'm a person.
> > I walk up to the vending machine.
> > And I look over what is available. I need to see the item name and price (at least that much).
> > I'd like to see how much cash I've put in the machine so far (if a machine has that capability).
> > After I've put in some cash, I may just want to press the coin return lever and come back later.
> > Otherwise, I select what I want.
> > And get it!
> > And I get my change back, for a change.

Right away, you can use the human scenario script to add depth to the OOA model. Add the corresponding attributes and services to the OOA model and you get Figure 2–7.

Note that the person selects an item. He really doesn't care which dispensing holder is holding that item. The person selects an item.

Now just a minute. The *person* selects an item. That sounds like something that a person does when he walks up and uses the vending machine.

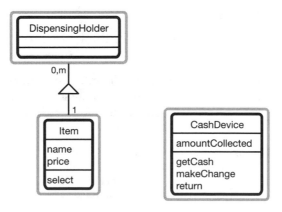

Figure 2–7: Adding things that a person using the system needs from the system.

An item *doesn't* select itself. In fact, no problem domain object selects itself.

The "select ain't my job, it's your job" principle. As a problem domain object, let me set you straight: "select" services aren't my job; it's a human interaction object's job.

The alternative? An item does something to itself (Figure 2–8).

"I'm an item. What do I do to myself? I *vend* myself."[2]

Wow! Note that with object-oriented development, you use problem domain classes and structures to architect a system. Then you consider what each object—the abstraction, not a real one—knows and does. And this means that even the abstractions of inanimate real objects come to life—knowing things and doing things.

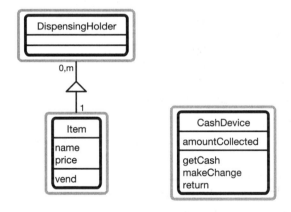

Figure 2–8: An item vends itself.

Acting out object interactions

Explore the object interactions in the OOA model, applying the following principle:

The "me, myself, and I" principle. Think about an object in the first person. Talk about an object in the first person. Write about an object in the first person. Put yourself in the midst of the architecture. "I'm a

---

[2]You could say that the dispensing holder has a name and a price. And get rid of the item class. But that decision limits the vending machine to columns with a fixed column name and column price. In contrast, a more general model (like the one in this chapter) supports columns and items, with each item having its own name and price.

_____ object; I know my _____ ; and here's what I do: _____." Keep "it, its, and itself" to a minimum.

Write a scenario script

Try it out. Repeat after me:

I'm an item.
　　Someone tells me to vend myself.
　　I need some help getting enough cash.
　　I tell my dispensing holder to dispense.
I'm a dispensing holder.
　　Someone tells me to dispense.
　　I look to see if the item that I'm told to dispense is
　　　　dispensable. If it is, then I dispense it.
　　I return a result to the sender—"dispensed" or "not
　　　　dispensed."
I'm an item.
　　If my dispensing holder returns "dispensed," then I
　　　　delete myself.
　　I need some help making change.
　　I return a "dispensed" or "not dispensed" result to the
　　　　sender.

What about interaction with the cash device?

I'm an item.
　　I know my price.
　　I know my corresponding cash device.
　　I send it a message to get the amount collected.
I'm a cash device.
　　I get cash.
　　I know the amount collected.
　　Someone asks me what amount I've collected; I
　　　　respond with that value.
I'm an item.
　　If the amount collected is greater than or equal to my price
　　　　I tell my dispensing holder to dispense.
　　　　I tell my cash device to make change.
　　Otherwise
　　　　I return a "not dispensed" result to the sender.
I'm a cash device.
　　I make change.
I'm an item.
　　I return a "dispensed" result to the sender.

Add interactions and services

Add object interactions and a "dispense" service to the OOA model. Label the scenario messages as scenario A, numbers 1, 2, and 3 (Figure 2–9).

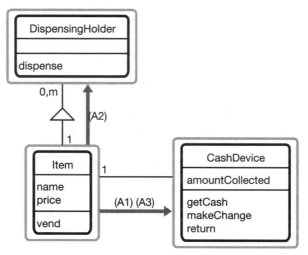

Figure 2–9: Adding object interactions.

Check out the constraints

As an item,

- I need to know about my cash device.
- I won't vend myself if the cash device doesn't have enough cash.

But does the cash device care about the item? In other words, do you need to add the connection variable and accessors to connect *from* a cash device *to* an item?

No. Why? Think about what a cash device does. "I'm a cash device. I get cash. I return cash. I check to see if I've got enough cash." None of these actions require a knowledge of an item.

For the scenario script, a cash device doesn't need to know about an item.

On the other hand, for free-form queries, you might choose to go ahead and implement the connection variable and the corresponding accessors; someone might come along just to query "for this cash device, what are your corresponding items." But such a query doesn't make a lot of sense, here.

So a cash device doesn't need to know about a connection to some number of items. Don't put a connection constraint next to cash device.

Refine who does what

Item is doing a lot of math—maybe too much math.
The principles are:

The "don't expect me to do all the work" principle. Don't just ask another object for its value(s), and then work on it yourself. Tell the object to do the work for you, giving you a more meaningful result.

And:

The "more than just a data hider" principle. If an object acts as just a data hider when an object sends it a message, check if it can do something more. Even if the work is modest, you may find a way to improve both distribution of responsibility, and encapsulation, partitioned by problem domain classes.

Make the cash device do the math:

> I'm an item.
>> I send a message "got enough (price)" to my cash device.
>
> I'm a cash device.
>> Someone asks me if I've got enough. If my amount collected is greater than or equal to the price he gives me, then I answer "yes." Otherwise, I answer "no."

Update the OOA model to reflect this new partitioning (Figure 2–10.)

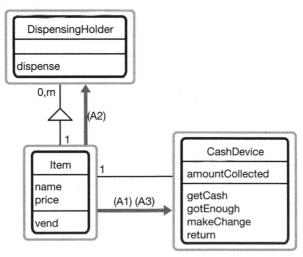

Figure 2–10: Getting the cash device to do more.

Sanity Check

Does this OOA model hold up across a family of systems?

How about a machine with columns and one kind of item in each column?

Item

name:	Coca-Cola
price:	$1
also knows:	its dispensing holder
also knows:	its cash device

name:	Coca-Cola
price:	$1
also knows:	its dispensing holder
also knows:	its cash device

name:	Coca-Cola
price:	$1
also knows:	its dispensing holder
also knows:	its cash device

Dispensing Holder

dispense:
> check to make sure that I'm not just empty
> dispense it

How about a spiral mechanism, one that just twists a full rotation to dispense whatever item happens to be there?

Item

name:	L4
price:	$1
also knows:	its dispensing holder
also knows:	its cash device

name:	L4
price:	$1
also knows:	its dispensing holder
also knows:	its cash device

Dispensing Holder

dispense:
> check to make sure that I'm not just empty
> dispense it

How about a column that may hold different items? No problem.

Item

name:	Coca-Cola
price:	$1
also knows:	its dispensing holder
also knows:	its cash device

name:	Pepsi
price:	$1
also knows:	its dispensing holder
also knows:	its cash device

name:	Jolt
price:	$1
also knows:	its dispensing holder
also knows:	its cash device

Dispensing Holder
  dispense:
    check to make sure that I'm not just empty
    check to make sure that the next one I'm holding is
        the one that I've been told to dispense
    dispense it

Wonderful.
Use these OOA results, do some OOD, and get into some OOP!

SOME PLANNING

You've worked out the OOA model quite a bit. Now you can go ahead and do some OOD and OOP, concurrently.

But if you're going to do some OOD and some OOP, where do you begin? How do you decide what to build first?

Two principles help you here:

The "good politics" principle. Design and code the capabilities that will most impress your customer (or perhaps your boss).

The "nice threads" principle. Design and code the capabilities that support a major thread of execution (a major scenario script).

For this example, begin with two core classes—dispensing holder and item. In other words, produce some tangible results more rapidly, by making a simplification: all items are free (just for this first round of OOD and OOP). Design and code as in Figure 2–11.

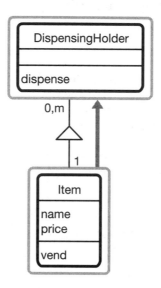

Figure 2–11: Planning for the first round of OOD and OOP.

For the second round, design and code the rest, as in Figure 2–12.

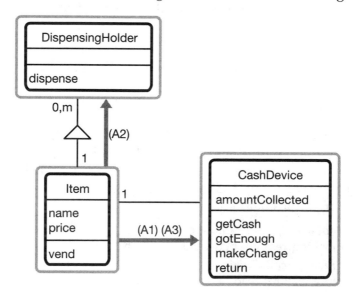

Figure 2–12: Planning for the second round of OOD and OOP.

Onward!

OOD—THE PROBLEM DOMAIN COMPONENT (THE FIRST ROUND)

The OOA results fit right into the midst of the OOA/OOD model, in a major component, called the problem domain component.

During OOD, you need to make certain additions and extensions to what was developed with OOA. Here, you need to add specific mechanisms for implementing whole-part structure.

About Designing a Whole-Part Structure

A whole-part structure is a mapping between objects. A whole knows about its parts; a part may know about its whole.

Design a whole-part structure by adding an attribute to the class of each participating object. Annotate each added attribute with "(d)," indicating it's there solely to support the design (Figure 2–13).

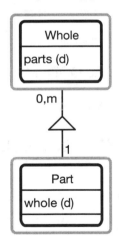

Figure 2–13: Implementing a whole-part structure.

Designing a Specific Whole-Part Structure

Add design attributes to dispensing holder and to item (Figure 2–14).

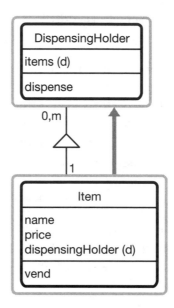

Figure 2–14: Implementing a whole-part structure for this example.

For now, that's it for the OOD additions to these two problem domain classes.

Onward to Smalltalk. And then to C++.

OOP—THE PROBLEM DOMAIN COMPONENT: SMALLTALK (THE FIRST ROUND)

What do you do at this point?

- Implement the problem domain classes as specializations of the model class.
- Implement the attributes in the OOA/OOD model as instance variables.
- Add methods to initialize the instance variables at the time an object is created.
- Add the methods to implement the services in the OOA/OOD model.

Here's a step-by-step guide:

For each class:
- Add a class and its instance variables.
- Add an intialization method.

- Add attribute accessors.
- Add connection accessors.
- Add a creation method.

And then for each class:

- Add methods to implement the services in an OOA/OOD model.

For this example, use the system browser and add a new class category, "Vending." Within that class category, you'll add the problem domain classes.

The Item Class

Add a class and its instance variables

Start with the item class. The class has two problem domain variables (name and price) and one connection variable (dispensing holder).

```
Model subclass: #Item
    instanceVariableNames: 'name price dispensingHolder '
    classVariableNames: ''
    poolDictionaries: ''
    category: 'Vending'
```

Add Initialization

To initialize an item, use this method:

```
Item methodsFor: 'initialize-release'
```

initialize
```
name := String new.
price := 0.0
```

When an item object is first created, the value of its dispensing holder variable is nil, meaning undefined. And that's just what you need here.

Add attribute accessors

Add accessors for the problem domain attributes. For accessors that set a value, add a line for model-view change notification.

```
Item methodsFor: 'accessing'
```

name
```
"Return the current value of name."

^name
```

name: aName
   "Set the value of name. Notify my dependents
        that I've changed."

   name := aName.
   self changed: #name

price
   "Return the current value of price."

   ^price

price: aPrice
   "Set the value of price. Notify my dependents
        that I've changed."

   price := aPrice.
   self changed: #price

Add connection accessors
(how to implement a single connection with other objects)

Add the connection accessors. Use a separate method category (protocol) called connections. Why? So you can separate the accessors for variables that describe an object from the accessors for variables that describe connections to other objects.

This section shows how to implement a single connection with other objects. Use this approach when implementing the side of a whole-part structure or an instance connection marked with a limit equal to one (for example, "0,1" or just plain "1").[3]

   Item methodsFor: 'connections'

connectToDispensingHolder: aDispensingHolder
   dispensingHolder := aDispensingHolder

dispensingHolder
   ^dispensingHolder

---

[3]OOA and OOD distinguish between whole-part structure and object connections. Here's why. Whole–part is one of the three basic methods of organization that people use. It's very strong semantically. It communicates part of the overall structure of the model. It provides a useful abstraction mechanism—a whole and its parts.

An object connection portrays something weaker. It models just an association, a tying together, of two objects because they are somehow associated and the objects need to remember that association.

Both whole-part structure and object connections are mappings between objects. The underlying meaning is quite different. This distinction is helpful in OOA and OOD. In OOP, you may end up using the same implementation approach for both.

Add object creation

Add a method which creates a new object and then tells that object to initialize itself.

Item class methodsFor: 'instance creation'

new
```
^super new initialize
```

Add more methods

You still need to add methods to implement each service in the OOA/OOD model. You're not quite ready to do so. Return to this after you've defined the dispensing holder class.

The Dispensing Holder Class

Program the dispensing holder class.

Add a class and its instance variables

```
Model subclass: #DispensingHolder
    instanceVariableNames: 'items '
    classVariableNames: ''
    poolDictionaries: ''
    category: 'Vending'
```

Add initialization

DispensingHolder methodsFor: 'initialize-release'

initialize
```
items := OrderedCollection new
```

A dispensing holder may be connected to more than one item. Hence, the items variable needs to hold a collection. In fact, it's an ordered collection.

An ordered collection is very much like a list, only smarter.

> As an ordered collection,
> I know my size.
> I know how to do things with each of my elements
>   (no more 'off by one' loop index errors, folks).

```
anOrderedCollection do: [:each | each printString]
```

This statement sends the message "printString" to each element in the ordered collection. The expression

```
:each |
```

creates a temporary variable. One by one, each element in the collection is assigned to that temporary variable; then the statements following the vertical bar are executed.

To collect the results of doing things with each element in a collection, use the "collect:" message.

```
anOrderedCollection collect: [:each | each printString].
```

This returns a new ordered collection containing the results of sending each element the "printString" message. So there should be one result for each element in "anOrderedCollection."

An ordered collection comes with a lot of capability. So when a variable needs to hold connections to some number of objects, let it hold an ordered collection.

Add attribute accessors

The dispensing holder class doesn't have any problem domain attributes.

On to the next step.

Add connection accessors
(how to implement a multiple connection with other objects)

This Smalltalk code shows how to implement a multiple connection with other objects. Use this approach when implementing the side of a whole-part structure or an instance connection marked with a limit greater than 1 (for example, "0, m" or "1, 5" or even just "2").

```
DispensingHolder methodsFor: 'connections'

connectToItem: anItem
    items add: anItem

disconnectWithItem: anItem
    items remove: anItem ifAbsent: []

items
    "Return the current value of items."

    ^items
```

Here's something new. As a dispensing holder, when I disconnect with an item, I need to remove that item from my list of connections. I do it with this statement:

```
items remove: anItem ifAbsent: []
```

This statement sends the message:

```
remove: ifAbsent:
```

to an ordered collection. And that ordered collection removes that object from itself.

There is a shorter message to remove an object from an ordered collection.

```
remove:
```

But if the object you want to remove is no longer in the collection, you'll get an error message. You're better off specifying what you want the software to do (or not do) if this occurs.

The statement:

```
items remove: anItem ifAbsent: []
```

tells the ordered collection, that if the object is absent, don't do anything special about it.

Add object creation

Add a method which creates a new object and then tells that object to initialize itself.

```
DispensingHolder class methodsFor: 'instance creation'
```

new
```
    ^super new initialize
```

Adding Methods to Implement Each OOA/OOD Service

All that's left now is to define methods that implement the services in the OOA/OOD model.

Write out what you want each method to do

Before you jump in and code, sit down and write out in your own words just what each method needs to do. Write it in the first person (me, myself, and I).

item
   vend
      I tell my dispensing holder to dispense me.
      If it succeeds, I release myself and return true.
      Otherwise, I return false.

   dispensing Holder

dispense: an item
I check if I'm empty.
    If so, I return false.
I check to see if an item is dispensable.
    If not, I return false.
I activate the dispenser.
I return true.

Identify the supporting methods

Identify the supporting methods that you need to program.

item
    vend
dispensing holder
    dispense
        test if I'm empty
        test if the requested item is dispensable
        activate the dispenser
        break this connection that I have with an item

Work backward through a key scenario script

Where do you begin? Start with the object at the end of a key scenario script and work backward. Implement all the methods for each class that you encounter; that's what will happen here. (An alternative: implement just those methods that affect the scenario script; add the other methods later.)

The "backward through the script" principle. When programming methods to implement the OOD services, work backward through the script. Why? This strategy lets you start small, try it, and test it; then you can add pieces that can invoke the methods you've already programmed.

So in this case, begin with what the dispensing holder needs to do. Then move back to what an item needs to do.

Add testing methods

Build the two testing methods.
Like so:

```
DispensingHolder methodsFor: 'testing'
```

isEmpty
```
^items isEmpty
```

```
itemIsDispensable: itemToDispense
    "Check if the first item and the item to dispense
        are the same object. Be sure to use == rather
        than =."

    ^items first == itemToDispense
```

Note that a dispensing holder considers an item as dispensable if it is the first item in its ordered collection of items.

Consider the equivalence operator, "==", in the statement:

```
    ^items first == itemToDispense
```

There are two ways to test the identity of an object, an equivalence test (==) and an equality test (=).

For this equivalence statement to return true:

```
    object1 == object2
```

just one object is held by (pointed to by) both of these variables.

For this equality statement to return true:

```
    object1 = object2
```

the objects held by these variables have the same structure and values.

Here's an example:

```
    |array1 array2|
    array1 := Array size: 4.
    array2 := Array size: 4.
    array1 = array2
```

Objects array1 and array2 are equal but not equivalent.

Add the activate method

Turn your attention to a method to activate the dispenser.

Even with an actual dispenser mechanism, you'd probably want to simulate telling it to dispense. And then you could hook up your software system with the actual dispenser mechanism after that.

In this example, you can simulate the actual dispensing by displaying something along the way, like some information about the item being dispensed.

Every object knows how to generate a printable string describing itself; the method is called "printString." For example, this is how to get a printed string for an item's price:

```
    item price printString
```

Remember that the evaluation sequence is from left to right, with precedence given to parentheses.

To get the printed result, you need to send a message to someone who can display a result for you. To do this, use the global variable "Transcript."

Aggghhhhh! Global variables? FORTRAN forever?

Oh, calm down a bit.

Yes, Smalltalk does have global variables. And each global variable begins with a capital letter.

Don't add your own global variables. Ugh! Good grief!

But there are some system-defined global variables that make life easier. "Transcript" is a good example. It holds the object that is responsible for the system transcript window. You need to know what that object is so that you can send it messages. The system creates that object, you don't. And the system needs to let you know what that object is. The global variable "Transcript" makes that possible.

You can write something on that system transcript object[4] by sending it a "show:" message with a string argument. For example,

```
Transcript show: 'Releasing item: '
```

The message "cr" adds a carriage return.

```
Transcript cr.
Transcript show: 'Releasing item: '
```

Strings are concatenated with the concatenation operator, "," .

```
| string1 string2 string3 |
string1 := 'Releasing '.
string2 := 'item'.
string3 := string1, string2.
Transcript cr.
Transcript show: string3
```

Here's a more compact way.

```
| string |
string := 'Releasing ', 'Item'.
Transcript cr; show: string
```

Note that this takes two statements:

```
Transcript cr.
Transcript show: string
```

and combines them into one statement:

---

[4]Using "Transcript" in Smalltalk is much like using the "cout" stream in C++.

```
Transcript cr; show: string
```

using the cascade operator, ";". The cascade operator is a shorthand way to send multiple messages to an object.

Here's how to display something about the item that's being dispensed.

```
DispensingHolder methodsFor: 'simulating'
```

printItem: itemToDispense
    Transcript cr.
    Transcript show: 'Releasing item: ' , itemToDispense
        name; space; space.
    Transcript space; show: 'price: ' , itemToDispense
        price printString

An alternate way to do this is to get "printString" to work for an item.[5] Do this by defining your own "printOn:" method (printString calls "printOn:" to get its job done).[6] Write a "printOn:" method for item.

```
Item methodsFor: 'printing'
```

printOn: aStream
    aStream nextPutOn: 'item:'; space; space.
    aStream nextPutOn: name printString; space; space;
        space.
    aStream nextPutOn: 'price:'; space; space.
    aStream nextPutOn: price printString

Then you can write the print item method like this:

printItem: itemToDispense
    Transcript cr.
    Transcript show: 'Releasing ', item printString

For the simulation, make the activate method itself just a no-op:

```
DispensingHolder methodsFor: 'dispensing'
```

activateDispenser
    ^self

Then invoke that method and the simulating method with the following statements:

---

[5]This is very much like overloading the insertion operator, "<<," in C++.

[6]Actually, "printString" is a system method. It sends its receiver the "printOn:" message. Various classes specialize the "printOn:" method.

```
printItem: itemToDispense.
self activateDispenser
```

Add the "break the connection" method

You already did this. It's the "disconnectWithItem" method.

Add the dispense method

Finally, you can program the dispense method itself.
Put it together:

```
DispensingHolder methodsFor: 'dispensing'
```

dispense: itemToDispense
  "Dispense the item.
  Return true if successful, otherwise false."

  self isEmpty ifTrue: [^false].
  (self itemIsDispensable: itemToDispense) ifFalse:
      [^false].
  self printItem: itemToDispense.
  self activateDispenser.
  self disconnectWithItem: itemToDispense.
  ^true

Run the code

Check out the interaction between a dispensing holder and an item.

```
| anItem aDispensingHolder |
aDispensingHolder := DispensingHolder new.
anItem := Item new.
anItem name: 'Jolt'; price: 0.75.
anItem connectToDispensingHolder: aDispensingHolder.
aDispensingHolder connectToItem: anItem.
aDispensingHolder dispense: anItem.
```

On the transcript window you should see something like this:

Releasing item: Jolt   price: 0.75

About Booleans and blocks

But wait. What are those "true" and "false" objects?
Smalltalk has a Boolean class. That class has two subclasses (specialization classes)—true and false (Figure 2–15).

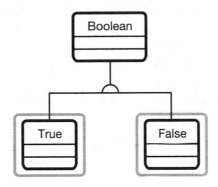

Figure 2–15: The Boolean hierarchy.

There is just one object in the "true" class. And there is just one object in the "false" class. The Smalltalk system creates these objects when it starts up. If you try to make a new true object or a new false object, you'll get an error message. (Look at the Boolean class; read the "new" method; you'll see why this happens.)

The variables "true" and "false" are special variables (the other special variables that you already know about are "self" and "super"). The "true" variable holds the only object in the true class; the "false" variable holds the only object in the false class.

Earlier you built:

```
DispensingHolder methodsFor: 'testing'
```

isEmpty
```
    ^items isEmpty
```

This method returns an object that is either "true" or "false."

```
aBoolean := items isEmpty
```

You'd like to know if "aBoolean" holds the true object or the false object. Just ask "aBoolean" if it's true or if it's false:

```
aBoolean ifTrue: [Transcript cr; printString: 'I"m true.']
         ifFalse: [Transcript cr; printString: 'I"m
            false.']
```

If "aBoolean" holds the true object, then that Boolean object executes the statements inside the brackets that follow "ifTrue:."

If "aBoolean" holds the false object, then that Boolean object executes the statements inside the brackets that follow "ifFalse:."

A pair of brackets and their enclosed statements is called a block closure or (more commonly) a *block*.

A block executes itself when someone sends it the message "value," meaning "execute your statements, returning the value of the last statement that you execute."

The full true–false message set consists of the following:

```
ifTrue:          "returns nil if it's false"
ifFalse:         "returns nil if it's true"
ifTrue: ifFalse:
ifFalse: ifTrue:
```

Take a look at the true class—and how it implements the "ifTrue:" and the "ifFalse:" methods[7]:

```
True methodsFor: 'controlling'

ifTrue: alternativeBlock
   "Answer the value of alternativeBlock."

   ^alternativeBlock value
```

In the "ifTrue:" method, do you see where the block is told to execute itself?

```
False methodsFor: 'controlling'

ifFalse: alternativeBlock
   "Since the condition is true, answer the value of the
       false alternative, which is nil."

   ^nil
```

Try out a few examples in a workspace.

```
true ifTrue: [1 + 3].
false ifFalse: ['hello'].
true ifFalse: ['hello'].
false ifTrue: [1 + 3].
true ifTrue: ['hello'] ifFalse: ['goodbye'].
false ifTrue: ['hello'] ifFalse: ['goodbye']
```

To really understand how blocks work, try this example:

```
|anInteger aBlock|
anInteger := 1.
```

---

[7]From ObjectWorks\Smalltalk, Version 4.1. Used with permission from ParcPlace Systems.

```
aBlock := [anInteger := 12].
anInteger inspect
```

The variable "anInteger" still equals 1 because you didn't tell the block to execute itself. This time, tell the block to do its thing:

```
|anInteger aBlock|
anInteger := 1.
aBlock := [anInteger := 12].
aBlock value.
anInteger inspect
```

The block executes itself. Now "anInteger" equals 12.

Many Smalltalk methods use Booleans and blocks. They are major components in the language's control structures. You'll need them whenever you want an object to perform a test and take an action based on the result.

Continuing backward through a key scenario script: back to item

You've programmed the methods for dispensing holder.

Now you can step back in the key scenario script to item. And implement the "vend" method.

By working backward through the scenario script, you built and tried out a small piece first. You can send a message to a dispensing holder; it will know what to do when it receives that message.

Now you can program and try out a larger piece.

    item
      → vend
    dispensing holder
      ✔ dispense

Add the vend method

Program the "vend" method.

You've already seen what this method is supposed to do:

    item
      vend
        I tell my dispensing holder to dispense me.
        If it succeeds, I release myself and return true.
        Otherwise, I return false.

So go ahead and write the code.

```
Item methodsFor: 'vending'
vend
    | success |
    success := dispensingHolder dispense: self.
    success ifFalse: [^false].
    ^true
```

You could write the code with fewer lines. Just be sure that mere mortals can understand what you're writing, though. Even in OOP, perhaps especially with OOP, this principle applies:

> *The "great code is readable code" principle.* Great code is readable. By you. By other members of the team. And by those who will read your work in the future.

Anyway, you really can write this method with fewer lines. And it's good Smalltalk code:

```
Item methodsFor: 'vending'

vend
    (dispensingHolder dispense: self) ifFalse: [^false].
    ^true
```

Look at the first statement:

```
(dispensingHolder dispense: self) ifFalse: [^false]
```

The expression in parentheses returns a Boolean that is sent the "ifFalse:" message. If it is false, the Boolean's "ifFalse:" method tells the block to execute itself.

An even shorter version? Here it is:

```
vend
    ^(dispensingHolder dispense: self)
```

or just:

```
vend
    ^ dispensingHolder dispense: self
```

Run the Code

Now that you've programmed both dispensing holder and item, try them out.

Plan the demo

Write out the plan in your own words.

> Create some items with names. Put them in an ordered collection.

Create a dispensing holder.

Connect the dispensing holder to each item in the collection; connect each item in the collection to the dispensing holder.

Iterate over the collection of items, sending each one a "vend" message.

Now program it in Smalltalk.

```
| item1 item2 item3 items aDispensingHolder |

item1 := Item new name: 'Coca-Cola'; price:  0.75.
item2 := Ttem new name: 'Pepsi'; price:  0.75.
item3 := Item new name: 'Jolt'; price:  0.75.
items := OrderedCollection with: item1 with: item2 with:
    item3.

aDispensingHolder := DispensingHolder new.

items do:
  [:each |
    aDispensingHolder connectToItem: each.
    each connectToDispensingHolder: aDispensingHolder].

items do:[:each | each vend]
```

As a vended item is dispensed, the code prints a description of it on the system transcript window.

Try it out

Do it.

On the transcript window you should see something like this:

```
Releasing item:  Coca-Cola   price: 0.75
Releasing item:  Pepsi   price: 0.75
Releasing item:  Jolt   price: 0.75
```

Way to go!

OOP—THE PROBLEM DOMAIN COMPONENT: C++ (THE FIRST ROUND)

Do something like what you did with C++ in Chapter 1:

- Implement the problem domain classes as C++ classes.
- Implement the attributes in the OOA/OOD model as data members.
- Add constructors, to initialize the data members at the time an object is created.

- Add implementors to implement the services in the OOA/OOD model.

Although this strategy achieves the same basic goal as the strategy described earlier in this chapter for Smalltalk, the details of this strategy are *very* different. And that's not too surprising. Smalltalk and C++ are very different languages.

Here's the step-by-step approach:

Declare each class
- Declare its constructors.
- Declare its destructor.
- Declare its implementors.
- Declare its accessors.
- Declare its data members.
- Declare its connection accessors.

Define the member functions for each class.

Note the words "declare" and "define."

In C++, a *declaration* makes known that a variable or function exists, has a certain form, and is defined elsewhere. A declaration for a variable or function may be used many times.

In C++, a *definition* of a variable, function, or class gets the compiler to allocate storage for that variable, function, or class. A definition for a variable, function, or class occurs one time only.

About types

So far you've built classes in C++ using the same basic types found in C, namely, int, float, array and char*.

But there's more! C++ class libraries include classes that implement strings, sets, linked lists, stacks, and queues, and many other very useful types.

As you become more comfortable programming in C++, start to replace the basic C types with object-oriented versions in C++. You'll notice a difference in how you think about your programs. Rather than call a function to concatenate two strings, you ask one string to concatenate itself to another. Instead of working with a position index when adding an item to an array, you tell a list to add an item to itself. It's the difference between "function think" and "object think."

At this point, start using a string class (rather than using the char* type). Here's the declaration:

```
class String {
public:
```

```
        // Constructors/destructors
        String() { character_array = new char[1];
               character_array[0] = '\0'; }
        String(char* new_string);
        String(String& new_string);

        String(int integer_to_convert);
        String(float float_to_convert);

        ~String() { }

        // Implementors
        int size() { return string_length; }
        String& copy();

        // Operators
        String& operator+ (String& a_string);
        String& operator+= (String& a_string);
        String& operator= (String& a_string);

        int operator< (String& a_string);
        int operator> (String& a_string);
        int operator== (String& a_string);

        operator char* () { return character_array; }
        friend ostream& operator<< (ostream& os, String&
               a_string);
    private:

        char* character_array;
        int string_length;
    };
```

This string class is included on the diskette that is included with this book.

You can learn a lot by reading a class declaration. By looking at the string class declaration, you see some different ways to create string objects:

```
String my_string;
String my_string("Hello, world.");
String my_string(String("Hello, world."));
String my_string(123);
String my_string(123.45);
```

Also, you discover overloaded operators, the ones that implement string operations like concatenation, assignment, and string comparisons (less than, equality, and greater than).

Declaring the Item and Dispensing Holder Classes

Declare the item class

Here's how to declare the item class:

```
class Item {
public:

    // Constructors/destructors
    Item() { price = 0.0; }
    Item(String new_name, float new_price)
        { name = new_name; price = new_price; }
    ~Item() { }


    // Implementors
    Boolean vend();

    // Accessors
    String& get_name() { return name; }
    void set_name(String& new_name) { name = new_name; }

    float get_price() { return price; }
    void set_price(float new_price) { price = new_price; }

private:

    // Data members
    String name;
    float price;
};
```

Note that the constructor that accepts an item name of type string also accepts an item name of type char*. The string class constructor immediately creates a string object, initialized with that char*.

The constructors use inline code to initialize an object.

The implementor

```
Boolean vend();
```

declares an implementor for implementing a service from the OOD model. It declares a return value of the type "Boolean." Use an enumeration or "enum" to define this type.

```
enum Boolean { false, true };
```

This makes Boolean a new enumerated type: false has the value

0 (zero); true has the value 1. Put this type definition in a header file so that it's available globally within your application.

The accessors get and set the values of the data members.

The private data members are name and price.

Declare the dispensing holder class

Next, program the declaration for the dispensing holder class.

```
class Dispensing_Holder {
public:

    // Constructors/destructors
    Dispensing_Holder() { }
    ~Dispensing_Holder() { }

    // Implementors
    Boolean dispense(Item& item_to_dispense);
};
```

The constructors need no inline code.

The destructor needs no inline code for deallocating dynamically allocated memory.

The class needs no accessors or private data members.

The implementor:

```
Boolean dispense(Item& item_to_dispense);
```

declares an implementor for implementing a service from the OOD model. What's special about this implementor declaration is that it takes an argument of the type "reference to item." A reference argument causes the function to act like "pass by reference" instead of "pass by value."

Like any other function in C++, you can't have an unknown type in the argument list. So how do you accommodate this restriction? You have two choices.

One, declare the item class first, in a header file.

```
class Item {
public:
    ...
private:
    ...
};

class Dispensing_Holder {
public:
    ...
```

```
    Boolean dispense(Item& item_to_dispense);
    ...
private:
    ...
};
```

Or two, use a forward reference to the item class at some time before declaring the dispensing holder class.

```
class Item;     // Forward reference
class Dispensing_Holder {
public:
    ...
    Boolean dispense(Item& item_to_dispense);
    ...
private:
    ...
};
```

About Implementing Connections with Other Objects

Earlier in this chapter, you worked through an OOD for a whole-part structure. How can you implement it in C++?

How to implement a multiple connection with other objects

A dispensing holder knows about some number of items.

This section shows how to implement a multiple connection with other objects. Use this approach when implementing the side of a whole-part structure or an instance connection marked with a limit greater than 1 (for example, "0,m" or "1,5" or even just "2").

Add a private data member called "items" to the dispensing holder class declaration.

C++ does not have a standard library with an ordered collection class. So what are your options? You can look for an available C++ class library that includes an ordered collection. Or you can use a standard data structure (an array or a stack) to implement a collection of items.

Use an array here.[8]

You can use an array of pointers that point to items:

```
Item* items[MAX_ITEMS_SIZE];
```

Admittedly, an array data type is just not as smart as an ordered

---

[8]In Chapter 3, you'll learn another way to implement a collection in C++.

collection class. For example, an array data type doesn't know how many items it holds. So you'll also need an integer data member, to keep track of the index of the last item added in the array:

```
int item_index;
```

Add these connection data members to the class declaration. More specifically, add them to the private data member section:

```
private:

    // Data members
    Item* items[MAX_ITEMS_SIZE];
    int item_index;
```

Next, add the corresponding accessors:

```
public:

    // Accessors
    Item** get_items() { return items; }
    Boolean connect_to_item(Item& anItem);
    Boolean disconnect_with_item(Item& anItem);
```

The accessors declared by

```
Boolean connect_to_item(Item& anItem);
Boolean disconnect_with_item(Item& anItem);
```

return a Boolean to indicate success or failure. For connect, "failure" means that the items array is full. For disconnect, "failure" means that it could not find the item.

The accessor declared by

```
Items** get_items() { return items; }
```

returns an array of pointers to items. (Note that, just like in C, an array name evaluates to the memory address of the first element of the array.)

When you add the connection accessors and data members, the dispensing holder class declaration looks like this:

```
class Dispensing_Holder {
public:

    // Constructors/destructors
    Dispensing_Holder() { item_index = 0; }
    ~Dispensing_Holder() { }
```

```
// Implementors
Boolean dispense(Item& item_to_dispense);

// Accessors
Item** get_items() { return items; }
Boolean connect_to_item(Item& anItem);
Boolean disconnect_with_item(Item& anItem);

private:

// Data members
Item* items[MAX_ITEMS_SIZE];
int item_index;
};
```

How to implement a single connection with other objects

An item knows about its dispensing holder.

This section shows how to implement a single connection with other objects. Use this approach when implementing the side of a whole-part structure or an object connection marked with a limit equal to one (for example, "0,1" or just plain "1").

Add a private data member to the item class to point to the item's dispensing holder:

```
private:

// Data members
Dispensing_Holder* a_dispensing_holder;
```

Add the connection accessors:

```
// Accessors
Dispensing_Holder& get_dispensing_holder()
    { return *a_dispensing_holder; }
void connect_to_holder(Dispensing_Holder&
    new_holder)
    { a_dispensing_holder = &new_holder; }
```

Oh-oh. The accessors can't return a pointer to a dispensing holder unless the dispensing holder class is already declared.

This puts you in a rather difficult situation!

```
class Item {
public:
   ...
   Dispensing_Holder& get_dispensing_holder()
       { return *a_dispensing_holder; }
```

```
    ...
  private:
    ...
  };

  class Dispensing_Holder {
  public:
    ...
    Item** get_items() { return items; }
    ...
  private:
    ...
  };
```

You want to declare the item class; but you must declare the dispensing holder class first. And you want to declare the dispensing holder class; but you must declare the item class first.

Ugh.

What's the solution?

About forward references and resolving order of declaration conflicts

Resolve order of declaration conflicts by using a forward reference. Just follow these guidelines:

> Use pointers and references, not objects.
> A class can include in its members a pointer or a reference to an object of a class that is declared but not defined. It can't include an object of that class.

> Access after definition, not declaration.
> A class can include data members declared through forward reference, but its member functions can't access the members of those data members until their classes are defined.

Use pointers and references, not objects

This is okay:

```
class First;  // Forward reference

class Second {
public:

  Second() { }
  ~Second() { }
```

```
First& get_first()  { return *my_first; }

private:

   First* my_first;            // A pointer to a first object
};
```

The first class is declared but not defined. The second class may contain in its members some pointers and references to an object of the first class.

This is not okay:

```
class First;  // Forward reference

class Second {
public:

   Second() { }
   ~Second() { }

   First& get_first()  { return my_first; }

private:

   First my_first;    // A first object
};                     // Dont do this!
```

The first class is forward-referenced but not declared. The second class contains a data member that is an object of the first class. Don't do this!

Access after definition, not declaration

This is okay:

```
class First;  // Forward reference
class Second {
public:

   Second() { }
   ~Second() { }

   First& get_first() { return *my_first; }

   int get_my_first_integer();

private:
```

```
   First* my_first;   // A pointer to a first object
};

class First {

public:

   First() { integer = 9999; }
   ~First() { }

   int get_integer() { return integer; }

private:

   int integer;
};

// Second class member functions

int Second::get_my_first_integer()
{
   // The first class is defined, so I
   // can call its member functions.
   return  my_first->get_integer();
}
```

The first class is defined before the member function in the second class accesses one of the member functions of the first class.

This is not okay:

```
class First;   // Forward reference

class Second {
public:

   Second() { }
   ~Second() { }

   First& get_first() { return *my_first; }

   int get_my_first_integer();

private:

   First* my_first;   // A pointer to a first object
};

// Second class member functions

int Second::get_my_first_integer()
```

```
{
    // The first class is not defined, so I
    // can't call its member functions.
    return my_first->get_integer();    // Don't do this!
}
```

The first class is not defined, so the member function in the second class can't access the member functions in the first class.

How to implement a single connection with other objects (cont.)

If you follow the guidelines, it doesn't matter which class you define first, item or dispensing holder.

Here, use a forward reference for dispensing holder and declare the item class first.

```
// Forward reference
class Dispensing_Holder;

class Item {
public:

    // Constructors/destructors
    Item() { price = 0.0; }
    Item(String new_name, float new_price)
            { name = new_name; price = new_price; }
    ~Item() { }

    // Accessors
    String& get_name() { return name; }
    void set_name(String new_name) { name = new_name; }

    float get_price() { return price; }
    void set_price(float new_price) { price = new_price; }

    Dispensing_Holder& get_dispensing_holder()
            { return *a_dispensing_holder; }
    void connect_to_dispensing_holder
            (Dispensing_Holder& new_holder )
                { a_dispensing_holder = &new_holder;}

private:

    // Data members
    String name;
    float price;
    Dispensing_Holder* a_dispensing_holder;
};
```

Defining the Member Functions for the Item Class

Define vend, the item class member function. Here's how:

```
// Implementors
Boolean Item::vend()
{
    Boolean success;

    success =
            a_dispensing_holder->dispense(*this);
    return success;
}
```

Take a look at this member function. In particular, examine one of its statements:

```
success =
        a_dispensing_holder->dispense(*this);
```

The part of the statement

```
*this
```

gets the object itself. The special variable "this" is a pointer to the object for which this member function has been invoked. To get the object that the special variable points to, just dereference it by using the dereference operator, "*." This results in "*this."[9]

Another part of the statement uses the class member access operator, "->." This lets you access the members of the object pointed to by the pointer.

To invoke a member function or to access a data member in the same class, you have a choice. You can use "this" plus the class member access operator plus the member name.

```
this->vend();      // Invoke a member function.
this->item_index;  // Access a data member.
```

Or just use the member name.

```
vend();         // Invoke a member function.
item_index;     // Access a data member.
```

This book includes "this->" to encourage "object think"—distinguishing members from just ordinary variables and functions within scope. (Over time, you may choose to drop this optional syntax.)

---

[9]"*this" in C++ is analogous to "self" in Smalltalk.

The syntax:

```
a_dispensing_holder->dispense(*this);
```

tells the dispensing holder to dispense this item.

Defining the Member Functions for the Dispensing Holder Class

Now define the dispensing holder class member functions. Here's what you need:

> connect to item; disconnect with item
> dispense
> > test if I'm empty
> > test if the requested item is dispensable
> > activate the dispenser
> > break the connection that I have with that item

Define the connect and disconnect member functions

Begin with the connection accessors. The first accessor adds a new item connection into the items array and increments the item index.

```
Boolean Dispensing_Holder::connect_to_item(Item& an_item)
{
  if (item_ptr < MAX_ITEMS_SIZE)
  {
    this->items[item_index++] = &an_item;
    return true;
  }
  return false;
}
```

The second accessor removes an item and shifts the array to fill in the gap.

```
Boolean Dispensing_Holder::disconnect_with_item(Item&
      an_item)
{
  for (int i = 0; i < item_index; i++)

    if (*(this->items[i]) == an_item)
    {
      for (int j = i; j < (item_index-1); j++)
        this->items[j] = this->items[j+1];
      item_index--;
      return true;
```

```
    }
    return false;
}
```

Define the testing member functions

A dispensing holder keeps track of the number of items it holds with its "item_index" data member. When that data member equals zero, the dispensing holder is empty.

Add this to the class declaration:

```
Boolean is_empty();
```

and then define it with the following:

```
Boolean Dispensing_Holder::is_empty()
{
    if (item_index == 0)
      return true;
    else
      return false;
}
```

An item is dispensable if it is the first element (actually, the zeroth element) in the items array. Use the equality operator "==":

Add this to the class declaration:

```
Boolean item_is_dispensable (Item& item_to_dispense);
```

and then define it with the following:

```
Boolean Dispensing_Holder::item_is_dispensable(Item&
        item_to_dispense)
{
    if (*(items[0]) == item_to_dispense)
      return true;
    else
      return false;
}
```

About overloading the equality operator

With C++, you can overload language operators, such as "+," "=," and "<."

Why? So you can assign your own meaning to these operators for the objects of a class.

For objects of a user-defined class, some operators have a

default meaning.[10] Most don't. For example, the equality operator, "==", is undefined for objects of a user-defined class. If you need that operator, you must define it yourself.

For items, overload the equality operator so it checks for equality of both item name and item price. (And use the equality operator for strings for comparing item names.)

Here's how:

```
Boolean Item::operator== (Item& an_item)
{
   if ((name == an_item.get_name()) &&
          (price == an_item.get_price()))
     return true;
   else
     return false;
}
```

Define the activate member functions

When a dispensing holder activates a dispenser, an item is dispensed. To simulate this dispensing, you can invoke an "activate dispenser" function (a no-op), and then just print the details about the dispensed item.

```
void Dispensing_Holder::activate_dispenser() { }
```

Note that the print item function uses the insertion operator, "<<."

```
void Dispensing_Holder::print_item(Item& item_to_dispense)
{
   cout << endl << "Releasing item: "
      << item_to_dispense << endl;
}
```

About overloading the insertion operator

You can override the insertion operator with something like this:[11]

```
ostream& operator<< (ostream& os, Item& an_item)
{
```

---

[10]The operators with default meanings are =, unary &, and comma.

[11]A member function requires that its left operand must be an object of the corresponding class. Here, the function is a binary operator. And its left operand is a reference to the predefined output stream class, "ostream." So this overloaded function must be defined as a non-member function.

```
    os << an_item.get_name() << " price: " <<
        an_item.get_price();
    return os;
}
```

Define the dispense member functions

Finally, put it all together with the dispense member function. Here's what it needs to do:

> dispense
> > test if I'm empty
> > test if the requested item is dispensable
> > activate the dispenser
> > break the connection that I have with that item

And so add this to the class declaration:

```
Boolean dispense(Item& item_to_dispense);
```

and then define it with the following:

```
Boolean Dispensing_Holder::dispense(Item& item_to_dispense)
{
    if (this->is_empty())
        return false;
    if (!this->item_is_dispensable(item_to_dispense))
        return false;

    this->activate_dispenser();
    this->print_item(item_to_dispense);
    this->disconnect_with_item(item_to_dispense);
    return true;
}
```

Run the Code

Check out the interaction between a dispensing holder and an item.

```
int main ()
{
    Dispensing_Holder a_dispensing_holder;
    Item an_item("Jolt", 0.75);

    a_dispensing_holder.connect_to_item(an_item);
    an_item.connect_to_dispensing_holder
            (a_dispensing_holder);

    a_dispensing_holder.dispense(an_item);

    return 0;
}
```

On the computer console you should see something like this:

Releasing item: Jolt   price: 0.75

OOD—THE PROBLEM DOMAIN COMPONENT (THE SECOND ROUND)

Adding the Cash Device

It's time to start charging for each and every item.

Add the cash device back into the model. Add connection attributes, too (Figure 2–16).

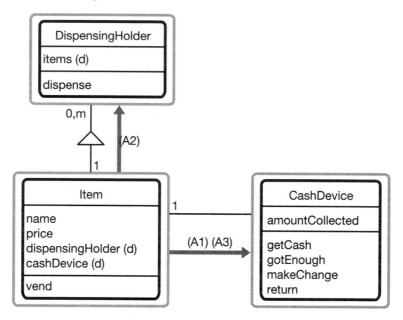

Figure 2–16: Ready for the second round of OOD and OOP.

Here's the plan.

First, build the cash device class.

Second, change the item class so its objects know about and interact with a cash device.

OOP—THE PROBLEM DOMAIN COMPONENT: SMALLTALK (THE SECOND ROUND)

The Cash Device Class

Review the basic approach for adding Smalltalk classes.

For each class:
- Add a class and its instance variables.
- Add an initialization method.
- Add attribute accessors.
- Add connection accessors.
- Add a creation method.

And then for each class
- Add methods to implement the services in an OOA/OOD model.

Add a class and its instance variables

Start by adding the cash device class. It has one instance variable.

```
Model subclass: #CashDevice
    instanceVariableNames: 'amountCollected '
    classVariableNames: ''
    poolDictionaries: ''
    category: 'Vending'
```

Add initialization

Initialization? Is it necessary? You bet.
A cash device collects cash. It better start collecting from zero.

```
CashDevice methodsFor: 'initialize-release'
```

initialize
```
    amountCollected := 0
```

Add attribute accessors

Add the accessors for amount collected, all by yourself. Remember to notify dependents when the amount collected is changed.
Do it.
Now take a look.

```
CashDevice methodsFor: 'accessing'
```

amountCollected
```
    "Return the current value of amount collected."

    ^amountCollected
```

amountCollected: newValue
```
    "Set the value of amount collected.
    Notify my dependents that I've changed."
```

```
amountCollected := newValue.
self changed: #amountCollected
```

Add connection accessors

No connection accessors are needed.

Add object creation

CashDevice class methodsFor: 'instance creation'

new
```
^super new initialize
```

Add the cash collecting methods

Implement the services. Remember to use the attribute accessor for changing the value of amount collected; that method includes the statement to broadcast a change.

CashDevice methodsFor: 'cash collecting'

gotEnough: amountToCollect
```
"Return true if the amount collected is greater than or
     equal to the amount to collect."

^amountCollected >= amountToCollect
```

return
```
"Reset the cash collected.
Return false to indicate cash not collected"

self amountCollected: 0.
^false
```

makeChangeFor: aPrice
```
self amountCollected: amountCollected - aPrice
```

Add a simulation method

How about "get cash"? That involves a physical interaction with some external device. You can simulate a limited form of this interaction. For simulation, you need a method that "feeds" cash into the cash device.

CashDevice methodsFor: 'simulating'

addCash
```
"Increase my amount collected by some default increment."

self amountCollected: (amountCollected +
     self cashIncrement)
```

```
cashIncrement
    ^0.25
```

Run the Code

That's it. The cash device is ready to go. Take it for a trial run. And enjoy your good work.

Take a trial run

```
| cashDevice price |
cashDevice := CashDevice new.
price := 1.00.
(cashDevice gotEnough: price)
    ifTrue: [Transcript cr; show: 'got enough!']
    ifFalse: [Transcript cr; show: 'need more!'].
```

On the transcript, you should see something like this:

need more!

Take a second trial run

Better put in some cash! Use the add cash message (it puts in 0.25 at a time). And try again.

```
| cashDevice price |
cashDevice := CashDevice new.
price := 1.0.
cashDevice addCash.
cashDevice addCash.
cashDevice addCash.
cashDevice addCash.
(cashDevice gotEnough: price)
    ifTrue: [Transcript cr; show: 'got enough!']
    ifFalse: [Transcript cr; show: 'need more!'].
```

On the transcript, you should see something like this:

got enough!

Take a third trial run—with blocks

This is a situation where blocks really pay off. Previously, you used:

```
cashDevice addCash
```

four times to set up the cash device with enough money for a demo.

Instead, you can put the statement in a block and execute the block four times.

```
4 timesRepeat: [cashDevice addCash]
```

This expression executes the statement in the block exactly four times.

But what if you don't know how many times you need to add cash to the cash device? Just check if the cash device has enough money for a demo. As long as the test returns false, just keep adding cash to the cash device.

Here's how to do it, using two blocks:

```
[cashDevice gotEnough: price]
   whileFalse: [cashDevice addCash]
```

The first block:

```
[cashDevice gotEnough: price]
```

is the test block. It's sent the message "whileFalse:" with another block, the loop block, as a message argument.[12]

Consider the loop block:

```
[cashDevice addCash]
```

As long as the test block is false, this loop block is executed. Program the cash device demo one more time:

```
| cashDevice price |
cashDevice := CashDevice new.
price := 1.0.
[cashDevice gotEnough: price]
   whileFalse: [Transcript cr; show: 'need more!'.
      cashDevice addCash].
Transcript cr; show: 'got enough!'
```

On the transcript you should see something like this:

```
need more!
need more!
need more!
need more!
got enough!
```

Adding the Cash Device Interaction to the Item Class

Your cash device works. It's time to add cash device interaction to the item class.

---

[12]Blocks also understand a "whileTrue:" message. You could write the same example, using "whileTrue" (just for fun!).

Add an instance variable

Add the "cash device" connection variable to the item class.

```
Model subclass: #Item
    instanceVariableNames: 'name price cashDevice
        dispensingHolder '
    classVariableNames: ''
    poolDictionaries: ''
    category: 'Vending'
```

Add connection accessors

Add connection accessors to the item class.

Item methodsFor: 'connections'

cashDevice
    "Return the current value of cash device."

    ^cashDevice

connectToCashDevice: aCashDevice
    cashDevice := aCashDevice

Add a testing method

An item is vendable if the cash device has enough cash to cover its price.

Item methodsFor: 'testing'

isVendable
    ^cashDevice gotEnough: price

Update the vend method

Update the vend method with "isVendable" and "makeChange."

Item methodsFor: 'vending'

vend
    | success |
    self isVendable ifFalse: [Screen default ringBell.
        ^false].
    success := dispensingHolder dispense: self.
    success ifFalse: [^false].
    cashDevice makeChangeFor: price.
    ^true

Run the Code

Set up a demo

Set up a vending machine with:

> 3 items to sell at the default price (0.75)
> 1.50 in the cash device

Create some items to sell. And put them in an array.

```
item1 := Item new name: 'Coca-Cola'; price: 0.75.
item2 := Item new name: 'Pepsi'; price: 0.75.
item3 := Item new name: 'Jolt'; price: 0.75.
items := Array with: item1 with: item2 with: item3
```

Create a dispensing holder for the items.

```
aDispensingHolder := DispensingHolder new
```

Create a cash device, with some cash already collected.

```
aCashDevice := CashDevice new.
aCashDevice amountCollected: 1.50
```

Connect the dispensing holder to each item in the collection; connect each item in the collection to the dispensing holder. Also, connect each item to a cash device.

```
items do:
  [:anItem |
     aDispensingHolder connectToItem: anItem.
     anItem connectToDispensingHolder: aDispensingHolder.
     anItem connectToCashDevice: aCashDevice]
```

Finally, one by one, tell each item to vend itself:

```
items do: [:anItem | anItem vend]
```

All together, it looks like this:

```
| item1 item2 item3 items aDispensingHolder aCashDevice |

item1 := Item new name: 'Coca-Cola'; price: 0.75.
item2 := Item new name: 'Pepsi'; price: 0.75.
item3 := Item new name: 'Jolt'; price: 0.75.
items := Array with: item1 with: item2 with: item3.

aDispensingHolder := DispensingHolder new.
aCashDevice := CashDevice new.
aCashDevice amountCollected: 1.50.
```

```
items do:
  [:anItem |
    aDispensingHolder connectToItem: anItem.
    anItem connectToDispensingHolder: aDispensingHolder.
    anItem connectToCashDevice: aCashDevice].

items do: [:anItem | anItem vend]
```

Try it out

You've got three items. Each one costs 0.75.

The cash device has 1.50 in it.

The dispensing holder dispenses what it can, printing what it dispenses each time:

```
Releasing item: Coca-Cola  price: 0.75
Releasing item: Pepsi  price: 0.75
```

Superb!

OOP—THE PROBLEM DOMAIN COMPONENT: C++ (THE SECOND ROUND)

Review the approach for adding each C++ class.

Declare each class.
- Declare its constructors and destructor.
- Declare its implementors.
- Declare its accessors.
- Declare its data members.
- Declare its connection accessors.

Define the member functions for each class.

Apply this approach to the cash device class.

The Cash Device Class

Declare the class

Start with the cash device class.

```
class Cash_Device {
public:

private:

};
```

Add constructors to initialize the amount collected.

You don't need to extend its destructor.

```
// Constructors/destructors
Cash_Device() { amount_collected = 0.0; }
Cash_Device(float cash_amount)
        { amount_collected = cash_amount; }
~Cash_Device() { }
```

Declare the implementors for the services in the OOA/OOD model.

Name the "return" function something like "return cash" (because the word "return" is a reserved word in C++).

Add an "add cash" implementor instead of a "get cash" implementor, to simulate putting cash into the cash device.

```
// Implementors
Boolean got_enough(float amount_to_collect);
float return_cash();

float make_change(float cash_amount);
void add_cash(float cash_amount);
```

Declare accessors for the amount collected.

```
// Accessors
float get_amount_collected() { return amount_collected; }
void set_amount_collected(float cash_amount)
  { amount_collected = cash_amount; }
```

The amount collected is private; it can be accessed only by its accessors.

```
private:

// Data members
float amount_collected;
```

Now put it all together—the declaration for the cash device class:

```
class Cash_Device {
public:

// Constructors/destructors
Cash_Device() { amount_collected = 0.0; }
Cash_Device(float cash_amount)
        { amount_collected = cash_amount; }
~Cash_Device() { }

// Implementors
Boolean got_enough(float amount_to_collect);
```

```
float return_cash();

float make_change(float cash_amount);
void add_cash(float cash_amount);

// Accessors
float get_amount_collected() { return amount_collected; }
void set_amount_collected(float cash_amount)
        { amount_collected = cash_amount; }
```

```
private:

    // Data members
    float amount_collected;
};
```

Define the class

Now it's time to define the member functions that implement the class.

An item asks a cash device, "do you 'got enough' cash collected to cover my price?" The cash device returns a Boolean response.

```
Boolean Cash_Device::got_enough(float amount_to_collect)
{
    if (amount_collected >= amount_to_collect)
        return true;
    else
        return false;
}
```

A cash device makes change:

```
float Cash_Device::make_change(float item_price)
{
    amount_collected -= item_price;
    return amount_collected;
}
```

The statement:

```
amount_collected -= item_price;
```

is a shorthand way of writing this:

```
amount_collected = amount_collected - item_price;
```

A cash device also knows how to return the amount collected. Simulate the cash return by setting the amount collected back to zero:

```
float Cash_Device::return_cash()
{
  float return_amount = amount_collected;
  amount_collected = 0.0;
  return return_amount;
}
```

A cash device knows how to get cash. Simulate adding cash with the following:

```
void Cash_Device::add_cash(float cash_amount)
{
  amount_collected += cash_amount;
}
```

Now try out your cash device.

Run the code

Write a program to test the device. Add cash into the cash device until it collects a requested amount.

```
int main ()
{
  Cash_Device a_cash_device;

  // Add cash until 1.0 collected.
  while (!a_cash_device.got_enough(1.0))
    {
    cout << "need more!" << endl;
    a_cash_device.add_cash(0.25);
    }
  cout << "got enough!" << endl;

  return 0;
}
```

On the console you'll see something like this:

need more!
need more!
need more!
need more!
got enough!

Adding the Cash Device Interaction to the Item Class

It's time to add the cash device into the rest of the vending system.

To implement a connection with a cash device, add connection accessors:

```
Cash_Device& get_cash_device() { return *a_cash_device; }
void connect_to_cash_device(Cash_Device& new_cash_device)
   { a_cash_device = &new_cash_device; }
```

Declare a corresponding private data member:

```
private:

    Cash_Device* a_cash_device;
```

What's needed here?

An item needs a function to check that its cash device has enough cash. Add this to the class declaration:

```
Boolean is_vendable ();
```

and then define it with the following:

```
Boolean Item::is_vendable()
{
    return a_cash_device->got_enough(price);
}
```

To vend itself, what does an item need to do?
• I check if I'm vendable.

```
    if (!this->is_vendable())
        return false;
```

• If I am vendable, I tell the cash device to make change.

```
    a_cash_device->(price);
```

The complete vend function definition looks like this:

```
Boolean Item::vend()
{
    Boolean success;

    if (!this->is_vendable())
        return false;
    success =
         a_dispensing_holder->dispense(*this);
    if (!success)
        return false;
    a_cash_device->(price);
    return true;
}
```

Run the Code

Put together a short demo so you can play with the interactions among the items, dispensing holder, and cash device.

Put the demo functions in a class somewhere. The item class is a good candidate—it's already working with dispensing holder and cash device.

Add a function to create and fully connect an item

Add a function to create an item from a name and price, add it into a dispensing holder, and connect it to a cash device:

Add this to the class declaration:

```
void add_item(String item_name, float item_price,
        Dispensing_Holder& holder, Cash_Device& device);
```

and then define it with the following:

```
void Item::add_item(String item_name, float item_price,
        Dispensing_Holder& item_holder, Cash_Device&
              device)
{
    Item* an_item = new Item(item_name, item_price);
    item_holder.connect_to_item(*an_item);
    an_item->connect_to_dispensing_holder(item_holder);
    an_item->connect_to_cash_device(device);
}
```

Here's how to call it within an item member function:[13]

```
add_item("Pepsi", 0.75, *dispensingHolder, *a_cash_device)
```

Set up a demo

Set up a vending machine with:

> 3 items to sell at the default price (0.75)
> 1.50 in the cash device

Create a dispensing holder for the items:

```
Dispensing_Holder a_dispensing_holder;
```

---

[13]The "add_item" function expects a string argument for the item name, but you can call it using a char*, instead. This is possible because there is a string constructor that knows how to create a string from a char*. When you call the function using a char*, the string constructor is automatically invoked to create a string from the char*.

Create a cash device, with some cash already collected.

```
Cash_Device a_cash_device;
a_cash_device.set_amount_collected(1.50);
```

Create some items, connected to a dispensing holder and to a cash device:

```
add_item("Coca-Cola", 0.75, a_dispensing_holder,
        a_cash_device);
add_item("Pepsi", 0.75, a_dispensing_holder, a_cash_device);
add_item("Jolt", 0.75, a_dispensing_holder, a_cash_device);
```

One by one, tell each item to vend itself:

```
a_dispensing_holder.vend_all(item_quantity);
```

Add this "vend all" demo member function to the dispensing holder class. First, declare it:

```
void vend_all(int item_quantity);
```

Then define it:

```
void Dispensing_Holder::vend_all(int item_quantity)
{
    for (int i = 0; i < item_quantity; i++)
        (this->items[0])->vend();
}
```

Return to the item class. Declare and define a "machine demo" member function. First, declare it:

```
void machine_demo();
```

Then define it:

```
void Item::machine_demo()
{
    Dispensing_Holder a_dispensing_holder;
    Cash_Device a_cash_device;
    a_cash_device.set_amount_collected(1.50);
    add_item("Coca-Cola", 0.75, a_dispensing_holder,
            a_cash_device);
    add_item("Pepsi", 0.75, a_dispensing_holder,
            a_cash_device);
    add_item("Jolt", 0.75, a_dispensing_holder,
            a_cash_device);
    a_dispensing_holder->vend_all(3);
}
```

Try it out

Put it all together now.

Place the class declarations in a header file. Put the class definitions in another file. Put the main program in a third file.

The main program creates an item and tells it to run its member function, "machine demo:"

```
#include <iostream.h>
#ifndef VEND_H
#include "vend.h"
#endif

int main ()
{
   // Run the demo.
   Item demo_item;
   demo_item.machine_demo();

   cout << endl << "Happy trails." << endl;
   return 0;
}
```

Run it.

In your console window, you should see something like this:

Releasing item: Coca-Cola   price: 0.75
Releasing item: Pepsi   price: 0.75
Happy trails.

Ah, sweet success … .

OOD—HUMAN INTERACTION COMPONENT

Identify What Needs Interaction

Identify the problem domain objects that a person needs to interact with.

Cash device
> A customer enters cash in me and can ask me to return some cash.

Item
> A customer needs to see my name and price.
> A customer needs some way to select me.

Design and program human interaction classes to provide interaction with a cash device and the items.

Design a Layout; Design Part of the Human Interaction Component

Design a layout—item

Begin with item. Design a display layout. The display contains an item's name and price. The display also includes a "select" button (Figure 2–17).

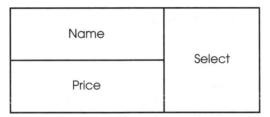

Figure 2–17: An item display.

In fact, you'll need some number of these item displays, one for each item at a "dispensable" position of a dispensing holder.

Design that part of the human interaction component

You need a container with three things in it—two display boxes and one button.

Put together an item view container (Figure 2–18).

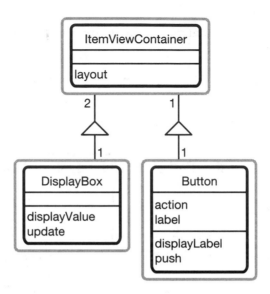

Figure 2–18: One container in the human interaction component.

Design a layout—cash device

Now do the same for cash device.

The display includes the amount collected. The display also needs buttons to "add cash" (at least to simulate that action) and to "return" (Figure 2–19).

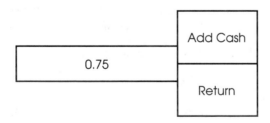

Figure 2–19: A cash device display.

Design that part of the human interaction component

You need a display box for the amount collected. You need "add cash" and "return" buttons.

Put together a cash device view container (Figure 2–20).

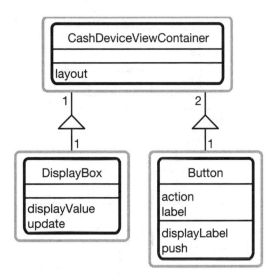

Figure 2–20: Another container in the human interaction component.

Containers, Containers, Containers

Have you just experienced a little *deja vu*? If not, go back and look at the last two OOD models. (You could even go back and look at the count view container back in Chapter 1.)

What's the same? What's different?

> Same: a container with some number of display boxes and
>   buttons
>
> Different: the names; the whole-part constraints

Wouldn't it be nice to have a reusable container, set up so it can handle some number of display boxes and buttons?

Yes!

You've just identified a reusable design component—a *model-value view container.*

What? That's right. Read it aloud as:

> "model-value <...pause...> view container"

It's a *view container* that is especially appropriate when you are presenting a view on a *model value.*

In its basic form, a model-value view container looks like Figure 2–21.

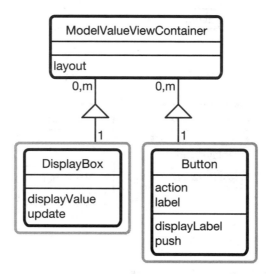

Figure 2–21: A model-value view container: a reusable design component.

Now you can show the human interaction component for the vending system like this (Figure 2–22):

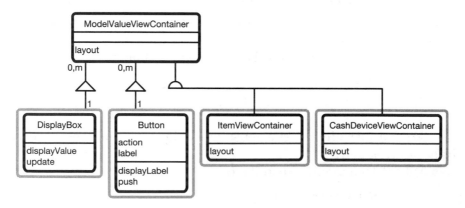

Figure 2–22: The human interaction component for the vending system.

OOD—THE HUMAN INTERACTION COMPONENT: SMALLTALK

A Small Problem

You're ready to go ahead and build a model-value view container.

But wait. Before you move ahead, there's a small problem with the display box that needs your help.

When you first built the display box, you overrode an inherited method, the one which displays a cursor for editing. The small problem is this: even though there is no longer a cursor inside the display box, you still can edit its value.

To really make a view read only, you need to do a bit more work. And this requires a little more understanding beyond model–view.

Model–View–Controller

In Smalltalk, a view object is connected to a controller object (Figure 2–23).[14]

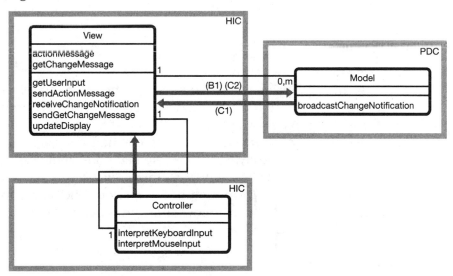

Figure 2–23: Model–View–Controller (MVC).

---

[14]More precisely, an object of a subclass (specialization class) of view is connected to an object of a subclass (specialization class) of controller.

Model and view

You applied model and view in Chapter 1.

A model[15] broadcasts any changes in its information. When a view receives a change notification, it sends a "get change" message to the model, to find the new information it needs. Then it uses the model's response to update itself (usually this means updating its display).

A view can also be used to change a model. And this is where a controller comes into play.

View and controller

A view gets user input via a controller. The controller knows how to interpret keyboard input (for example, delete key means cut, enter key means accept) and mouse input (for example, left button means select, right button means show window menu). How the input is interpreted depends on the type of view, too. A mouse click on a button is interpreted differently from a mouse click in a text editing window. As you might expect, each kind of controller is for use with a corresponding kind of view.

Controller and model

A controller also knows about its model.

So a view and a controller both know about the same model. A view displays the information in the model. A controller determines how the information can be manipulated.

Here's an example of controller–model interaction.

One kind of controller knows how to dispatch pop-up menus in response to certain mouse clicks. Such pop-up menus usually consist of commands for changing information in the model. When a menu option is selected, this kind of controller sends the command directly to the model (Figure 2–24).

---

[15]More precisely: an object of a subclass (specialization class) of model.

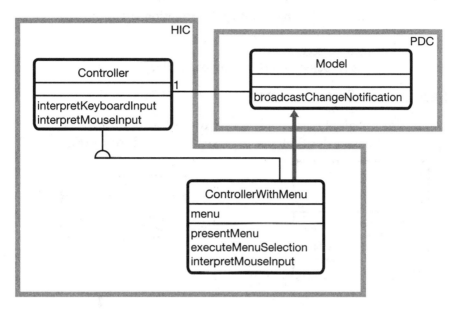

Figure 2–24: A controller with menu.

The text editor in the Smalltalk system browser is a good example of a "controller with pop-up" in action:

> A model is responsible for finding the information to show
> (a class definition, for example).
> A text view displays the information, including
> any highlight regions.
> A controller handles the pop-up menu used for
> accepting text.
> When a menu option is selected, the controller sends a
> corresponding command directly to the model.

Method categories (protocols) for model–view–controller

At times, you'll add a method just to support model–view–controller interaction. When this happens, put it into one of these method categories (protocols):

> model access
> (as a view or controller object) get or set the model on
> which I am dependent
> view access

(as a model object) return information about me that the
view wants to display

controller access

(as an object) get or set my controller

Resolving the Small Problem

To get a display box that does not allow user type-in, create a
specialized controller that ignores user keyboard input (Figure 2–25).

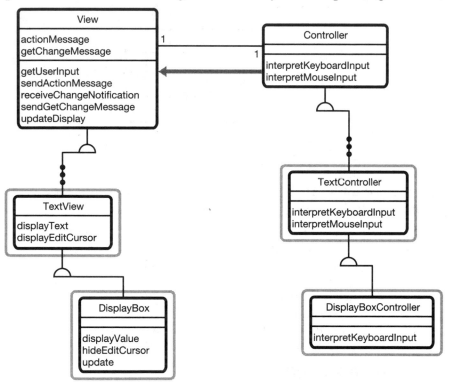

Figure 2–25: Adding a display box controller.

Add your own controller

Add a method so a display box (view) can attach a display box
controller to itself.

```
DisplayBox methodsFor: 'controller access'

defaultController
    ^DisplayBoxController new
```

Define your own controller

Define a display box controller as a specialization of text controller.

A display box controller is just like a text controller, except it needs to override two things:[16]

First:

> I'm a text controller.
>> When someone gives me some new text, I normally send
>>> the text to a view so it can display it.
> I'm a display box controller.
>> I override that behavior.
>> I just return back to the sender, in the same way that the
>>> method does for a text controller.

Second:

> I'm a text controller.
>> When someone gives me an "accept" command,
>>> I normally send a message to my model.
> I'm a display box controller.
>> I override that behavior.
>> I just flash the view (make it blink on the screen).

And so:

```
TextController subclass: #DisplayBoxController
    instanceVariableNames: ''
    classVariableNames: ''
    poolDictionaries: ''
    category: 'Vending Views'

DisplayBoxController methodsFor: 'private'

doAccept
"Ignore the user's input.  Flash my view."

    self view flash.
    ^false

replaceSelectionWith: aText saveSelectionForUndo:
        aBoolean
"Disable the sending of user text input to a view."

    ^self
```

[16]This design problem came up before. You saw it in the text view class. Here it is again, this time in the text view controller class. The class library design puts too much responsibility into the text view controller class. With generalization-specialization, one could have designed it with at least two classes, perhaps something like a text view controller class *and* a text view with input controller class. So what should you do at this point? Inherit from text view controller and override unwanted methods.

Remember:

> A model contains some information.
>
> A view displays that information.
>
> A controller determines how a user can manipulate the information with the keyboard and the mouse.[17]

OOP—HUMAN INTERACTION COMPONENT: SMALLTALK

The Model-Value View Container Class

You worked through some OOD for the human interaction component. You discovered a reusable design component, something called a model-value view container. And you understand the "controller" part of the model-view-controller triad.

What's next?

Build a reusable model-value view container.

Add a class and its instance variables

Add a new class—a specialization of the composite part class, in the class category called "model views":

```
CompositePart subclass: #ModelValueViewContainer
    instanceVariableNames: ''
    classVariableNames: ''
    poolDictionaries: ''
    category: 'Model Views'
```

What's special about this class? Just this: it will reduce the amount of effort it takes to make some number of buttons and display boxes—things that are very helpful when dealing with an underlying model that has a value that needs to be displayed.

You've programmed something like this before: the count view container. Cut and paste in the methods that can be used again and again; in some cases, all you need to do is pass in and use a parameter that holds the model.

Add view creation methods

For buttons and display boxes, just pass in and use a parameter that holds a model.

---

[17]A controller does some other things, too. "When a mouse enters my view, I become active. While active, I can receive events from the keyboard and the mouse. I interpret inputs and pass results to my corresponding model."

ModelValueViewContainer methodsFor: 'view creation'

makeButton: buttonLabel **on:** aModel **for:** action
   "Make a button to send a message to aModel to perform
         an action."

   | buttonView buttonAdaptor |
   buttonAdaptor := (PluggableAdaptor on: aModel)
         performAction: action.
   buttonView := LabeledBooleanView new.
   buttonView model: buttonAdaptor.
   buttonView label: buttonLabel.
   buttonView beTrigger.
   buttonView controller beTriggerOnUp.
   ^buttonView

makeDisplayBoxOn: aModel **for:** aspect
   "Make a value view that displays that value indicated by
         aspect, but has no message for changing a value."

   | itemView |
   itemView := DisplayBox
         on: aModel
         aspect: aspect
         change: nil
         menu: nil.
   ^itemView

Add window opening methods

In addition to passing in and using a parameter that holds a
model, you might also need to reorganize a method or two so that
things like window label and window minimum size are not hard-
wired just to a single value—like so:

ModelValueViewContainer methodsFor: 'window opening'

openOn: aModel
"Build the views for the model inside me.
Place myself in a window, with my default label.
Open the window on the screen."

   self openOn: aModel
      labeled: self windowLabel

openOn: aModel **labeled:** aLabel
"Build the views for the count inside me.
Place myself in a window, with label, aLabel.
Open the window on the screen."

```
| window |
window := ScheduledWindow new.
window component: self.
self buildViewOn: aModel.
window label: aLabel.
window minimumSize: self windowSize.
window open
```

windowLabel
```
^'Model Value'
```

windowSize
```
^100 @ 100 "pixels"
```

A note. In a specialization class, for a specific kind of model-value view container, you can override the window label and window size methods with whatever you need.

And another note. Two "open on" methods are defined; only the "openOn: labeled:" method is really needed; the other is defined as a matter of convenience, so you don't have to specify a label if you don't want to. Two other combinations could be added— "openOn: sized:" and "openOn: labeled: sized:." But they're not. Why? Those combinations are just not likely to be used very often; so no convenient shortcut is provided.

Add a view layout method

Some methods just come across "as is" from your earlier work with count view container.

ModelValueViewContainer methodsFor: 'view layout'

addView: view **in:** area
```
| wrapper |
wrapper := BorderedWrapper on: view in: area.
self addWrapper: wrapper
```

Add a constraint frame method

Along the way, you may uncover a helper method, a little piece of functionality you'd like to make easier to do again and again. Here's one:

ModelValueViewContainer methodsFor: 'private'

constraintFrame: originConstraints **corner:**
```
        cornerConstraints
    ^LayoutFrame originFractions: originConstraints
        cornerFractions: cornerConstraints
```

The Cash Device View Container Class

Now put your reusable model-value view container to work. Build a cash device view container.

Design a layout

Next, design what you'd like the view to look like. And mark its constraint frame dimensions (Figure 2–26).

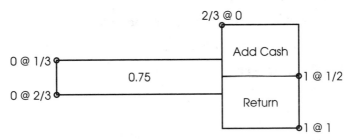

Figure 2–26: The cash device display layout.

Add a class and its instance variables

Begin by adding a new class:

```
ModelValueViewContainer subclass: #CashDeviceViewContainer
    instanceVariableNames: ''
    classVariableNames: ''
    poolDictionaries: ''
    category: 'Vending Views'
```

Add view layout methods

Build a display box to show the amount collected.

CashDeviceViewContainer methodsFor: 'view layout'

addValueViewOn: aCashDevice
    | itemView itemArea |
    itemView := self makeDisplayBoxOn: aCashDevice
            for: #amountCollected.
    itemArea := self constraintFrame: 0 @ (1/3)
            corner: 2/3 @ (2/3).
    self addView: itemView in: itemArea

Build a button to increment the amount collected.

CashDeviceViewContainer methodsFor: 'view layout'

```
addIncrementButtonOn: aCashDevice
    | button buttonArea |
    button := self
    makeButton: 'Add Cash'
            on: aCashDevice
            for: #addCash.
    buttonArea := self constraintFrame: 2/3 @ 0
            corner: 1 @ (1/2).
    self addView: button in: buttonArea
```

Build a button to return the amount collected.

CashDeviceViewContainer methodsFor: 'view layout'

```
addReturnButtonOn: aCashDevice
    | button buttonArea |
    button := self
            makeButton: 'Return'
            on: aCashDevice
            for: #return.
    buttonArea := self constraintFrame: 2/3 @ (1/2)
            corner: 1 @ 1.
    self addView: button in: buttonArea
```

Add a view creation method

Put all three views into a cash device container.

CashDeviceContainer methodsFor: 'view creation'

```
buildViewOn: aCashDevice

    self addValueViewOn: aCashDevice.
    self addIncrementButtonOn: aCashDevice.
    self addReturnButtonOn: aCashDevice.
```

Add window parameter methods

Customize the appearance of the window for an item:

CashDeviceViewContainer methodsFor: 'window opening'

```
windowLabel
    ^'Cash Device'
```

```
windowSize
    ^250 @ 50 pixels
```

Try it out

Go ahead. Do it.

```
CashDeviceViewContainer new openOn: CashDevice new
```

It should look something like Figure 2–27.

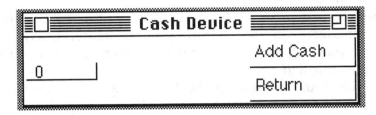

Figure 2–27: A cash device view container at work.

The Item View Container Class

Next, put the model-value view container to work again. This time, build an item view container.

How to get an item name and item price for the display boxes

Each item view container holds the name and price of the dispensable item in the corresponding dispensing holder.

Once an item is successfully vended, each display box needs to update itself with the name and price of the new dispensable item in the corresponding dispensing holder.

Who knows which item is the dispensable one? The dispensing holder knows.

One approach

You could ask the dispensing holder what the dispensable item is; then you could send messages to that item to get what you need—name and price.

Yet to work with the way that model–view–controller is implemented in Smalltalk, you must connect a view object with just one model object.

There *is* a way to get around this limitation—although it requires more conceptualization time and more code than one would like. You can use a third party, a "model holder," whenever a view needs to work with more than one model. In this case, you connect a view object to a model holder. The model holder holds whatever model object is currently of interest.

You'll apply that approach in Chapter 3. For now, consider a simpler approach.

A simpler approach

Who knows which item is the dispensable one? The dispensing holder knows.

So, connect each display box (a view) to its corresponding dispensing holder object (the sole corresponding model object).

A display box needs to ask for the dispensable item name and the dispensable item price.

And a button needs to tell the dispensing holder to vend its dispensable item.

So add some capability to the dispensing holder class to support this human interaction approach:

```
DispensingHolder methodsFor: 'view access'
```

dispensableItemName
```
^self isEmpty
    ifTrue: ['Empty']
    ifFalse: [items first name]
```

dispensableItemPrice
```
^self isEmpty
    ifTrue: [0]
    ifFalse: [items first price]
```

vendTheDispensableItem
```
self isEmpty ifTrue: [^false].
items first vend ifFalse: [^false].
self changed: dispensableItemName.
self changed: dispensableItemPrice.
^true
```

Design a layout

Next, design what you'd like the view to look like. And mark its constraint frame dimensions (Figure 2–28).

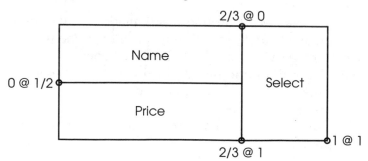

Figure 2–28: The item display layout.

Add a class and its instance variables

Add a new class:

```
ModelValueViewContainer subclass: #ItemViewContainer
    instanceVariableNames: ''
    classVariableNames: ''
    poolDictionaries: ''
    category: 'Vending Views'
```

Add view layout methods

Build a name display box.

ItemViewContainer methodsFor: 'view layout'

addNameViewOn: aDispensingHolder
```
| itemView itemArea |
itemView := self makeDisplayBoxOn: aDispensingHolder
        for: #dispensableItemName.
itemArea := self constraintFrame: 0 @ 0 corner: 2/3 @
        (1/2).
self addView: itemView in: itemArea
```

Build a price display box.

ItemViewContainer methodsFor: 'view layout'

addPriceViewOn: aDispensingHolder
```
| itemView itemArea |
itemView := self makeDisplayBoxOn: aDispensingHolder
        for: #dispensableItemPrice.
itemArea := self constraintFrame: 0 @ (1/2) corner:
        2/3 @ 1.
self addView: itemView in: itemArea
```

Build a select button.

ItemViewContainer methodsFor: 'view layout'

addSelectButtonOn: aDispensingHolder
```
| button buttonArea |
button := self
        makeButton: 'Select'
        on: aDispensingHolder
        for: #vendTheDispensableItem.
buttonArea := self constraintFrame: 2/3 @ 0
        corner: 1 @ 1.
self addView: button in: buttonArea
```

Add a view creation method

Put all three views into an item view container.

ItemViewContainer methodsFor: 'view creation'

```
buildViewOn: aDispensingHolder
    self addNameViewOn: aDispensingHolder.
    self addPriceViewOn: aDispensingHolder.
    self addSelectButtonOn: aDispensingHolder
```

Add window parameter methods

Customize the appearance of an item window:

ItemViewContainer methodsFor: 'window opening'

```
windowLabel
    ^'Items'
```

```
windowSize
    ^200 @ 66   "pixels"
```

Run the Code (Part I)

Put together a simple demo

Create some items.

```
item1 := Item new name: 'Coca-Cola'; price: 0.
item2 := Item new name: 'Pepsi'; price: 0.
item3 := Item new name: 'Jolt'; price: 0.
items := Array with: item1 with: item2 with: item3.
```

Create a dispensing holder and a cash device.

```
aDispensingHolder := DispensingHolder new.
aCashDevice := CashDevice new.
```

Connect the items to a dispensing holder and a cash device; and connect the dispensing holder to each item.

```
items
    do:
        [:anItem |
        anItem connectToDispensingHolder:
                aDispensingHolder.
        anItem connectToCashDevice: aCashDevice.
        aDispensingHolder connectToItem: anItem]
```

And then open up the views in an item view container on the dispensing holder:

```
^ItemViewContainer new openOn: aDispensingHolder
```

Put this all together into a simple demo.

Item class methodsFor: 'vending demos'

simpleDemo
```
| item1 item2 item3 items aDispensingHolder aCashDevice |
    item1 := Item new name: 'Coca-Cola'; price: 0.
    item2 := Item new name: 'Pepsi'; price: 0.
    item3 := Item new name: 'Jolt'; price: 0.
    items := Array with: item1 with: item2 with: item3.

    aDispensingHolder := DispensingHolder new.
    aCashDevice := CashDevice new.
items
    do:
        [:anItem |
            anItem connectToDispensingHolder: aDispensingHolder.
            anItem connectToCashDevice: aCashDevice.
            aDispensingHolder connectToItem: anItem].
```

```
^ItemViewContainer new openOn: aDispensingHolder
```

Try it out

Do the following:

```
Item simpleDemo
```

And you should see something like Figure 2–29.

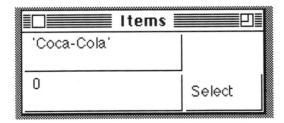

Figure 2–29: An item view container at work.

Run the Code (Part II)

Put together an overall demo. Include:

> Multiple dispensing holders, with some items
> 　　　in each holder
> A cash device

An item view container for each dispensing holder
A cash device view container

Demo methods are typically class methods. It's a convenient place to keep them.

Build some items, some dispensing holders, and a cash device

Add methods to build some fully-connected demo items:

Item class methodsFor: 'vending demos'

connectItem: name **price:** price **to:** aDispensingHolder
    and: aCashDevice

  | anItem |

anItem := self new name: name; price: price.
anItem connectToHolder: aDispensingHolder.
anItem connectToCashDevice: aCashDevice.
aDispensingHolder connectToItem: anItem

vendingMachineDemo

  | dispensingHolders aDispensingHolder aCashDevice |

dispensingHolders := OrderedCollection new.
aCashDevice := CashDevice new.

aDispensingHolder := DispensingHolder new.
dispensingHolders add: aDispensingHolder.
4 timesRepeat: [self connectItem: 'Coca-Cola' price: 0.75
    to: aDispensingHolder and: aCashDevice].

aDispensingHolder := DispensingHolder new.
dispensingHolders add: aDispensingHolder.
6 timesRepeat: [self connectItem: 'Pepsi' price: 0.75
    to: aDispensingHolder and: aCashDevice].

aDispensingHolder := DispensingHolder new.
dispensingHolders add: aDispensingHolder.
3 timesRepeat: [self connectItem: 'Jolt' price: 0.75
    to: aDispensingHolder and: aCashDevice].

ItemViewContainer vendingMachineDemoFor:
    dispensingHolders and: aCashDevice

Build the views

With three dispensing holders, you need three corresponding item view containers.

This also means that you need a container of item view containers!

Build some item view containers

You need to build a number of item value view containers. Write a supporting method.

> I build an item value view container.
>
> I use a fraction that I'm given to build a constraint frame.
>
> I put the view in a container that I'm given.

Here it is:

```
viewFor: dispenser in: container at: topFraction
       to: bottomFraction
| itemContainer frame |
itemContainer := ItemViewContainer new buildViewOn:
       dispenser.
frame := container constraintFrame: 0 @ topFraction
       corner: 1 @ bottomFraction.
container addView: itemContainer in: frame
```

Now use that supporting method to build a view for each dispensing holder:

```
| composite rowFraction |
composite := ModelValueViewContainer new.

rowFraction := 1.0 / dispensingHolders size.
1 to: dispensingHolders size do: [:index | self
       viewFor: (dispensingHolders at: index)
       in: composite
       at: index - 1 * rowFraction
       to: index * rowFraction]
```

Then place the whole thing in a window and tell it to open itself.

```
window := ScheduledWindow new.
window component: composite.
window minimumSize: 200 @ 200.
window label: 'Vending Machine'.
window open
```

Build a cash view container

Building a cash device view container is a little bit easier. There's just one cash device. And so:

```
CashDeviceContainer new openOn: cashDevice
```

does the job.

Build the views—the demo method

Finally, put together the complete class method for building the views for the demo:

```
ItemViewContainer class methodsFor: 'demos'

vendingMachineDemoFor: dispensingHolders and:
        cashDevice
    | composite rowFraction window |
    composite := ModelValueViewContainer new.
    rowFraction := 1.0 / dispensingHolders size.
    1 to: dispensingHolders size do: [:index | self
        viewFor: (dispensingHolders at: index)
        in: composite
        at: index - 1 * rowFraction
        to: index * rowFraction].
    window := ScheduledWindow new.
    window component: composite.
    window minimumSize: 200 @ 200.
    window label: 'Vending Machine'.
    window open.
    CashDeviceContainer new openOn: cashDevice
```

Try it out

Now for the kick-off command. Ready, set, go!

```
Item vendingMachineDemo
```

You should see something like Figure 2–30.

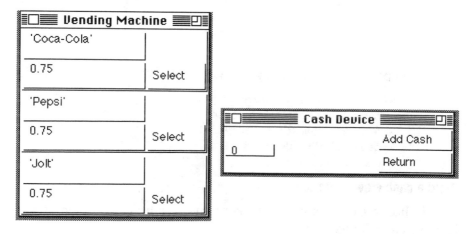

Figure 2–30: The vending machine demo.

Congratulations!

Go down the hallway and buy something nice for yourself—from a vending machine!

OOD—HUMAN INTERACTION COMPONENT: C++

The Cash View Container

In Chapter 1, you developed a human interaction component for a count view container.

Earlier in this chapter, you developed a human interaction component for an item view container (Figure 2-18).

Now look at the OOD for the cash device view container (Figure 2–31).

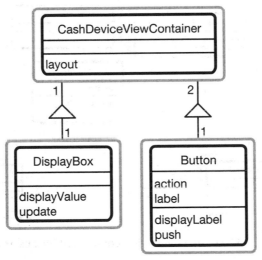

Figure 2–31: A cash device view container.

All three designs follow the same basic pattern.

So what should you do?

Take your human interaction component from chapter 1.

And repeat that same pattern—for a cash device view container and an item view container (Figure 2–32).

When you do this, the human interaction component looks like this:

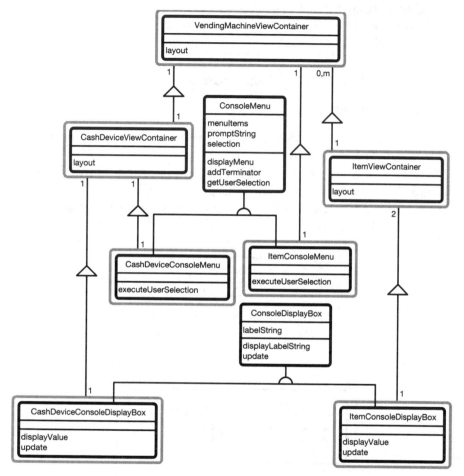

Figure 2–32: Human interaction component for this example.

And the interaction between the human interaction component and the problem domain component looks like this (Figure 2–33):

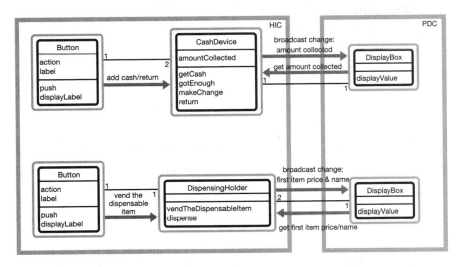

Figure 2–33: The interaction between the human interaction component and the problem domain component.

OOP—HUMAN INTERACTION COMPONENT: C++

Wow! You've got quite a bit to tackle here:

> add member functions to the dispensing holder class
> build the cash view container class
> > build the cash device console display box class
> > build the cash device console menu class
> > build the cash device view container class itself
> build the item view container class
> > build the item console display box class
> > build the item view container class itself
> build the item console menu class
> build the vending machine view container class

Adding Member Functions to the Dispensing Holder Class

Add functions to get a dispensable item name, get a dispensable item price, and vend a dispensable item.

First add member functions to return the dispensable item price and name.

Declare the member functions.

```
float dispensable_item_price();
String dispensable_item_name();
```

And define them.

```
float Dispensing_Holder::dispensable_item_price()
{
  if (this->is_empty())
    return 0.0;
  else
    return ((items[0])->get_price());
}

String Dispensing_Holder::dispensable_item_name()
{
  if (this->is_empty())
    return String ("Empty");
  else
    return ((items[0])->get_name());
}
```

Next, add a member function to vend a dispensable item.
Declare it.

```
Boolean vend_the_dispensable_item();
```

And define it.

Add a dispensing holder member function that vends a dispensable item.

```
Boolean Dispensing_Holder::vend_the_dispensable_item()
{
  Boolean success;

  if (this->is_empty())
    return false;
  success = ((items[0])->vend());
  if (!success)
    return false;
  else
    return true;
}
```

The Cash Device Console Display Box Class

Consider the specific responsibilities:

> I'm a cash device console display box.
>> I know about a cash device.
>> I display a value.
>>> ask the cash device for amount collected
>>> display my label string
>>> display the amount collected

Declare the class

Declare the cash device console display box class as a specialization of the console display box class.

```
class Cash_Device_Console_Display_Box : public
        Console_Display_Box {
public:

    // Constructors/destructors
    Cash_Device_Console_Display_Box() { }
    ~Cash_Device_Console_Display_Box() { }

    // Implementors
    void display_value();

    // Accessors
    Cash_Device& get_cash_device() { return *a_cash_device; }
    void set_cash_device(Cash_Device& new_device)
            { a_cash_device = &new_device; }
private:

    // Data members
    Cash_Device* a_cash_device;
};
```

Define the member functions

```
void Cash_Device_Console_Display_Box::display_value()
{
    float amount;

    amount = a_cash_device->get_amount_collected();
    this->display_label_string();
    cout << amount;
}
```

The Cash Device Console Menu Class

Consider the specific responsibilities:

> I'm a cash device console menu.
> I know about a cash device.
> Here's what I do:
> make my menu items for a cash device
> get the user's selection
> execute the user's selection

But first, refine the console menu class from Chapter 1.

Refine the console menu class

Before you create a menu for the cash device, refine the console menu. Use objects instead of char*.

The old console menu stores its menu items as an array of char*, and uses a char* for its prompt string. Simplify the code and increase its level of abstraction by using string objects instead.

First, update the console menu class declaration. Change the parameter list of any member function that includes a parameter of type char*.

```
void add_item(String new_item);
void add_prompt(String menu_prompt);
void add_terminator(String quit_label);
```

Next, change the types of the data members.

```
String menu_items[MAX_CONSOLE_MENU_SIZE];
String prompt_string;
```

Finally, change the member function definitions.
Just change the parameter lists for these two member functions:

```
void Console_Menu::add_prompt(String new_prompt)
{
   prompt_string = new_prompt;
}

void Console_Menu::add_terminator(String quit_label)
{
   this->add_item(quit_label);
}
```

Simplify the add item member function. Use the string constructor that accepts an integer argument. And use the string concatenation operator, "+."

```
void Console_Menu::add_item(String new_item)
{
   menu_items[menu_size] =
         String(menu_size + 1) + String(". ") + new_item;
   menu_size++;
}
```

"Object think" really does make things *simpler*!

Declare the class

```
class Cash_Device_Console_Menu : public Console_Menu {
public:

  // Constructors/destructors
  Cash_Device_Console_Menu() { }
  ~Cash_Device_Console_Menu() { }

  // Implementors
  void make_items(Cash_Device& new_device);
  void execute_selection();

  // Accessors
  Cash_Device& get_cash_device() { return *a_cash_device; }
  void set_cash_device(Cash_Device& new_device)
      {a_cash_device = &new_device;}

private:

  // Data members
  Cash_Device* a_cash_device;
};
```

Define the member functions

Start with make menu items.

```
void Cash_Device_Console_Menu::make_items
      (Cash_Device& new_device)
{
    a_cash_device = &new_device;
    this->add_item("Add cash (0.25): ");
    this->add_item("Return cash ");
}
```

"Get user's selection" is inherited from the console menu class. Build the code to execute a user selection.

```
void Cash_Device_Console_Menu::execute_selection()
{
  switch (selection) {
    case 1:
      a_cash_device->add_cash(0.25);
      break;
    case 2:
      a_cash_device->return_cash();
      break;
  };
}
```

The Cash Device View Container Class

Consider the specific responsibilities:

I'm a cash device view container.
  I create a console menu and a console display box.
    make cash device console menu
    make cash device console display box

Declare the class

```
class Cash_Device_View_Container {
public:

    // Constructors/destructors
    Cash_Device_View_Container(){ }
    ~Cash_Device_View_Container(){ }

    // Implementors
    void build_views(Cash_Device& a_cash_device);
    void make_amount_box(Cash_Device& a_cash_device);
    void make_cash_device_menu
            (Cash_Device& a_cash_device);

    void display_components();

private:

    Cash_Device_Console_Display_Box* amount_box;
    Cash_Device_Console_Menu* cash_device_menu;
};
```

Define the member functions

First, write the member function that makes the cash device console menu.

```
void Cash_Device_View_Container::
        make_cash_device_menu(Cash_Device&
        a_cash_device)
{
    cash_device_menu = new Cash_Device_Console_Menu();
    cash_device_menu->make_items(a_cash_device);
    cash_device_menu->add_terminator("Done");
    cash_device_menu->add_prompt("Enter cash, please: ");

}
```

Next, program the member function that builds a cash device console display box.

```
void Cash_Device_View_Container::make_amount_box
      (Cash_Device& a_cash_device)
{
   amount_box = new Cash_Device_Console_Display_Box();
   amount_box->set_cash_device(a_cash_device);
   amount_box->set_label_string("Amount entered: " );
}
```

Build the views on a cash device.

```
void Cash_Device_View_Container::build_views
      (Cash_Device& a_cash_device)
{
   this->make_amount_box(a_cash_device);
   this->make_cash_device_menu(a_cash_device);
}
```

Finally, add a member function to do the following:

> Do until finished:
>> tell the menu to get a selection
>> execute the selection
>> tell the display box to display the value

```
void Cash_Device_View_Container::display_components()
{
   while (cash_device_menu->get_user_selection())
      {
      cash_device_menu->execute_selection();
      amount_box->display_value();
      }
}
```

Run the code

Write a simple demo program.

Make a cash device and a cash device view container. Have the cash device view container build its views for the cash device and then display its components.

```
int main ()
{
   Cash_Device a_cash_device;
   Cash_Device_View_Container a_cash_device_view_container;

   a_cash_device_view_container.
         build_views(a_cash_device);
   a_cash_device_view_container.display_components();

   return 0;
}
```

On your computer screen you should see something like this:

1. Add cash (0.25)
2. Return cash
3. Done

Enter cash, please: 1

Amount entered: 0.25

The Item Console Display Box Class

Consider the specific responsibilites:

> I'm an item console display box.
> I know about a dispensing holder.
>> I display a value.
>>> I can display a dispensable item name
>>> I can display a dispensable item price

Make the item console display box smart.

> I know if I am to display a price or a name.
>> I have a flag.
>>> if the display flag = "name," I display the name.
>>> if the display flag = "price," I display the price.

Declare the class

```
class Item_Console_Display_Box : public
      Console_Display_Box {
public:

   // Constructors/destructors
   Item_Console_Display_Box() { display_flag =
         String("name"); }
   ~Item_Console_Display_Box() { }

   // Implementors
   void display_value();
   String get_value();

   void set_display_flag_to_name(){ display_flag =
         String("name"); }
   void set_display_flag_to_price(){ display_flag =
         String("price"); }
   String get_dispensable_price();
   String get_dispensable_name();
```

```
    // Accessors
    void set_dispensing_holder(Dispensing_Holder&
            new_holder)
                { a_dispensing_holder = &new_holder; }
    Dispensing_Holder& get_dispensing_holder()
                { return *a_dispensing_holder; }
private:
    // Data members
    Dispensing_Holder* a_dispensing_holder;
    String display_flag;
};
```

Set the display flag with the set display flag functions; don't add accessors for it.

Note that the constructor initializes an item console display box so that it displays an item name (as a default).

Define the member functions

Start with how an item console display box gets its value:

get value
    if the display_flag = "name,"
        get the dispensable item name
    if the display_flag = "price,"
        get the dispensable item price

Get the dispensable item name from a dispensing holder.

```
String Item_Console_Display_Box::
        get_dispensable_name()
{
    String name =
            a_dispensing_holder->dispensable_item_name();
    return name;
}
```

Get the dispensable item price from a dispensing holder.

```
String Item_Console_Display_Box::get_dispensable_price()
{
    float price = a_dispensing_holder->
            dispensable_item_price();
    // Create a string from a float.
    String price_string(price);
    return price_string;
}
```

Get a value to display.

```
String Item_Console_Display_Box::get_value()
{
  if (display_flag == String("price"))
    return (this->get_dispensable_price());
  else
    return (this->get_dispensable_name());
}
```

Display a value.

```
void Item_Console_Display_Box::display_value()
{
  cout << this->get_value();
}
```

The Item View Container Class

Consider the specific responsibilities:

I'm an item view container.
   I create two console display boxes.
   Here's how:
      build views on a dispensing holder
         make 2 item view console display boxes
            to show the dispensable item price
            to show the dispensable item name
   Then:
   lay out my component views on the display.

Declare the class

```
class Item_View_Container {
public:

  // Constructors/destructors
  Item_View_Container() { }
  ~Item_View_Container() { }

  // Implementors
  void build_views(Dispensing_Holder&
        a_dispensing_holder);
  void make_price_box(Dispensing_Holder&
        a_dispensing_holder);
  void make_name_box(Dispensing_Holder&
        a_dispensing_holder);
  void display_components();

private:
```

```
Item_Console_Display_Box* price_box;
Item_Console_Display_Box* name_box;
```

```
};
```

Define the member functions

Make a display box for the dispensable item name.

```
void Item_View_Container::make_name_box
        (Dispensing_Holder& a_dispensing_holder)
{
    name_box = new Item_Console_Display_Box();
    name_box->set_dispensing_holder(a_dispensing_holder);
    name_box->set_display_flag_to_name();
}
```

Make a display box for the dispensable item price.

```
void Item_View_Container::make_price_box
        (Dispensing_Holder& a_dispensing_holder)
{
    price_box = new Item_Console_Display_Box();
    price_box->set_dispensing_holder(a_dispensing_holder);
    price_box->set_display_flag_to_price();
}
```

Build the views on a dispensing holder.

```
void Item_View_Container::build_views
        (Dispensing_Holder& a_dispensing_holder)
{
    this->make_name_box(a_dispensing_holder);
    this->make_price_box(a_dispensing_holder);
}
```

Finally, display the component views. Draw a border around them.

```
void Item_View_Container::display_components()
{
    char*  border  =  "——————————————";

    cout << border;
    cout << endl;
    name_box->display_value();
    cout << "\t";
    price_box->display_value();
    cout << endl << border << endl;
}
```

Great. You've finished another major part of the vending machine.

Run the code

Create an item, a dispensing holder, and an item view container. Connect the dispensing holder to the item, and create the item views for the dispensing holder. Finally, display the item views.

```
int main ()
{
    Item an_item("Coca-Cola", 0.75);
    Dispensing_Holder a_dispensing_holder;
    Item_View_Container an_item_view_container;

    a_dispensing_holder.connect_to_item(an_item);
    an_item_view_container.build_views
            (a_dispensing_holder);

    an_item_view_container.display_components();

    return 0;
}
```

On your computer screen, you should see something like this:

Coca-Cola   0.75

The Item Console Menu Class

Consider the specific responsibilities:

> I'm an item console menu.
> > I know about a set of dispensing holders.
> > I know how to build my menu.
> > > My menu items are the dispensing holders' dispensable item names.
> > I execute the user's selection.
> > > I tell the dispensing holder selected to vend the dispensable item.
> > I update my menu items.
> > > After I execute a selection I update my menu items, since one of the dispensable items has changed.

Declare the class

```
class Item_Console_Menu : public Console_Menu {
public:
```

```
// Constructors/destructors
Item_Console_Menu() { }
~Item_Console_Menu() { }

// Implementors
void make_items(Dispensing_Holder**
        dispensing_holders, int number_of_holders);

void update_items();
void update_item(int item_number);
void replace_item(String new_item, int item_number);

Boolean sold_out_selection();
void execute_selection();

// Accessors
void set_dispensing_holders(Dispensing_Holder**
        new_value, int number_of_holders);

private:

// Data members
Dispensing_Holder*
        dispensing_holders[MAX_CONSOLE_MENU_SIZE];
};
```

Define the "make menu items" member functions

Create a list of dispensable item names from the dispensing holders. Remember the set of dispensing holders for use once a selection is made.

```
void Item_Console_Menu::make_items
        (Dispensing_Holder** dispensing_holders,
          int number_of_holders)
{
    Dispensing_Holder* a_dispensing_holder;

    // For each dispensing holder, add its dispensable
    // item name to the menu.
    for (int i = 0; i < number_of_holders; i++)
      {
      a_dispensing_holder = dispensing_holders[i];
      String name =
            a_dispensing_holder->dispensable_item_name();
      this->add_item(name);
      }
    this->set_dispensing_holders(dispensing_holders,
          number_of_holders);
}
```

Store the dispensing holders in an array of dispensing holder pointers.

```
void Item_Console_Menu::set_dispensing_holders
        (Dispensing_Holder** new_holders,
              int number_of_holders)
{
    for (int i = 0; i < number_of_holders; i++)
        dispensing_holders[i] = new_holders[i];
}
```

Define the "execute selection" member function

To execute a user's selection, tell a dispensing holder to vend its dispensable item.

```
void Item_Console_Menu::execute_selection()
{

    Dispensing_Holder* a_dispensing_holder =
            dispensing_holders[selection-1];

    a_dispensing_holder->vend_the_dispensable_item();
    this->update_items();
}
```

Define the "update menu items" member functions

Delete the old menu item and add a new menu item.

```
void Item_Console_Menu::replace_item(String& new_item,
        int item_number)
{
    menu_items[item_number] =
            String(item_number + 1) + String(". ") +
            new_item;
}
```

Update an item by getting the current dispensable item name and using it.

```
void Item_Console_Menu::update_item(int item_number)
{
    Dispensing_Holder* a_dispensing_holder;

    a_dispensing_holder = dispensing_holders[item_number];
    String name = a_dispensing_holder->
            dispensable_item_name();
    this->replace_item(name, item_number);
}
```

Update a menu's items by updating the last one selected.

```
void Item_Console_Menu::update_items()
{
   if (selection == 0)
      return;
   this->update_item(selection - 1);
}
```

Run the code

Plan:

> Create an array for three dispensing holders.
> Create a cash device with some money already in it.
> Add an item into each holder.
> Build an item console menu on each dispensing holder.
> Run the menu.

Create an array for three dispensing holders.

```
Dispensing_Holder* holders[3];
```

Create a cash device with some money already in it.

```
Cash_Device a_cash_device;
a_cash_device.set_amount_collected(1.25);
```

Use the Item::add_item function you wrote while testing the problem domain component. Use it to add items into the dispensing holders.

```
Item item;
item.add_item("Coca Cola", 0.75, holder, a_cash_device);
```

Store the holder in the array.

```
holders[0] = holder;
```

Repeat two more times; then create the item console menu.

```
item_menu.make_items(holders, 3);
item_menu.add_terminator("Quit");
item_menu.add_prompt("Pick your favorite: ");
```

Run the menu.

```
item_menu.get_user_selection();
item_menu.execute_selection();
```

Put the demo code together.

```
int main () {

    Dispensing_Holder* holders[3];
    Item_Console_Menu item_menu;

    Cash_Device a_cash_device;
    a_cash_device.set_amount_collected(1.25);

    Item item;
    Dispensing_Holder* holder = new Dispensing_Holder();

    item.add_item("Coca-Cola", 0.75, *holder,
            a_cash_device);
    holders[0] = holder;

    holder = new Dispensing_Holder();
    item.add_item("Pepsi", 0.75, *holder, a_cash_device);
    holders[1] = holder;

    holder = new Dispensing_Holder();
    item.add_item("Jolt", 0.75, *holder, a_cash_device);
    holders[2] = holder;

    item_menu.make_items(holders, 3);
    item_menu.add_terminator("Quit");
    item_menu.add_prompt("Pick your favorite: ");

    item_menu.get_user_selection();
    item_menu.execute_selection();

    return 0;

}
```

On your console, you should see something like this:

1. Coca-Cola
2. Pepsi
3. Jolt
4. Quit

Pick your favorite: 3

Releasing item: Jolt price: 0.75

Now all that remains is the final vending machine container, itself.

The Vending Machine View Container Class

Consider the specific responsibilities:

I'm a vending machine view container.

I create a cash device view container, an item console
menu, and a set of item views.
I know how to lay these out on the console.

Declare the class

```
class Vending_Machine_View_Container {
public:

    // Constructors/destructors
    Vending_Machine_View_Container()
            { component_count = -1; }
    ~Vending_Machine_View_Container() { }

    // Implementors

    // View builders
    void build_view_containers(Dispensing_Holder**
            dispensing_holders, Cash_Device& a_cash_device,
            int number_of_holders);
    void make_cash_device_view_container
            (Cash_Device& a_cash_device);
    void make_item_view_container
            (Dispensing_Holder& a_dispensing_holder);
    void make_item_menu
            (Dispensing_Holder** dispensing_holders,
            int number_of_holders)

    // Displaying
    void display_components();
    void display_item_view_containers();

private:

    // Data members
    Item_Console_Menu* menu;
    Item_View_Container*
            item_view_containers[MAX_CONTAINER_SIZE];
    Cash_Device_View_Container* a_cash_device_view_container;
    int component_count;

};
```

Define the "make menu item" member function

```
void Vending_Machine_View_Container::make_item_menu
        (Dispensing_Holder** dispensing_holders,
        int number_of_holders)
```

```
   {
   menu = new Item_Console_Menu();
   menu->make_items
           (dispensing_holders, number_of_holders);
   menu->add_terminator("Quit");
   menu->add_prompt("Select an item: ");
   }
```

Define the "make view containers" member functions

Make an item view container. Store it in an array of item view containers.

```
void Vending_Machine_View_Container::
       make_item_view_container (Dispensing_Holder&
       dispensing_holder)
   {
   Item_View_Container* item_view_container;

   item_view_container = new Item_View_Container();
   item_view_container->build_views(dispensing_holder);
   item_view_containers[++component_count] =
           item_view_container;
   }
```

Create a cash device view container for the cash device it's given.

```
void Vending_Machine_View_Container
       ::make_cash_device_view_container(Cash_Device&
       a_cash_device)
   {
   a_cash_device_view_container =
           new Cash_Device_View_Container();
   a_cash_device_view_container->
           build_views(a_cash_device);
   }
```

Define the "build views" member function

Create all the view containers needed for the vending machine system. This means that you need to create a new container for an array of filled dispensing holders and for a cash device.

```
void Vending_Machine_View_Container::build_view_containers
       (Dispensing_Holder** dispensing_holders,
       Cash_Device& a_cash_device, int number_of_holders)
   {
   this->make_cash_device_view_container(a_cash_device);
```

```
    this->make_item_menu(dispensing_holders,
        number_of_holders);

    for (int i= 0; i < number_of_holders; i++)
      this->make_item_view_container
          (*dispensing_holders[i]);
}
```

Define the "display containers" member functions

Lay out the container components on the display.

> Do until finished:
>> show the item view containers
>> tell menu to get user selection
>>> it's a good selection, display the cash device
>>>> to get the money
>> tell the menu to execute the selection

Show all the item view containers telling each one to display its components.

```
void Vending_Machine_View_Container::
        display_item_view_containers()
{
  // I'm empty! I won't make any item view containers.
  if (component_count == -1)
    return;
  cout << endl;
  for(int i = 0; i <= component_count; i++)
    (item_view_containers[i])->display_components();
}
```

Determine if a selection is sold out.

```
Boolean Item_Console_Menu:: sold_out_selection()
{
  if (dispensing_holders[selection - 1]->is_empty())
    return true;
  else
    return false;
}
```

Loop until the user quits.

```
void Vending_Machine_View_Container::
        display_components()
```

```
{
   this->display_item_view_containers();
   while (menu->get_user_selection())
      {
      if (!menu->sold_out_selection())
        {
        a_cash_device_view_container->display_components();
        menu->execute_selection();
        }
      this->display_item_view_containers();
      }
}
```

Run the Code

Create dispensing holders with items for the demo

Add a "machine demo" member function. Put this member function into the item class. It's a convenient place to coordinate all the work to set up the demo.

Declare it.

```
int machine_demo(DispensingHolder**
       dispensing_holders, cashDevice& a_cash_device);
```

And define it.

```
int Item::machine_demo(Dispensing_Holder**
       dispensing_holders, Cash_Device& a_cash_device)
{
   Dispensing_Holder* a_dispensing_holder;

   // Make three dispensing holders and put
   // them in the array.
   for (int i = 0; i < 3; i++)
     dispensing_holders[i] = new Dispensing_Holder();

   // Fill the holders with my special demo items.

   a_dispensing_holder = dispensing_holder[0];
   for (i = 0; i < 4; i++)
     this->add_item("Coca-Cola", 0.75,
             *a_dispensing_holder, a_cash_device);

   a_dispensing_holder = dispensing_holder[1];
   for (i = 0; i < 6; i++)
     this->add_item("Pepsi", 0.75,
             *a_dispensing_holder, a_cash_device);
```

```
   a_dispensing_holder = dispensing_holder[2];
   for (i = 0; i < 3; i++)
     this->add_item("Jolt", 0.75,
             *a_dispensing_holder, a_cash_device);

   // Return the number of dispensing holders that
   // I've filled.
   return 3;
}
```

Invoke it like this:

```
an_item->machine_demo(dispensing_holder_array,
     a_cash_device);
```

Put the demo together

Start the vending machine demo by building and displaying the view containers.

```
void Vending_Machine_View_Container::vending_machine_demo
        (Dispensing_Holder** dispensing_holders,
        Cash_Device& a_cash_device,
        int number_of_holders)
{
   this->build_view_containers(dispensing_holders,
         a_cash_device, number_of_holders);
   this->display_components();
}
```

Finally, program the vending machine demo:

```
void Vending_Machine_View_Container::
        vending_machine_demo()
{
   // Create a cash device.
   Cash_Device a_cash_device;

   // Create an array for dispensing holders.
   Dispensing_Holder** dispensing_holders =
         new Dispensing_Holder*[MAX_CONTAINER_SIZE];

   Item an_item;
   int number_of_holders;

   // Get the dispensing holders from an item.
   // I need to know how many, please.
   number_of_holders = an_item.machine_demo
         (dispensing_holders, a_cash_device);
```

```
    // Build my human interface for these
    // dispensing holders and start it running.
    this->vending_machine_demo(dispensing_holders,
            a_cash_device, number_of_holders);

    // I'm all done. I'll clean up after myself.
    delete[] dispensing_holders;
}
```

Try it out

At last, the vending machine is complete.

```
int main ()
{
    // Create a vending machine view.
    Vending_Machine_View_Container vending_machine_view;

    // Run the demo.
    vending_machine_view.vending_machine_demo();

    cout << endl << "Happy trails." << endl;

    return 0;
}
```

And on your computer screen you should see something like this:

Coca-Cola0.75

Pepsi   0.75

Jolt   0.75

---

1. Coca-Cola
2. Pepsi
3. Jolt
4. Quit

Select an item: 3

Go for the Jolt!

1. Add cash (0.25)
2. Return cash
3. Done

Enter cash, please:

Add enough money.

Amount entered: 0.75

And voila!

Releasing item: Jolt   price: 0.75

ABOUT MAKING CHANGE

Think about this for a bit.

You've just completed a vending machine. You exerted extra effort to develop an architecture that might apply across a family of systems.

It vends items.

The same architecture applies to more than just cans of soda. It applies to candy, cookies, beer, theater tickets, sports tickets, and songs in a jukebox.

What happens when you need to make change? What are its items? What is its dispensing holder?

A cash device that can make change is just another vending system!!! That's a peek at reuse in the large.

SUMMARY

In this chapter, you did some amazing things.

OOA and OOD
- Finding more effective class names
- Acting out key scenario scripts
- Architecting for reuse
- Designing whole-part structures and object connections
- Applying the model-view-controller pattern
- Planning and doing concurrent development

OOP (Smalltalk)
- Implementing whole-part structures and object connections
- Using ordered collections
    adding/removing elements
    iterating over all elements
- Implementing a thread of execution
    writing out the thread

finding supporting methods
working backwards through the scenario
- Testing object identity: equality vs. equivalence
- Printing an object on the transcript window
    the default approach
    how to specialize
- Using the cascade operator to send multiple messages
- Writing conditional tests with boolean and block objects
- Repeating statements with conditional loops
    while loop
    times repeat
- Building a reusable container class
    creating buttons
    creating display boxes
    opening a window with a label and a size
- Adding the controller to the model-view-controller pattern

OOP (C++)

- Class libraries: object-oriented versions of basic types
- Replacing char* variables with string objects
- Using reference variables for pass-by-reference function calls
- Declaring a class with a forward reference
- Implementing whole-part structures and object connections
- Resolving order of declaration conflicts
    using pointers and references, not objects
    accessing after definition, not declaration
- Writing member functions
    using the "this" pointer
    using the class member access operator
    accessing data members and invoking member functions
- Overloading operators—equality insertion
- Refining the human interaction classes, using string objects
- Using display flags to build multi-purpose human-
    interaction classes

You also learned and applied these principles:

The "pay up" principle. Pay me now. Or pay much, much more later.

The "haste makes waste" principle. Haste makes waste, even with objects.

The "hacker's paradise" principle. No matter what the language, the universal cry for hackers is "I just code it up." Systems built this way are truly a hacker's paradise.

The "change, change, change, change, change" principle. Use a simple set of pictures to architect a system. Use a medium that you can inexpensively change again and again, encouraging and supporting creativity and innovation. Simple, flexible notation is essential.

The "emotionally attached" principle. Architect with OOA and OOD. Look for innovative ideas and apply them early in your work (while the project is young and your emotional investment in a particular solution is not as great). A warning sign? Rejecting new ideas with the words "after all, I've already built this much and it runs just fine." Such emotional attachment can be very counterproductive to finding new, breakthrough ideas on how to best architect a system.

The "perpetual employment" principle. Years ago, assembly language programmers learned that obscure coding resulted in perpetual employment. By shortcutting past OOA and OOD, you can do the same; the code will be so obscure and so brittle that you'll be sorely needed, forevermore.

The "Frankenstein" principle. Be careful what you hack up one night in the lab; the result may follow you for years to come.

The "variety pack" principle. Consider a series of human interaction alternatives, from simple to futuristic. If you are already familiar with just one or two approaches, work through a family of possibilities.

The "it's my name; generalize it" principle. Take all or part of a class name. Generalize it into a new name. If both names imply identical system responsibilities, then just use the more general name (encourage wider reuse). However, if the names imply different system responsibilities, use both classes in your model (increase the problem domain partitioning of system responsibilities).

The "service with a smile" principle. As an object, I know things and I do things, all for the direct or indirect benefit of someone who uses the system.

The "select ain't my job, it's your job" principle. As a problem domain object, let me set you straight: "select" services aren't my job; it's a human interaction object's job.

The "me, myself, and I" principle. Think about an object in the first person. Talk about an object in the first person. Write about an object in the first person. Put yourself in the midst of the architecture. "I'm a _____ object; I know my _____ ; and here's what I do: _____." Keep "it, its, and itself" to a minimum.

The "don't expect me to do all the work" principle. Don't just ask another object for its value(s), and then work on it yourself. Tell the object to do the work for you, giving you a more meaningful result.

The "more than just a data hider" principle. If an object acts as just a data hider when an object sends it a message, check if it can do something more. Even if the work is modest, you may find a way to improve both distribution of responsibility, and encapsulation, partitioned by problem domain classes.

The "good politics" principle. Design and code the capabilities that will most impress your customer (or perhaps your boss).

The "nice threads" principle. Design and code the capabilities that support a major thread of execution (a major scenario script).

The "backward through the script" principle. When programming methods to implement the OOD services, work backward through the script. Why? This strategy lets you start small, try it, and test it; then you can add pieces that can invoke the methods you've already programmed.

The "great code is readable code" principle. Great code is readable. By you. By other members of the team. And by those who will read your work in the future.

3

Sales, Sales, Sales

In this chapter, you'll experience:

OOA and OOD
- Applying a high-speed approach to finding problem domain classes
- Designing a human interaction component with multiple containers
- Designing human interaction for a model collection
- Designing data management classes

OOP (Smalltalk)
- Enforcing subclass responsibility
- Creating a scrolling list
- Coordinating human interaction objects
- Reading from and writing to files
- Using the dictionary class
- Storing objects on a file with an object tag format
- Restoring objects from a file

OOP (C++)
- Using library classes
- Formatting stream output
- Coordinating human interaction objects
- Reading from and writing to files
- Using heterogeneous collections and the virtual function mechanism
- Storing objects on a file with an object tag format
- Restoring objects from a file

Just do it.

SOME OOA

Begin with some OOA. This time, you'll apply an OOA strategy that emphasizes high-speed OOA class identification.

Suppose that you want to build a system to support a sales organization.

What's the purpose of the system (in 25 words or less)? How about this: to process and record sales transactions.

Are you ready to look for objects—and identify classes of objects? Consider person, place, and thing.

The "person, place, thing" principle. Find initial classes by listing potential classes of objects—objects which may be a person, place, or thing.

Start with some of the classes that are needed to support basic sales transactions:

> Person
> > Customer
> > Sales rep
>
> Place
> > Store
>
> Thing
> > Product
> > Transaction

Now expand the scope, with added breadth.

The "high-speed breadth" principle. Push person, place, and thing. Go wild, identifying many, many classes.

Add additional classes, ones that add to the breadth of subject matter coverage in this problem domain.

> Person
> > Customer
> > Sales rep
> > Supervisor
>
> Place
> > Store
> > Billing location
> > Ship-to location
> > Warehouse location
>
> Thing
> > Authorization
> > Discount agreement

Distributor
Product
Promotion
Supplier
Sales transaction

Again expand the scope, this time with added depth.

The "high-speed depth" principle. Apply generalization–specialization and whole–part to each class. New generalizations, specializations, wholes, and parts add depth to your OOA model.

Apply generalization–specialization and whole–part.

In the list that follows, each added class includes how it was found—generalization, specialization, whole, part.

Person
Customer
Gold customer (specialization)
Spouse (part)
Child (part)
Sales rep
Trainee sales rep (specialization)
Supervisor
Trainee supervisor (specialization)

Place
Point of sale (generalization)
Store
Wholesale store (specialization)
Discount store (specialization)
Retail store (specialization)
Other sales location (specialization)
Billing location
Ship-to location
Warehouse location

Thing
Authorization
Credit authorization (specialization)
Credit card authorization (specialization)
Check authorization (specialization)
Discount agreement
OEM agreement (specialization)
Volume discount agreement (specialization)
Distributor
National distributor (specialization)
International distributor (specialization)

Product
    Hazardous product (specialization)
    Incentive (a better generalization name than
            "promotion")
    Customer incentive (specialization)
    Sales person incentive (specialization)
Supplier
Transaction (generalization)
    Sales transaction
    Return transaction (specialization)
    Line item (part)

So where should you begin? What's a reasonable strategy for accelerated delivery of working results?

Apply this principle:

The "heart and soul" principle. Make an extensive list of classes in a problem domain. Then select a small number of classes . . . ones that together represent the heart and soul, the core of the problem domain under consideration. Do OOA and OOD on these first. Build them. Demonstrate working results. Then go for more.

Select some core classes for this problem domain:

Person
    Customer
Thing
    Product
    Sales transaction
    Transaction line item

Any generalization classes of these core classes should be brought along so that the class architecture will remain the same—for this first pass of OOA to OOD to OOP, and for subsequent passes, too. And so, refine the core classes to the following:

Person
    Customer
Thing
    Product
    Transaction
        Sales transaction
        Line item

Begin to put these core classes together, piece by piece (Figure 3–1).

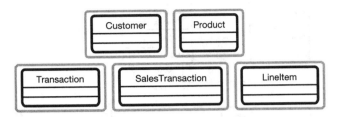

Figure 3–1: Putting together some core classes.

Next, interconnect the classes with gen–spec structure; and interconnect the objects with whole-part structure and object connections (Figure 3–2).

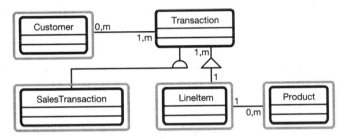

Figure 3–2: Adding interconnections.

For this core OOA model, just add enough attributes and services to make the initial development interesting to your client. Suppose you worked this out with your client and together you came up with something like this:

Person
    Customer ... name and address

Thing
    Product ... name and price
    Transaction ... date and time; calculate total
        Sales transaction ... method of payment; calculate total
        Line item ... quantity; calculate total

Add these details to the OOA model; add message connections too (Figure 3–3).

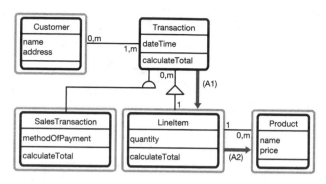

Figure 3–3: An OOA model for sales transactions.

Note that "as a line item, I know how to calculate my own total —a line item total." This is much better than making the transaction do all of the totaling work all by itself.

The "behavior across a collection" principle. Let a collection do just the work that applies across a collection. Push work down into each part.

This principle becomes especially important when a collection has different kinds of parts. If the collection does all the work, it will be riddled with "case," "switch," or "if-then-else if" statements, just to help it decide which computation to apply to which part. Ugh! It's much better to distribute responsibility down into the parts.

SOME PLANNING

Make a few simplifying assumptions about the problem domain to reduce the time and effort it will take to do OOD and OOP, producing frequent, tangible, working results. How about this:

Just one customer per transaction
Just one product

Begin with the problem domain component. Then do the human interaction component. And just to make things interesting, plan on doing the data management component, too!

OOD—PROBLEM DOMAIN COMPONENT

Add the design variables needed to implement whole-part structure and object connections (Figure 3–4).

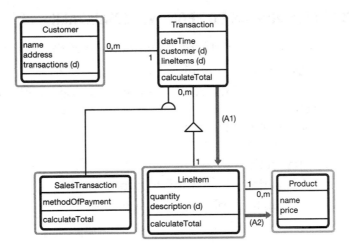

Figure 3–4: Adding design variables.

The Plan

Build the classes backwards through the key scenario, trying out the code along the way.

The scenario?

> I'm a sales transaction.
> > Someone just told me to calculate my total.
> > I send a message to each of my transaction line items,
> > > telling each one to calculate its total.
> > I tally up the results and return the total to the sender.
> I'm a line item.
> > Someone just told me to calculate my total.
> > I send a message to my product, telling it to calculate
> > > its total.
> > I calculate a total and return the total to the sender.
> I'm a product.
> > Someone just asked me for my price.
> > I return my price to the sender.

So, build the classes in this order:

> product
> transaction line item
> transaction
> sales transaction

and finally:

> customer

And away you go!

OOP—PROBLEM DOMAIN COMPONENT: SMALLTALK

You should be getting a good idea on what to do at this point.

- Specialize from the model class.
- Add variables and the corresponding accessor methods.
  For attributes
  For whole-part structures
  For object connections
- Add initialization methods.
- Override the default creation method, "new."
- Add methods to implement the services.

The Product Class

Add a class and its instance variables

Here it is:

```
Model subclass: #Product
    instanceVariableNames: 'name price '
    classVariableNames: ''
    poolDictionaries: ''
    category: 'Transactions'
```

Add initialization

Initialize a product.

```
Product methodsFor: 'initialize-release'

initialize
    name := String new.
    price := 0.0
```

Add attribute accessors

Do it.

Add connection accessors

Define accessors for adding or removing a connection: None.

Add object creation

Do it.

The Line Item Class

Add a class and its instance variables

Here it is:

```
Model subclass: #LineItem
    instanceVariableNames: 'quantity product lineNumber '
    classVariableNames: ''
    poolDictionaries: ''
    category: 'Transactions'
```

Add initialization

Initialize a line item.

```
LineItem methodsFor: 'initialize-release'
```

initialize
```
    quantity := 0.
    lineNumber := 0
```

Add attribute accessors

Do it.

Add connection accessors

Define accessors for adding or removing a connection:

```
LineItem methodsFor: 'connections'
```

connectToProduct: aProduct
```
    "Set the connection to product"
    product := aProduct
```

product
```
    ^product
```

Add object creation

Do it.

Add a "calculate total" method

The algorithm is pretty simple.
Program the method:

```
LineItem methodsFor: 'calculations'
```

calculateTotal
```
    ^quantity * product price
```

Run the code

Make a line item for a product whose price is 1.5. Set the quantity of the line item to 5. Then tell the line item to calculate its total.

```
| product lineItem total|
product := Product new.
product name: 'SuperWidget'; price: 1.5.
lineItem := LineItem new.
lineItem connectToProduct: product.
lineItem quantity: 5.
total := lineItem calculateTotal.
Transcript cr; show: total printString
```

You should see 7.5 printed on the transcript window.

The Transaction Class

Add a class and its instance variables

Here it is:

```
Model subclass: #Transaction
    instanceVariableNames: 'dateTime customer lineItems '
    classVariableNames: ''
    poolDictionaries: ''
    category: 'Transactions'
```

Add initialization

Initialize a transaction.

Transaction methodsFor: 'initialize-release'

initialize
```
|dateAndTimeArray|
lineItems := OrderedCollection new.
dateAndTimeArray := Time dateAndTimeNow.
dateTime := (dateAndTimeArray at: 1) printString,'',
        (dateAndTimeArray at: 2) printString.
```

Add attribute accessors

Add read and write accessors for the date time variable. Be sure to notify dependents of a change when it occurs.

Transaction methodsFor: 'accessing'

dateTime
```
^dateTime
```

```
dateTime: newValue
   dateTime := newValue.
   self changed: #dateTime.
```

Add connection accessors

Define accessors for adding or removing a connection:

Transaction methodsFor: 'connections'

connectToCustomer: aCustomer
```
customer := aCustomer
```

connectToLineItem: aLineItem
```
lineItems add: aLineItem.
aLineItem lineNumber: lineItems size.
```

disconnectWithLineItem: aLineItem
```
lineItems remove: aLineItem ifAbsent: [nil].
self renumberLineItems.
```

customer
```
^customer
```

lineItems
```
^lineItems
```

renumberLineItems
```
"After a line item is deleted, renumber the remaining
      items"

1 to: lineItems size do: [:index | (lineItems at: index)
      lineNumber: index]
```

Add object creation

Here it goes:

Transaction class methodsFor: 'instance creation'

new
```
^super new initialize
```

Add a "calculate total" method

This method establishes that all of its specializations must define what it means to "calculate total."

Transaction methodsFor: 'calculations'

calculateTotal
```
^self subclassResponsibility
```

The Sales Transaction Class

Add a class and its instance variables

Here it is:

```
Transaction subclass: #SalesTransaction
    instanceVariableNames: 'methodOfPayment '
    classVariableNames: ''
    poolDictionaries: ''
    category: 'Transactions'
```

Add initialization

Initialize a sales transaction.

```
SalesTransaction methodsFor: 'initialize-release'
```

initialize
```
    methodOfPayment := 'cash'.
    super initialize
```

Add attribute accessors

Do it.

Add connection accessors

You don't need to add any here; the sales transaction class inherits its connections accessors from the transaction class.

Add object creation

Not needed. It is inherited from the transaction class.

Add a "calculate total" method

The algorithm is pretty simple.
Program the method:

```
SalesTransaction methodsFor: 'calculations'
```

calculateTotal
```
    | subTotal |
    subTotal := 0.
    lineItems do: [:anItem | subTotal := subTotal +
            anItem calculateTotal].
    ^subTotal
```

Run the code

Create a sales transaction with two line items. Make the first a line item with quantity 5 and a product whose price is 1.5. Make the second a line item with quantity 2. Tell the sales transaction to calculate its total.

```
| product lineItem1 lineItem2 salesTransaction total |
product := Product new.
product name: 'SuperWidget'; price: 1.5.
lineItem1 := LineItem new quantity: 5.
lineItem1 connectToProduct: product.
lineItem2 := LineItem new quantity: 2.
lineItem2 connectToProduct: product.
salesTransaction := SalesTransaction new.
salesTransaction connectToLineItem: lineItem1.
salesTransaction connectToLineItem: lineItem2.
total := salesTransaction calculateTotal.
Transcript cr; show: total printString
```

You should see 10.5 printed on the transcript window.

The Customer Class

Add a class and its instance variables

Here it is:

```
Model subclass: #Customer
    instanceVariableNames: 'name address transactions '
    classVariableNames: ''
    poolDictionaries: ''
    category: 'Transactions'
```

Add initialization

Initialize a transaction.

Customer methodsFor: 'initialize-release'

initialize
```
    name := String new.
    address := String new.
    transactions := OrderedCollection new
```

Add attribute accessors

Do it.

Add connection accessors

Define accessors for adding or removing a connection:

Customer methodsFor: 'connections'

connectToTransaction: aTransaction
    transactions add: aTransaction.

disconnectWithTransaction: aTransaction
    transactions remove: aTransaction ifAbsent: [nil].

transactions
    ^transactions

Add object creation

Do it.

Run the Code

Create a customer with several sales transactions, each with two to three line items connected to different products.

When you need a more elaborate demo, go ahead and build some demonstration methods.

First, add some demo methods which create line items for different types of products.

LineItem class methodsFor: 'demo'

forProductMegaWidget: quantity
    | lineItem product|
    lineItem := LineItem new quantity: quantity.
    product := Product new name: 'MegaWidget'; price: 3.0.
    lineItem connectToProduct: product.
    ^lineItem

forProductSaladShooter: quantity
    | lineItem product|
    lineItem := LineItem new quantity: quantity.
    product := Product new name: 'SaladShooter'; price: 19.99.
    lineItem connectToProduct: product.
    ^lineItem

forProductSuperWidget: quantity
    | lineItem product|
    lineItem := LineItem new quantity: quantity.
    product := Product new name: 'SuperWidget'; price: 1.5.
    lineItem connectToProduct: product.
    ^lineItem

Now add a demonstration method which creates sales transactions with these line items, and then connects the sales transactions to a customer.

Customer class methodsFor: 'demo'

customerDemo

```
| customer lineItem1 lineItem2 lineItem3
      salesTransaction |
customer := Customer new name: 'Barney Rubble'.
customer address: 'Bedrock'.

salesTransaction := SalesTransaction new.
lineItem1 := LineItem forProductSuperWidget: 5.
lineItem2 := LineItem forProductMegaWidget: 3.
lineItem3 := LineItem forProductSaladShooter: 1.

salesTransaction connectToLineItem: lineItem1.
salesTransaction connectToLineItem: lineItem2.
salesTransaction connectToLineItem: lineItem3.
customer connectToTransaction: salesTransaction.

salesTransaction := SalesTransaction new.
lineItem1 := LineItem forProductMegaWidget: 6.
lineItem2 := LineItem forProductSaladShooter: 2.

salesTransaction connectToLineItem: lineItem1.
salesTransaction connectToLineItem: lineItem2.
customer connectToTransaction: salesTransaction.

salesTransaction := SalesTransaction new.
lineItem1 := LineItem forProductSuperWidget: 4.

salesTransaction connectToLineItem: lineItem1.
customer connectToTransaction: salesTransaction.

^customer
```

Now run your customer demo.

```
| customer |
customer := Customer customerDemo.
customer transactions do: [:aSaleTransaction |
   Transcript cr; show: aSaleTransaction calculateTotal
         printString].
```

You should see these totals printed on the transcript window:

```
36.49
57.98
6.0
```

OOP—PROBLEM DOMAIN COMPONENT: C++

About Using Some C++ Library Classes

You should be feeling pretty confident by now. You've already defined C++ classes for two major examples. So what's the next step?

Find a class library, or several, and use the library classes to reduce the data manipulation in your own C++ classes.

In the source code diskette included with this book, you'll find a library directory with some C++ classes for frequently needed data structures.

You can use these (or similar ones) to simplify your code, reducing the amount of data structure bookkeeping in your classes.

An ordered list class

So far, you have implemented whole-part structures and object connections using arrays of pointers. There's nothing wrong with that. Yet you can simplify the code in the connection accessors and increase its understandability by using a library class, such as a list.

Here's the declaration for an ordered list class.

```
template<class Item_Type>
class Ordered_List {
public:
   Ordered_List() { first_element = NULL_ELEMENT;
       current_element - NULL_ELEMENT;
       last_element = NULL_ELEMENT;
       number_of_items = 0; }
   ~Ordered_List() { this->delete_items(); }

   void add(const Item_Type& new_item);
   Boolean remove(const Item_Type& an_item);
   void reset() { current_element = first_element; }

   Item_Type current();
   Item_Type item_at(int location);

   Boolean is_empty();
   Boolean includes(const Item_Type& an_item);
   Boolean end_of_list();

   int size() { return number_of_items; }

   Item_Type operator++ ();   // Prefix increment
   Item_Type operator++ (int);       // Postfix increment

   friend ostream& operator<<(ostream& os,
           Ordered_List<Item_Type>&);
  private:
   // Utility functions
   void delete_items();
   void remove_after(Ordered_List_Element<Item_Type>*
           previous_element);
```

```
Ordered_List_Element<Item_Type>* locate(const Item_Type&
    an_item);

// Data members
Ordered_List_Element<Item_Type>* first_element;
Ordered_List_Element<Item_Type>* current_element;
Ordered_List_Element<Item_Type>* last_element;

int number_of_items;
};
```

Notice that the list is parameterized. You can use it to create different lists holding different types of items:

```
Ordered_List<int> integer_list;
Ordered_List<Integer_Count> integer_count_list;
Ordered_List<Dispensing_Holder*> dispensing_holder_list;
```

It's easy to tell a list to add and remove items:

```
dispensing_holder_list.add(a_holder);
dispensing_holder_list.remove(a_holder);
```

You can tell a list to test for an object in itself:

```
integer_list.includes(5);
```

You can tell a list to find an object at a given location:

```
integer_count_list.item_at(3);
```

Best of all, a list is easy to iterate through. It remembers its beginning, its current position, and its end.

```
while( !integer_list.end_of_list() )
    {
    // Get the current element.
    cout << integer_list.current();
    // Move the current element.
    integer_list++;
    }
```

Just remember to tell it to reset its current element back to the beginning when you're through.

```
integer_list.reset();
```

A time class

This class is similar to the date class. It hides all the details of manipulating C time structures.

```
class Time {
public:
```

```cpp
        // Constructors/destructors
        Time(){ time_of_day = time(NULL);}
        Time(time_t a_time) { time_of_day = a_time; }
        Time(int hours, int minutes = 0, int seconds = 0);
        ~Time() { }

        // Implementors
        void set_time(int hours, int minutes, int seconds);
        int hours();
        int minutes();
        int seconds();

        String print_string();

        // Arithmetic
        Time add_time(int hour = 0, int minutes = 0, int
                seconds = 0);
        Time subtract_time(int hour = 0, int minutes = 0,
                int seconds = 0);

        // Arithmetic operators
        friend Time operator+ (Time& time1, Time& time2);
        friend Time operator- (Time& time1, Time& time2);

        // Increment/decrement operators
        Time operator++();         // prefix
        Time operator++(int);      // postfix

        Time operator--();         // prefix
        Time operator--(int);      // postfix

        // Comparison operators
        friend Boolean operator< (Time& time1, Time& time2);
        friend Boolean operator> (Time& time1, Time& time2);
        friend Boolean operator== (Time& time1, Time& time2);

        // Conversion operator: converts to long
        long as_seconds();

        friend ostream& operator<< (ostream& os, Time& aTime);
private:
    time_t time_of_day;
    static long seconds_in_hour;
    static long seconds_in_minute;
};
```

The default constructor uses the current time value. The other
constructors allow you to set the time.

```cpp
        Time now;                           // Current time
        Time present( time(NULL) );         // Current time
        Time(12, 30, 0)                     // 12:30:00 p.m.
```

You can add and subtract times:

```
Time now;
Time two_hours_from_now = now + Time(2, 0, 0);
Time four_and_a_half_hours_ago = now - Time(4, 30, 0);
Time thirty_minutes_later = now.add_time(0, 30, 0);
```

and compare times:

```
now < thirty_minutes_later;
now == present;
now > four_and_a_half_hours_ago;
```

You can use the increment and decrement operators to adjust time in one second increments:

```
Time midnight(0, 0, 0);
midnight--;                          // 11:59:59 p.m.
```

A boolean class

Here's the Boolean class:

```
class Boolean {
public:

    Boolean() { truth_value = 0; }
    Boolean(Boolean& a_boolean)
            { truth_value = a_boolean.is_true(); }
    Boolean (int an_integer) { truth_value = (an_integer
            != 0); }
    ~Boolean() { }

    int be_true() { truth_value = 1; return truth_value; }
    int be_false() { truth_value = 0; return truth_value; }

    int is_true() { return (truth_value != 0); }
    int is_false() { return (truth_value == 0); }

    int operator! () { return !truth_value; }
    operator int () { return truth_value; }

    friend ostream& operator<< (ostream& os, Boolean&
            a_boolean);

private:

    int truth_value;
};
```

The default constructor creates a false boolean object:

```
Boolean george;  // Boolean george is false.
```

The other constructors create a boolean object, initialized with the result from a conditional test:

```
// later is true if a_time > now
Boolean later( a_time > now );
```

Instead of comparing a boolean object to zero or one, just ask if it is true or false:

```
if (later.is_true() && found.is_false()) { }
```

or you can use short-hand notation:

```
if (later && !found) { }
```

You can set booleans by using a member function or by using an assignment:

```
Boolean later.be_true();
Boolean greater = 1;
Boolean lesser = true;
```

Where the variables true and false are defined to be boolean objects:

```
#define false Boolean(0);
#define true Boolean(1);
```

Finally, when you output a boolean, it prints as "true" or "false":

```
cout << later    // Prints either "true" or "false"
```

The Product Class

Declare the class

```
class Product {
public:

    // Constructors/destructors
    Product();
    Product(String a_name, float a_price);
    ~Product() { }

    // Accessors
    String get_name() { return name; }
    void set_name(String new_value) { name = new_value; }

    float get_price() { return price; }
    void set_price(float new_value) { price = new_value; }

private:

    // Data members
    String name;
```

```
    float price;
};
```

Define the constructor member functions

```
Product::Product()
{
  name = "Widget";
  price = 2.5;
}

Product::Product(String a_name, float a_price)
{
  name = a_name;
  price = a_price;
}
```

Declare and define the insertion operator

You can do some pretty fancy stream formatting in C++. Define the insertion operator for the product class so that it outputs its name in a left-justified field and its price with two decimal places.

Declare the insertion operator:

```
friend ostream& operator<< (ostream& os, Product&
     a_product);
```

Then define it:

```
ostream& operator<< (ostream& os, Product& a_product)
{
  os.width(12);                     // Field width of 12
                                    // Left justified
  os.setf(ios::left, ios::adjustfield);
  os << a_product.name;
  os.width(0);                      // Restore default.
                                    // Restore default.
  os.setf(ios::right, ios::adjustfield);
  os << " price: ";
  os.precision(2);                  // Two decimal places
  os.width(5);
  os.setf(ios::showpoint);          // Show trailing zeros.
  os << a_product.price << "   ";
  os.setf(0, ios::floatfield);      // Restore default.
  os.precision(6);                  // Restore default.
  return os;
}
```

All the pre-defined C++ types use different versions of the insertion operator.

When you define an insertion operator for a class, you're overloading this output stream member function:

```
ostream& operator<< (ostream& os, Product& a_product);
```

If you then make this function a friend of your class, the operator can access all the members of the class directly, even the non-public ones.

Also, remember the insertion operator is really a member function for an output stream class. So you can't declare it as a member function of your own class.

Declare and define the equality operator

Declare the equality operator:

```
Boolean operator== (Product& a_product);
```

Define it:

```
Boolean Product::operator== (Product& a_product)
{
    Boolean same_name(name == a_product.get_name());
    Boolean same_price(price == a_product.get_price());

    return(same_name && same_price);
}
```

The Line Item Class

Declare the class

```
class Line_Item {
public:

    // Constructors/destructors
    Line_Item() { quantity = 0; line_number = 0;}
    Line_Item(Product& a_product, int product_quantity);
    ~Line_Item() { }

    // Implementors
    float calculate_total();

    // Accessors
    int get_quantity() { return quantity; }
    void set_quantity(int new_value) { quantity =
            new_value; }

    int get_line_number() { return line_number; }
```

```
void set_line_number(int new_value)
      { line_number = new_value; }

Product& get_product() { return *product; }
void connect_to_product(Product& a_product);

private:

   // Data members
   Product* product;
   int line_number;
   int quantity;

};
```

Define the constructor member function

```
Line_Item::Line_Item(Product& a_product, int
      product_quantity)
{
   product = &a_product;
   quantity = product_quantity;
   line_number = 0;
}
```

Define the connection accessor member function

Define accessors for adding or removing a connection:

```
void Line_Item::connect_to_product(Product& a_product)
{
   product = &a_product;
}
```

Add the insertion operator

Declare the insertion operator.

```
friend ostream& operator<< (ostream& os, Line_Item&
      a_line_item);
```

Define the line item insertion operator so that it prints the line item's product, its quantity, and its total.

```
ostream& operator<< (ostream& os, Line_Item& a_line_item)
{
   os << a_line_item.line_number
      << ". "
      << *a_line_item.product
      << " quantity: "
```

```
          << a_line_item.quantity << "   "
          << " total: ";
    os.precision(2);
    os.width(5);
    os.setf(ios::showpoint);
    os << a_line_item.calculate_total()
       << endl;
    os.setf(0, ios::floatfield);      // Restore default.
    os.precision(6);                  // Restore default.
    return os;
}
```

Add the equality operator

Declare the equality operator:

```
Boolean operator== (Line_Item& a_line_item);
```

Then define it:

```
Boolean Line_Item::operator== (Line_Item& a_line_item)
{
    return(line_number ==
        a_line_item.get_line_number())
}
```

Define the "calculate total" member function

Define the member function—calculate a line item total.

```
float Line_Item::calculate_total()
{
    return (quantity * product->get_price());
}
```

Run the code

Try out a line item and a product.

```
int main ()
{
    Product good_food("Peanut butter", 2.25);
    Line_Item food_line_item(good_food, 2);

    food_line_item.set_line_number(1);
    cout << food_line_item;
    return 0;
}
```

On the screen you should see:

1. Peanut butter   price: 2.25   quantity: 2   total: 4.50

The Transaction Class

Here's your first chance to use the parameterized list class.

A transaction has a list of line items. You could declare the data member like this:

```
Ordered_List<Line_Item*> line_items;
```

But that's a "finger-ful" to type. An easier approach? Define a synonym for the list class parameterized over line items:

```
typedef Ordered_List<Line_Item*> Line_Item_List;
```

Now you can use the name "Line_Item_List" instead:

```
Line_Item_List line_items;
```

Declare the class

```cpp
// Forward reference
class Customer;

// List synonyms
typedef Ordered_List<Line_Item*> Line_Item_List;

class Transaction {
public:

    // Constructors/destructors
    Transaction() { }
    ~Transaction() { };

    // Implementors
    virtual float calculate_total() = 0;

    // Accessors
    Date get_date() { return date; }
    Time get_time() { return time; }
    void set_date(Date new_value) { date = new_value; }
    void set_time(Time new_value) { time = new_value; }

    void connect_to_customer(Customer& a_customer)
            { customer = &a_customer; }
    Customer& get_customer() { return *customer; }

    void connect_to_line_item(Line_Item& a_line_item);
    void disconnect_with_line_item(Line_Item& a_line_item);
    Line_Item_List& get_line_items(){ line_items.reset();
            return line_items; }

protected:

    // Supporting member functions
    void renumber_line_items();
```

```
// Data members
Date date;
Time time;
Customer* customer;
Line_Item_List line_items;

};
```

Note that the constructor is defined inline this time.

Define the connection accessor member functions

Define accessors for adding or removing a connection:

```
void Transaction::connect_to_line_item(Line_Item&
      a_line_item)
{
   line_items.add(&a_line_item);
   a_line_item.set_line_number(line_items.size());
}

void Transaction::disconnect_with_line_item(Line_Item&
      a_line_item)
{
   line_items.remove(&a_line_item);
   this->renumber_line_items();
}

void Transaction::renumber_line_items()
{
   int number_of_items = line_items.size();
   Line_Item* a_line_item;
   for (int i = 0; i < number_of_items; i++)
      {
      a_line_item = line_items.item_at(i);
      a_line_item->set_line_number(i + 1);
      }
}
```

Add the insertion operator

Declare the insertion operator:

```
friend ostream& operator<< (ostream& os, Transaction&
      a_transaction);
```

Then define it:

```
ostream& operator<< (ostream& os, Transaction&
      a_transaction)
{
```

```
os << a_transaction.date << "   "
   << a_transaction.time << endl;
a_transaction.line_items.reset();
while(!a_transaction.line_items.end_of_list())
   {
   os << *a_transaction.line_items.current();
   a_transaction.line_items++;
   }
   os.precision(2);
   os.width(5);
   os.setf(0, ios::showpoint);
os << "Total cost:   "
   << a_transaction.calculate_total()
   << endl;
   os.setf(0, ios::floatfield);
   os.precision(6);
   return os;
}
```

Add the equality operator

Declare the equality operator:

```
Boolean operator== (Transaction& a_transaction);
```

Then define it:

```
Boolean Transaction::operator== (Transaction&
        a_transaction)
{
   return ((date == a_transaction.get_date()) &&
        (time == a_transaction.get_time()));
}
```

Define the "calculate total" member function

The specific "calculate total" behavior is defined in each specialization class.

The Sales Transaction Class

Declare the class[1]

```
class Sales_Transaction : public Transaction {
public:
```

---

[1]This derived class—like most derived classes—is publicly derived. This means that all public and protected members in its base class are public and protected in the derived class, too. In contrast, private derivation means that all public and protected members in the base class are private in the derived class, inaccessible to others.

```
// Constructors/destructors
Sales_Transaction() { method_of_payment = "cash"; }
~Sales_Transaction() { }

// Implementors
float calculate_total();

// Accessors
String get_method_of_payment() { return
        method_of_payment; }
void paid_with_cash() { method_of_payment = "cash"; }
void sold_on_credit() { method_of_payment = "credit"; }

private:

    // Data members
    String method_of_payment;
};
```

Add the insertion operator

Declare the insertion operator:

```
friend ostream& operator << (ostream& os,
        Sales_Transaction& a_sales_transaction);
```

Then define it:

```
ostream& operator << (ostream& os, Sales_Transaction&
        a_transaction)
{
  os << a_transaction.date << "   "
     << a_transaction.time << endl;
  a_transaction.line_items.reset();
  while(!a_transaction.line_items.end_of_list())
    {
    os << *a_transaction.line_items.current();
    a_transaction.line_items++;
    }
    os.precision(2);
    os.width(5);
    os.setf(0, ios::showpoint);
  os << "Total cost:   "
     << a_transaction.calculate_total()
     << endl;
    os.setf(0, ios::floatfield);
    os.precision(6);
  os << "Method of payment:   "
     << a_transaction.method_of_payment
     << endl;
```

```
    return os;
}
```

Add the equality operator

Declare the equality operator:

```
Boolean operator== (Sales_Transaction&
      a_sales_transaction);
```

Then define it:

```
Boolean Transaction::operator== (Sales_Transaction&
      a_sales_transaction)
{
   Boolean same_date_time = ((date ==
         a_transaction.get_date())
         &&(time == a_transaction.get_time())));
   return (same_date_time &&
         (method_of_payment ==
         a_sales_transaction.get_method_of_payment())));
}
```

Define the "calculate total" member function

Define the member function that calculates a sales transaction total.

```
float Sales_Transaction::calculate_total()
{
   float subtotal = 0.0;
   Linc_Item* a_line_item;

   line_items.reset();
   while(!line_items.end_of_list())
      {
      a_line_item = line_items.current();
      subtotal = subtotal + a_line_item->calculate_total();
      line_items++;
      }
   return subtotal;
}
```

Run the code

Try out a sales transaction, a line item, and a product.

```
int main ()
{
   Sales_Transaction a_sale;

   Product sporting_good("Bowling shoes", 22.50);
   Product good_food("Peanut butter", 2.25);
```

```
        Line_Item sporting_line_item(sporting_good, 1);
        Line_Item food_line_item(good_food, 2);

        a_sale.connect_to_line_item(sporting_line_item);
        a_sale.connect_to_line_item(food_line_item);
        cout << a_sale;
        return 0;
    }
```

You should see something like this on the console:

Fri Sep 11, 1998 22:48:53
1. Bowling shoes   price: 22.50   quantity: 1 total: 22.50
2. Peanut butter   price: 2.25   quantity: 2 total: 4.50
Total cost: 27.00
Method of payment: cash

The Customer Class

A customer remembers a list of sales transactions. Use a parameterized list. Create a synonym for it.

```
        typedef Ordered_List<Sales_Transaction*>Transaction_List;
```

Declare the class

```
    class Customer {
    public:

        // Constructors/destructors
        Customer();
        Customer(String a_name, String an_address);
        ~Customer() { }

        // Implementors

        // Accessors
        String get_name() { return name; }
        void set_name(String new_value) { name = new_value; }

        String get_address() { return address; }
        void set_address(String new_value) { address =
                new_value; }

        Transaction_List& get_transactions();
        void connect_to_transaction(Sales_Transaction&
                a_transaction);
        void disconnect_with_transaction
                (Sales_Transaction& a_transaction);

    private:

        // Data members
```

```
    String name;
    String address;
    Transaction_List transactions;
};
```

Define the constructor member functions

```
Customer::Customer()
{
    name = String("Barney Rubble");
    address = String("Bedrock");
}

Customer::Customer(String a_name, String an_address)
{
    name = a_name;
    address = an_address;
}
```

Define the connection accessor member functions

Define accessors for adding or removing a connection:

```
void Customer::connect_to_transaction
        (Sales_Transaction& a_sales_transaction)
{
    transactions.add(&a_sales_transaction);
}

void Customer::disconnect_with_transaction
        (Sales_Transaction& a_sales_transaction)
{
    transactions.remove(&a_sales_transaction);
}
```

Add the insertion operator

Declare the insertion operator:

```
friend ostream& operator<< (ostream& os, Customer&
        a_customer);
```

Then define it:

```
ostream& operator<< (ostream& os, Customer& a_customer)
{
    os << endl << "Name: " << a_customer.name << "\t"
        << "Address: " << a_customer.address << endl;
    a_customer.transactions.reset();
    while(!a_customer.transactions.end_of_list())
```

```
    {
    cout << *a_customer.transactions.current();
    a_customer.transactions++;
    }
  return os;
}
```

Add the equality operator

Declare the equality operator:

```
Boolean operator== (Customer& a_customer);
```

Then define it:

```
Boolean Customer::operator== (Customer& a_customer)
{
   return ((name == a_customer.get_name()) &&
       (address == a_customer.get_address()) );
}
```

Run the Code

Your system is large enough that it makes sense to write some functions to generate the objects in your demonstration.

First, write some demo member functions that generate line items for different products. Add these demo member functions to the line item class itself.

Declare the demo member functions:

```
// Demo member functions
Line_Item* for_product_mega_widget(int quantity);
Line_Item* for_product_super_widget(int quantity);
Line_Item* for_product_bowling_shoes(int quantity);
```

Then define them:

```
Line_Item* Line_Item::for_product_mega_widget(int
      quantity)
{
  Product* mega_widget = new Product("MegaWidget", 3.0);
  Line_Item* new_line_item =
        new Line_Item(*mega_widget, quantity);
  return new_line_item;
}

Line_Item* Line_Item::for_product_super_widget(int
      quantity)
{
  Product* super_widget = new Product("SuperWidget", 1.5);
```

```
        Line_Item* new_line_item =
                new Line_Item(*super_widget, quantity);
        return new_line_item;
    }

Line_Item* Line_Item::for_product_bowling_shoes(int
        quantity)
{
    Product* bowling_shoes = new Product("Bowling shoes",
            22.5);
    Line_Item* new_line_item =
            new Line_Item(*bowling_shoes, quantity);
    return new_line_item;
}
```

Now write a demo member function that creates a customer with sales transactions—plus line items from the item class demo member functions.

Add this demo member function to the customer class itself.

```
Customer& Customer::customer_demo()
{
    Customer* mr_rubble = new Customer();
    Line_Item dummy_line_item;
    Line_Item* line_item1;
    Line_Item* line_item2;
    Line_Item* line_item3;

    // Make a sales transaction with line items.
    Sales_Transaction* a_sale_transaction =
            new Sales_Transaction();
    line_item1 =
            dummy_line_item.for_product_super_widget(5);
    line_item2 = dummy_line_item.for_product_mega_widget(3);
    line_item3 =
            dummy_line_item.for_product_bowling_shoes(1);
    a_sale_transaction->connect_to_line_item(*line_item1);
    a_sale_transaction->connect_to_line_item(*line_item2);
    a_sale_transaction->connect_to_line_item(*line_item3);

    // Connect the sales transaction to the customer.
    mr_rubble->connect_to_transaction(*a_sale_transaction);
    // Make a sale transaction with line items
    a_sale_transaction = new Sales_Transaction();
    line_item1 = dummy_line_item.for_product_mega_widget(6);
    line_item2 =
            dummy_line_item.for_product_bowling_shoes(2);
```

```
    a_sale_transaction->connect_to_line_item(*line_item1);
    a_sale_transaction->connect_to_line_item(*line_item2);

    // Connect the sales transaction to the customer.
    mr_rubble->connect_to_transaction(*a_sale_transaction);

    // Make a sales transaction with line items.
    a_sale_transaction = new Sales_Transaction();
    line_item1 =
            dummy_line_item.for_product_super_widget(4);
    a_sale_transaction->connect_to_line_item(*line_item1);

    // Connect the sales transaction to the customer.
    mr_rubble->connect_to_transaction(*a_sale_transaction);
    return *mr_rubble;
}
```

Okay. Finally, write a program to run your demonstration:

```
int main ()
{
    Customer dummy_customer;
    Customer& mr_rubble = dummy_customer.customer_demo();

    cout << mr_rubble << endl;

    Transaction_List& transactions = mr_rubble.
            get_transactions();

    while(!transactions.end_of_list())
        {
        cout << *transactions.current();
        transactions++;
        }

    return 0;
}
```

You should see something like this on the console:

Name: Barney Rubble   Address: Bedrock
Fri Sep 11, 1998 6:08:41
1. SuperWidget   price: 1.50   quantity: 5 total: 7.50
2. MegaWidget   price: 3.00   quantity: 3 total: 9.00
3. Bowling shoes   price: 22.50   quantity: 1 total: 22.50
Total cost: 39.00
Method of payment: cash

Fri Sep 11, 1998 9:45:59
1. MegaWidget   price: 3.00   quantity: 6 total: 18.00
2. Bowling shoes   price: 22.50   quantity: 2 total: 45.00

Total cost: 63.00
Method of payment: cash

Fri Sep 11, 1998 22:05:13
1. SuperWidget   price: 1.50   quantity: 4 total: 6.00
Total cost: 6.00
Method of payment: cash

OOD—HUMAN INTERACTION COMPONENT

Deciding What to Design and Build

Previously, you took a problem domain component and built human interaction classes for each class whose objects needed a way to interact with a physical device.

Sales transactions are different. A sales transaction is an event which is remembered over time. Such remembered events require a different kind of human interface. They need an interface that organizes and displays information, data entry, or data lookup.

Think about some of the ways you could present the information for a sales transaction system:

> A transactions window
>> List all the transactions for a given time period.
>> For a selected transaction show:
>>> its customer's name and address
>>> its line items
>>> its total cost.
> A line item window
>> List all the line items for a specific product.
>> For a selected transaction show:
>>> the quantity sold.
> A customer window
>> Show a customer's name and address.
>> List the customer's transactions.
>> For a selected transaction show:
>>> its line items
>>> its total cost.

What should you design and build first? Work it out with the people who will use the automated system. You might even get to something like this: You need a selection criterion. Here's one: "Ask the end-user!" He's the one who needs to use the information in the display.

> I need to see a customer's name and address, plus all of his transactions. When I select a transaction, I'd like to see its line items. When I select a line item, I'd like to see its quantity and total.

Designing the Customer Window

Identify the human interaction classes

Sketch out what you need. Begin by writing down each problem domain class that has objects that the human interaction component needs to work with. List what information each object contributes and establish how you'd like to present it.

Customer
    name   display a value
    address   display a value
    transactions   display a list
Transaction
    line items   display a list
    total   display a value
Line item
    quantity   display a value
    total   display a value

Add human interaction classes to satisfy your display and interaction needs (Figure 3–5):

Figure 3–5: A selectable list and a display box.

Connect the human interaction objects

Consider how each human interaction component finds the information it displays.

Draw connections between the problem domain objects and the human interaction objects.

Add human interaction for a customer object (Figure 3–6):

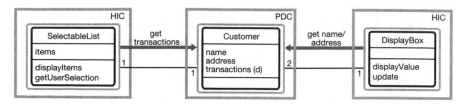

Figure 3–6: Connecting the human interaction for a customer.

Next, add human interaction for a sales transaction object (Figure 3–7):

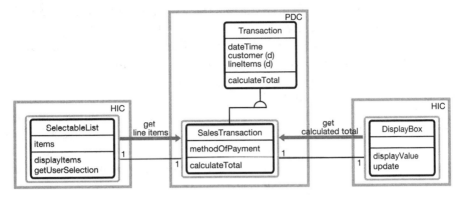

Figure 3–7: Human interaction for a sales transaction.

Finally, add human interaction for a line item (Figure 3–8):

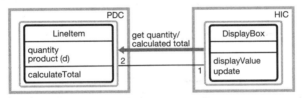

Figure 3–8: Human interaction for a line item.

Coordinate the human interaction objects

You've designed the individual parts of a customer window. The next step is to make those parts work together.

What are your choices?

One approach: hire a window manager. That manager oversees the entire window. That's okay, but it does mean some centralized control (ugh). And it does mean limited reuse (double ugh), because future reuse is an "all or nothing" proposition.

What's the alternative?

You can design smaller human interaction pieces, ones that communicate and coordinate via mailboxes. Here, you distribute responsibility. And you build-in a finer granularity of reusable components for the future.

Ahhh. A principle!

The "mail dominance" principle. Design small, domain-based human interaction containers that communicate and coordinate via mailboxes. Why? Better distribution of responsibility. And increased likelihood of reuse.

How do you do this?

Divide the human interaction into domain-related pieces. In this case, it's customer, transaction, and line item.

Next, consider what selections might be made. In this case, for a customer window, it's a transaction selection and a line item selection.

Make those selections—or rather, the corresponding selection holders—into your "mailbox" objects.

Then, whenever a selection occurs, change the selection holder. Whenever that happens, the selection holder in turn notifies all of its dependents—those who need to know about the new selection.

Add a transaction selection holder (Figure 3–9) and a line item selection holder (Figure 3–10).

Figure 3–9: Adding a transaction selection holder.

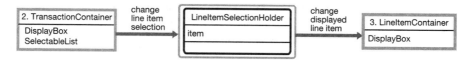

Figure 3–10: Adding a line item selection holder.

OOD—HUMAN INTERACTION COMPONENT: SMALLTALK

Design a Layout; Design the Human Interaction Component

Design a layout

Organize this human interaction content:

Customer
    name   a display box
    address   a display box
    transactions   a selectable list

Transaction
    line items   a selectable list
    total   a display box

Line item
    quantity   a display box
    total   a display box

into an initial display layout for a customer screen, something like Figure 3–11.[2]

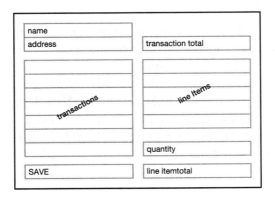

Figure 3–11: An initial display layout for a customer screen.

(You could use the "save" button to save this information to a file.) What container(s) should you use here? And why?

You could use just one container, called a customer window (Figure 3–12).

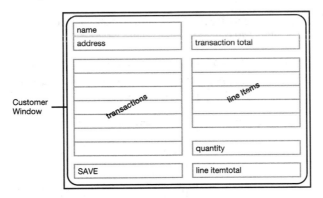

Figure 3–12: One big container.

And this is a very common design approach.

But if you look ahead toward reuse, you could take another approach. It would be nice if you could partition the display into smaller containers—ones that might be useful for building other displays in the same problem domain. But where should you turn for help?

The problem domain classes!

[2]For human interface design ideas and principles, see [Laurel] and [Apple].

The "let the problem domain classes be your guide" principle. Let the problem domain classes guide you in organizing the classes in each design component.

What does this mean for human interaction? It means that you'll want to grab all of the human interaction objects that correspond to a problem domain object and put them into a container. Why? Someone will be much more likely to use that container in the future, achieving a larger scale of reuse. You'll be more likely to reuse those containers when you build other displays for this system (and for other systems in the same problem domain).

Apply this principle to the customer window. Consider its selectable lists and its display boxes:

> As a customer
> > I know my name and address—two display boxes.
> > I know my transactions—a selectable list.
>
> As a transaction
> > I know my line items—a selectable list.
> > I know my calculated total—a display box.
>
> As a line item
> > I know my quantity and calculated total—two
> > > display boxes.

So, what should you do? Use a customer container, a transactions container, and a line items container—all inside a container of containers, a customer window (Figure 3–13).

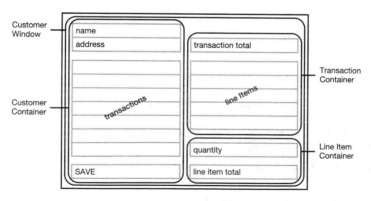

Figure 3–13: A number of containers.

Design the human interaction component

Use model view container classes. Why? Because applying model view container classes provides a simple and repeatable approach to putting together "chunks" of a display.

You used them a bit in Chapter 2. You'll apply them even more aggressively here.

What kind of model view containers do you need?

You need a special container, a model-value view container (Figure 3–14). It's a view container that is suited for presenting a view on a model value. It holds some number of display boxes and buttons.

You've built this one before. Reuse it!

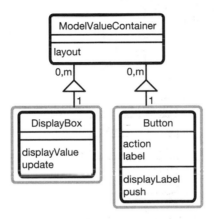

Figure 3–14: A model-value view container.

You also need another special container, a model-collection view container. It's another view container, one suited for presenting a view on a model collection. It holds selectable lists, along with display boxes (totals, counts) and action buttons (save, cancel).

Design a model-collection view container to hold display boxes, buttons, and selectable lists. Connect each display box to a model value; connect each button to a model action; connect each selectable list to a model collection.

What you need is something like a model-value view container plus a bit more. Here's an opportunity to reuse by specializing. Do it!

Recognizing that a collection is a special kind of value, you can make a model-collection view container a specialization of a model-value view container.

Add a model-collection view container (Figure 3–15).

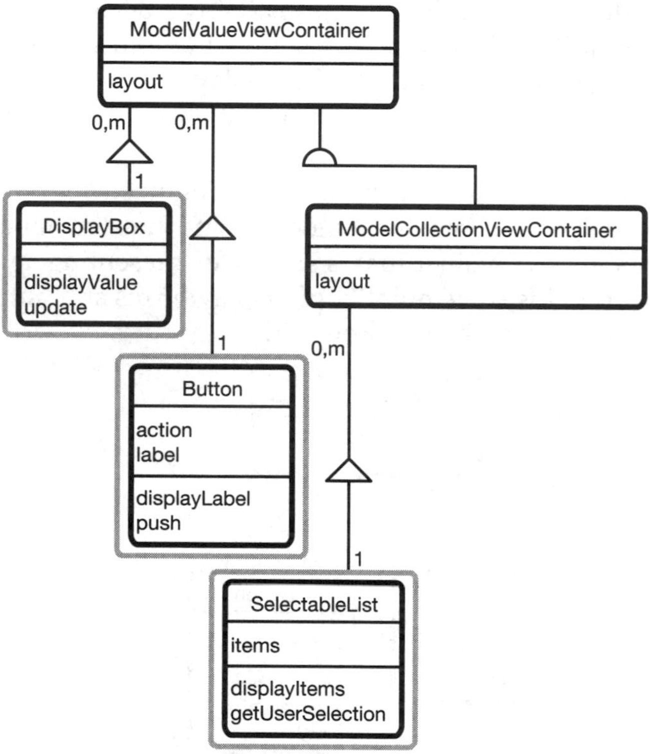

Figure 3–15: Adding a model-collection view container.

So far, so good.

Add the application-specific specialization containers to the human interaction component (Figure 3–16).

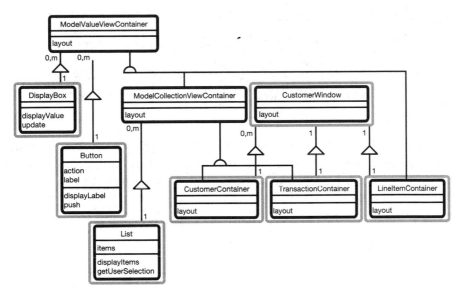

Figure 3–16: Adding application-specific containers.

OOP—HUMAN INTERACTION COMPONENT: SMALLTALK

The Plan

Build the model-collection view container class.
Then build these specializations:

>   customer container class
>   transaction container class

Next, get the views in different containers working together.

Finally, build a class whose objects are containers of containers—
the customer window class.

The Model-Collection View Container Class

Add a class and its instance variables

Build a model-collection view container, a specialization of a
model-value view container.

```
ModelValueViewContainer subclass:
        #ModelCollectionViewContainer
    instanceVariableNames: ''
    classVariableNames: ''
    poolDictionaries: ''
    category: 'Model Views'
```

Add a "make list on" method

Write a method to add a selectable list to a container class. This time, you'll need scroll bars.

To get scroll bars for a selectable list, you need to put a selectable list inside a special kind of wrapper, a border decorator:

```
wrapper := BorderDecorator on: listView.
```

Using the border decorator, you can create a selectable list with no scroll bars, vertical scroll bars, horizontal scroll bars, or both vertical and horizontal scroll bars. The default configuration is "with vertical scroll bars."

ModelCollectionViewContainer methodsFor: 'view layout'

addListView: listView **in:** area
  | wrapper |
  wrapper := BorderDecorator on: listView.

  self add: wrapper in: area

Next, write the methods to create the selectable list. Selectable lists have many options which are normally set during creation, but you won't need them here.[3]

> I'm a selectable list.
>   I *find* the items to display by sending my model a
>   "get list" message.
>   I *show* the items in a list format.
>   I *change* my model, by sending it a "selected item"
>   message with the index of the selected item.
>   I know I must find and show again when my model
>   broadcasts a "changed:" message with my
>   "aspect" as an argument.

ModelCollectionViewContainer methodsFor: 'view creation'

makeListOn: aModel **showing:** getListMsg **selecting:**
  selectedItemMsg **updateFor:** aspect

---

[3]Here are the other options you can set when creating a selectable list:

  printItems: When true, I convert the list items to strings using the "printString" method.

  oneItem: When true, I act as a read-only list; no items are selectable.

  menu: This is the message that I send to my model to get a pop-up menu for editing the list items.

  initialSelection: This is the message that I send to my model to find the initial selection.

  useIndex: When true, I return the index of the selected item; otherwise, I return the selected item.

```
| listView |
listView := SelectionInListView
        on: aModel
        printItems: false
        oneItem: false
        aspect: aspect
        change: selectedItemMsg
        list: getListMsg
        menu: nil
        initialSelection: nil
        useIndex: true.
^listView
```

The Customer Container Class

A customer container holds two display boxes (one for name, the other for address) and a selectable list (for the collection of transactions).

Add a class and its instance variables

```
ModelCollectionViewContainer subclass: #CustomerContainer
instanceVariableNames: "
class VariableNames: "
poolDictionaries: "
category: 'Transaction Views'
```

Add an "add transaction list on" method

CustomerContainer methodsFor: 'view layout'

addTransactionListViewOn: aCustomer

```
| itemView listArea |
itemView := self
        makeListOn: aCustomer
        showing: #transactionCollection
        selecting: #changeTransactionSelection:
        updateFor: #transactions.
listArea := self constraintFrame: 0 @ (2/9) corner: 1 @ 1.
self addListView: itemView in: listArea.
^itemView
```

Add view layout methods

CustomerContainer methodsFor: 'view layout'

addAddressViewOn: aCustomer

```
| itemView itemArea |
itemView := self makeDisplayBoxOn: aCustomer
        for: #address.
itemArea := self constraintFrame: 0 @ (1/9)
        corner: 1 @ (2/9).
self addView: itemView in: itemArea
```

addNameViewOn: aCustomer

```
| itemView itemArea |
itemView := self makeDisplayBoxOn: aCustomer for: #name.
itemArea := self constraintFrame: 0 @ 0 corner: 1 @ (1/9)
self addView: itemView in: itemArea
```

Add a view creation method

CustomerContainer methodsFor: 'view creation'

buildViewOn: aCustomer

```
self addNameViewOn: aCustomer.
self addAddressViewOn: aCustomer.
self addTransactionListViewOn: aCustomer
```

Who holds a collection of transactions?

A transaction list view needs some help. "As a transaction list view, I need to ask someone in the model about a collection of transactions." For each transaction, I need a description that I can display.

Who knows the transactions for a customer? A customer does.

Add a "transactionCollection" method to customer, to return a collection of transaction descriptions. Use the transaction's date and time for a transaction description.

Customer methodsFor: 'view access'

transactionCollection
```
^transactions collect: [:each | each dateTime]
```

Holding a Transaction Selection

A transaction selection holder

A view in a customer container gets a new transaction selection. Views in a transaction container need that transaction selection, too.

What mechanism can you use to communicate and coordinate effectively?

Use a mail box, known in Smalltalk as a value holder. A value holder holds a value and knows how to interact with views on that value.

Name the value holder something like "transaction selection holder" (Figure 3–17).

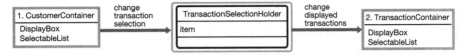

Figure 3–17 : Adding a transaction selection holder.

Here's what happens:

I'm a transaction list view.
    I get a transaction selection.
    I send a change message to my transaction selection
        holder object, telling it to change its value.

I'm a transaction selection holder object.
    Someone tells me to change my value.
    I change my value.
    I tell my transaction container to change the displayed
        transaction.

I'm a transaction container.
    Someone told me to change my displayed transaction.
    I tell my display box and selectable list to display the
        new transaction.

Who holds a transaction selection holder?

Who in the model holds a transaction selection holder object? It's whoever holds the collection that it is a selection of.

In this case, a customer holds a collection of transactions. And so it's a customer who holds a transaction selection holder object.

Add a transaction selection to the customer class

A customer object needs to know about its transactions and its transaction selection.

Add a "transaction selection" variable.

```
Model subclass: #Customer
    instanceVariableNames: 'name address transactions
        transactionSelection '
    classVariableNames: ''
    poolDictionaries: ''
    category: 'Transactions'
```

Add a line to the initialize method.

```
transactionSelection := TransactionSelectionHolder new
```

Add an accessor so a view can change the transaction selection.

Customer methodsFor: 'view access'

changeTransactionSelection: indexSelected
    indexSelected = 0
        ifTrue: [transactionSelection value: nil]
        ifFalse: [transactionSelection value:
            (transactions at: indexSelected)]

The Transaction Selection Holder Class
Add a class and its instance variables

```
ValueHolder subclass: #TransactionSelectionHolder
    instanceVariableNames: 'transactionContainer '
    classVariableNames: ''
    poolDictionaries: ''
    category: 'Transaction Holders'
```

Add connection accessors

TransactionSelectionHolder methodsFor: 'connections'

connectToTransactionContainer: newValue
    transactionContainer := newValue

transactionContainer
    ^transactionContainer

Add a "value update" method

Add a method to "update my value."

TransactionSelectionHolder methodsFor: 'accessing'

value: selectedTransaction
    super value: selectedTransaction.
    transactionContainer isNil ifTrue: [^self].
    transactionContainer changeDisplayedTransaction:
        selectedTransaction

The Transaction Container Class

Ahhh. A similar pattern.

You've just added a selection holder to the customer container class. Now it's time to add another class—the transaction container class—and a selection holder.

Add a class and its instance variables

When a transaction container is told to change its displayed transaction selection it updates its selectable list, and its display box.

Add instance variables, so a transaction container can talk directly to its selectable list and display box.[4]

```
ModelCollectionViewContainer subclass: #TransactionContainer
    instanceVariableNames: ' lineItemList totalBox '
    classVariableNames: ''
    poolDictionaries: ''
    category: 'Transaction Views'
```

The transaction container communicates to the line item container through a line item selection holder. Add an instance variable to hold the connection to the line item selection holder.

```
ModelCollectionViewContainer subclass: #TransactionContainer
instanceVariableNames: 'lineItemList totalBox
        lineItemSelectionHolder '
    classVariableNames: ''
    poolDictionaries: ''
    category: 'Transaction Views'
```

Add connection accessors

Don't add connection accessors for the line item list and the total box. They're private parts of the transaction container.

Do add connection accessors for the line item selection holder, since it represents a public mailbox.

TransactionContainer methodsFor: 'connections'

connectToLineItemSelectionHolder: aLineItemSelectionHolder
    lineItemSelectionHolder := aLineItemSelectionHolder

lineItemSelectionHolder
    ^lineItemSelectionHolder

Add a view layout method

TransactionContainer methodsFor: 'view layout'

addLineItemListOn: aTransaction
    | listArea |

---

[4]A visual container keeps a list, called its components, of the views inside it. To avoid searching the list for a particular component, add instance variables when a container needs to communicate with a particular component.

```
lineItemList := self
   makeListOn: aTransaction
   showing: #lineItemCollection
   selecting: #changeLineItemSelection:
   updateFor: #lineItems.
listArea := self constraintFrame: 0 @ (1/3) corner: 1 @ 1.
self addListView: lineItemList in: listArea.
^lineItemList
```

Add an "add total box on" method

Set up a display box so that "as a display box, I display the results I get when I send a 'calculate total' message to my model object."

TransactionContainer methodsFor: 'view layout'

```
addTotalBoxOn: aTransaction
   | itemArea |
   totalBox := self makeDisplayBoxOn: aTransaction
         for: #calculateTotal.
   itemArea := self constraintFrame: 0@(1/9) corner: 1@(2/9)
   self addView: totalBox in: itemArea.
   ^totalBox
```

Add a "build view on" method

Add a method to create a transaction container for a transaction.

TransactionContainer methodsFor: 'view creation'

```
buildViewOn: transaction
   self addLineItemListOn: transaction.
   self addTotalBoxOn: transaction
```

Add a "change the displayed transaction" method

Add a method so the transaction container can update its selectable list and its display box when the displayed transaction changes.

First, connect the selectable list and the display box to the new selected transaction:

```
lineItemList  model: selectedTransaction.
totalBox model: selectedTransaction.
```

Next, tell the selectable list and display box to update what it displays:

```
lineItemList update: #lineItems.
totalBox update: #calculateTotal.
```

Finally, connect the line item selection holder to the selected transaction, so that the line item selection holder can hold the selected line item for the selected transaction.

```
selectedTransaction lineItemSelection:
    lineItemSelectionHolder.
```

Add an overall "change displayed transaction" method

Now put it all together:

```
TransactionContainer methodsFor: 'view selections'

changeDisplayedTransaction: selectedTransaction
    selectedTransaction isNil ifTrue: [^self].
    lineItemList model: selectedTransaction.
    totalBox model: selectedTransaction.
    lineItemList update: #lineItems.
    totalBox update: #calculateTotal.
    selectedTransaction lineItemSelection:
        lineItemSelectionHolder
```

Holding a Line Item Selection

A line item selection holder

Here's the picture (Figure 3–18):

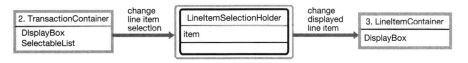

Figure 3–18: Adding a line item selection holder.

Who holds a line item selection holder?

A transaction holds a line item selection holder.

Add a line item selection to the transaction class

Add a selected line item instance variable:

```
Model subclass: #Transaction
    instanceVariableNames: 'dateTime customer lineItems
        lineItemSelection '
    classVariableNames: ''
    poolDictionaries: ''
    category: 'Transactions'
```

Add a statement to the initialize method, initializing the line item selection:

```
lineItemSelection := LineItemSelectionHolder new.
```

Add view access to its collection of line items.

Transaction methodsFor: 'view access'

lineItemCollection
```
^lineItems collect: [:each | each lineNumber
printString]
```

Add view access to set the value of the selected line item.

Transaction methodsFor: 'view access'

changeLineItemSelection: indexSelection

```
indexSelected = 0
    ifTrue: [lineItemSelection value: nil]
    ifFalse: [lineItemSelection value:
        (lineItems at: indexSelection)]
```

The Line Item Selection Holder Class

Add a class and its instance variables

```
ValueHolder subclass:  #LineItemSelectionHolder
    instanceVariableNames: 'lineItemContainer '
    classVariableNames: ''
    poolDictionaries: ''
    category: 'Transaction Holders'
```

Add connection accessors

LineItemSelectionHolder methodsFor: 'connections'

connectToLineItemContainer: newValue
```
    lineItemContainer := newValue
```

lineItemContainer
```
    ^lineItemContainer
```

Add a "value update" method

LineItemSelectionHolder methodsFor: 'accessing'

value: selectedLineItem
```
    super value: selectedLineItem.
    lineItemContainer isNil ifTrue: [^self].
    lineItemContainer changeDisplayedLineItem:
        selectedLineItem.
```

The Line Item Container Class

A line item container holds two display boxes (for line item total and line item quantity).

Add a class and its instance variables

Make line item container a specialization of model-value view container. Add instance variables, so a line item container can update its display boxes when a new line item is selected.

```
ModelValueViewContainer subclass: #LineItemContainer
    instanceVariableNames: 'totalBox quantityBox '
    classVariableNames: ''
    poolDictionaries: ''
    category: 'Transaction Views'
```

Add view layout methods

Add a view layout method, "add total box on."

LineItemContainer methodsFor: 'view layout'

addTotalBoxOn: lineItem
   | itemArea |
   totalBox := self makeDisplayBoxOn: lineItem
        for: #calculateTotal.
   itemArea := self constraintFrame: 0 @ (1/2)
        corner: 1 @ 1.
   self addView: totalBox in: itemArea.
   ^totalBox

Add a view layout method, "add quantity box on."

LineItemContainer methodsFor: 'view layout'

addQuantityBoxOn: lineItem
   | itemArea |
   quantityBox := self makeDisplayBoxOn: lineItem
        for: #quantity.
   itemArea := self constraintFrame: 0 @ 0
        corner: 1 @ (1/2).
   self addView: quantityBox in: itemArea.
   ^quantityBox

Add a view creation method

LineItemContainer methodsFor: 'view creation'

buildViewOn: aLineItem
   self addQuantityBoxOn: aLineItem.
   self addTotalBoxOn: aLineItem

Add a view selection method

Add a method that changes the displayed line item to some other one.

LineItemContainer methodsFor: 'view selections'

```
changeDisplayedLineItem: selectedLineItem
    selectedLineItem isNil ifTrue: [^self].
    totalBox model: selectedLineItem.
    quantityBox model: selectedLineItem.
    totalBox update: #calculateTotal.
    quantityBox update: #quantity
```

Getting the Views in Different Containers Working Together

The approach

The transaction selection holder and the line item selection holder each provide a way to synchronize the views in different containers (Figure 3–20).

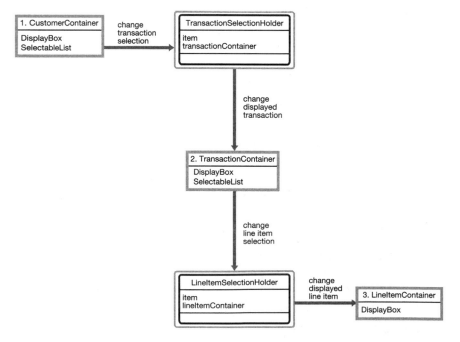

Figure 3–20: Synchronizing the views in the different containers.

A transaction selection holder is connected to a transaction container. So "as a transaction selection holder, when I change my value, I tell my transaction container to change its displayed transaction."

Likewise, a line item selection holder is connected to a line item container. So, when a line item is selected, the value of the line item selection holder changes, and the line item container is told to change its displayed line item.

The Customer Window Class

Put it all together in one container of containers.

Build a container class that builds the three containers for a customer, hooks them up so that they work together, and physically arranges them in a window.

Add a class and its instance variables

```
CompositePart subclass: #CustomerWindow
    instanceVariableNames: ''
    classVariableNames: ''
    poolDictionaries: ''
    category: 'Transaction Views'
```

Add methods to create the views inside a customer window

Here's the plan:

> Add a customer container.
> Add a transaction container.
> Add a line item container.

Add an "add customer container" method

Add a method to create a customer container and place it inside the customer window.

```
CustomerWindow methodsFor: 'view layout'
```

addCustomerContainer: customer
```
    | customerView  frame |
    customerView := CustomerContainer new.
    customerView buildViewOn: customer.
    frame := self constraintFrame: 0 @ 0 corner: 1/2 @ 1.
    self addView: customerView in: frame.
    ^customerView
```

Add an "add transaction container" method

Set up the transaction container so it *receives* the selected transaction from the transaction selection holder, and it *sends* the selected line item to the line item selection holder.

Here's how:

> Create a transaction container to display an initial transaction:
>
> Connect the transaction container to the transaction selection holder:
>
> Connect the line item selection holder to the transaction container

Now, write the method:

```
CustomerWindow methodsFor: 'view layout'
```

```
addTransactionContainer: transaction
        and: transactionSelectionHolder
        and: lineItemSelectionHolder
    | transactionContainer frame |
    transactionContainer := TransactionContainer new.
    transactionContainer buildViewOn: transaction.
    transactionSelectionHolder
      connectToTransactionContainer: transactionContainer.
    transactionContainer
      connectToLineItemSelectionHolder:
            lineItemSelectionHolder.
    frame := self constraintFrame: 1/2 @ 0
            corner: 1 @ (7/9).
    self addView: transactionContainer in: frame.
    ^transactionContainer
```

Add an "add line item container" method

Set up the line item container so it receives the selected line item from the line item selection holder.

Follow the same pattern you used to create the preceding container:

```
CustomerWindow methodsFor: 'view layout'
```

```
addLineItemContainer: lineItem and: lineItemSelectionHolder
    | lineItemContainer  frame |
    lineItemContainer := LineItemContainer new.
    lineItemContainer buildViewOn: lineItem.
```

```
lineItemHolder connectToLineItemContainer:
        lineItemContainer.
frame := self constraintFrame: 1/2 @ (7/9)
        corner: 1 @ 1.
self addView: lineItemContainer in: frame.
^lineItemContainer
```

Add a "build the views inside a customer window" method

Let a customer's first transaction be the default selection transaction. Using the transaction selection holder connect the views in a customer container to the views in a transaction container. Using the line item selection holder connect the views in a transaction container to the views in a line item container.—Whew!

CustomerWindow methodsFor: 'build views'

buildViewOn: aCustomer
```
    | transaction lineItem transactionSelectionHolder
        lineItemSelectionHolder |
    transaction := aCustomer transactions first.
    lineItem := transaction lineItems first.
    transactionSelectionHolder := aCustomer
        transactionSelection.
    lineItemSelectionHolder := transaction lineItemSelection.
    self addCustomerContainer: aCustomer.
    self
      addTransactionContainer: transaction
      and: transactionSelectionHolder
      and: lineItemSelectionHolder.
    self addLineItemContainer: lineItem and:
        lineItemSelectionHolder
```

Add a window opening method

CustomerWindow methodsFor: 'window opening'

openOn: aCustomer

```
    | window |
    window := ScheduledWindow new.
    window component: self.
    self buildViewOn: aCustomer.
    window label: 'Customer demo'.
    window minimumSize: 300@200.
    window open
```

Run the Code

What can you do? How about this:

Create a customer with transactions and line items.
Open a customer window for this customer.

Use the customer demo you wrote earlier, the one that creates a customer. And open a customer window on it.
Try it out.
In a system workspace, evaluate:

```
CustomerWindow new openOn: Customer customerDemo
```

You should see something like Figure 3–21.

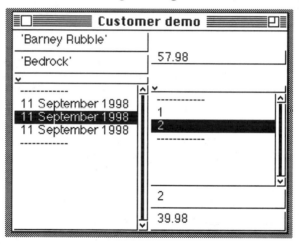

Figure 3–21: The customer demo.

OOD—HUMAN INTERACTION COMPONENT: C++

Grouping the Human Interaction Content into Containers

Partition the human interaction component into "chunks" using the problem domain classes as your guide:

```
Customer
    name            a display box
    address         a display box
    transactions    a selectable list
```

Transactions
    line items   a selectable list
    total   a display box

Line item
    quantity   a display box
    total   a display box

Building your human interaction component in chunks reduces risk—you can build and test incrementally—and it increases the likelihood of reuse—you can use the chunks again within the same problem domain.

Add a visual container to your OOA/OOD model for each chunk in the human interaction component. Here's the customer container (Figure 3–22):

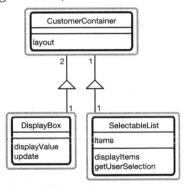

Figure 3–22: Adding a customer container.

Add a similar design for the transaction container and the line item container.

Connecting the Containers

The views inside the transaction container depend upon the customer container to tell them which transaction to display.

The transaction selection (from a selectable list) is the one that the views need to display.

Use a transaction selection holder to get the transaction selection from the selectable list and pass it along to the transaction container (Figure 3–23).

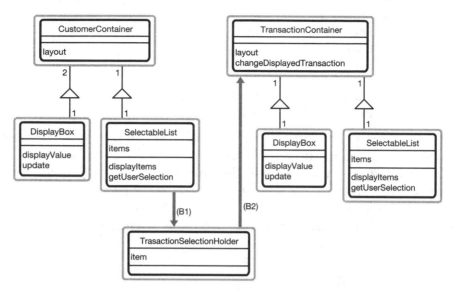

Figure 3–23: Connecting the customer container and the transaction container.

Similarly, the views inside the line item container depend upon the transaction container to tell them which line item to display.

Use a line item selection holder to get the line item selection from the selectable list and pass it along to the line item container (Figure 3–24).

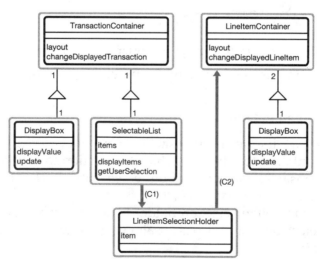

Figure 3–24: Connecting the transaction container and the line item container.

Using Console Menus and Console Display Boxes

Match the needed human interaction classes to your growing library of reusable human interaction classes:

> display box → console display box
> selectable list → console menu

Design the customer, transaction, and line item containers using the console display boxes and console menus. For example, for the customer container (Figure 3–25):

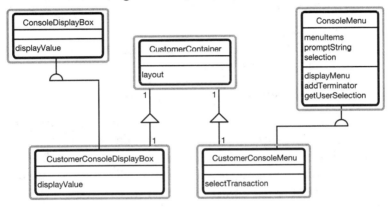

Figure 3–25: Using your reusable console classes within the customer container.

Add a similar design for the transaction container and the line item container.

OOP—HUMAN INTERACTION COMPONENT: C++

The Plan

> Create a transaction selection holder and a line item
>   selection holder.
> Create a customer container, a transaction container, and a
>   line item container.
> Use the selection holders to connect the containers.
> Create a customer window to hold all of the containers.

But, before you start, take some time out to consider how you might improve your console display box class. Spending a bit of time every now and then to refactor your reusable class library can simplify your work and save you a lot of time later.

Time for a principle!

The reclassifying principle. As you learn more about a problem domain and build more classes for it, take time again and again to reclassify and reorganize, increasing understandability and the likelihood of reuse.

Improving the Console Display Box Class

Look at all the console display boxes you need for this human interaction component:

> customer name → console display box
> customer address → console display box
> transaction total → console display box
> line item total → console display box
> line item quantity → console display box

What's the same about each of these console display boxes? Each one gets a value from an object and displays it.

What's different about each of these console display boxes? The type of object it displays and the function it calls to get its value.

Sounds like you need a parameterized class, doesn't it?

Change your console display box class to a template class, parameterized over its object type and its value function type:

```
template<class Object_Type, class Value_Function_Type>
class Console_Display_Box {
public:

  // Constructors/destructors
  Console_Display_Box() { label_string = ""; }
  ~Console_Display_Box() { }

  // Accessors
  String get_label_string() { return label_string; }
  void set_label_string(String a_string)
    { label_string = a_string; }

  Object_Type& get_object() {return *object;}
  void set_object (Object_Type& an_object)
    { object = &an_object; }

  Value_Function_Type get_value_function()
    { return value_function; }
```

```
void set_value_function(Value_Function_Type a_function)
   { value_function = a_function; }

void display_label_string();
void display_value();
```

```
private:

   // Data members
   String label_string;
   Object_Type* object;
   Value_Function_Type value_function;
};
```

Here's how it works:

> I'm a console display box.
> > I know about an object and a value function.
> > I determine my value to display by telling the object to
> > > call the value function.

About parameterizing a class over a function

How can you assign a function to a class data member? It's fairly simple. Just use a pointer to the function. Then, when you're ready to call the function, just dereference its pointer.

Here's how the console display box calls a function by dereferencing a pointer:

```
template<class Object_Type, class Value_Function_Type>
void Console_Display_Box<Object_Type, Value_Function_Type>
   ::display_value()
{
   this->display_label_string();
   cout << (object->*value_function)();
}
```

Notice that the value function is really a pointer to a member function of the object. The console display box tells the object to call the function pointed to by the value function pointer.

About working with pointers to functions

In C++, a pointer to a function is a derived type. A pointer to a function looks something like this:

```
String (*get_string)();
```

This statement declares the "get_string" identifier as a pointer to a function; moreover, that member function takes no arguments and returns a string.

To create a pointer to a class member function, use the class name and the scope resolution operator:

```
String (Customer::*get_string)();
```

This statement declares the "get_string" identifier as a pointer to a customer member function; moreover, that member function takes no arguments and returns a string.

You can assign pointers to functions just like you can for any other pointer. Remember to use the class name and scope resolution operator for member functions:

```
get_string = &Customer::get_name;
```

An example—a console display box for a customer's name

Now you can create a specialized console display box without defining a new class.

How?

First, create a synonym type to represent a pointer to a customer member function:

```
typedef String (Customer::*Customer_String_Function)();
```

Next, create a console display box parameterized for the customer class and the customer string function.

```
Console_Display_Box <Customer,
        Customer_String_Function> a_console_display_box;
```

To use the console display box, assign it a customer object and a customer member function.

```
Customer mr_rubble("Barney Rubble", "Bedrock");
a_console_display_box.set_object(mr_rubble);
a_console_display_box.set_value_function
        (&Customer::get_name);
```

That's all there is to it! Your console display box is ready to go to work.

Tell it display its value:

```
a_console_display_box.display_value();
```

The display box tells its object (a customer) to execute its member function ("get_name") and prints the result on the console:

Barney Rubble

No sweat!

Now, use the new console display box to build your human interaction component.

The Transaction Selection Holder Class

I'm a transaction selection holder.
I hold a transaction selection for a customer.
When someone tells me to change my selection, I get my
new transaction selection from my customer's
list of transactions.

Declare the class

```
class Transaction_Selection_Holder {
public:
  // Constructors/destructors
  Transaction_Selection_Holder() { }
  ~Transaction_Selection_Holder() { }

  // Accessors
  Transaction& get_selection()
    { return *transaction_selection; }
  void set_selection(Transaction& a_transaction)
    { transaction_selection = &a_transaction; }

  Customer& get_customer()
    { return *a_customer; }
  void connect_to_customer(Customer& new_customer)
    { a_customer = &new_customer; }

private:
  Transaction* transaction_selection;
  Customer* a_customer;
};
```

Add the "change selection" member function

Somebody, probably a human interaction object, tells the transaction selection holder the index of the selected transaction.

Add a member function, so a transaction selection holder can get its new transaction selection from its customer, using the selection index.

Declare the member function:

```
void change_selection(int selection_index);
```

Then define it:

```
void Transaction_Selection_Holder::change_selection
        (int selection_index)
{
  //(List indices start at zero).
  int list_selection = selection_index - 1;
  Transaction_List& transactions =
    a_customer->get_transactions();
  transaction_selection =
    transactions.item_at(list_selection);
}
```

The Line Item Selection Holder Class

Follow the same pattern you used to build the transaction selection holder.

Declare the class

```
class Line_Item_Selection_Holder {
public:
  //Constructors/destructors
  Line_Item_Selection_Holder() { }
  ~Line_Item_Selection_Holder() { }

  // Accessors
  Line_Item& get_selection()
    { return *line_item_selection; }
  void set_selection(Line_Item& new_selection)
    { line_item_selection = &new_selection; }

  Transaction& get_transaction()
    { return *a_transaction; }
  void connect_to_transaction(Transaction&
        new_transaction)
    { a_transaction = &new_transaction; }
private:

  Line_Item* line_item_selection;
  Transaction* a_transaction;
};
```

Add the "change selection" member function

Declare the member function:

```
void change_selection(int new_selection);
```

Then define it:

```
void Line_Item_Selection_Holder::change_selection
        (int selection_index)
{
    int list_selection = selection_index - 1;
    Line_Item_List& line_items =
        a_transaction->get_line_items();
    line_item_selection =
        line_items.item_at(list_selection);
}
```

Planning for the Customer Container Class

Build the customer container class. For an object in that class, consider its parts:

> I'm a customer container. I hold:
> > two container console display boxes (for customer name
> > > and address)
> > a transaction console menu (for customer transactions)

Build the parts, then the container.

The Customer Console Display Box Class

Use your parameterized console display box class. Make the customer console display box a synonym type for the console display box class, parameterized for the customer class and a customer string function:

```
typedef String (Customer::*Customer_String_Function)();
typedef Console_Display_Box <Customer,
        Customer_String_Function>
            Customer_Console_Display_Box;
```

The Transaction Console Menu Class

Build the transaction console menu class. Consider an object in that class:

> I'm a transaction console menu.
> I know about a customer.

> I display its transactions in my menu list.
> When someone selects one of the transactions, I notify
> my transaction selection holder.

Declare the class

```
class Transaction_Console_Menu : public Console_Menu {
public:
  // Constructors/destructors
  Transaction_Console_Menu() { }
  ~Transaction_Console_Menu() { }

  // Implementors
  void make_items(Customer& new_customer);
  void execute_selection();

  // Accessors
  Customer& get_customer()
    { return *a_customer; }
  void connect_to_customer(Customer& new_customer)
    { a_customer = &new_customer; }

  Transaction_Selection_Holder& get_transaction_holder()
    { return *a_transaction_holder; }
  void connect_to_transaction_holder
    (Transaction_Selection_Holder& new_holder)
    { a_transaction_holder = &new_holder; }

private:

  // Data members
  Customer* a_customer;
  Transaction_Selection_Holder* a_transaction_holder;
};
```

Define the "make items" member function

Write a member function to create menu items describing a customer's transactions. Use each transaction's date and time as its description.

```
void Transaction_Console_Menu::make_items
      (Customer& a_customer)
{
  menu_size = 0;
  Transaction_List& transactions =
        a_customer.get_transactions();
  while(!transactions.end_of_list())
  {
```

```
        String transaction_description =
                transactions.current()->get_date_time();
        this->add_item(transaction_description);
        transactions++;
    }
    this->connect_to_customer(a_customer);
}
```

Add the "get date time" member function to the transaction class

To the transaction class, add a member function to return a transaction's date and time as a string.

Declare the member function:

```
String get_date_time();
```

Then define it:

```
String Transaction::get_date_time()
{
    return String(date.print_string()) + String(" ") +
        String(time.print_string());
}
```

Add the "execute selection" member function

A transaction console menu responds to a user's selection by telling its corresponding transaction selection holder to change.

```
void Transaction_Console_Menu::execute_selection()
{
    if (selection == 0)
        return;
    a_transaction_holder->change_selection(selection);
}
```

You now have all the pieces in place so you can build the customer container class.

The Customer Container Class

Declare the class

```
class Customer_Container {
public:
    // Constructors/destructors
    Customer_Container() { }
    ~Customer_Container() {}
```

```
private:

    // Data members
    Customer_Console_Display_Box* name_box;
    Customer_Console_Display_Box* address_box;
    Transaction_Console_Menu* transaction_menu;
};
```

Add the "make display boxes" member functions

Add a member function to create a customer console display box, one that gets and displays a customer's name.

Declare the member function:

```
void make_name_box(Customer& a_customer);
```

Then define it:

```
void Customer_Container::make_name_box(Customer&
        a_customer)
{
    name_box = new Customer_Console_Display_Box();

    name_box->set_value_function(&Customer::get_name);
    name_box->set_label_string("Name:   ");
    name_box->set_object(a_customer);
}
```

Add a member function to create a customer console display box to display a customer's address.

Declare the member function:

```
void make_address_box(Customer& a_customer);
```

Then define it:

```
void Customer_Container::make_address_box
        (Customer& a_customer)
{
    address_box = new Customer_Console_Display_Box();

    address_box->set_value_function(&Customer::get_address);
    address_box->set_label_string("Address:   ");
    address_box->set_object(a_customer);
}
```

Add the "make transaction console menu" member function

Add a member function to create a customer console menu box to display a customer's transactions and get a user's selection.

Declare the member function:

```
void make_transaction_console_menu(Customer& a_customer);
```

Then define it:

```
void Customer_Container
    ::make_transaction_console_menu(Customer& a_customer)
{
    transaction_menu = new Transaction_Console_Menu();

    transaction_menu->make_items(a_customer);
    transaction_menu->add_terminator("Quit");
    transaction_menu->add_prompt("Select a transaction:  ");
}
```

Add the "build views" member function

Now add a member function that builds all the component views inside a customer container.

Declare the member function:

```
void build_views(Customer& a_customer);
```

Then define it:

```
void Customer_Container::build_views
        (Customer& a_customer)
{
    this->make_name_box(a_customer);
    this->make_address_box(a_customer);
    this->make_transaction_console_menu(a_customer);
}
```

Add the "connect to transaction holder" member function

Add a member function to connect the transaction console menu inside a customer container to a corresponding transaction selection holder.

Declare the member function:

```
void connect_menu_to_holder
        (Transaction_Selection_Holder&
            a_transaction_holder);
```

Then define it:

```
void Customer_Container::connect_menu_to_holder
        (Transaction_Selection_Holder&
            a_transaction_holder)
{
   transaction_menu->
      connect_to_transaction_holder(a_transaction_holder);
}
```

Add the "display customer components" member function

When someone tells a customer container to display its components, the first thing it does is tell each of its customer console display boxes to display itself.

Declare the member function:

```
void display_customer_components();
```

Then define it:

```
void Customer_Container::display_customer_components()
{
   char* border = "---------------------------";

   cout << border << endl;
   name_box->display_value();
   cout << endl;
   address_box->display_value();
   cout << endl << border << endl;
}
```

Add the "display components" member function

Finally, add a member function so a customer container can repeatedly (1) tell each of its customer components to display itself and (2) get and execute a user selection.

Declare the member function:

```
void display_components();
```

Then define it:

```
void Customer_Container::display_components()
{
    this->display_customer_components();
    while(transaction_menu->get_user_selection() != 0)
        {
        transaction_menu->execute_selection();
        this->display_customer_components();
        }
}
```

Run the Code

Create a customer container for a customer. And use the customer demo you defined earlier.

```
int main ()
{
    Customer a_customer;
    Customer_Container a_customer_container;
    Customer& mr_rubble = a_customer.customer_demo();

    Transaction_Selection_Holder* transaction_holder =
        new Transaction_Selection_Holder();
    transaction_holder->connect_to_customer(mr_rubble);

    a_customer_container.build_views(mr_rubble);
    a_customer_container.
        connect_menu_to_holder(*transaction_holder);

    a_customer_container.display_components();
    return 0;
}
```

On the console, you should see something like this:

```
----------------------------
Name:  Barney Rubble
Address:  Bedrock
----------------------------


1. Fri Sep 11 1998        09:04:15
2. Fri Sep 11 1998        09:04:15
3. Fri Sep 11 1998        09:04:15
4. Quit


Select a transaction:
```

Planning for the Transaction Container Class

Build the transaction container class. For an object in that class, consider its parts:

> I'm a transaction container. I hold:
>> a transaction console display box (for transaction total)
>> a transaction console menu (for transaction line items)

Build the parts, then the container.

The Transaction Console Display Box Class

Use your parameterized console display box class. Make the transaction console display box a synonym type for the console display box class, parameterized for the transaction class and a transaction string function:

```
typedef String
        (Transaction::*Transaction_String_Function)();
typedef Console_Display_Box <Transaction,
        Transaction_String_Function>
                Transaction_Console_Display_Box;
```

Add the "total string" member function to the transaction class

A console display box expects its value function to return a string.

Add a member function to the transaction class to return a string representing the transaction's calculated total.

Declare and define the member function:

```
String total_string() { return
        String(this->calculate_total()); }
```

The Line Item Console Menu Class

Build the line item console menu class. Consider an object in that class:

> I'm a line item console menu.
> I know about a transaction.
> I get and display its line items in my menu list.
> When someone selects one of my line items, I notify my
>> line item selection holder.

Declare the class

```
class Line_Item_Console_Menu : public Console_Menu {
public:
```

```
    // Constructors/destructors
    Line_Item_Console_Menu() { }
    ~Line_Item_Console_Menu() { }

    // Implementors
    void make_items(Transaction& new_transaction);
    void execute_selection();

    // Accessors
    Transaction& get_transaction()
       { return *a_transaction; }
    void connect_to_transaction
            (Transaction& new_transaction)
       { a_transaction = &new_transaction; }

    Line_Item_Selection_Holder& get_line_item_holder()
       { return *a_line_item_holder; }
    void connect_to_line_item_holder
        (Line_Item_Selection_Holder& new_holder)
       { a_line_item_holder = &new_holder; }

private:

    // Data members
    Transaction* a_transaction;
    Line_Item_Selection_Holder* a_line_item_holder;

};
```

Add the "make items" member function

Write a member function to create menu items which describe a transaction's line items. Use a line item's line number as its description.

```
void Line_Item_Console_Menu::make_items
        (Transaction& new_transaction)
{
    Line_Item_List& line_items =
            new_transaction.get_line_items();
    menu_size = 0;
    String item_number_string;

    while(!line_items.end_of_list())
        {
        item_number_string = String("Line Item:  ") +
                String(line_items.current()->
                        get_line_number());
        this->add_item(item_number_string);
```

```
        line_items++;
        }
    this->connect_to_transaction(new_transaction);
}
```

Add the "execute selection" member function

A line item console menu responds to a user's selection by telling its line item selection holder to change.

```
void Line_Item_Console_Menu::execute_selection()
{
    if (selection == 0)
        return;
    a_line_item_holder->change_selection(selection);
}
```

You now have all the pieces in place so you can build the transaction container class.

The Transaction Container Class

Declare the class

```
class Transaction_Container {
public:

    // Constructors/destructors
    Transaction_Container() { }
    ~Transaction_Container() {}

private:

    // Data members
    Transaction_Console_Display_Box* total_box;
    Line_Item_Console_Menu* line_item_menu;
};
```

Add the "make total box" member function

Add a member function to create a transaction console display box, one that gets and displays a transaction's total.

Declare the member function:

```
void make_total_box();
```

Then define it:

```
void Transaction_Container::make_total_box()
{
```

```
    total_box =
        new Transaction_Console_Display_Box();
    total_box->
        set_value_function(&Transaction::total_string);
    total_box->set_label_string("Transaction total:   ");
}
```

Add the "make line item console menu" member function

Declare the member function:

```
void make_line_item_console_menu();
```

Then define it:

```
void Transaction_Container::make_line_item_console_menu()
{
    line_item_menu = new Line_Item_Console_Menu();
    line_item_menu->add_prompt("Select a line_item:   ");
}
```

Add the "build views" member function

Declare the member function:

```
void build_views();
```

Then define it:

```
void Transaction_Container::build_views()
{
    this->make_total_box();
    this->make_line_item_console_menu();
}
```

Add the "change the displayed transaction" member function

Add a member function so a transaction container can tell its line item menu and its total box to change.
Declare the member function:

```
void Transaction_Container::change_displayed_transaction
        (Transaction& selected_transaction)
```

Then define it:

```
void Transaction_Container::change_displayed_transaction
        (Transaction& selected_transaction)
{
```

```
        line_item_menu->make_items(selected_transaction);
        line_item_menu->add_terminator("Quit");
        total_box->set_object(selected_transaction);
        this->display_components();
    }
```

Add the "connect to line item holder" member function

Add a member function to connect the line item console menu inside a transaction container to a corresponding line item selection holder.

Declare the member function:

```
void connect_menu_to_holder
        (Line_Item_Selection_Holder& a_line_item_holder);
```

Then define it:

```
void Transaction_Container::connect_menu_to_item_holder
        (Line_Item_Selection_Holder& a_line_item_holder)
{
    line_item_menu->
        connect_to_line_item_holder(a_line_item_holder);
}
```

Add the "display components" member function

Declare the member function:

```
void display_components();
```

Then define it:

```
void Transaction_Container::display_components()
{
    cout << endl;
    total_box->display_value();
    cout << endl;
    if (line_item_menu->get_user_selection() != 0)
        line_item_menu->execute_selection();
}
```

Run the Code

Create a sales transaction with line items. Create a line item selection holder. And create a transaction container.

Finally, tell the transaction container to change its displayed transaction to the sales transaction that you created.

```
int main ()
{
   // Create a sales transaction with line items.
   Sales_Transaction a_sale_transaction;
   Line_Item a_line_item;
   Line_Item* line_item1 =
         a_line_item.for_product_super_widget(5);
   Line_Item* line_item2 =
         a_line_item.for_product_mega_widget(3);
   Line_Item* line_item3 =
         a_line_item.for_product_bowling_shoes(1);

   a_sale_transaction.connect_to_line_item(*line_item1);
   a_sale_transaction.connect_to_line_item(*line_item2);
   a_sale_transaction.connect_to_line_item(*line_item3);

   // Create a line item selection holder.
   Line_Item_Selection_Holder* line_item_holder =
      new Line_Item_Selection_Holder();
   line_item_holder->connect_to_transaction
         (a_sale_transaction);

   // Create a transaction container.
   Transaction_Container a_transaction_container;

   a_transaction_container.build_views();
   a_transaction_container.
      connect_menu_to_holder(*line_item_holder);

   // Tell it to change its displayed transaction.
   a_transaction_container.
      change_displayed_transaction(a_sale_transaction);
   return 0;
}
```

On the console, you should see something like this:

Transaction Total: 39.00

1. Line Item: 1
2. Line Item: 2
3. Line Item: 3
4. Quit

Select a line item:

Planning for the Line Item Container Class

Here you go again.

Build the line item container class. For an object in that class, consider its parts:

> I'm a line item container. I hold:
> > two console display boxes for line item quantity and
> > > total

The Line Item Console Display Box Class

Use your parameterized console display box class. Make the line item console display box a synonym type for the console display box class, parameterized for the line item class and a line item string function:

```
typedef String (Line_Item::*Line_Item_String_Function)();
typedef Console_Display_Box <Line_Item,
    Line_Item_String_Function>
        Line_Item_Console_Display_Box;
```

Add the "quantity string and total string" member function to the line item class

The console display box expects its value function to return a string. Add member functions to the line item class to return strings representing a line item's quantity and its calculated total.

Declare and define the member functions:

```
String quantity_string() { return String(quantity); }
String total_string() { return
        String(this->calculate_total()); }
```

The Line Item Container Class

Declare the class

```
class Line_Item_Container {
public:

  //Constructors/destructors
  Line_Item_Container() { }
  ~Line_Item_Container() {}

private:

  // Data members
  Line_Item_Console_Display_Box* total_box;
  Line_Item_Console_Display_Box* quantity_box;
};
```

Add the "make display boxes" member functions

Declare the member functions:

```
void make_total_box();
void make_quantity_box();
```

Then define them:

```
void Line_Item_Container::make_total_box()
{
    total_box = new Line_Item_Console_Display_Box();

    total_box->set_value_function(&Line_Item::total_string);
    total_box->set_label_string("Line item total:   ");
}

void Line_Item_Container::make_quantity_box()
{
    quantity_box = new Line_Item_Console_Display_Box();

    quantity_box->
       set_value_function(&Line_Item::quantity_string);
    quantity_box->set_label_string("Line item quantity:   ");
}
```

Add the "build views" member function

Declare the member function:

```
void build_views();
```

Then define it:

```
void Line_Item_Container::build_views()
{
    this->make_total_box();
    this->make_quantity_box();
}
```

Add the "change displayed line item" member function

Add a member function so a line item container can tell its quantity box and its total box to change.

Declare the member function:

```
void Line_Item_Container::change_displayed_line_item
        (Line_Item& selected_line_item)
```

Then define it:

```
void Line_Item_Container::change_displayed_line_item
      (Line_Item& selected_line_item)
{
   total_box->set_object(selected_line_item);
   quantity_box->set_object(selected_line_item);
   this->display_components();
}
```

Add the "display components" member function

Declare the member function:

```
void display_components();
```

Then define it:

```
void Line_Item_Container::display_components()
{
   cout << endl;
   total_box->display_value();
   cout << "    ";
   quantity_box->display_value();
   cout << endl;
}
```

Run the Code

Create a demo line item. Create a line item container.

Tell the line item container to change its displayed line item to the one you just created.

```
int main ()
{
   Line_Item a_line_item;
   Line_Item* demo_line_item =
      a_line_item.for_product_super_widget(5);
   Line_Item_Container a_line_item_container;

   a_line_item_container.build_views();
   a_line_item_container.
      change_displayed_line_item(*demo_line_item);

   return 0;
}
```

On the console, you should see something like this:

Line item total: 7.50 Line item quantity: 5

Connecting the Containers

Here's how the containers work together:

> I'm a customer container.
>> When someone selects a transaction from my transaction
>> console menu, I send a change message to my
>> corresponding transaction container.
>
> I'm a transaction container.
>> I tell my total box and my line item menu to display the
>> new transaction.

and

> I'm a transaction container.
>> When someone selects a line item from my line item
>> console menu, I send a change message to my
>> corresponding line item container.
>
> I'm a line item container.
>> I tell my total box and my quantity to display the new
>> line item.

Connecting a Customer Container and a Transaction Container

Who in the model sends a transaction selection to a transaction container?

Who knows about a transaction selection? A transaction selection holder knows.

Use a transaction selection holder to connect a customer container to a transaction container.

Adding to the Transaction Selection Holder Class

Declare a "transaction container" data member

Add a data member to the transaction selection holder class, to hold a connection to a transaction container.

```
Transaction_Container* a_transaction_container;
```

Add the connection accessor member functions

Declare and define the connection accessors:

```
void connect_to_transaction_container
        (Transaction_Container& a_container);
        { a_transaction_container = &a_container; }
Transaction_Container& get_transaction_container()
        { return *a_transaction_container; }
```

Add change notification

When a transaction selection holder changes, it tells its corresponding transaction container to change its displayed transaction.

So, for the transaction selection holder class, add a statement to the change selection member function:

```
a_transaction_container->
    change_displayed_transaction(*transaction_selection);
```

Run the Code

First, create a customer. Create the selection holders. And connect the transaction holder to a customer.

Next, create a customer container. Create a transaction container. Connect the transaction console menu (inside a customer container) to the transaction selection holder. Connect the transaction selection holder to the transaction container. And connect the line item console menu (inside a transaction container) to the line item selection holder.

Finally, tell the customer container to display its components.

```
int main ()
{
    // Create a customer.
    Customer a_customer;
    Customer mr_rubble = a_customer.customer_demo();

    // Create the selection holders.
    // Connect the transaction holder to the customer.
    Transaction_Selection_Holder* transaction_holder =
        new Transaction_Selection_Holder();

    transaction_holder->connect_to_customer(mr_rubble);

    Line_Item_Selection_Holder* line_item_holder =
        new Line_Item_Selection_Holder();

    // Create the customer container.
    Customer_Container* a_customer_container =
        new Customer_Container ();

    a_customer_container->build_views(mr_rubble);

    // Create the transaction container.
    Transaction_Container* a_transaction_container =
        new Transaction_Container();

    a_transaction_container->build_views();
```

```
// Connect the transaction console menu (inside a
// customer container) to the transaction selection
// holder.
a_customer_container->
   connect_menu_to_holder(*transaction_holder);

// Connect the transaction selection holder to the
// transaction container.
transaction_holder->connect_to_transaction_container
        (*a_transaction_container);

// Connect the line item console menu
// (inside a transaction container) to the line item
// selection holder.
a_transaction_container->
   connect_menu_to_holder(*line_item_holder);

a_customer_container->display_components();

return 0;

}
```

Try it out. You should see something like this:

```
- - - - - - - - - - - - - - - - - - - - - - - - - - - -
Name:  Barney Rubble
Address:  Dedrock
- - - - - - - - - - - - - - - - - - - - - - - - - - - -

1. Fri Sep 11 1998    09:04:15
2. Fri Sep 11 1998    09:04:15
3. Fri Sep 11 1998    09:04:15
4. Quit

Select a transaction:  1

Transaction total:  39.00

1. Line item: 1
2. Line item: 2
3. Line item: 3
4. Quit

Select a line item:
```

Connecting a Transaction Container and a Line Item Container

Who in the model sends a line item selection to a line item container?

Who knows about a line item selection? A line item selection holder knows.

Use a line item selection holder to connect a transaction container to a line item container.

Adding to the Line Item Selection Holder Class

Declare a "line item container" data member

Add a data member to the line item selection holder class, to hold a connection to a line item container.

```
Line_Item_Container* a_line_item_container;
```

Add the connection accessor member functions

Declare and define the connection accessors:

```
void connect_to_line_item_container
    (Line_Item_Container& a_container);
        { a_line_item_container = &a_container; }
Line_Item_Container& get_line_item_container()
    { return *a_line_item_container; }
```

Add change notification

When a line item selection holder changes, it tells its line item container to change its displayed line item.

So, for the line item selection holder class, add a statement to the change selection member function:

```
a_line_item_container->
    change_displayed_line_item(*line_item_selection);
```

Adding to the Transaction Container Class

When the displayed transaction changes, the transaction container tells its line item selection holder.

Declare a "line item selection holder" data member

Add a data member to the transaction container class, to hold a connection to a line item selection holder.

```
Line_Item_Selection_Holder* a_line_item_selection_holder;
```

Add the connection accessor member functions

Do it.

When a transaction container connects to a line item selection holder, it connects its line item console menu to that line item selection holder, too.

So, add this statement to the connect to line item holder accessor:

```
this->connect_menu_to_holder(a_line_item_holder);
```

Add change notification

When a transaction container changes, it tells its corresponding line item selection holder.

For the transaction container class, add a statement to its change displayed transaction member function.

```
a_line_item_selection_holder->
    connect_to_transaction(selected_transaction);
```

Run the Code

Add a line item container to your previous demo.

```
// Create a line item container.
Line_Item_Container* a_line_item_container =
    new Line_Item_Container();
a_line_item_container->build_views();
```

Connect a line item selection holder to a corresponding line item container.

```
line_item_holder->
    connect_to_line_item_container(*a_line_item_container);
```

On the console, you should see something like this:

```
- - - - - - - - - - - - - - - - - - - - - - - - - - - - - -
Name:  Barney Rubble
Address: Bedrock
- - - - - - - - - - - - - - - - - - - - - - - - - - - - - -
1. Fri Sep 11 1998    09:04:15
2. Fri Sep 11 1998    09:04:15
3. Fri Sep 11 1998    09:04:15
4. Quit

Select a transaction:  1

Transaction total:  39.00
```

1. Line item: 1
2. Line item: 2
3. Line item: 3
4. Quit

Select a line item: 1

Line item quantity: 5   Line item total: 7.50

The Customer Window Class

One more time!

Build the customer window class. For an object in that class, consider its parts:

> I'm a customer window. I hold:
> a customer container
> a transaction container
> a line item container

A customer window builds these containers and connects them with a transaction selection holder and a line item selection holder.

Declare the class

```
class Customer_Window {
public:

  // Constructors/destructors
  Customer_Window() { }
  ~Customer_Window() { }

private:

  // Data members
  Customer_Container* a_customer_container;
  Transaction_Container* a_transaction_container;
  Line_Item_Container* a_line_item_container;
};
```

Add the "make customer container" member function

Create a customer container. Connect its transaction console menu to a corresponding transaction selection holder.

Declare the member function:

```
void make_customer_container (Customer& a_customer,
    Transaction_Selection_Holder* a_transaction_holder);
```

Then define it:

```
void Customer_Window::make_customer_container
  (Customer& a_customer,
  Transaction_Selection_Holder* a_transaction_holder)
{
  a_customer_container = new Customer_Container();

  a_customer_container->build_views(a_customer);
  a_customer_container->
    connect_menu_to_holder(*a_transaction_holder);
}
```

Add the "make transaction container" member function

Create a transaction container. Connect a corresponding transaction selection holder to the transaction container. And connect the transaction container and its transaction console menu to a line item selection holder.

Declare the member function:

```
void
make_transaction_container(Transaction_Selection_Holder*
        a_transaction_holder,
        Line_Item_Selection_Holder*
        a_line_item_holder);
```

Then define it:

```
void Customer_Window::make_transaction_container
  (Transaction_Selection_Holder* a_transaction_holder,
  Line_Item_Selection_Holder* a_line_item_holder)
{
  a_transaction_container = new Transaction_Container;

  a_transaction_container->build_views();
  a_transaction_holder->
    connect_to_transaction_container
      (*a_transaction_container);
  a_transaction_container->
    connect_to_line_item_holder
      (*a_line_item_holder);
}
```

Add the "make line item container" member function

Create a line item container. Connect a line item selection holder to the line item container.

Declare the member function:

```
void make_line_item_container
  (Line_Item_Selection_Holder* a_line_item_holder);
```

Then define it:

```
void Customer_Window::make_line_item_container
   (Line_Item_Selection_Holder* a_line_item_holder)
{
   a_line_item_container = new Line_Item_Container();

   a_line_item_container->build_views();
   a_line_item_holder->
         connect_to_line_item_container
               (*a_line_item_container);
}
```

Add the "build views" member function

Create a transaction selection holder and a line item selection holder. Create the containers.

Connect the containers with the selection holders.

Declare the member function:

```
void build_views(Customer& a_customer);
```

Then define it:

```
void Customer_Window::build_views(Customer& a_customer)
{
   Transaction_Selection_Holder* a_transaction_holder =
      new Transaction_Selection_Holder();
   Line_Item_Selection_Holder* a_line_item_holder =
      new Line_Item_Selection_Holder();

   this->make_customer_container(a_customer,
         a_transaction_holder);
   this->make_transaction_container(a_transaction_holder,
         a_line_item_holder);
   this->make_line_item_container(a_line_item_holder);
}
```

Add the "display components" member function

Start the display by telling the customer container to display its components. The application ends when the customer container's transaction menu is told to quit.

Declare the member function:

```
void display_components();
```

Then define it:

```
void Customer_Window::display_components()
{
  a_customer_container->display_components();
}
```

Run the Code

```
int main ()
{
  Customer a_customer;
  Customer& mr_rubble = a_customer.customer_demo();
  Customer_Window a_customer_window;

  a_customer_window.build_views(mr_rubble);
  a_customer_window.display_components();
  return 0;
}
```

On the console, you should see something just like you did before (this time, you used a customer window as an overall container).

OOD—DATA MANAGEMENT COMPONENT

A Plan

For this example, design the capability to save and restore a customer object, its sales transactions, and its line items in a file.

You could choose to work with a flat file, a relational DBMS, or an object DBMS.

For simplicity and platform-independence, this example uses a flat file and an object tag format. Many of the same lessons apply when using a relational DBMS. With an object-oriented DBMS, much of the work is done for you.

Time to begin.

Designing the Data Management Component

Data management consists of two major activities: storing and restoring.

A format object

Begin with a format object—one that knows how to store and restore.

What does each format object know and do?

> I'm a format object.
> I know about a corresponding problem domain object.

I know how to save:
    its values
    its connections to other objects.
I get what needs to be saved, format it, and save it.
I know how to restore that object, too.

Design the format classes

In this example, you need format classes that define how to save:

- a customer's attribute values and connections to each corresponding collection of transactions
- each transaction's attribute values and connections to its collection of line items
- and each line item's attribute values.

To support the idea of saving and restoring objects and their connections, add an explicit object identifier to the problem domain classes (Figure 3–26).

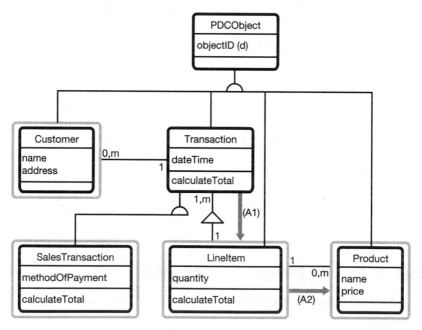

Figure 3–26: Adding an object identifier to each problem domain class.

Use the object identifier to store the connections between objects. For example, here's what a file in object tag format looks like for a customer with two transactions:

```
<ObjectDefn>
<className>Customer
<objectID><id>57
<name>Barney Rubble
<address>Bedrock
<transaction><id>64
<transaction><id>49
<\ObjectDefn>
```

For the data management component, introduce an object tag format class and its specializations (Figure 3–27):

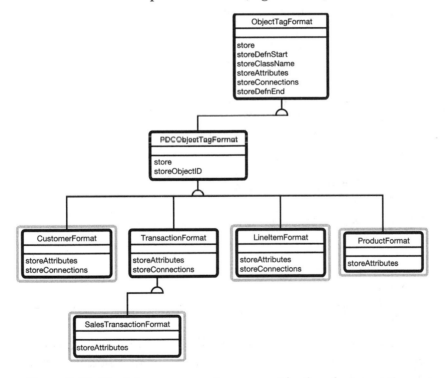

Figure 3–27: The data management component for the sales transaction system.

Save objects to a flat file

In data management, you need to design for effective object storage *and* object retrieval.

Try to design the file layout in such a way that all the objects can be restored in one pass, reading the file only one time. This gets a bit tricky when dealing with the connections between objects. But it can be done.

To make this happen, consider a format which includes an initial object table, followed by the details for each object. For example:

```
<ObjectTable>
<className>SalesTransaction
<objectID><id>148
<className>LineItem
<objectID><id>150
<className>Customer
<objectID><id>141
<\ObjectTable>

<ObjectDefn>
<className>SalesTransaction
<objectID><id>148
<dateTime>19 February 1996  11:59:15 pm
<lineItem><id>150
<lineItem><id>151
<lineItem><id>152
<\ObjectDefn>

<ObjectDefn>
<className>LineItem
<objectID><id>150
<line number>1
<item quantity>5
<product><id>149
<\ObjectDefn>
```

The file begins with an object table. It includes the class name and object identifier for each object in the file. So, when it's time to restore the objects in the file, you can:

- read in the object table;
- use the class name to decide what kind of object to create;
- create a new object for each table entry;
- and give the new object its object identifier.

For example, upon encountering the table entry:

```
<className>SalesTransaction
<objectID><id>148
```

a restore service creates a new sales transaction object and gives it object identifier 148.

After the object table, the file consists of object definitions. In the object definitions, connections to other objects are stored as object identifiers. For example, the file entry:

```
<lineItem><id>150
<lineItem><id>151
<lineItem><id>152
```

shows how an object might store its connections to line items.

To restore the connections, a restore service just looks up the connecting objects (in this case, with identifiers 150, 151, and 152) in the object table.

Note that it's important that only references to objects registered in the object table appear in the file.

Design the object table

A vital part of this object tag format data management scheme is the object table itself: how it is created, how it is saved, and how it is restored.

Develop a scenario script for registering (script D, with step numbers along the way).

I'm a PDC object.
  I register myself by telling (D10) an object table about me.

So far, so good. Now develop a scenario script for storing (script E).

I'm an object table.
  I know my PDC object identifiers.
  When told to save to a file,
    I open the file.
    I save my values.
    I tell (E10) each PDC object to save itself.
    I close the file.

I'm a PDC object.
  I know my object identifier.
  When told to save myself,
    I tell (E20) my corresponding object tag format
      object to store itself.

I'm a PDC object tag format object.
   When told to do so, I store my PDC object by doing the following:
      store the definition start
      store the class name
      store the object identifier
      store the attribute values
      store the connection values
      store the definition end.

Put together a corresponding data management component (Figure 3–28).

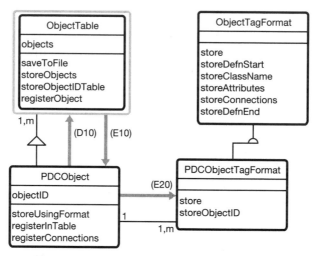

Figure 3–28: Storing PDC objects.

Next, develop a scenario script for restoring (script F).

I'm an object table.
   When told to read from a file,
      I open the file.
      I restore my values.
      I create each of my PDC objects.
      I tell (F10) each object to restore itself, using a specific format.
      I close the file.

I'm a PDC object.
   When told to restore myself,
      I tell (F20) my corresponding object tag format object
            to restore itself.

I'm a PDC object tag format object.
   When told to do so, I restore my PDC object by doing the following:
      read the definition start

restore the class name
retore the object identifier
restore the attribute values
restore the connection values
read the definition end.

Add to the data management component (Figure 3–29).

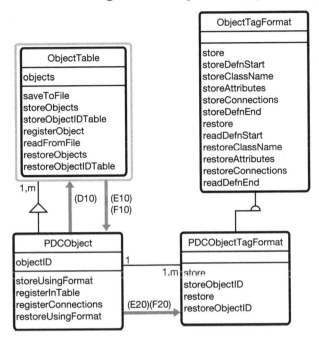

Figure 3–29: Restoring PDC objects.

Extend the architecture to work with other formats

To save the object table using a different format than the object tag format, you would need to tell each PDC object to store itself using a different format.

For example, you might want to apply a binary format, using these classes:

CustomerBinaryFormat
TransactionBinaryFormat
LineItemBinaryFormat

To support a variety of potential formats, an object table needs to know how to map a class name read from a file to a corresponding format.

So, add a class map, one that maps a set of problem domain classes to their corresponding formats (Figure 3–30).

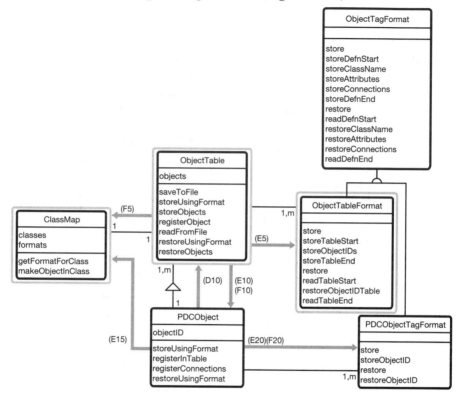

Figure 3–30: Extending the architecture with a class map.

And to support saving an object table itself, in different formats, add an object table format to your model.

Add the class map and object table format into the scenario script.

Here's the complete scenario script at this point:

I'm a PDC object.
   I register myself by telling (D10) an object table about me.

I'm an object table.
   I know my PDC object identifiers.
   I know my corresponding class map.
   When told to save to a file,
      I open the file.
      I tell (E5) my corresponding object tag format to save my values.
      I tell (E10) each PDC object to save itself, using a specific class map.
      I close the file.

I'm an object table format object.
   When told to do so, I store my object table by doing the following:
      store the definition start
      store the class name
      store the table start
      store the object identifiers
      store the table end
      store the definition end.

I'm a PDC object.
   I know my object identifier.
   When told to save myself,
      I tell (E15) the class map (the one that the sender told me about)
            to get my format.
      I tell (E20) my corresponding object tag format object to store itself.

I'm a class map object.
   I know my classes and my corresponding formats.
   When someone tells me to get the format for a class, I do so.

I'm an object tag format object.
   When told to do so, I store my PDC object by doing the following:
      store the definition start
      store the class name
      store the object identifier
      store the attribute values
      store the connection values
      store the definition end.

I'm an object table.
   When told to read from a file,
      I open the file.
      I tell my corresponding object tag format to restore my values.
      I create each of my PDC objects.
      Once I know the class name, I tell (F5) the class map to create
            a new object in that class.
      I tell (F10) each object to restore itself, using a specified class map.
      I close the file.

I'm an object table format object.
   When told to do so, I restore my object table object by doing the
            following:
      read the definition start
      read the class name
      read the table start
      restore the object identifiers
      read the table end
      read the definition end.

I'm a class map object.
   When someone tells me to create an object in a class, I do so.

I'm a PDC object.
   When told to restore myself,
      I tell (F20) my corresponding object tag format object
         to restore itself.

I'm an object tag format object.
   When told to do so, I restore my PDC object by doing the following:
      read the definition start
      restore the class name
      restore the object identifier
      restore the attribute values
      restore the connection values
      read the definition end.

Wow! Time for some OOP.

OOP—PROBLEM DOMAIN COMPONENT UPDATE: SMALLTALK

Update the problem domain component with what's needed to support the data management component.

The PDC Object Class

Add a class, its class variables, and its instance variables

Add an object identifier.

Also, add a class variable, one that holds a single value, the next object identifier.

```
Model subclass: #PDCObject
   instanceVariableNames: 'objectID '
   classVariableNames: 'NextObjectID '
   poolDictionaries: ''
   category: 'Transactions'
```

Add class initialization

Add a class initialization method to initialize the class variable.

PDCObject class methodsFor: 'class initialization'

initialize
   NextObjectID := 0

Later, you'll initialize the class with the following:

```
PDCObject initialize
```

Add object creation

PDCObject class methodsFor: 'instance creation'

getNextID
```
NextObjectID := NextObjectID + 1.
^NextObjectID
```

assignID: pdcObject
```
pdcObject objectID: self getNextID
```

new
```
| newOne |
newOne := super new initialize.
self assignID: newOne.
^newOne
```

restore
```
"Create a new object without an objectID."

^super new initialize
```

Establish the specializations of the PDC object class

Now establish customer, transaction, sales transaction line item, and product classes as specializations of the PDC object class.

Here's how, using the customer class as an example.

```
PDCObject subclass: #Customer
    instanceVariableNames: 'name address transactions
        transactionSelection '
    classVariableNames: ''
    poolDictionaries: ''
    category: 'Transactions'
```

Run the code

Try it out! Make a customer object with an identifier.

```
| aCustomer |
aCustomer := Customer new.
Transcript cr; show: aCustomer objectID printString
```

You should see a "1" on the transcript. Onward!

OOP—PROBLEM DOMAIN COMPONENT UPDATE: C++

Update the problem domain component with what's needed to support the data management component.

The PDC Object Class

Declare the class

Add an object identifier.

Also, add a static data member, one that holds a single value, the next object identifier. A static variable has just one value—and that variable and its value is known by every object in the class.

```
class PDC_Object {
public:

    // Constructors/destructors
    PDC_Object() { }
    ~PDC_Object() { };

    // Accessors
    int get_object_ID(){ return object_ID; }
    void set_object_ID(int new_ID) { object_ID = new_ID; }

protected:

    // Data members
    int object_ID;
    static int next_object_ID;

};
```

Define the static data member initialization

Define the static data member initialization along with the member function definitions.

Define (initialize) the static member.

```
// Initialize static members
int PDC_Object::next_object_ID = 0;
```

Add object identifier assignment

Define a class constructor that uses the static data member to assign identifiers.

First, declare and define an inline member function to assign object identifiers.

```
int get_next_object_ID() { return ++next_object_ID; }
```

Next, use that member function in the class constructor.

```
PDC_Object() { object_ID = this->get_next_object_ID(); }
```

The complete class declaration looks like this:

```
class PDC_Object {
public:

  // Constructors/destructors
  PDC_Object() { object_ID = this->get_next_object_ID(); }
  ~PDC_Object() { };

  // Accessors
  int get_object_ID(){ return object_ID; }
  void set_object_ID(int new_ID) { object_ID = new_ID; }

protected:

  int get_next_object_ID( return ++next_object_ID; );

  int object_ID;
  static int next_object_ID;
};
```

OOP—DATA MANAGEMENT COMPONENT: SMALLTALK

Overview

For the data management component, you need to build these classes:

- object tag format
- PDC object tag format
- transaction format
- sales transaction format
- the other format classes
- object table
- object table format
- class map

In addition, you need to modify the problem domain classes to support data management.

Time to begin!

The Object Tag Format Class

Begin by building a general-purpose object tag format class.

Add a class and its instance variables

Add an object tag format class.

```
Object subclass: #ObjectTagFormat
    instanceVariableNames: ''
    classVariableNames: ''
    poolDictionaries: ''
    category: 'Transaction Formats'
```

Apply four message categories (protocols) for its specializations: storing, storing-private, restoring, and restoring-private.

For methods which *must* be implemented by a specialization with objects, add code that generates an error if that method is not implemented and yet is accidentally invoked.

Add storing methods

Start with the storing methods first.

```
ObjectTagFormat methodsFor: 'storing'
```

storeAttributesFor: anObject **on:** stream
```
    "Subclasses must implement.
    Raise an error signal if this method is invoked."

    self subclassResponsibility
```

storeClassNameFor: anObject **on:** stream
```
    self
        storeTag: 'className'
        value: anObject class name
        on: stream
```

storeConnectionsFor: anObject **on:** stream
```
    "Optional. Subclasses need to implement only if they
    have connected objects that need saving."

    ^self
```

storeDefnEndOn: stream
```
    self storeTag: '\ObjectDefn' on: stream.
    stream cr
```

storeDefnStartOn: stream
```
    self storeTag: 'ObjectDefn' on: stream.
    stream cr
```

Add the method which stores an object. Use these steps:

I'm an object tag format.
> I save my object to a file.
>> store the definition start
>> store the class name
>> store the attribute values
>> store the connections
>> store the definition end

and put it into code.

```
ObjectTagFormat methodsFor: 'storing'

store: anObject on: stream

    self storeDefnStartOn: stream.
    self storeClassNameFor: anObject on: stream.
    self storeAttributesFor: anObject on: stream.
    self storeConnectionsFor: anObject on: stream.
    self storeDefnEndOn: stream
```

The formatting methods rely upon these private methods:

```
ObjectTagFormat methodsFor: 'storing-private'

storeTag: tagName on: stream
    stream nextPutAll: '<', tagName, '>'

storeTagValue: tagValue on: stream
    "Write a value on the stream. Any < characters in
        tagValue are stored as <<."

    | readStream |
    readStream := tagValue readStream.
    [readStream atEnd]
      whileFalse:
        [readStream peek = $< ifTrue: [stream nextPut: $<].
        stream nextPut: readStream next].
    stream cr

storeTag: tagName value: tagValue on: stream
    self storeTag: tagName on: stream.
    self storeTagValue: tagValue on: stream
```

The "peek" message tells the stream to return its next character, without changing position in the stream. The "nextPutAll:" message tells a stream to write a string to itself. The "nextPut:" message tells a stream to write a character to itself. And the "cr" message tells a stream to write a carriage return character to itself.

Add restoring methods

Now add the restoring methods.

ObjectTagFormat methodsFor: 'restoring'

restoreAttributesFor: anObject **on:** stream
  ^self subclassResponsibility

restoreClassNameFrom: stream
  ^self restoreTagValue: 'className' from: stream

restoreConnectionsFor: anObject **from:** stream **using:**
      objectTable
  "Optional"

  ^self

readDefnEndFrom: stream
  self restoreTag: '\ObjectDefn' from: stream.
  stream atEnd ifFalse: [stream next]

readDefnStartFrom: stream
  self restoreTag: 'ObjectDefn' from: stream.
  stream atEnd ifFalse: [stream next]

restore: anObject **from:** stream **using:** objectTable

  self readDefnStartFrom: stream.
  self restoreClassNameFrom: stream.
  self restoreAttributesFor: pdcObject from: stream.
  self restoreConnectionsFor: pdcObject
      from: stream using: objectTable.
  self readDefnEndFrom: stream

The restoring methods rely on these private methods:

ObjectTagFormat methodsFor: 'restoring-private'

restoreTag: tagName **from:** stream
  "Read a tag from stream. If the tag read does not
  match the expected tag name, reset the stream to
  original position, and return nil. Otherwise
  return tag name."

  | writeStream position |
  position := stream position.
  stream next.
  writeStream := WriteStream on: (String new: 300).
  writeStream nextPutAll: (stream upTo: $>).
  (writeStream contents sameAs: tagName)

```
    ifFalse:
      [stream position: position.
      ^nil].
  ^tagName
```

restoreTagValue: tagName **from:** stream
```
  (self restoreTag: tagName from: stream) isNil ifTrue:
      [^nil].
  ^self restoreTagValueFrom: stream
```

restoreTagValueFrom: stream
```
  "Read a value from stream.  Any < characters in
  tagValue are stored as <<, so drop extra one, and keep
  reading. Otherwise, quit when I hit < by itself,and skip
  back one to put the < back on the stream."

  | writeStream done |
  writeStream := WriteStream on: (String new: 300).
  done := false.
  [done or: [stream atEnd]]
    whileFalse:
      [writeStream nextPutAll: (stream upTo: $<).
      stream peek = $<
        ifTrue: [writeStream nextPut: stream next]
        ifFalse·
          [stream skip: -1.
          done := true]].
  writeStream contents last = Character cr
    ifTrue: [writeStream skip: -1].
  ^writeStream contents
```

The "upTo:" message tells the stream to read itself, up to the designated character.

The PDC Object Tag Format Class

Now specialize the general-purpose object tag format class, adding the PDC object tag format class.

Add a class and its instance variables

```
ObjectTagFormat subclass: #PDCObjectTagFormat
  instanceVariableNames: ''
  classVariableNames: ''
  poolDictionaries: ''
  category: 'Transaction Formats'
```

Add storing methods

PDCObjectTagFormat methodsFor: 'storing'

```
storeObjectIDFor: pdcObject on: stream
    self storeTag: 'objectID' on: stream.
    self storeID: pdcObject objectID on: stream
```

PDCObjectTagFormat methodsFor: 'storing-private'
```
storeID: id on: stream
    self
       storeTag: 'id'
       value: id printString
       on: stream
```

Add the method which stores a PDC object. Use these steps:

I'm a PDC object tag format.
  I save my PDC object to a file.
     store the definition start
     store the class name
     store the object id
     store the attribute values
     store the connections
     store the definition end

and put it into code.

PDCObjectTagFormat methods For: 'storing'

```
store: pdcObject on: stream
    self storeDefnStartOn: stream.
    self storeClassNameFor: pdcObject on: stream.
    self storeObjectIDFor: pdcObject on: stream.
    self storeAttributesFor: pdcObject on: stream.
    self storeConnectionsFor: pdcObject on: stream.
    self storeDefnEndOn: stream
```

Add restoring methods

PDCObjectTagFormat methods For: 'restoring'

```
restoreObjectIDFor: pdcObject from: stream
    | objectID |
    (self restoreTag: 'objectID' from: stream) isNil ifTrue:
         [^nil].
    objectID:= (self restoreIDFrom: stream).
    objectID isNil ifTrue: [^nil].
```

```
    pdcObject objectID: objectID
```

restore: pdcObject **from:** stream **using:** objectTable
```
    self readDefnStartFrom: stream.
    self restoreClassNameFrom: stream.
    self restoreObjectIDFor: pdcObject from: stream.
    self restoreAttributesFor: pdcObject from: stream.
    self restoreConnectionsFor: pdcObject from: stream
            using: objectTable.
    self readDefnEndFrom: stream
```

PDCObjectTagFormat methodsFor: 'restoring-private'

restoreIDFrom: stream
```
    | idString |
    idString := self restoreTagValue: 'id' from: stream.
    idString isNil ifTrue: [^nil].
    ^Integer readFrom: idString readStream
```

The Transaction Format Class

Add a class and its instance variables

```
    PDCObjectTagFormat subclass: #TransactionFormat
      instanceVariableNames: ''
      classVariableNames: ''
      poolDictionaries: ''
      category: 'Transaction Formats'
```

The transaction format class specializes the storing and restoring methods.

Add storing methods

```
    TransactionFormat methodsFor: 'storing'
    storeAttributesFor: transaction on: stream
      self
        storeTag: 'dateTime'
        value: transaction dateTime
        on: stream

    storeConnectionsFor: transaction on: stream
      transaction lineItems
        do:
          [:anItem |
          self storeTag: 'lineItem' on: stream.
          self storeID: anItem objectID on: stream]
```

Add restoring methods

TransactionFormat methodsFor: 'restoring'

restoreAttributesFor: transaction **from:** stream
```
| dateTime |
dateTime := self restoreTagValue: 'dateTime' from:
      stream.
transaction dateTime: dateTime
```

restoreConnectionsFor: transaction **from:** stream **using:**
      objectTable

```
[(self restoreTag: 'lineItem' from: stream) isNil
   or: [stream atEnd]]
   whileFalse:
      [| lineItemID lineItem |
      lineItemID := self restoreIDFrom: stream.
      lineItemID isNil ifTrue: [^self].
      lineItem := objectTable objectAt: lineItemID.
      lineItem isNil
         ifFalse: [transaction connectToLineItem:
                  lineItem]]
```

Note how the transaction format restores connections for a transaction. First, it reads the next tag from the stream.

```
(self restoreTag: 'lineItem' from: stream)
```

If that tag does not equal "lineItem," then the transaction format (namely, the behavior described by this method) is done. Otherwise, the transaction format reads in the object identifier for the line item. It then looks up the line item in an object table.

```
lineItemID := self restoreIDFrom: stream.
lineItemID isNil ifTrue: [^self].
lineItem := objectTable objectAt: lineItemID.
```

Finally, once the line item is located successfully, the transaction connects itself to the line item.

```
lineItem isNil
   ifFalse: [transaction connectToLineItem: lineItem]
```

The Sales Transaction Format Class

The sales transaction format class is a specialization of the transaction format class.

Add a class and its instance variables

```
TransactionFormat subclass: #SalesTransactionFormat
   instanceVariableNames: ''
   classVariableNames: ''
   poolDictionaries: ''
   category: 'Transaction Formats'
```

Add storing methods

SalesTransactionFormat methodsFor: 'storing'

storeAttributesFor: salesTransaction **on:** stream
```
   super storeAttributesFor: salesTransaction on: stream.
   self
      storeTag: 'methodOfPayment'
      value: salesTransaction methodOfPayment
      on: stream
```

Add restoring methods

SalesTransactionFormat methodsFor: 'restoring'

restoreAttributesFor: transaction **from:** stream
```
   | methodOfPayment |
   super restoreAttributesFor: transaction from: stream.
   methodOfPayment := self restoreTagValue:
         'methodOfPayment' from: stream.
   transaction methodOfPayment: methodOfPayment
```

The Other Format Classes

In a similar fashion, add customer format, line item format, and product format classes.

The Object Table Class

Now add the object table class. An object table knows the PDC object identifiers and its corresponding class map. It knows how to register objects, store objects, and restore objects.

Add a class and its instance variables

Add an object table class.

```
Object subclass: #ObjectTable
   instanceVariableNames: 'objects classMap '
   classVariableNames: ''
   poolDictionaries: ''
   category: 'Transaction Formats'
```

Add initialization

Objects are stored in the object table using object identifiers as keys. Initialize the objects' instance variable to be a dictionary object.

ObjectTable methodsFor: 'initialize-release'

```
initialize
    objects := Dictionary new
```

Add a registering method

Dictionaries hold key and value pairs, called associations. The dictionary "at: put:" method stores a value with a key.

```
objects at: objectID put: object
```

So add a method that registers objects, using object identifiers as keys.

ObjectTable methodsFor: 'object registering'

```
registerObject: object with: objectID
    ^objects at: objectID put: object
```

Add finding methods

Using object identifiers as keys simplifies finding objects.

ObjectTable methodsFor: 'object finding'

```
objectAt: objectID
    "Return the object associated with the object id; or
    return nil, if I don't contain the object."

    ^objects at: objectID ifAbsent: []

containsObject: objectID
    ^(self objectAt: objectID) notNil
```

Now add the methods to store the object table. The object table has its own format, one which defines how to save its objects' identifiers.

Add storing methods

ObjectTable methodsFor: 'storing'

```
storeOn: stream
    | format |
    format := self classMap getFormatFor: self class name.
    format store: self on: stream
```

Write another method to store all the objects on a file stream, using the object table. Remember that the objects are stored as values in a dictionary.

```
ObjectTable methodsFor: 'storing'
```

storeObjectsOn: stream
    objects values do:
        [:object | object storeOn: stream using: self]

Add the method to open a file for writing.

```
ObjectTable methodsFor: 'storing'
```

saveToFile: fileNameString
    | fileStream |
    Cursor write
        showWhile:
            [fileStream :=
                (Filename named: fileNameString) writeStream.
            self storeOn: fileStream.
            self storeObjectsOn: fileStream.
            fileStream close]

Add restoring methods

Similarly, add methods for reading an object table.

```
ObjectTable methodsFor: 'restoring'
```

readFromFile: fileNameString
    | fileStream |
    Cursor read
        showWhile:
            [fileStream :=
                (Filename named: fileNameString) readStream.
            self restoreFrom: fileStream.
            self restoreObjectsFrom: fileStream.
            fileStream close]

restoreFrom: fileStream
    | format |
    format := self classMap getFormatFor: self class name.
    format restore: self from: fileStream

restoreObjectsFrom: fileStream
    objects values do:
        [:each | each restoreFrom: fileStream using: self]

Add a method to create a restored object. Once the object table know the class name, it tells its class map to create an object in that class.

```
ObjectTable methodsFor: 'object creating'
```

createObject: className
    ^classMap makeObjectInClass: className

The Object Table Format Class

The object table format class defines how to store and restore an object table, such as:

```
<ObjectTable>
<className>SalesTransaction
<objectID><id>148
<className>LineItem
<objectID><id>150
<className>Customer
<objectID><id>141
<\ObjectTable>
```

No object identifier is needed here.

Add a class and its instance variables

Add an object table format class, a specialization of the object tag format class.

```
ObjectTagFormat subclass: #ObjectTableFormat
    instanceVariableNames: ''
    classVariableNames: ''
    poolDictionaries: ''
    category: 'Transaction Formats'
```

Add storing methods

```
ObjectTableFormat methodsFor: 'storing'
```

storeAttributesFor: objectTable **on:** stream
    ^self

storeTableEndOn: stream
    self storeTag: '\ObjectTable' on: stream.
    stream cr

```
storeTableStartOn: stream
    self storeTag: 'ObjectTable' on: stream.
    stream cr
```

Add a store method to write out the class names and object identifiers for the objects stored in the object table.

ObjectTableFormat methodsFor: 'storing'

storeObjectIDsFor: objectTable **on:** stream

```
objectTable objects
    do:
        [:pdcObject
        |objectFormat|
        objectFormat := pdcObject getFormatFrom:
                objectTable classMap.
        objectFormat storeClassNameFor: pdcObject on: stream.
        objectFormat storeObjectIDFor: pdcObject on: stream]
```

Add the method that stores an object table. Use these steps:

> I'm an object table format.
> I save my object table to a file.
> > store the definition start
> > store the class name
> > store the table start
> > store the object identifiers
> > store the table end
> > store the definition end

and put it into code.

ObjectTableFormat methodsFor: 'storing'

store: objectTable **on:** stream

```
    self storeDefnStartOn: stream.
    self storeClassNameFor: objectTable on: stream.
    self storeTableStartOn: stream.
    self storeObjectIDsFor: objectTable on: stream.
    self storeTableEndOn: stream.
    self storeDefnEndOn: stream
```

Add restoring methods

Add the corresponding restore methods.

ObjectTableFormat methodsFor: 'restoring'

restoreAttributesFor: objectTable **from:** stream
  ^self

readTableEndFrom: stream
  self restoreTag: '\ObjectTable' from: stream.
  stream atEnd ifFalse: [stream next]

readTableStartFrom: stream
  self restoreTag: 'ObjectTable' from: stream.
  stream atEnd ifFalse: [stream next]

Add a restore method to read in the class names and object identifiers for the objects to be restored in the object table.

```
. restoreObjectIDsFor: objectTable from: stream
  | className newOne objectFormat |

  [stream atEnd]
    whileFalse:
      [className := self restoreClassNameFrom: stream.
      className isNil ifTrue:
        [^self].
      newOne := objectTable createObject: className.
      objectFormat := newOne getFormatFrom: objectTable
          classMap.
      (objectFormat restoreObjectIDFor: newOne from:
          stream) isNil
        ifTrue: [^self].
      objectTable registerObject: newOne
        at: newOne objectID]
```

Take a close look at this method. After an object table format reads a class name, it tells the object table to create an object in that class.

```
newOne := objectTable createObject: className.
```

Then it assigns that new object the next object identifier restored from the file.

```
(objectFormat restoreObjectIDFor: newOne from: stream)
  isNil ifTrue: [^self].
```

Adding to the Problem Domain Component to Support Data Management

You've already added an attribute to the problem domain classes to support data management. Now you need to add several methods.

Add registering methods

A "register myself in the object table" behavior is the same for each problem domain object.

Each problem domain object registers itself in the object table. In addition, some objects register their connecting objects, too.

Here's the basic pattern:

```
PDCObject methodsFor: 'data management'

registerInTable: objectTable
    (objectTable containsObject: self objectID)
        ifTrue: [^self].
    objectTable registerObject: self at: self objectID.
    self registerConnectionsIn: objectTable
```

Make the register connections method a "no-op" since it is an optional method for specialized classes (some will need to register connections, others won't).

```
PDCObject methodsFor: 'data management'

registerConnectionsIn: objectTable
    ^self
```

Specialize the register connections method for customer, transaction, and transaction line item.

```
Customer methodsFor: 'data management'

registerConnectionsIn: objectTable
    self transactions do: [:each | each registerInTable:
        objectTable]
```

```
Transaction methodsFor: 'data management'

registerConnectionsIn: objectTable
    self lineItems do: [:each | each registerInTable:
        objectTable]
```

```
LineItem methodsFor: 'data management'
```

registerConnectionsIn: objectTable
    product registerInTable: objectTable

Add a "get format" method

Each problem domain object gets its format object from a class map. Add a method to get the format.

```
PDCObject methodsFor: 'data management'
```

getFormatFrom: aClassMap
    ^aClassMap getFormatFor: self class name

Add a storing method

The behavior of storing and restoring itself is also the same for all problem domain objects.

```
PDCObject methodsFor: 'data management'
```

storeOn: stream **using:** objectTable
    | format |
    format := self getFormatFrom: objectTable classMap.
    format store: self on: stream

Add a restoring method

```
PDCObject methodsFor: 'data management'
```

restoreFrom: stream **using:** objectTable
    | format |

    format := self getFormatFrom: objectTable classMap
    format restore: self from: stream using: objectTable

The Class Map Class

A class map remembers associations between problem domain classes and format objects.

Add a class and its instance variables

Add the class map class. Include one instance variable to hold the associations between classes and formats.

```
Object subclass: #ClassMap
    instanceVariableNames: 'classFormats '
    classVariableNames: ''
```

```
poolDictionaries: ''
category: 'Transaction Formats'
```

Add initialization

Initialize the class formats instance variable to be a dictionary.

ClassMap methodsFor: 'initialize-release'

initialize
```
classFormats := Dictionary new
```

Add mapping methods

The keys to the dictionary are the problem domain class names. The values are the corresponding format objects.

ClassMap methodsFor: 'mapping'

getFormatFor: className
```
^classFormats at: className ifAbsent: []
```

putFormat: formatObject **at:** className
```
^classFormats at: className put: formatObject
```

Add a restoring method

The class map also knows how to create (restore) an object in a named class. Add a method that takes a class name as a parameter and returns a restored object of that class. Remember that a restored object doesn't get an object identifier immediately at the time of creation.

ClassMap methodsFor: 'restoring'

makeObjectInClass: objectClassNameString
```
| objectClassSymbol objectClass |
objectClassSymbol := objectClassNameString asSymbol.
objectClass := Smalltalk at: objectClassSymbol
        ifAbsent: [nil].
^objectClass isNil
  ifTrue: [nil]
  ifFalse: [objectClass restore]
```

The global variable, Smalltalk, is a dictionary whose keys are symbols and whose values are classes. This method converts the class name string into a symbol; then it looks in the Smalltalk dictionary for a matching class. Once it finds a matching class, it sends a restore message to that class. (Note: the restore method is defined only for the specializations of the PDCObject class.)

Add a method to define a specific domain map

For the sales transaction system, define a class method to create the sales class map.

ClassMap class methodsFor: 'defaults'

salesClassMap
```
    | newOne |
    newOne := self new.
    newOne putFormat: CustomerFormat new at: Customer name.
    newOne putFormat: SalesTransactionFormat new
        at: SalesTransaction name.
    newOne putFormat: LineItemFormat new
        at: LineItem name.
    newOne putFormat: ProductFormat new at: Product name.
    newOne putFormat: ObjectTableFormat new at: ObjectTable
        name.
    ^newOne
```

Run the Code

In a workspace, type and evaluate the following code:

```
| customer objectTable classMap |

customer := Customer customerDemo.
objectTable := ObjectTable new.
classMap := ClassMap salesClassMap.

objectTable classMap: classMap.
customer registerInTable: objectTable.
objectTable saveToFile: 'tagFile.fmt'
```

The program creates a "tagFile.fmt" file. It should look something like this:

```
<ObjectDefn>
<className>ObjectTable
<ObjectTable>
<className>Customer
<objectID><id>141
<className>SalesTransaction
<objectID><id>142
<\ObjectTable>
<\ObjectDefn>
<ObjectDefn>
<class>Customer
```

```
<objectID><id>141
<name>Barney Rubble
<address>Bedrock
<transaction><id>142
<\ObjectDefn>
<ObjectDefn>
<class>SalesTransaction
<objectID><id>142
<dateTime>11 September 1998  3:27:34 pm
<methodOfPayment>cash
<lineItem><id>36
<lineItem><id>39
<\ObjectDefn>
```

Super. Now try restoring the objects.

```
| objectTable classMap |

objectTable := ObjectTable new.
classMap := ClassMap salesClassMap.

objectTable classMap: classMap.
objectTable readFromFile: 'tagFile.fmt'
```

To see how it worked, inspect the object table:

```
objectTable inspect
```

and look at its dictionary instance variable.
You might also write the new object table out to a second file:

```
objectTable saveToFile: 'tagFile2.fmt'
```

and compare it to the first file.

Congratulations! You did it.

OOP—DATA MANAGEMENT COMPONENT: C++

Overview

For the data management component, build these classes:

- object tag format
- PDC object tag format
- transaction format
- sales transaction format
- the other format classes

- object table
- object table format
- class map

About Heterogeneous Collections and the Virtual Function Mechanism

About heterogeneous collections

A heterogeneous collection is a collection of different kinds of objects. In the sales transaction system, both object table and class map are heterogeneous collections.

In building the data management component, you'll use heterogeneous collections and the virtual function mechanism.

An object table contains different kinds of PDC objects—customers, sales transactions, line items, and products. And that is a problem.

So far, you've implemented a whole-part connection using an array or a list. But in a strongly typed language such as C++, arrays and lists can only hold one type of object.

Here, you need an array or list that can hold different kinds of PDC objects.

The solution? Use a base class pointer. Since all of the PDC objects have the same base class, declare an array or list of pointers to the corresponding base class:

```
PDC_Object* pdc_objects[10];
```

Use this array to hold pointers to objects that belong to classes derived from the PDC object class. Include pointers to different kinds of PDC objects—customers, sales transactions, line items, and products.

Similarly, a class map holds different types of object tag formats. They can all be held in a list of pointers to the corresponding base class:

```
Ordered_List<Object_Tag_Format*> formats;
```

About the virtual function mechanism

You can use the virtual function mechanism to delay until runtime the decision of which member function is invoked.

You need this capability when you are using a base class pointer to point to a derived class object. For example, suppose you have an object tag format pointer which is pointing to a customer format object:

```
Object_Tag_Format* an_object_tag_format;
an_object_tag_format = new Customer_Format();
```

When you tell the object tag format object to store itself:

```
an_object_tag_format->store(a_stream);
```

the virtual function mechanism ensures that the store member function for a customer format is invoked, rather than the store member function in the object tag format class.

The virtual function mechanism only works for the member functions that you declare "virtual" in the corresponding base class. For the preceding example to work, you must declare the store member function as a virtual function in the object tag format class:

```
virtual void store(ofstream& a_stream);
```

The virtual function mechanism is important for effectively working with heterogeneous collections.

In this example, you'll use heterogeneous collections and the virtual function mechanism for the object table and the class map.

The Object Tag Format Class

Add an object tag format class for C++.

> I'm an object tag format.
> I save my object to a file:
> > store the definition start
> > store the class name
> > store the attribute values
> > store the connections
> > store the definition end

A plan

The object tag format class is the root class for all object tag format classes. That class establishes the basic behavior for storing and restoring objects in the object tag format. The specializations of that class add to that behavior.

What's different about each specialization? Each specialization class defines how to store and restore a specific kind of object.

Ahh. Familiar territory. Or is it?

What do you do when a group of classes are the same *except* for the type of a data member? Create a template class. But should you implement the object tag format class as a template class parameterized over the type of object to be stored or restored?

Before you decide, make certain that the parameterization applies across all specializations of the object tag format class.

Take a look at the object tag format gen-spec structure. (Figure 3–31) Two specialization branches coming out from the object tag format class—the PDC object tag formats, and the object table format:

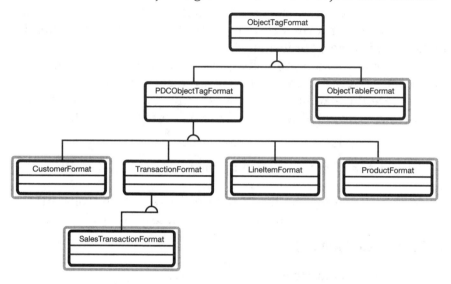

Figure 3– 31: The object tag format class and its two specialization branches.

If both branches have similar behavior for storing and restoring objects, then you have a strong case for implementing the object tag format object as a template class.

Now look at the model after with storing services for each class (Figure 3–32):

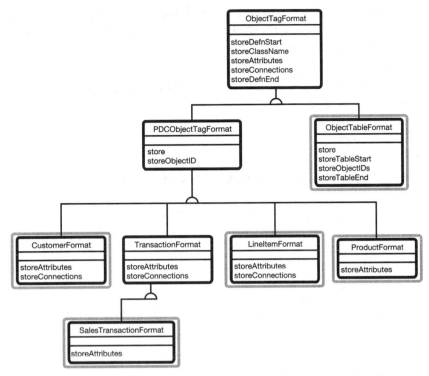

Figure 3–32: The object tag format class and its specializations, with the storing services.

Uh-oh. The behavior for the two different branches is very different. How a PDC object format stores its corresponding PDC object is different from how an object table format stores its corresponding object table.

So, don't implement the object tag format class as a template class.

Instead, you'll need to add specialization classes, each with its own data member that holds the object it stores and restores.

Declare the class

All specializations of the object tag format class must implement certain functions.

Do you remember how to force a concrete derived (specialization) class to implement a member function? Do it with a pure virtual function.

```
virtual void my_function() = 0;
```

Back in the count example, you used these pure virtual functions:

```
virtual void increment() = 0;
virtual void decrement() = 0;
```

What about now? Use pure virtual functions in the object tag format class to declare a member function which *must* be implemented by a concrete derived class.

> I'm an object tag format.
>> I know how to store object definitions on an output
>>> file stream.
>> I have some helpful ways of storing tag names
>>> and values.

Put the general-purpose member functions for storing and restoring data in a protected section (accessible to all derived classes).

```
// Forward references
class Object_Table;

class Object_Tag_Format {
public:

    // Constructors/destructors
    Object_Tag_Format() { }
    ~Object_Tag_Format() { }
    virtual

    // Implementors
    // Storing objects
    // Same for all
    void store_defn_start(ofstream& a_stream);
    void store_defn_end(ofstream& a_stream);

    // May be specialized
    virtual_void store(ofstream& a_stream);
    // Optional
    virtual void store_connections(ofstream& a_stream) { }

    // Must be implemented by specialized classes
    virtual void store_class_name(ofstream& a_stream) = 0;
    virtual void store_attribute_values(ofstream& a_stream)
            = 0;

    // Restoring objects
    // Same for all
    void read_defn_start(ifstream& a_stream);
    void read_defn_end(ifstream& a_stream);
    String restore_class_name(ifstream& a_stream);

    // May be specialized
    virtual void restore(ifstream& a_stream, Object_Table*
            an_object_table);
```

```
// Optional
virtual void restore_connections(ifstream& a_stream,
        Object_Table* an_object_table){ }

// Must be implemented by specialized classes
virtual void restore_attribute_values(ifstream&
        a_stream) = 0;

protected:

// Supporting member functions
void store_tag(ofstream& a_stream,
        String tag_name);
void store_value(ofstream& a_stream,
        String tag_value);
void store_tag_value(ofstream& a_stream,
        String tag_name,
        String tag_value);
void store_ID(ofstream& a_stream,
        int object_ID);
void store_date(ofstream& a_stream, Date& a_date);
void store_time(ofstream& a_stream, Time&  a_time);

String restore_value(ifstream& a_stream);
Boolean restore_tag(ifstream& a_stream, String tag_name);
String restore_tag_value(ifstream& a_stream, String
        tag_name);
int restore_ID(ifstream& a_stream);
Date& restore_date(ifstream& a_stream);
Time& restore_time(ifstream& a_stream);
};
```

Define the storing member functions

Store a tag name and a value

Add member functions for storing a tag name and a value. Define the functions inline. Each function inserts information into an output file stream, an "ofstream."

```
void inline Object_Tag_Format::store_tag(ofstream&
        a_stream, String tag_name)
{
    a_stream <<  "<" << tag_name <<  ">";
}

void inline Object_Tag_Format::store_value(ofstream&
        a_stream, String tag_value)
{
```

```
    a_stream << tag_value << endl;
}

void inline Object_Tag_Format::store_tag_value(ofstream&
      a_stream, String tag_name, String tag_value)
{
  this->store_tag(a_stream, tag_name);
  this->store_value(a_stream, tag_value);
}
```

Store an object identifier

Add a member function to store an identifier.

```
void Object_Tag_Format::store_ID(ofstream& a_stream,
      int object_ID)
{
  // Create a string from the object ID.
  String id_string(object_ID);

  this->store_tag_value(a_stream, "id", id_string);
}
```

Store a date and a time

Some common data types require special treatment for storing and restoring. To handle these special cases, add member functions to the object tag format class, so specialized format classes can use them, too.

Add a member function to store a date using the format "month number/day of month/year".

```
void Object_Tag_Format::store_date(ofstream& a_stream,
      Date& a_date)
{
  String& separator = String("/");
  String& date_string = String(a_date.day_of_month())
    + separator
    + String(a_date.day_of_month())
    + separator
    + String(a_date.year());

  this->store_tag_value(a_stream, "date", date_string);
}
```

Add a member function to store a time using the format "hours:minutes:seconds".

```
void Object_Tag_Format::store_time(ofstream& a_stream,
        Time& a_time)
{
    this->store_tag_value(a_stream, "time"
        a_time.print_string());
}
```

Store on a file stream

Define how an object tag format stores an object.

```
void Object_Tag_Format::store(ofstream& a_stream,
{
    this->store_defn_start(a_stream);
    this->store_class_name(a_stream);
    this->store_attribute_values(a_stream);
    this->store_connections(a_stream);
    this->store_defn_end(a_stream);
}
```

You need to define the store class name, store attribute values, and store connections member functions in the derived (specialized) format class definitions.

Meanwhile, go ahead and define the other storing functions here.

```
void inline Object_Tag_Format::store_defn_start
        (ofstream& a_stream)
{
    this->store_tag(a_stream, "ObjectDefn");
    a_stream << endl;
}

void inline Object_Tag_Format::store_defn_end(ofstream&
        a_stream)
{
    // Use two backslashes. The first backslash indicates a
    // special character follows. This allows the second
    // backslash to be printed.
        this->store_tag(a_stream, "\\ObjectDefn");
        a_stream << endl;
}
```

Define the restoring member functions

Restore tag names and values

Here's how to read one character from an input file stream:

```
a_stream.get(ch);
```

and this is how to read all characters up to a designated last character:

```
a_stream.get(character_array, 80, last_char);
```

In this statement, characters are placed into a character array until 80 characters are read or the last character is encountered, whichever comes first.

Next, define the member functions for restoring tags and values. Give each function an input file stream, an "ifstream," as a parameter.

Restore a tag.

```
Boolean Object_Tag_Format::restore_tag(ifstream& a_stream,
        String tag_name)
{
  char ch, last_char = '>';
  char tag_read[80];

  // Current position in the stream
  long position = a_stream.tellg();

  // Read the first character, '<'.
  a_stream.get(ch);

  // Read the tag name up to the '>'.
  a_stream.get(tag_read, 80, last_char);

  // Check if tag read is the same as tag name.
  if (String(tag_read) == tag_name)
    {
    // The same. Get the '>' from the stream.
    a_stream.get(ch);
    return true;
    }
  else
    {
    // Not the same. Reset stream position.
    a_stream.seekg(position);
    return false;
    }
}
```

Similarly, restore a tag value.

```
String Object_Tag_Format::restore_value(ifstream&
a_stream)
{
    char ch, last_char = '<';
    char* tag_value = new char[80];

    // Read up to the start of the next tag.
    a_stream.get(tag_value, 80, last_char);

    // Drop the last character, if it's a newline character.
    int size = strlen(tag_value);
    if (tag_value[size-1] == '\n')
        tag_value[size-1] = '\0';
    return tag_value;
}

String Object_Tag_Format::restore_tag_value(ifstream&
        a_stream, String tag_name)
{
    this->restore_tag(a_stream, tag_name);
    return this->restore_value(a_stream);
}
```

Restore object identifiers

Add the member function to restore an object identifier.

```
int Object_Tag_Format::restore_ID(ifstream& a_stream)
{
    if (!(this->restore_tag(a_stream, "id")))
        return -1;
    String& id_string = this->restore_value(a_stream);
    int object_ID = id_string.as_integer();
    return object_ID;
}
```

Restore a date and a time

A date is stored as a string. For example, September 11, 1998 is stored as "9/11/98".

To restore a date, parse a date string into numbers for month, day, and year. It's easy to do. Just break the string into substrings, using the forward slash,/, as the substring boundary, like this:

```
"9/11/98" -> "9", "11", "98"
```

Then convert each substring into an integer:

```
int month_number = month_string.as_integer();
```

Who knows how to break a string into substrings? A string knows how. The string class provided on the source diskette has a member function for breaking a string into two strings:

```
String& break_at(char delimiter);
```

All characters before the delimiter character are returned by the member function. They are also deleted from the string, along with the delimiter.[5] For example:

```
String date_string("9/11/98");
// Set month string to "9".
String& month_string = date_string.break_at('/');
// The date string is now "11/98".
```

Add a member function that restores a date object from a file stream.

```
Date& Object_Tag_Format::restore_date(ifstream& a_stream)
{
  char separator = '/';
  String& date_string =
        this->restore_tag_value(a_stream, "date");
  String& month_string = date_string.break_at(separator);
  String& day_string = date_string.break_at(separator);
  String& year_string = date_string;
  Date* restored_date = new Date(day_string.as_integer(),
        month_string.as_integer(),
        year_string.as_integer());
  return *restored_date;
}
```

Times are also stored as strings. For example, 11:59:02 p.m. is stored as "23:59:02".

To restore a time, parse a time string into numbers for hour, minute, and second.

```
Time& Object_Tag_Format::restore_time(ifstream& a_stream)
{
  char separator = ':';
  String& time_value_string =
        this->restore_tag_value(a_stream, "time");
```

---

[5]The string class also has a member function for returning the characters before the delimiter, without deleting them from the string: `String& read_up_to(char delimiter);`

```
    String& hour_string =
            time_value_string.break_at(separator);
    String& minute_string =
            time_value_string.break_at(separator);
    String& second_string = time_value_string;
    Time* restored_time = new Time(hour_string.as_integer(),
        minute_string.as_integer(),
        second_string.as_integer());
    return *restored_time;
}
```

Restore an object from a file stream

Define how an object tag format restores an object.

```
void Object_Tag_Format::restore(ifstream& a_stream,
        Object_Table* an_object_table)
{
    this->read_defn_start(a_stream);
    this->restore_class_name(a_stream);
    this->restore_attribute_values(a_stream);
    this->restore_connections(a_stream,
            an_object_table);
    this->read_defn_end(a_stream);
}
```

You need to define the restore attribute values, and restore connections in the derived (specialized) format class definitions.

Meanwhile, go ahead and define the other restoring functions.

```
void Object_Tag_Format::read_defn_start(ifstream&
        a_stream)
{
    char ch;
    this->restore_tag(a_stream, "ObjectDefn");
    a_stream.get(ch);
}

void Object_Tag_Format::read_defn_end(ifstream&
        a_stream)
{
    char ch;
    this->restore_tag(a_stream, "\\ObjectDefn");
    a_stream.get(ch);
}
```

```
String Object_Tag_Format::restore_class_name(ifstream&
        a_stream)
{
    this->restore_tag(a_stream, "className");
    return this->restore_value(a_stream);
}
```

Which object is the one to store?

How does an object tag format object know which object to store and to restore? Since the object tag format class is an abstract class, this may not seem relevant. But specialized formats do need to know what object they'll be storing.

Here's what happens:

I'm a PDC object.
> Somebody tells me to store myself on a file.
> I ask a class map for a format object that knows how to store an object of my class.
> When I get the format object, I tell it to set the object it holds to me.
> Then I tell that format object to store itself on the file.

Remember that the class map returns a pointer to an object tag format. To make certain that the member function for the object actually pointed is invoked, use the virtual function mechanism.

The impact? Declare the store and set object member functions as virtual functions in the object tag format class.

You've already handled this for the store member function. Now do it for the set object member function.

Add a pure virtual member function to the object tag format class. Use a generic point, void*, so the function can be called with any type of object pointer:

```
virtual void set_object(void* new_object) = 0;
```

The PDC Object Tag Format Class

Declare the class

All the PDC object tag formats follow the same pattern for storing and restoring their PDC object.

Ahh. This is familiar territory.

Declare the PDC object tag format class as a template class.

```
template<class PDC_Type>
class PDC_Object_Tag_Format : public Object_Tag_Format
{
```

```
public:

    // Constructors/destructors
    PDC_Object_Tag_Format() { }
    ~PDC_Object_Tag_Format() { }
    virtual

    // Implementors
    virtual void store(ofstream& a_stream);
    virtual void restore(ifstream& a_stream,
            Object_Table* an_object_table);

    void store_object_ID(ofstream& a_stream);
    void restore_object_ID(ifstream& a_stream);
    void set_object(void* new_object)
        { pdc_object = (PDC_Type*)new_object; }

    // Accessors
    void set_pdc_object(PDC_Type& new_object)
        { pdc_object = &new_object ; }
    PDC_Type& get_pdc_object()
        { return *pdc_object; }

protected:

    PDC_Type* pdc_object;
};
```

Define the storing member functions

Store a PDC object identifier

Add a member function to store a PDC object identifier.

```
template<class PDC_Type>
void PDC_Object_Tag_Format<PDC_Type>::store_object_ID
        (ofstream& a_stream)
{
    int object_ID = pdc_object->get_object_ID();
    this->store_tag(a_stream, "objectID");
    this->store_ID(a_stream, object_ID);
}
```

Store a PDC object

Define the member function which stores a PDC object. Use these steps:

I'm a PDC object tag format.
I save my PDC object to a file.

store the definition start
store the class name
store the object identifier
store the attribute values
store the connections
store the definition end

And put it into code:

```
template<class PDC_Type>
void PDC_Object_Tag_Format<PDC_Type>::store(ofstream&
     a_stream)
{
   this->store_defn_start(a_stream);
   this->store_class_name(a_stream);
   this->store_object_ID(a_stream);
   this->store_attribute_values(a_stream);
   this->store_connections(a_stream);
   this->store_defn_end(a_stream);
}
```

Define the restoring member functions

Restore a PDC object identifier

Add a member function to restore a PDC object identifier.

```
template<class PDC_Type>
void
PDC_Object_Tag_Format<PDC_Type>::restore_object_ID
     (ifstream& a_stream)
{
   if (!(this->restore_tag(a_stream, "objectID")))
     return;
   int object_ID = this->restore_ID(a_stream);
   pdc_object->set_object_ID(object_ID);
}
```

Restore a PDC object

Define the member function which restores a PDC object.

```
template<class PDC_Type>
void PDC_Object_Tag_Format<PDC_Type>::restore(ifstream&
     a_stream, Object_Table* an_object_table)
{

   this->read_defn_start(a_stream);
```

```
      this->restore_class_name(a_stream);
      this->restore_object_ID(a_stream);
      this->restore_attribute_values(a_stream);
      this->restore_connections(a_stream, an_object_table);
      this->read_defn_end(a_stream);
   }
```

The Transaction Format Class

The transaction format class is a specialization of the pdc object tag format class.

A transaction format consists of the following:

> class name
> > "Transaction"
>
> attribute values
> > date
> > time
>
> connections
> > line items

The transaction format class is an abstract class, derived from a parameterized class. You need to be careful how you declare it. For example, if you declare it like this:

```
Transaction_Format : public PDC_Object_Tag_Format
      <Transaction> {
   . . .
};
```

then all specializations of the transaction format class are parameterized over the transaction class. But that's not what you need! Instead, you need a more specific parameterization. For example, you need a sales transaction format class to be parameterized over the sales transaction class.

The solution? Declare the transaction format class itself as a parameterized class.

Declare the class

```
      template<class Transaction_Type>
      class Transaction_Format : public
            PDC_Object_Tag_Format<Transaction_Type> {
      public:

        // Constructors/destructors
        Transaction_Format() { }
        ~Transaction_Format() { }
```

```
    // Implementors
    void store_class_name(ofstream& a_stream);
    void store_attribute_values(ofstream& a_stream);
    void store_connections(ofstream& a_stream) ;
    void restore_connections(ifstream& a_stream,
            Object_Table* an_object_table);
    void restore_attribute_values(ifstream& a_stream);

};
```

Define the storing member functions

Store a class name

```
template<class Transaction_Type>
void
Transaction_Format<Transaction_Type>::store_class_name
        (ofstream& a_stream)
{
    this->store_tag_value(a_stream, "className",
            "Transaction");
}
```

Store attribute values

```
template<class Transaction_Type>
void Transaction_Format<Transaction_Type>::
        store_attribute_values(ofstream& a_stream)
{
    Date& a_date = pdc_object->get_date();
    Time& a_time = pdc_object->get_time();

    this->store_date(a_stream, a_date);
    this->store_time(a_stream, a_time);
    }
```

Store connection values

```
template<class Transaction_Type>
void Transaction_Format<Transaction_Type>::
        store_connections(ofstream& a_stream)
{
    Line_Item_List& line_items =
            pdc_object->get_line_items();
    Line_Item* item;
    int line_item_ID;
```

```
while (!line_items.end_of_list())
  {
  item = line_items.current();
  line_item_ID = item->get_object_ID();
  this->store_tag(a_stream, "lineItem");
  this->store_ID(a_stream, line_item_ID);
  line_items++;
  }
}
```

Define the restoring member functions

Restore attribute values

```
template<class Transaction_Type>
void Transaction_Format<Transaction_Type>::
      restore_attribute_values(ifstream& a_stream)
{
  Date& a_date = this->restore_date(a_stream);
  Time& a_time = this->restore_time(a_stream);

  pdc_object->set_date(a_date);
  pdc_object->set_time(a_time);
}
```

Restore connection values

The transaction format restores the connections between the transaction and its line items.

```
template<class Transaction_Type>
void Transaction_Format::restore_connections(ifstream&
      a_stream, Object_Table* an_object_table)
{
  int object_ID;
  Line_Item* line_item;

  while ((this->restore_tag(a_stream, "lineItem")) != 0)
    {
    object_ID = this->restore_ID(a_stream);
    line_item =
      (Line_Item*)an_object_table->
            object_at_ID(object_ID);
    pdc_object->connect_to_line_item(*line_item);
    }
}
```

That finishes the transaction format.

The Sales Transaction Format Class

To save a particular kind of transaction, add a corresponding specialization from the transaction format class.

A sales transaction's format consists of the following:

> class name
> "SalesTransaction"
> attribute values
> date
> time
> methodOfPayment
> connections
> line items

A sales transaction format stores everything that a transaction format stores, plus an extra attribute value for the method of payment. It also stores its own value for the class name.

Declare the class

```
class Sales_Transaction_Format : public
        Transaction_Format<Sales_Transaction> {
public:

    // Constructors/destructors
    Sales_Transaction_Format() { }
    ~Sales_Transaction_Format() { }

    // Implementors
    void store_class_name(ofstream& a_stream);
    void store_attribute_values(ofstream& a_stream);

    void restore_attribute_values(ifstream& a_stream,);

private:

};
```

Define the storing member functions

Store the class name

Specialize the "store class name" member function to store the sales transaction class name.

```
void Sales_Transaction_Format::store_class_name
    (ofstream& a_stream)
{
```

```
        this->store_tag_value(a_stream, "className",
            "Sales_Transaction");
}
```

Store attribute values

Write a statement to invoke the inherited "store attribute values" function for a sales transaction:

```
Transaction_Format<Sales_Transaction>::
    store_attributes_values(a_stream);
```

Then add a statement to take care of getting the attribute value for method of payment:

```
String& payment_string =
    pdc_object->get_method_of_payment();
```

Put these together in the "store attribute values" member function.

```
void Sales_Transaction_Format::store_attribute_values
        (ofstream& a_stream)
{
    Transaction_Format<Sales_Transaction>::
            store_attribute_values(a_stream);

    String& payment_string =
        pdc_object->get_method_of_payment();
    this->store_tag_value(a_stream, "methodOfPayment",
        payment_string);
}
```

Define the restoring member functions

Write a method to invoke the transaction format member function and then restore the "method of payment" attribute value.

```
void Sales_Transaction_Format::restore_attribute_values
            (ifstream& a_stream)
{
    Transaction_Format<Sales_Transaction>::
            restore_attribute_values(a_stream);
    String& payment_method =
        this->restore_tag_value(a_stream, "methodOfPayment");
    pdc_object->set_method_of_payment(payment_method);
}
```

The Other Format Classes

This is really pretty simple to do. Just follow the same basic pattern. Go ahead and create formats for the customer, transaction line item, and product classes.

The Object Table Class

Add an object table class, so that an object table can:

```
register my objects by their identifiers
save myself in a file
   store the class codes and object identifiers of my
           PDC objects
   store my PDC objects
read myself from a file
   restore the class codes and object identifiers
   restore the PDC objects
```

With some of these chores, it'll need help from its format and the class map.

About representing a collection of PDC objects

The object table is a collection of PDC objects, indexed by object identifiers.

One way that you can implement this in C++ is by using parallel arrays—one for the object identifiers, one for the PDC objects.

```
// Data members
int object_IDs[MAX_TABLE_SIZE];
PDC_Object* objects[MAX_TABLE_SIZE];
```

To find a PDC object by its identifier, find the location of the identifier in the object identifiers array. The corresponding PDC object will be in the same location in the objects array.

Declare the class

Declare the object table class.

```
// Forward reference
class Object_Table_Object_Iterator;

class Object_Table {
public:

    // Constructors/destructors
```

```
        Object_Table() { table_index = -1; }
        ~Object_Table() { }

        // Implementors
        Boolean save_to_file(char* filename);
        void register_object(int object_ID, PDC_Object*
                pdc_object);

        void store(ofstream& a_stream);
        void store_objects(ofstream& a_stream);

        Boolean read_from_file(char* filename);
        void restore(ifstream& a_stream);
        void restore_objects(ifstream& a_stream);

        Object_Table_Object_Itcrator& get_objects();

        Class_Map* get_class_map() { return class_map; }
        void set_class_map(Class_Map* new_value)
                    { class_map = new_value; }

        void* object_at_ID(int object_ID);

    private:

        // Supporting member functions
        Boolean find_ID(int object_ID);

        // Supporting class
        friend class Object_Table_Object_Iterator;

        // Data members
        int object_IDs[MAX_TABLE_SIZE];
        PDC_Object* objects[MAX_TABLE_SIZE];
        Class_Map* class_map;
        int table_index;
    };
```

Add a supporting class

Declare a supporting class. This class is used to iterate through the PDC objects in the object table.

```
    class Object_Table_Object_Iterator {
    public:

        // Constructors/destructors
        Object_Table_Object_Iterator(Object_Table& new_table)
                { an_object_table = &new_table;
                  position = 0; }
```

```
~Object_Table_Object_Iterator() { }

// Overloaded function call operator
PDC_Object* operator() ()
  { if (position <= an_object_table->table_index)
    return an_object_table->objects[position++];
    else return 0;
  }
void reset() { position = 0; }
int size ()   {return an_object_table->table_index; }

private:

  Object_Table* an_object_table;
  int position;
};
```

Define the member function for accessing the PDC objects stored inside an object table. Instead of returning the actual array of PDC objects, return an iterator object.

```
Object_Table_Object_Iterator& Object_Table::get_objects()
{
  Object_Table_Object_Iterator object_iterator =
        new Object_Table_Object_Iterator(*this);
  return object_iterator;
}
```

A new iterator object is returned for each access because the array of PDC objects may change frequently, possibly invalidating an iterator's position within the array.

Define the finding member functions

Continue with the object table class.

Add a member function to see if an object identifier is already present.

```
Boolean Object_Table::find_ID(int object_ID)
{
  // Check if empty.
  if (table_index == -1)
    return false;
  int i = 0;
  Boolean found = false;
```

```
while ( (i <= table_index) && (!found) )
  {
  if (object_IDs[i] == object_ID)
     found = true;             // found it!
  else
     found = false;
  i++;
  }
return found;
}
```

Add a member function to handle a request for a specific object with a specific object identifier.

Notice that when the object table is asked to return an object with a given identifier, it actually returns a void*, a generic pointer.

Why not return a PDC object pointer instead? Consider the alternatives.

Returning a generic pointer makes it easier to use the object returned. If the member function requesting the object knows what type the object returned should be, then it can cast the generic pointer to a pointer of the right type, like this:

```
Customer* a_customer =
  (Customer*)an object_table->object_at_ID(6);
```

Returning a pointer to a PDC object isn't very helpful here. Once you get it, you're stuck; there is no way to figure out what kind of PDC object that its really pointing to (it's unsafe to cast from a base class pointer to a derived class pointer).

```
void* Object_Table::object_at_ID(int object_ID)
{
  int i = 0;

  PDC_Object* pdc_object;
  while ((i <= table_index) &&
    (object_IDs[i] != object_ID))
     i = i++;
  pdc_object = objects[i];
  return (void*)pdc_object;
}
```

Define the registering member functions

Register an object by its object identifier.
Add the "register object" member function.

```
void Object_Table::register_object(int object_ID,
    PDC_Object* pdc_object)
{
  if (!this->find_ID(object_ID))
    {
    // Didn't find the object_id; register the object.
    object_IDs[++table_index] = object_ID;
    objects[table_index] = pdc_object;
    }
}
```

Define the storing member functions

Store objects and object identifiers

An object table stores the class name and the object identifier for each of its objects, using its corresponding object table format.

```
void Object_Table::store(ofstream& a_stream)
{
  Object_Tag_Format* format =
      class_map->get_format_for_table();
  format->set_object(this);
  format->store(a_stream);
}
```

And an object table tells each of its objects to store itself. Add a member function for storing objects.

```
void Object_Table::store_objects(ofstream& a_stream)
{
  // Get my object iterator.
  Object_Table_Object_Iterator next_object =
                  this->get_objects();
  PDC_Object* pdc_object;

  // Use my iterator to step through my objects.
  while ((pdc_object = next_object()) != 0)
    pdc_object->store_using_table(a_stream, this);
}
```

Save to a file

Just open an output file stream, store the object identifiers, and store the PDC objects.

```
Boolean Object_Table::save_to_file(char* filename)
{
```

```
    // Open the file and get its output file stream.
    ofstream a_stream(filename, ios::out);

    // Check that the file has been opened successfully.
    if (!a_stream)
      {
      cout << "Cannot open " << filename << "for output"
            << endl;
      return false;
      }

    this->store(a_stream);
    this->store_objects(a_stream);
    a_stream.close();
    return true;
}
```

Define the restoring member functions

Restore objects and object identifiers

Most of the work is done by the format objects for the object table and the PDC objects.

Add the member functions.

```
void Object_Table..restore(ifstream& a_stream)
{
    Object_Tag_Format* format =
            class_map->get_format_for_table();
    format->set_object(this);
    format->restore(a_stream, this);
}

void Object_Table::restore_objects(ifstream& a_stream)
{
    Object_Table_Object_Iterator next_object =
      this->get_objects();
    PDC_Object* pdc_object;
    while ((pdc_object = next_object()) != 0)
      pdc_object->restore_using_table(a_stream, this);
}
```

Read from a file

```
Boolean Object_Table::read_from_file(char* filename)
{
    // Open the file and get its output file stream.
    ifstream a_stream(filename);
```

```
    // Check that the file has been opened successfully.
    if (!a_stream)
        {
        cout << "Cannot open" << filename << "for input"
                << endl;
        return false;
        }

    this->restore(a_stream);
    this->restore_objects(a_stream);
    a_stream.close();
    return true;
    }
```

The Object Table Format Class

The object table format class defines how to store and restore an object table.

About class codes for storing objects

Part of an object table format's job is to store a reference to a class and an object identifier, for each and every PDC object in an object table.

A class reference indicates which class an object belongs to. During the restoring activity, a new object in that class is created and assigned its attribute values and connection values.

For a class reference, you can use a class name stored as a string. You can then look up the proper class by comparing the class name string against a set of strings.

For a more efficient approach you can assign an integer code for each class. Use this approach for an object table.

Hence, store a class code, along with the object identifier, for every PDC object in the object table.

Declare the class

Declare the object table format class

```
class Object_Table_Format : public Object_Tag_Format
{
public:
    Object_Table_Format() { }
    ~Object_Table_Format() { }
    void store(ofstream& a_stream);
    void restore(ifstream& a_stream,
        Object_Table* new_object_table);
```

```
      void store_class_name(ofstream& a_stream);
      void store_attribute_values(ofstream& a_stream) {}
      void store_table_start(ofstream& a_stream);
      void store_object_IDs(ofstream& a_stream);
      void store_table_end(ofstream& a_stream);
      void store_class_code(ofstream& a_stream, int
            class_code);

      void restore_attribute_values(ifstream& a_stream) { }
      void read_table_start(ifstream& a_stream);
      void restore_object_IDs(ifstream& a_stream,
            Object_Table* some_object_table);
      void read_table_end(ifstream& a_stream);
      int restore_class_code(ifstream& a_stream);

      void set_object(void* new_object)
         { an_object_table = (Object_Table*)new_object; }

      // Accessors
      void set_object_table(Object_Table& new_object_table)
         { an_object_table = *new_object_table; }
      Object_Table& get_object_table()
         { return *an_object_table; }
   private:
      Object_Table* an_object_table;
   };
```

Define the storing member functions

Store a class name

First, add the easy one, storing the class name.

```
   void Object_Table_Format::store_class_name(ofstream&
         a_stream)
   {
      this->store_tag_value(a_stream, "className",
            "Object_Table");
   }
```

Store a class code

Add a member function to store a class code.

```
   void Object_Table_Format::store_class_code
         (ofstream& a_stream, int class_code)
   {
      String code_string(class_code);
```

```
    this->store_tag_value(a_stream, "classCode",
        code_string);
}
```

Store the table start and table end

Add member functions to store the start and end of the object table.

```
void Object_Table_Format::store_table_start(ofstream&
    a_stream);
{
  this->store_tag(a_stream, "ObjectTable");
  a_stream << endl;
}
void Object_Table_Format::store_table_end(ofstream&
    a_stream);
{
  this->store_tag(a_stream, "\\ObjectTable");
  a_stream << endl;
}
```

Store the object identifiers

Next, add a member function for storing the object identifiers.

```
void Object_Table_Format::store_object_IDs(ofstream&
    a_stream)
{
  PDC_Object* pdc_object;

  // Get the iterator for the object table's PDC objects.
  Object_Table_Object_Iterator next_object =
            an_object_table->get_objects();

  int class_code;

  while ((pdc_object = next_object()) != 0)
    {
    // Store the pdc object's class code.
    class_code = pdc_object->get_class_code();
    store_class_code(a_stream,class_code);

    // Store the PDC object's object identifier.
    this->store_tag(a_stream, "objectID");
    int id = pdc_object->get_object_ID();
    this->store_ID(a_stream, id);
    }

}
```

Store an object table

Add the member function which stores an object table. Use these steps:

> I'm an object table format.
> > I store my object table to a file.
> > > store the definition start
> > > store the class name
> > > store the table start
> > > store the object identifiers
> > > store the table end
> > > store the definition end

And put it into code:

```
void Object_Tag_Format::store(ofstream& a_stream)
{
   this->store_defn_start(a_stream);
   this->store_class_name(a_stream);
   this->store_table_start(a_stream);
   this->store_object_IDs(a_stream);
   this->store_table_end(a_stream);
   this->store_defn_end(a_stream);
}
```

Define the restoring member functions

Restore a class code

Add a member function to restore a class code.

```
int Object_Table_Format::restore_class_code(ifstream&
      a_stream)
{
   if (!(this->restore_tag(a_stream, "classCode")))
      return -1;
   String& code_string = this->restore_value(a_stream);
   int class_code = code_string.as_integer();
   return class_code;
}
```

Read the table start and table end

Add member functions to read the start and end of the object table.

```
void Object_Table_Format::read_table_start
      (ifstream& a_stream);
{
```

```
    char ch;

    this->restore_tag(a_stream, "ObjectTable");
    a_stream.get(ch);
}
void Object_Table_Format::read_table_end(ifstream&
        a_stream);
{
    char ch;

    this->restore_tag(a_stream, "\\ObjectTable");
    a_stream.get(ch);
}
```

Restore the object identifiers

```
void Object_Table_Format::restore_object_IDs(ifstream&
        a_stream, Object_Table* new_object_table)
{
    an_object_table = new_object_table;

    // Get the class map for the object table.
    Class_Map* class_map = an_object_table->get_class_map();

    int class_code, object_ID;

    // Read the next class code from the stream.
    // Stop when I encounter something other than a class
    // code.
    while ((class_code = this->restore_class_code(a_stream))
            != -1)
      {
      // Read the object identifier.
      this->restore_tag(a_stream, "objectID");
      object_ID = this->restore_ID(a_stream);

      // Ask the class map to recreate the object using
      // its class code and object identifier. The class
      // map then registers the object in the object table.
      class_map->restore_object(object_ID, class_code,
            an_object_table);
      }
}
```

Restore an object table

Add a member function that restores an object table.

```
void Object_Table_Format::restore(ifstream& a_stream,
        Object_Table* object_table)
{
    this->read_defn_start(a_stream);
```

```
    this->restore_class_name(a_stream);
    this->read_table_start(a_stream);
    this->restore_object_IDs(a_stream, object_table);
    this->read_table_end(a_stream);
    this->read_defn_end(a_stream);
}
```

The Class Map Class

Add a way to map problem domain classes to format objects. And add a way to restore (re-create) a new object for each problem domain class.

Create a specialized map for each set of problem domain classes that you want to use with this data management approach. Each specialized map needs its own member functions for restoring (creating) an object.

Declare the class

Declare a general class map. Include a variable for storing format objects.

```
typedef Ordered_List<Object_Tag_Format*>
        Object_Tag_Format_List;

class Class_Map {
public:

    // Constructors/destructors
    Class_Map() { }
    virtual ~Class_Map() { }

    // Implementors
    Object_Tag_Format* get_format_for(int class_code);
    Object_Tag_Format* get_format_for_table()
            {return get_format_for(table_class_code());}

    // Can be specialized by derived classes
    virtual int table_class_code(){return 0;}
    virtual void restore_object(int object_ID, int
            class_code, Object_Table* an_object_table) { }

protected:

    Object_Tag_Format_List formats;
};
```

Define the member functions

Assign an integer code to each problem domain class. This makes associating formats with problem domain classes fairly easy to do.

```
Object_Tag_Format* Class_Map::get_format_for(int
        class_code)
{
    Object_Tag_Format* format;

    format = formats.item_at(class_code)
    return format;
}
```

The generalized class map can't do much work. You need a specialized version for the sales transaction system.

The Sales Domain Class Map

First, establish the class codes. Use an enumerated type.

```
enum Sales_Domain_Class { TRANSACTION, SALES_TRANSACTION,
LINE_ITEM, CUSTOMER, PRODUCT, OBJECT_TABLE}
```

Declare the class

```
class Sales_Domain_Class_Map : public Class_Map {
public:

    // Constructors/destructors
    Sales_Domain_Class_Map();
    ~Sales_Domain_Class_Map() { }

    // Implementors
    int table_class_code() {return OBJECT_TABLE;}
    void restore_object(int object_ID, int class_code,
            Object_Table* an_object_table);
};
```

The constructor for the class creates the format objects.

```
Sales_Domain_Class_Map::Sales_Domain_Class_Map()
{
    formats.add(new Transaction_Format<Transaction>());
    formats.add(new Sales_Transaction_Format());
    formats.add(new Line_Item_Format());
    formats.add(new Customer_Format());
    formats.add(new Product_Format());
    formats.add(new Object_Table_Format());
}
```

Define the member functions

The restore object member function creates a new object, assigns its object identifier, and registers it in an object table. The member function uses the class code to decide what kind of object to create.

```cpp
void Sales_Domain_Class_Map::restore_object(int object_ID,
             int class_code, Object_Table* an_object_table)
{
   PDC_Object* pdc_object;

   // Create the new PDC object based on its class code.
   switch (class_code)
      {
      case SALES_TRANSACTION:
         pdc_object = new Sales_Transaction ();
         break;
      case LINE_ITEM:
         pdc_object = new Transaction_Line_Item ();
         break;
      case CUSTOMER:
         pdc_object = new Customer ();
         break;
      case PRODUCT:
         pdc_object = new Product ();
         break;
      }

   // Assign the object's identifier.
   pdc_object->set_object_ID(object_ID);

   // Register the object in the object table.
   an_object_table->
         register_object(object_ID, pdc_object);
}
```

Adding to the Problem Domain Component to Support Data Management

You've already added an attribute to the problem domain classes to support data management. Now you need to add several member functions.

Add the "register a PDC object in an object table" member function

First, a PDC object needs to know how to register itself and its connections in a corresponding object table.

Derived classes need to specialize the register connections member function; declare it as a virtual function.

```
// Data management
void register_in_table(Object_Table* an_object_table);
virtual void register_connections(Object_Table*
        an_object_table) { }
```

Add the member function for registering an object and its connections in a table.

```
void PDC_Object::register_in_table(Object_Table*
        an_object_table)
{
  an_object_table->register_object(object_ID, this);
  this->register_connections(an_object_table);
}
```

For the transaction, customer, and line item classes, add member functions for registering connections. For example, here's the member function for the customer class:

```
void Customer::register_connections(Object_Table*
        an_object_table)
{
  Transaction* transaction;

  // Tell my sales transactions to register themselves in
  // the table.
  transactions.reset();
  while (!transactions.end_of_list())
    {
    transaction = transactions.current();
    transaction->register_in_table(an_object_table);
    transactions++;
    }
}
```

Add the "get class code" member function

Class codes distinguish the different types of PDC objects.

Add a member function to return the class code for each PDC object. Add it to the PDC object class. Make it a pure virtual member function:

```
// Must be implemented by specialized classes
virtual int get_class_code() = 0;
```

Add the member function to the transaction class:

```
int get_class_code() {return TRANSACTION;}
```

Repeat for the other classes which are specializations of PDC object:

```
// Sales transaction
int get_class_code() {return SALES_TRANSACTION ;}
// Customer
int get_class_code() {return CUSTOMER;}
// Line Item
int get_class_code() {return LINE_ITEM;}
// Product
int get_class_code() {return PRODUCT;}
```

Add the "store and restore a PDC object using an object table" member function

First, put together the declarations.

```
// Data management functions
void store_using_table(ofstream& a_stream, Object_Table*
        an_object_table);
void restore_using_table(ifstream& a_stream,
        Object_Table* an_object_table);
```

Next, develop the definitions.

A PDC object gets its storage format from the class map of the object table.

To store, a PDC object tells its format to store it and its designated class code.

```
void PDC_Object::store_using_table(ofstream& a_stream,
        Object_Table* an_object_table)
{
    int class_code = this->get_class_code();
    Class_Map* class_map = an_object_table->get_class_map();
    Object_Tag_Format* format =
            class_map->get_format_for(class_code);
    format->set_object(this);

    format->store(a_stream);
}
```

To restore, a PDC object tells its format to restore it, using the format corresponding to its class code.

```
void PDC_Object::restore_using_table(ifstream& a_stream,
        Object_Table* an_object_table)
{
```

```
    int class_code = this->get_class_code();
    Class_Map* class_map = an_object_table->get_class_map();
    Object_Tag_Format* format =
            class_map->get_format_for(class_code);
    format->set_object(this);

    format->restore(a_stream, an_object_table);
}
```

Run the Code

To try it out, use your customer demo program to create a customer with some sales transactions and line items. Then save the customer using an object table with a sales domain class map.

```
int main ()
{
    // Create the demo customer.
    Customer customer;
    Customer& mr_rubble = customer.customer_demo();

    // Create an object table and its sales class map.
    Object_Table an_object_table;
    Sales_Domain_Class_Map* a_class_map =
            new Sales_Domain_Class_Map();

    an_object_table.set_class_map(a_class_map);

    // Register the customer in the object table.
    // Save the object table to a file.
    mr_rubble.register_in_table(&an_object_table);
    an_object_table.save_to_file("tagFile.fmt");
    return 0;
}
```

The program creates a "tagFile.fmt" file, whose contents will look something like this:

```
<ObjectDefn>
<className>Object_Table
<ObjectTable>
<classCode>3
<objectID><id>1
<classCode>1
<objectID><id>2
<\ObjectTable>
<\ObjectDefn>
<ObjectDefn>
```

```
<className>Customer
<objectID><id>1
<name>Barney Rubble
<address>Bedrock
<transaction><id>2
<\ObjectDefn>
<ObjectDefn>
<className>Sales_Transaction
<objectID><id>2
<dateTime>Tue Sep 29 21:09:13 1992
<methodOfPayment>cash
<lineItem><id>3
<\ObjectDefn>
```

Create a second object table. Read in the tag file you have just created.

```
// Create another object table.
   Object_Table another_object_table;

   another_object_table.set_class_map(class_map);

   // Read the object from a file,
   another_object_table.read_from_file("tagFile.fmt");
```

Finally, save the contents of the second table to another file.

```
   another_object_table.save_to_file("tagFile2.fmt");
```

Do the files match? Yes?
Excellent.

SUMMARY

In this chapter, you learned and applied:

OOA and OOD
- Applying a high-speed approach to finding problem domain classes
- Designing a human interaction component with multiple containers
- Designing human interaction for a model collection
- Designing data management classes

OOP (Smalltalk)
- Enforcing subclass responsibility
- Creating a scrolling list

- Coordinating human interaction objects
- Reading from and writing to files
- Using the dictionary class
- Storing objects on a file with an object tag format
- Restoring objects from a file

OOP (C++)

- Using library classes
- Formatting stream output
- Coordinating human interaction objects
- Reading from and writing to files
- Using heterogeneous collections and the virtual function mechanism.
- Storing objects on a file with an object tag format
- Restoring objects from a file

You also learned and applied these principles:

The "person, place, thing" principle. Find initial classes by listing potential classes of objects—objects which may be a person, place, or thing.

The "high-speed breadth" principle. Push person, place, and thing. Go wild, identifying many, many classes.

The "high-speed depth" principle. Apply generalization–specialization and whole–part to each class. New generalizations, specializations, wholes, and parts add depth to your OOA model.

The "heart and soul" principle. Make an extensive list of classes in a problem domain. Then select a small number of classes . . . ones that together represent the heart and soul, the core of the problem domain under consideration. Do OOA and OOD on these first. Build them. Demonstrate working results. Then go for more.

The "behavior across a collection" principle. Let a collection do just the work that applies across a collection. Push work down into each part.

The "mail dominance" principle. Design small, domain-based human interaction containers that communicate and coordinate via mailboxes. Why? Better distribution of responsibility. And increased likelihood of reuse.

The "let the domain classes be your guide" principle. Let the problem domain classes guide you in organizing the classes in each design component.

4

Go With The Flow

The example in this chapter? Go with the flow: a traffic flow management system.

You'll experience:

OOA and OOD
- Identifying and applying system purpose
- Applying the targeted analogy strategy
- Improving your model with scenario scripts
- Working with object interactions to explore what an object needs to do

OOP (Smalltalk)
- Generating random numbers
- Working with dates and times
- Writing timed simulations using delay objects
- Creating graphics objects
- Working with shapes, colors, and graphics context
- Implementing state-dependent rules (using blocks)
- Adding methods to display a view
- Adding methods to respond to model broadcasts

OOP (C++)
- Using default arguments in member functions
- Writing parameterized functions
- Generating random numbers
- Working with dates and times
- Implementing state-dependent rules (using pointers to member functions)
- Building human interaction classes that respond to notify messages

SOME OOA

A Modest Beginning

A client needs you to build a traffic flow system.
Where should you begin?

Just hearing the name of the system, you might picture something like Figure 4–1.

Figure 4–1: A traffic light system—a first impression?

And so you could begin with a single class—expecting it to be the core class in this new system (Figure 4–2).

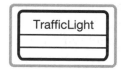

Figure 4–2: The core class in the traffic light system?

Without any further discussion or correspondence with the client (caution: this means trouble!), you walk through a scenario script.

> I'm a traffic light.
>> I know how many lamps I have, what color they are, and what state each is in.

Whoops. Wait a minute. That traffic light knows too much about its parts. Try again.

> I'm a traffic light.
>> I know about my corresponding lamps.
> I'm a traffic lamp.
>> I know my state (on, off).
>> I know my duration (how long I stay in my "on" state).
>> When told to, I run myself in my state for my duration.

Now the OOA model looks something like Figure 4–3:

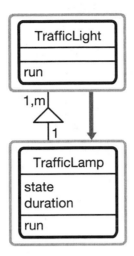

Figure 4–3: A traffic light is a collection of traffic lamps.

So far so good.

What happens if you want to use this traffic light system in an intersection?

You could add an "intersection" class, with some number of traffic lights as its parts.

But wait. Is intersection the right grouping?

The "dig yourself a large enough whole" principle. Whenever you name the "whole" in a whole-part structure, use a name that is applicable (large enough to apply) across the variety of collections that you may need to support.

Is an intersection the best collection to use here? What would be larger? How about some number of intersections? Or no intersections at all—traffic flow management for a single special lane, with traffic lights every block for 3 miles?

What's the name for a collection of traffic lights? Try something like "traffic device group" (Figure 4–4).

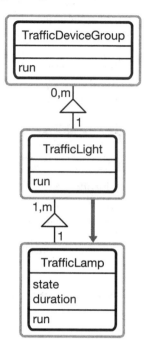

Figure 4–4: Adding a traffic device group.

Walk around and take a second look. What else is in the problem domain? How about the classes shown in Figure 4–5.

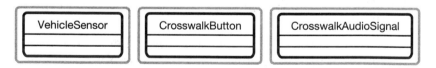

Figure 4–5: Some additional classes?

What's the same? What's different?

Both vehicle sensor and crosswalk button are requesting devices, used to detect a request from someone interacting with an automated system.

A crosswalk audio signal is just like traffic signal. In fact, it's exactly the same; the only difference is how the information is presented to a human being!

Oh-oh. You've been modeling human interaction devices. And this means that you've missed the problem domain—the *real* problem domain—entirely!

Is this system *really* about traffic lamps? No way!

The "pay attention to the man behind the curtains" principle. Look past the current human interaction wizardry—and get to the underlying problem domain.

Take a closer look.

What's the Purpose of the System?

The need

How did you get into so much trouble?

Perhaps you lost sight of what the purpose of the system is all about!

The "25 words or less" principle. Always, always, always begin by asking "What's the purpose of the system, in 25 words or less?" Put that purpose on a decorative poster! And use the purpose of the system to guide your every move.

Just what is the purpose of this system?

"To run traffic lights." No! This scope is too limiting. Traffic lights, vehicle sensors, crosswalk buttons, crosswalk audio signals, and even people sensors could be part of the system under consideration—now or in the future.

Who you gonna call?

To crisply define the purpose of the system, who are you going to call? Your problem domain experts!

YOU:
Hello. I'm ... . Can you describe the business that you're in?

Problem Domain Expert (PDE):
Thanks for calling. Yes, I know this business well.

I work for the city. This business at hand is traffic flow management. We configure the traffic signals at each intersection with one purpose in mind: the safe and expedient flow of traffic. Safety is a must.

YOU:
So the purpose of the system might be stated as "to provide safe and expedient traffic flow."

PDE:
Right. With extra emphasis on safety.

YOU:
Okay: "to provide *safe* and expedient traffic flow."

PDE:
Yes. And we define steps for each intersection.

We take into account the traffic signals, crosswalk signals, crosswalk buttons, and electromagnetic vehicle sensors.

We use different steps for different time periods during a single day, and often for different days during a week.

Putting together a system purpose statement

Put this information to work—and develop a clear statement of system purpose.

Establishing a system purpose statement is essential. It helps team members understand more, since listening (and reading) with a purpose is the one great key to improved listening (and reading) comprehension.

System purpose keeps you on track during development. Many, many things may be enticing, intriguing, or just plain fun to explore. But again and again, a clearly defined system purpose can help you rein yourself back in, keeping you focused on what the system is all about.

However, identifying system purpose does you little good—if it's something that you find, muse over it for a while, drop it into a folder somewhere, and forget its existence.

Just to encourage yourself to keep the system purpose in mind, you might want to include it as an annotation on an OOA model. You might even tape the purpose statement just below the screen on your workstation (Figure 4–6).

> *"...to provide <u>safe</u> and expedient traffic flow."*

Figure 4–6: The purpose of the system, in 25 words or less.

The system or systems you build to satisfy this purpose might use a wide variety of human interaction technologies—traffic lights, electronic traffic signs, audio tone signals (to help the sight-impaired make safe intersection crossings), and others in the future (for example, sensors that interact directly with computing systems running a vehicle).

Applying the system purpose

Consider the classes that you looked at earlier—traffic device group, traffic light, and traffic lamp. These classes are human interaction classes. That's great news for the human interaction component. But without them, what's left? What goes in the OOA model?

What abstraction do you use in the OOA model, independent of how the information might be presented to someone?

In other words, where do you turn when the problem domain seems rather abstract and not very tangible? What should you do when the human interaction devices are so prominent that they make it hard to look past them to see the real business at hand?

Apply another strategy for architecting an object-oriented system: the targeted analogy.

Targeted Analogy

What it is

Here's the principle:

The "targeted analogy" principle. When the true underlying problem domain is unclear, look for analogous systems that exist to achieve a similar purpose. Learn from the parallels between the systems.

First, you identify the purpose of the system.

Then, you look for targeted analogies—analogous systems that achieve a similar purpose. A targeted analogy can help you gain the the problem domain understanding that you need (plus the core classes, too).

Apply the principle here. Examine several targeted analogies for the system under consideration.

Targeted analogy 1

The purpose of this system is "to provide *safe* and expedient traffic flow."

What other systems monitor and control traffic flow?

How about a hall monitor, a student on duty at the local high school?

"I'm a hall monitor. I adjust (or in this problem domain, *try* to adjust!) the flow rate of traffic. I tell dawdlers to go faster and runners to go slower (in other words, I generally make a nuisance of myself)."

Model the core class of this analogous system (Figure 4–7).

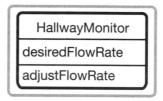

Figure 4–7: A targeted analogy: the hallway monitor.

That OOA model needs to be refined a bit. It could use some help from some principles.

The "my oh my" principle. Every service name should make perfect sense when the words "I" or "me" or "my" or "myself" are added alongside the verb in the service name. If not, change the service or change the class name so that it does make sense.

Applying this principle, "adjust flow rate" becomes:

adjust my flow rate

Whose flow rate? The flow rate of the hallway monitor? Or something else? What really has a flow rate?

The service name "adjust my flow rate" points to the need for a different class name. Do you know what it is?

Here's another principle to help you get there:

The "I'd rather do it to myself" principle. If an object in an OOA/OOD model acts on something not yet in the model, replace the object in the model with one that acts on itself. And let the new object do the action on itself.

The hallway monitor and the "adjust flow rate" service work *on* something. That object is the hallway itself. Let the hallway adjust its own doggone flow rate (Figure 4–8)!

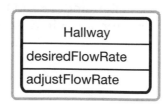

Figure 4–8: A targeted analogy, refined: a hallway.

Transferring what you learn from a targeted analogy

Okay, okay. That's all fine and good. You can now "object think" even in the strangest of places. But how do you transfer a lesson learned in a targeted analogy over to the system you have at hand?

Remember your high school days? It's likely that some wonderful grammar teacher tried to teach you about figures of speech—something out of the ordinary, used for emphasis.

Just hearing the phrase "figures of speech" might make you want to shut down and sleep. But hold on! Just listen to this:

A metaphor. A figure of speech in which a word denoting a class is used in place of another, suggesting an analogy between them.

Wow!

A metaphor uses one class in place of another, suggesting an analogy between them. The sequence is:

metaphor—>class—>analogy

Ah, but how do you find a metaphor—and the class name it reveals? Just reverse the process:

analogy—>class—>metaphor

Look at an analogy. Consider each class. And answer the question, "What class in the problem domain is a metaphor for this class?"

The "analogy to class to metaphor" principle. Find a targeted analogy. Identify core classes. Identify which problem domain class and targeted analogy class are metaphors for each other. Add what you learned from the targeted analogy to your OOA/OOD model.

This principle is the key to getting tremendous value out of a targeted analogy.

Apply it here.

The *analogy* is hallway traffic flow management.

Its core *class* is hallway.

The core *metaphor* is lane (Figure 4–9). Hallway and lane are metaphors for each other.

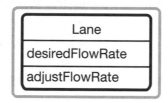

Figure 4–9: "As a lane, this is what I know and do."

"As a lane, I know my own flow rate. And I know how to adjust my own flow rate."

So far, so good.

Targeted analogy 2

What other kind of system exists "to provide *safe* and expedient traffic flow?"

How about an air traffic control system? Yes, such a system is used to provide safe and expedient air traffic flow.

What are some of the core classes in that problem domain? Aircraft. Airport. Airspace volume. Flight path.

An air traffic control system directs and monitors aircraft, providing safe and expedient traffic flow within an airspace volume along certain defined flight paths.

Take a closer look at flight paths.

Typically, a defined flight path has a name (for easy referencing).

Also, flight paths intersect each other. For safety, one of the things that would be nice for each flight path to know is its own crossing flight paths (Figure 4–10).

"I'm a flight path. I know my name. And I know my crossing flight paths."

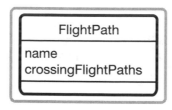

Figure 4–10: A targeted analogy: a flight path.

A flight path knows its own crossing flight paths. So do you need a flight path intersection, too? The key issue is this: does an intersection know or do anything that the flight path cannot do for itself? After all, a flight path can monitor itself for what is inside of it. And if it knows its own crossing flight paths, it can check itself for current and potential conflicts. At least at this point, there doesn't seem to be a compelling reason to include an intersection in this OOA model.

Move on back to the problem domain at hand—traffic flow management.

What targeted analogy class (flight path) and problem domain class are metaphors for each other?

Yes, it's lane. Again.

Add what you learned from the targeted analogy. Here, each lane needs to know its crossing lanes. From a safety perspective, this makes good sense, too (Figure 4–11).

"I'm a lane. And I know my crossing lanes."

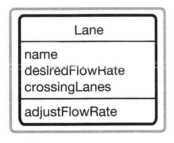

Figure 4–11: Adding to what a lane knows.

Targeted analogy 3

Go after one more targeted analogy.

How about a sprinkler system?

It's purpose is to control water flow. It's a water flow management system. To do its work, it uses a script (a collection of steps and applicable intervals).

The core classes? Valve. Step. Script. And active interval.

Valve? A valve adjusts a pipe's flow rate. Apply the "I'd rather do it to myself" principle. "I'm a pipe and I know how to adjust my own flow rate."

The core classes? Pipe. Step. Script. And active interval (Figure 4–12).

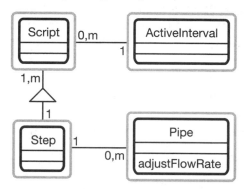

Figure 4–12: Targeted analogy: a sprinkler system.

Consider what each script, step, pipe, and active interval might know and do. "I'm a *script*. I run myself" (Figure 4–13).

Figure 4–13: "As a script, this is what I do."

"I'm a *step*. I run myself. I know my desired flow rate and duration" (Figure 4–14).

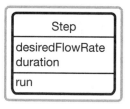

Figure 4–14: "As a step, this is what I know and do."

"I'm a *pipe*. I adjust my flow rate, based on whatever desired flow rate and duration I'm told to apply to myself" (Figure 4–15).

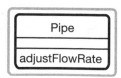

Figure 4–15: "As a pipe, this is what I do."

"As a pipe, I know my own maximum flow rate—and won't allow it to be exceeded. And when someone tells me to adjust my flow rate to my maximum, I do it" (Figure 4–16).

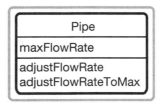

Figure 4–16: "As a pipe, this is what I know and do."

"As an *active interval*, I know my days of the week, my start time, and my end time" (Figure 4–17).

Figure 4–17: "As an active interval, this is what I know."

"As an active interval, I can check to see whether I'm active for a given day and time that someone gives to me" (Figure 4–18).

Figure 4–18: "As an active interval, this is what I know and do."

Consider the *object interactions:*
> I'm a script.
>> I send a message to each of my active intervals, telling it
>>> to check if it is active.
> I'm an active interval.
>> I check if I'm active; I return the result to the sender.
> I'm a script.
>> I send a message to step, telling it to run.

I'm a step.
　　I send a message to my pipe, telling it to adjust
　　　　　its flow rate.
I'm a pipe.
　　I adjust my flow rate.

Putting this all together, you get Figure 4–19.

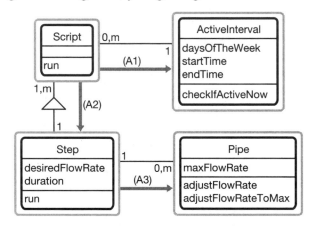

Figure 4–19: Targeted analogy: a sprinkler system (with lots more detail).

Note that this message scenario (A) and its steps (1, 2, 3) are included on the model.

Now go back to the traffic flow management system. Pipe and lane are metaphors. Add in the observations from the targeted analogy (Figure 4–20).

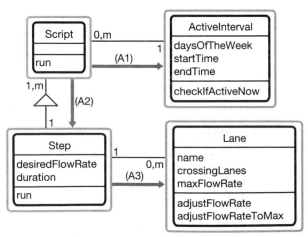

Figure 4–20: Adding in the lessons learned from the sprinkler system analogy.

But wait a moment. A step, you say? Why bother with a step? Hold on there! And watch out!

The "I'll be back" principle. If I'm a problem domain class, don't throw me away just because you think you can smash me in with another class. I'm probably needed. I'll be back.

Why not just have a lane that knows its own desired flow rate and duration? You could model a lane this way. And *if* those values always apply to that lane—whenever it is used—that's okay. But desired flow rate and duration are attributes of a *step*, not a lane; many steps can apply to a single lane. Both step and lane are important. And needed.

On another matter: safety.

"As a lane, I know my maximum flow rate." That makes a lot of sense. It's a *safety* constraint on a lane.

"As a lane, I know my crossing lanes." That also makes a lot of sense. It's another *safety* constraint on a lane.

This gives *safety* constraints very high visibility—from the very start. And that practically applies the purpose of the system: to provide *safe* and expedient traffic flow.

Additional targeted analogies

You could consider other targeted analogies, including telecommunications (the flow of telephone calls), power distribution systems (the flow of electrons), railways (the flow of trains), and even ant farms (the flow of ants).

But for this book, three targeted analogies are enough.

So what's next?

Develop a Scenario Script and Refine the Model

Develop and act out a scenario script, to discover more details that you need in the model.

> I'm a script.
> > I send a message to each of my active intervals, telling it
> > > to check if it is active.
>
> I'm an active interval.
> > I know my days of the week, start time, and end time.
> > I check if I'm active; I return the result to the sender.
>
> I'm a script.
> > Once I find an active interval,
> > > I send a message to a step, telling it to run.

> I'm a step.
>> I know my desired flow rate and my duration.
>> I send a message to my lane, telling it to adjust its flow
>>> rate to a desired flow rate for a duration.
> I'm a lane.
>> I tell each of my crossing lanes to close itself.
>> I adjust my flow rate.

Hold it! There's more to it than that. After all, a sudden transition from opened to closed is not a safe thing to do. You need a duration. And you need a *transition* duration.

Try again.

> I'm a step.
>> I know my transition duration, desired flow rate, and
>>> my duration.
>> I send a message to my lane, telling it to adjust its
>>> flow rate.
> I'm a lane.
>> I tell each of my crossing lanes to close itself.
>> I adjust my flow rate.

So step now looks like Figure 4–21.

Figure 4–21: "As a step, this is what I know and do."

And lane now looks like Figure 4–22.

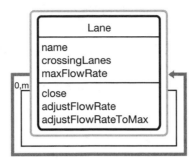

Figure 4–22: "As a lane, I tell each of my crossing lanes to close itself."[1]

"I'm a (crossing) lane. Someone just told me to close myself over a transition duration. I adjust my own flow rate from my current flow rate down to zero." Oh! "As a lane, something else that I need to know is my current flow rate" (Figure 4–23).

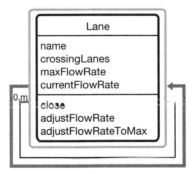

Figure 4–23: "As a lane, I know my current flow rate, too."

What else can you learn from a lane?

"One more thing. I might get requested by a pedestrian waiting at the curbside or by a vehicle passing over some sort of sensor. When this happens, I need to remember that someone has requested me. After all, certain steps might tell me to adjust my flow rate only when I've been requested."

And what's the impact on step?

"As a step, I may be applicable only when my corresponding lane has been requested by someone. I need to let the lane know this; it knows enough to know what to do about it."

---

[1]When an object needs to know about one or some number of other objects in the same class, you can model it just like this. Use an attribute *and* an object connection. Why? To effectively communicate the meaning behind this kind of mapping.

The message from a step to a lane looks like this:

```
adjustFlowRate
    (desired flow rate, transition duration, duration,
        onlyWhenRequested)
```

Add attributes and a service to make this happen (Figure 4–24).

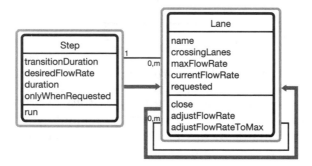

Figure 4–24: Adding the fact that some steps apply only when a lane has been requested.

Putting the lessons from the targeted analogies together with the scenario script results, you get Figure 4–25.

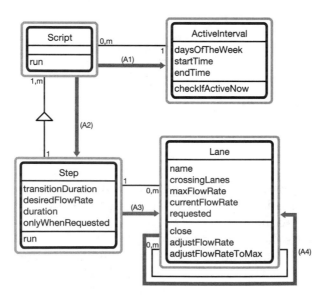

Figure 4–25: Traffic flow management: the OOA model.

Walking through Some Examples

Check out the OOA model by walking through some examples.

Four lanes

This example consists of four lanes (Figure 4–26).

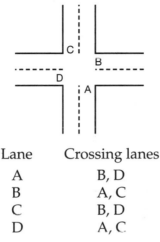

Lane	Crossing lanes
A	B, D
B	A, C
C	B, D
D	A, C

Figure 4–26: The four lanes.[2]

Do the steps run in sequence? Or do they run at the same time, in parallel?

An OOA model can reflect one or the other. The key issue is: which one is easier to understand? Effective communication is a must.

With OOD, the added key issue is: to simulate parallel behavior, what language and operating system constructs are available? If operating system independence is an issue, parallel behavior can be a real pain.

Keep it simple. Only do things in parallel when it pays for itself by *significantly* simplifying what you would otherwise have to do sequentially.[3]

Just to show that you could apply either one here, this section walks through both sequential and parallel steps. But the rest of the

---

[2] This same example applies to both left-side and right-side driving conventions.

[3] With concurrency, you'll also have to design in the usual safeguards to avoid the usual parallel processing pitfalls, including things like deadly embraces and starved requesters.

chapter applies sequential steps. It's simpler to understand. And it's easier to get it right. And it's operating system independent.

Define the steps—running *in parallel*:

Step	Transition Duration	Duration	Desired Flow Rate	Only When Requested	For Lane
1	5	30	max	no	A
2	5	30	max	no	C
3	5	30	max	no	B
4	5	30	max	no	D

It works like this:

> As a script
> I tell my steps to run.
>
> As a step
> I tell my lane to adjust its flow rate.
>
> As a lane
> I tell my crossing lanes to close.
> Then I wait for them to close (the transition duration).
>
> Suppose that lanes A and C get serviced first, and get
>   their crossing lanes closed.
>
> Then for A and C
> I adjust my flow to maximum.
> Then I stay open for 30 seconds.
> Then I honor the pending 'close' request
>   (from lanes B and D).
>
> Then for B and D
> I adjust my flow to maximum.
> Then I stay open for 30 seconds.
> Then I honor the pending 'close' request
>   (from lanes A and C).

Define the steps—running *sequentially*:

Step	Transition Duration	Duration	Desired Flow Rate	Only When Requested	For Lane
1	5	0	max	no	A
2	0	30	max	no	C
3	5	0	max	no	B
4	0	30	max	no	D

It works like this, repeating again and again:

> As a script
>> I tell my next step to run itself.
>
> As a step
>> I tell my lane to adjust its flow rate.
>
> As a lane
>> If I'm told to run only when requested and I'm not
>> requested, I just return.
>> I tell my crossing lanes to close over the transition
>> duration.
>> If my duration > 0, then I set:
>>> current flow rate =
>>>> min (desired flow rate, max flow rate)
>> I wait for the duration.

Five lanes

Extend the previous example. Add another lane—a pedestrian lane (Figure 4–27).

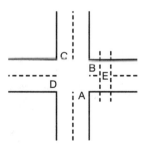

Figure 4–27: Adding a pedestrian lane

So the new lane is:

Lane	Crossing Lanes
E	B, D

Another step is needed:

Step	Transition Duration	Duration	Desired Flow Rate	Only When Requested	For Lane
5	5	15	max	yes	E

And it fits right into the previous example.

OOD—PROBLEM DOMAIN COMPONENT

Add design details to the OOA model.

Add Connection Details

Add connection attributes

To begin with, go ahead and add the connection attributes (Figure 4–28).

Further constrain the object connections

Check out each connection. Each message sender needs to know to whom to send a message. That means:

> As a script, I need to know my steps.
> As a step, I need to know my lane.
> As a lane, I need to know my crossing lanes.

Update the object connection constraints accordingly (Figure 4–28). And verify that each sender has an attribute to capture this need to know.

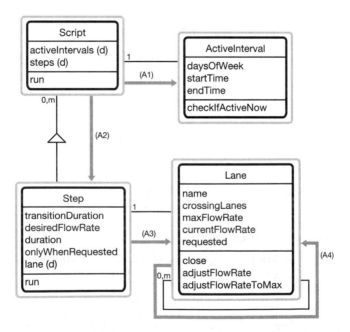

Figure 4–28: Adding connection attributes and updating object connection constraints.

Working with Object Interactions

Apply the "interaction then action" principle:

The "interaction then action" principle. Examine needed object inter-actions. And add the corresponding actions.

Work the message from script to active interval

Work the message from the sender's perspective:

> I send a message to each of my active intervals, to "check if active now," until one of them answers that it is active now.
> Arguments? None.

Then work the message from the receiver's perspective:

> I check to see if I'm active now.
> I return my response to the sender.

Add what you learned to step and to active interval (Figure 4-29).

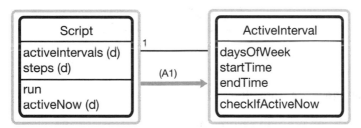

Figure 4–29: Adding to step and active interval.

Work the message from script to step

Work the message from the sender's perspective:

> I send a message to a step, telling it to run.
> Any arguments? None.
> But which step do I send that message to? To select the next step, I need to know where I am in the step sequence.

Then work the message from the receiver's perspective:

> I run myself.
> Once done, I return a response to the sender.

Add what you learned to script and to step (Figure 4–30).

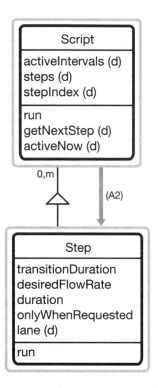

Figure 4–30: Adding to script and step.

Work the message from step to lane

Work the message from the sender's perspective:

> I send a message to a lane, telling it to adjust its flow.
>
> Any arguments? Yes: flow rate, transition duration, duration, only when requested.
>
> But which lane do I send the message to? I need to know which lane that is.

Then work the message from the receiver's perspective:

> Someone just told me to adjust my flow rate over a transition duration to a new rate, and stay there for a given duration.

Working this interaction doesn't add anything new. However, it does corroborate earlier design additions to the model.

Work the message from lane to lane

> I tell each of my crossing lanes to close itself.
> I adjust my current flow rate to the desired flow rate.
> I wait for the desired duration.

Now put it all together (Figure 4–31).

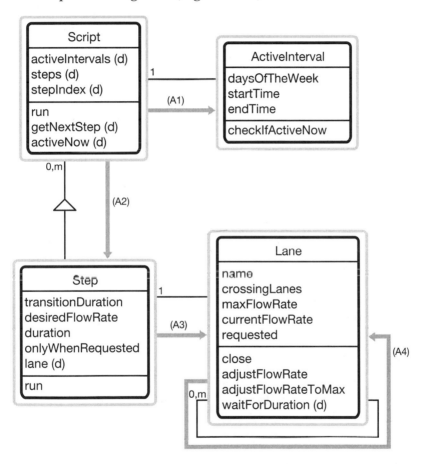

Figure 4–31: The OOA/OOD model at this point.

OOP—THE PROBLEM DOMAIN COMPONENT: SMALLTALK

You're ready to start building the problem domain component classes in Smalltalk.

What order should you build the classes in?

Apply the "backward through the script" principle. Build the classes in this order: lane, step, active interval, and sequence.

The Lane Class

Add a class and its instance variables

Start by adding the lane class. It has five problem domain variables and one simulation variable.

```
Model subclass: #Lane
    instanceVariableNames: 'name currentFlowRate
            maxFlowRate crossingLanes requested
            laneRequester '
    classVariableNames: ''
    poolDictionaries: ''
    category: 'Traffic Flow'
```

The "laneRequester" instance variable holds an object that is a random-number generator; you'll use it to simulate lane requests.

Add initialization

Initialize a lane object.

Lane methodsFor: 'initialize-release'

initialize
```
    laneRequester := Random new.
    requested := false.
    crossingLanes := OrderedCollection new.
    currentFlowRate := 0.
    maxFlowRate := 0.
    name := String new
```

Add attribute accessors

You can do this one yourself! Add read and write accessors. Be sure to notify dependents of a flow rate change; use the symbol "#currentFlowRate."

Add connection accessors

The "crossing lanes" variable holds the connections to the crossing lanes. Define connection accessors for adding or removing a connection to crossing lane:

Lane methodsFor: 'connections'

connectToCrossingLane: aLane
```
    crossingLanes add: aLane
```

disconnectWithCrossingLane: aLane
```
    crossingLanes remove: aLane ifAbsent: []
```

Add object creation

By now, you should know how to do this one in your sleep. Here it goes:

```
Lane class methodsFor: 'instance creation'

new
    ^super new initialize
```

Add the "adjust flow rate" methods

"I'm a lane. I adjust my flow rate." Here's how:

> adjust flow rate (desired flow rate, transition duration,
>   duration, only when requested).
>   if I'm told to run only when requested,
>   and I'm not, I'm done.
>   Tell each of my crossing lanes to close itself over the
>   transition duration.
>   Set my flow to the desired flow rate,
>   using whichever is less:
>   the desired flow rate
>   my maximum flow rate.
>   Wait for the duration.

The closing methods

You need to tell each lane just to go ahead and close. But you can still do this gradually. How?

> Tell each crossing lane to partially close, cutting
>   its flow rate by some reduced amount
>   for part of the transition duration.
>   Tell each crossing lane to close itself completely.
>   Wait for the remaining part of the transition duration.

For example: "As a lane, when someone tells me to close myself, I cut the flow rate by half, wait for the transition duration, and close."

```
Lane methodsFor: 'rate adjustment'

closeCrossingLanesFor: transitionDuration

    | statusMsg |
statusMsg := 'I"m closing my crossing lanes in ',
        transitionDuration printString, ' seconds.'.
    self printStatusMsg: statusMsg.
    crossingLanes do: [:aLane | aLane cutFlowRateInHalf].
```

```
    self waitFor: transitionDuration / 2.
    crossingLanes do: [:aLane | aLane close].
    self waitFor: transitionDuration / 2
```

cutFlowRateInHalf
```
    self currentFlowRate: currentFlowRate / 2
```

close
```
    self currentFlowRate: 0.
    self printStatusMsg: 'I''m closed.'
```

And for good measure:

Lane methodsfor: 'rate adjustment'

open
```
    self currentFlowRate: maxFlowRate.
    self printStatusMsg: 'I''m open.'
```

Both open and close use this:

printStatusMsg: statusMsg

```
    Transcript cr; show: name, '.'; space; space.
    Transcript show: statusMsg; cr
```

The "cut flow rate in half" method is added to fit the design within the limitations imposed by a sequential architecture.

The waiting method

Lane methodsFor: 'rate adjustment'

waitFor: durationInSeconds
```
    (Delay forSeconds: durationInSeconds) wait
```

This method creates a delay object that knows about a specific duration. Then it tells that delay object to wait.

The "adjust flow rate" method itself

Your lane is now ready to respond to the adjust flow rate message. Define the overall methods:

Lane methodsFor: 'rate adjustment'

adjustFlowRateTo: desiredRate **transitionFor:**
```
        transitionDuration duration: aDuration
    self closeCrossingLanesFor: transitionDuration.
    self currentFlowRate: (desiredRate min: maxFlowRate).
```

```
    self waitFor: aDuration.
    ^true

adjustFlowRateTo: desiredRate transitionFor:
        transitionDuration duration: aDuration
        onlyWhenRequested: onlyWhenRequested
    (onlyWhenRequested and: [self requested not])
      ifTrue: [^false].
    ^self
      adjustFlowRateTo: desiredRate
        transitionFor: transitionDuration
        duration: aDuration

adjustFlowRateToMax: transitionDuration duration:
        aDuration onlyWhenRequested: onlyWhenRequested
    (onlyWhenRequested and: [self requested not])
      ifTrue: [^false].
    ^self
      adjustFlowRateTo: maxFlowRate
        transitionFor: transitionDuration
        duration: aDuration
```

Run the code

One lane is kind of ho-hum. Go for two!
Set up two lanes that cross each other:

```
| laneA laneB |
laneA := Lane new.
laneB := Lane new.
laneA connectToCrossingLane:  laneB.
laneB connectToCrossingLane:  laneA
```

Tell one lane to immediately open itself to its maximum flow rate.

```
laneB open
```

Tell the other lane to adjust its flow rate to max:

```
laneA adjustFlowRateToMax: 2 duration: 5
        onlyWhenRequested: false
```

Next, add a method so "as a lane, I display my current flow rate whenever I change it."

Lane methodsFor: 'demo'

```
printFlowRate: flowRate duration: duration
    | newRate |
    newRate := flowRate min: maxFlowRate.
    Transcript cr; show: self name,'.'; space.
    Transcript space; show: 'I"m adjusting to ', newRate
          printString.
    Transcript show: ' for ', duration printString.
    Transcript show: ' seconds.'
```

(Note that to get a single quotation mark within a string, use a single quotation mark immediately followed by another one.)
Finally, add this expression:

```
self printFlowRate: desiredRate duration: aDuration
```

to the "adjustFlowRate: transitionFor: duration: " method. Now do it.

```
| laneA laneB |
laneA := Lane new maxFlowRate: 40; name: 'Lane A'.
laneB := Lane new maxFlowRate: 40; name: 'Lane B'.
laneA connectToCrossingLane:  laneB.
laneB connectToCrossingLane:  laneA.
laneB open.
laneA adjustFlowRateToMax: 2 duration: 5
        onlyWhenRequested: false
```

On the system transcript, you should see something like this:

Lane B
I'm open.

Lane A
I'm closing my crossing lanes in 5 seconds.

Lane A
I'm adjusting my current flow rate to 40
for a duration of 5 seconds.

Add the "simulate lane requests" methods

First, write out a scenario script for lane requests:

> I'm a lane.
> > From time to time, someone might request me.
> > I need to remember that I've been requested; I set my "requested" variable to true.

I also need to be able to clear requests.

Add these two methods:

```
Lane methodsFor: 'lane requests'
```

request
```
    self requested: true
```

```
Lane methodsFor: 'lane requests'
```

clearRequests
```
    self requested: false
```

Now consider how to simulate lane requests:

> I'm a lane.
>> I can simulate receiving requests with my "lane requester," which is really a random-number generator object.
>> When I check if I have any waiting requests, my "lane requester" will simulate a random yes/no response.

```
Lane methodsFor: 'simulating'
```

getAnyWaitingRequests
```
    laneRequester next > 0.5 ifTrue: [self request]
```

And consider when the lane is no longer being requested:

> I'm a lane.
>> I reset my "requested" variable right at the end of one of my "adjust flow rate" services.

Run the Code

So how many times does a lane look before it finds that it has been requested? Try out the simulation and see for yourself.

```
| laneA messageCount |
laneA := Lane new.
messageCount := 0.
[laneA requested not]
    whileTrue:
        [messageCount := messageCount + 1.
        laneA getAnyWaitingRequests].
Transcript cr; show: 'Messages sent:  ', messageCount
        printString
```

Take a look at this code. It sends the message "whileTrue:" to the block:

```
[laneA requested not]
```

As long as the block evaluates to true, the block executes the argument following "whileTrue:"

```
[messageCount := messageCount + 1.
laneA getAnyWaitingRequests]
```

When you try it out, you'll see something like this in the transcript window:

Messages sent: 7

The Step Class

Add a class and its instance variables

```
Model subclass: #Step
    instanceVariableNames: 'transitionDuration
            desiredFlowRate duration
            onlyWhenRequested lane '
    classVariableNames: ''
    poolDictionaries: ''
    category: 'Traffic Flow'
```

Add initialization

```
Step methodsFor: 'initialize-release'
```

initialize
```
    transitionDuration := 0.
    desiredFlowRate := 0.
    duration := 0.
    onlyWhenRequested := false
```

Add attribute accessors

Add read and write accessors for the problem domain variables.
Plus, for convenience, add an accessor that sets all four variables at once.

flowRate: aFlowRate **transition:** aTransitionDuration
        duration: aDuration **onlyWhenRequested:** aBoolean
    self desiredFlowRate: aFlowRate.

```
self transitionDuration: aTransitionDuration.
self duration: aDuration.
self onlyWhenRequested: aBoolean
```

Add connection accessors

Add the connection accessors.

Step methodsFor: *'connections'*

connectToLane: aLane
    lane := aLane

lane
    ^lane

Add object creation

Do it.

Add the run methods

"I'm a step. I run myself." Here's how:

> If my desired flow rate is "maximum," then I tell my lane
>   to adjust to its maximum flow rate
> else
>   I tell my lane to adjust to my desired flow rate.

The alternative? Well, you could ask each lane whether or not it's been requested. Then you could ask each lane what its maximum flow rate is. And finally, you could send a message to do what you want it to do.

Such an approach violates encapsulation. And the "don't expect me to do all the work" and the "more than just a data hider" principles. So what? Are you going to be struck by a bolt of lightning? Nope. But what happens is this: step ends up knowing too much about the internal details of lane. Step and lane get entangled together. And that decreases understandability, testability, reusability, extensibility, and maintainability. Ugh!

The "don't butt into someone else's business" principle. As an object, I don't butt into another object's business, sending it a message to peek at its values and then another message to get the real work done. Instead, I just send one message, telling the object what I want it to do (let it check its own status).

The "desired rate is max" method

Here's what it looks like in Smalltalk, using a symbol to represent the desire for maximum flow rate:

```
Step methodsFor: 'testing'
```

desiredFlowRateIsMax
```
^desiredFlowRate = #maxFlow
```

The run method itself

```
Step methodsFor: 'running'
```

run
```
self desiredFlowRateIsMax
  ifTrue: [
    ^lane
      adjustFlowRateToMax: transitionDuration
      duration: duration
      onlyWhenRequested: onlyWhenRequested]
  ifFalse: [
    ^lane
      adjustFlowRateTo: desiredFlowRate
      transitionFor: transitionDuration
      duration: duration
      onlyWhenRequested: onlyWhenRequested]
```

Run the code

Run, step, run. Run a step and a corresponding lane.

Build a step with a 5-second duration and a "#maxFlow" desired flow rate. Connect that step to a lane. Then tell the step to run.

```
| laneA step |
laneA := Lane new name: 'Lane A'.
laneA maxFlowRate: 25.
step := Step new.
step flowRate: #maxFlow  transition: 4 duration: 5
     onlyWhenRequested: false.
step connectToLane: laneA.
step run
```

On the system transcript, you should see something like this:

Lane A. I'm adjusting to 25 for 5 seconds.

What's next?

You've completed the lane and the step classes, but there's more to traffic flow than lanes and steps. Onward! To script!

But wait. Script sends messages to both active interval and step. Both messages are part of this thread of execution.

As long as you're working backward through the script, do active interval. Then script.

The Active Interval Class

Time for time

In Smalltalk, you can get today's date and time by sending a message to the time class:

```
Time dateAndTimeNow
```

A time object is an array with the date (the first element) and the time (the second element).

You can create a time object for a specific time. For example, to create a time object for 90 seconds after midnight, use this:

```
Time readFrom: ('12:01:30 am' readStream).
```

Or this:

```
Time fromSeconds: 90
```

You can add times:

```
| time1 time2 time3 |
time1 := Time readFrom: ('12:01:30 am' readStream).
time2 := Time fromSeconds: 90.
time3 := time1 addTime: time2
```

subtract times:

```
time2 subtractTime: time1
```

and even compare times:

```
time3 > time1
```

Add a class and its instance variables

```
Model subclass: #ActiveInterval
    instanceVariableNames: 'daysOfWeek startTime
        endTime '
    classVariableNames: ''
```

```
poolDictionaries: ''
category: 'Traffic Flow'
```

Add initialization

Add initialization:

ActiveInterval methodsFor: 'initialize-release'

initialize
```
daysOfWeek := OrderedCollection new.
startTime := Time readFrom: '12:00 am' readStream.
endTime := Time readFrom: '11:59 pm' readStream
```

Add attribute accessors

Add read and write accessors for the problem domain variables.
The days of week attribute is a collection of integers:

1 Monday
2 Tuesday
3 Wednesday
4 Thursday
5 Friday
6 Saturday
7 Sunday

Add a convenient accessor method for adding days to the days
of the week collection:

ActiveInterval methodsFor: 'accessing'

startDayIndex: dayIndex1 **endDayIndex:** dayIndex2
     byStep: stepInteger
```
"Store the integers from dayIndex1 to dayIndex2 by
     stepInteger in the days of week collection."
dayIndex1
  to: dayIndex2
  by: stepInteger
  do: [:index | daysOfWeek add: index]
```

Add some other convenient accessors, for setting days of the
week. For example:

```
ActiveInterval methodsFor: 'accessing'
```

forMWF
```
^self
   startDayIndex: 1
   endDayIndex: 5
   byStep: 2
```

forToday
```
^self
   startDayIndex: Date today weekdayIndex
   endDayIndex: Date today weekdayIndex
   byStep: 1
```

Add object creation

Do it.

Add a "check if active now" method

"I'm an active interval. I check myself to see if I'm active now." Here's how to get the job done:

> I'm active if
> (days of the week includes today's day of the week)
> and
> (start time < now < end time)
> otherwise I'm inactive.

The "contains day" method

Does the days of the week collection include today's day of the week?

Date objects know their weekday index—the same indexing scheme (1 to 7) that you've already applied.

You can send a message to a date object and ask it for its weekday index:

```
anIndex := date weekdayIndex
```

Add a supporting method to see if an interval contains a specific day of the week index:

```
ActiveInterval methodsFor: 'testing'
```

containsDay: weekdayIndex
```
^daysOfWeek includes: weekdayIndex
```

The time method

Add a supporting method for converting a time name into an object of the class time with the corresponding internal time value:

ActiveInterval methodsFor: 'converting'

```
startTime: hourName1 endTime: hourName2
    self startTime: (Time readFrom: hourName1 readStream).
    self endTime: (Time readFrom: hourName2 readStream)
```

The "before time" and "after time" methods

ActiveInterval methodsFor: 'comparing'

```
afterTime: aTime
    ^startTime > aTime
```

```
beforeTime: aTime
    ^endTime < aTime
```

The "check if active now" method itself

ActiveInterval methodsFor: 'testing'

```
checkIfActiveNow
    | dateAndTimeArray |
    dateAndTimeArray := Time dateAndTimeNow.
    ^(self containsDay: (dateAndTime at: 1) weekdayIndex)
        and: [self containsTime: (dateAndTime at: 2)]
```

Run the Code

Make an active interval for today, with start time equal to now and end time equal to now plus 2 minutes. Check if it is active now.

```
| interval1 |
interval1 := ActiveInterval new forToday.
interval1 startTime: (Time now).
interval1 endTime: (Time now addTime: (Time fromSeconds:
120)).
interval1 checkIfActiveNow
    ifTrue: [Transcript cr; show: 'Yes, I"m active now.']
    ifFalse: [Transcript cr; show: 'No, I"m not active now.']
```

And on the transcript window,

Yes, I'm active now.

Increase the start and end times.

```
interval1 startTime: (Time now addTime: (Time fromSeconds:
    120)).
interval1 endTime: (Time now addTime: (Time fromSeconds:
    240)).
interval1 checkIfActiveNow
  ifTrue: [Transcript cr; show: 'Yes, I"m active now.']
  ifFalse: [Transcript cr; show: 'No, I"m not active now.']
```

And on the transcript window,

No, I'm not active now.

The Script Class

Finally, you're ready to build the script class.

Add a class and its instance variables

```
Model subclass: #Script
    instanceVariableNames: 'activeIntervals steps stepIndex '
    classVariableNames: ''
    poolDictionaries: ''
    category: 'Traffic Flow'
```

Add initialization

```
Script methodsFor: 'initialize-release'
```

initialize
```
    self initializeActiveIntervals.
    self initializeConnections
```

initializeConnections
```
    stepIndex := 1.
    steps := OrderedCollection new
```

initializeActiveIntervals
```
    | interval |
    activeIntervals := OrderedCollection new.
    interval := ActiveInterval new forToday.
    interval startTime: '8:00am' endTime: '12:00pm'.
    activeIntervals add: interval
```

Add attribute accessors

Add read and write accessors.
But don't add accessors for the step index (keep it private).

Add connection accessors

Add the connection accessors (just like before), this time for steps and for active intervals.

Add object creation

Do it.

Add the run methods

"I'm a script. I run myself. And I keep doing this same old thing."
Here's how:

> look for an active interval that's active now
> get the next step
> run the next step
> increment the step index

The "check if active now" method

```
checkIfActiveNow
    "Tell the active intervals collection to detect if
        any of its members are active now."

    | activeOne |
    activeOne := activeIntervals
        detect: [:anInterval | anInterval checkIfActiveNow]
        ifNone: [nil].
    ^activeOne notNil
```

The "get next step" method

```
Script methodsFor: 'private'
```

```
getNextStep
    ^steps at: stepIndex
```

The "run next step" method

```
Script methodsFor: 'scheduling'
```

```
runNextStep
    self runStep: self getNextStep
```

```
runStep: aStep
   aStep run.
   self incrementStepIndex
```

The "increment step index" method

Program it, using a wraparound on the step index.

```
Script methodsFor: 'private'
```

incrementStepIndex
```
   | newValue |
   stepIndex = steps size
        ifTrue: [newValue := 1]
        ifFalse: [newValue := stepIndex + 1].
   stepIndex := newValue
```

Note that the starting index for arrays is 1.
You could also write the "ifTrue: ifFalse:" statement this way:

```
stepIndex := (stepIndex = steps size
        ifTrue: [1]
        ifFalse: [stepIndex + 1])
```

but the first approach seems easier to read and understand.

About supporting methods

You've built a number of methods, to get a number of little things done.

- ✔ look for an active interval that's active now
- ✔ get the next step
- ✔ run the next step
- ✔ increment the step index

Ah. So many little methods. Why?
Here's the principle:

The "I get by with a little help from my friends" principle. Methods that get help from little methods that do one thing, and one thing well, facilitate reuse.

Here's how.
Suppose that you want to inherit a substantial behavior, *except* that some small piece of it has changed.

If that code was written as one big blob, the best you can do is cut-and-paste for a reuse mechanism. That requires redundant code. And that requires extra effort when you test and maintain a system. Ugh! Barf!

But if that code was written with small, single-minded methods, then you have a fine granularity of selection over that which you inherit as-is and that which you redefine for yourself. And that's wonderful because you are much more likely to be able to apply inheritance as your reuse mechanism.

An example? Suppose that at some future time—next week, next month, or next year—you need to add a specialization of script. And perhaps it's exactly the same as script, except that this time you want to use a different way to determine the next step. With what you've done here (using little methods), you only need to redefine one little method, rather than cut-and-paste and redo all the functionality of script.

The run method itself

```
Script methodsFor: 'stepping'
```

run

```
    [self checkIfActiveNow] whileTrue: [self runNextStep]
```

Run the code

Create two lanes. Set their maximum flow rate values. Connect them so they cross each other. Open one lane.

Set up two steps, each with a desired flow rate of "#maxFlow." Connect one step to one lane; connect the other step to the other lane.

Create a script. Connect a script to a step. Tell the script to run the next step. And again, tell the script to run the next step.

```
| laneA script laneB stepA stepB |
laneA := Lane new name: 'Lane A'.
laneB := Lane new name: 'Lane B'.
laneA maxFlowRate: 25.
laneB maxFlowRate: 35.
laneA connectToCrossingLane: laneB.
laneB connectToCrossingLane: laneA.
laneB open.
```

```
stepA := Step new
        flowRate: #maxFlow
        transition: 2
        duration: 4
        onlyWhenRequested: false.
stepB := Step new
        flowRate: #maxFlow
        transition: 3
        duration: 6
        onlyWhenRequested: false.
stepA connectToLane: laneA.
stepB connectToLane: laneB.
script := Script new.
script connectToStep: stepA.
script connectToStep: stepB.
script runNextStep.
script runNextStep.
Transcript cr; show: 'Happy trails.'
```

On the transcript window, you should see something like the following:

Lane B. I'm open.

Lane A. I'm closing my crossing lanes in 3 seconds.

Lane A. I'm adjusting to 25 for 4 seconds.

Lane B. I'm closing my crossing lanes in 2 seconds.

Lane B. I'm adjusting to 35 for 6 seconds.

Happy trails.

Run the Code—Four Lane Demo

Build a flow management demo for a four lane intersection (Figure 4–32).

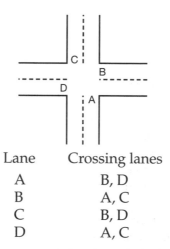

Lane	Crossing lanes
A	B, D
B	A, C
C	B, D
D	A, C

Figure 4–32: A four lane intersection.

Use a sequential script.

Step	Transition Duration	Duration	Desired Flow Rate	Only When Requested	For Lane
1	3	0	max	no	A
2	0	6	max	no	C
3	3	0	max	no	B
4	0	6	max	no	D

Where to put demo methods

Where do you put the demo methods? Use class methods to implement demo needs across a collection of objects in a class. Use instance methods to implement demo needs that apply to just a single object in a class.

The plan

Here's the plan:

the script demo class method:
  create the lanes
  create the steps
  create the script
  tell a script to start its demo
the script demo instance method:
  create a short active interval
  tell myself to run
  ring a bell when I'm done

Create the lanes

This is a fitting job for a class method in the lane class.

Lane class methodsFor: 'demo'

fourLaneDemo
```
| laneA laneB laneC laneD |
laneA := Lane new maxFlowRate: 25; name: 'Lane A'.
laneB := Lane new maxFlowRate: 35; name: 'Lane B'.
laneC := Lanc new maxFlowRate: 25; name: 'Lane C'.
laneD := Lane new maxFlowRate: 35; name: 'Lane D'.
laneB open.
laneD open.
laneA connectToCrossingLane:  laneB;
       connectToCrossingLane:  laneD.
laneC connectToCrossingLane:  laneB;
       connectToCrossingLane:  laneD.
laneB connectToCrossingLane:  laneA;
       connectToCrossingLane:  laneC.
laneD connectToCrossingLane:  laneA;
       connectToCrossingLane:  laneC.
^OrderedCollection
       with: laneA
       with: laneB
       with: laneC
       with: laneD
```

Create the steps

Add a method to the step class to create steps for paired lanes.

Step class methodsFor: 'demo'

demoStepsFor: lane1 **and:** lane2
```
| step stepCollection |
stepCollection := OrderedCollection new.
step := Step new
        flowRate: #maxFlow
        transition: Step demoTransitionDuration
        duration: 0
        onlyWhenRequested: false.
step connectToLane: lane1.
stepCollection add: step.
step := Step new
        flowRate: #maxFlow
        transition: 0
```

```
                duration: Step demoStepDuration
                onlyWhenRequested: false.
        step connectToLane: lane2.
        stepCollection add: step.
        ^stepCollection
```

demoStepDuration
```
    ^6
```

demoTransitionDuration
```
    ^3
```

Create the script

Create a method that adds a collection of steps to a script.

Script methodsFor: 'demo'

addStepConnections: stepCollection
```
    stepCollection do: [:aStep | self connectToStep: aStep]
```

Finally, you're ready to add the method that creates a script for the four lanes.

Script class methodsFor: 'demo'

fourLaneDemo: fourLanes
```
    | laneA laneC laneD laneB stepsAC stepsBD script |
    laneA := fourLanes at: 1.
    laneB := fourLanes at: 2.
    laneC := fourLanes at: 3.
    laneD := fourLanes at: 4.
    stepsAC := Step demoStepsFor: laneA and: laneC.
    stepsBD := Step demoStepsFor: laneB and: laneD.
    script := Script new.
    script addStepConnections: stepsAC.
    script addStepConnections: stepsBD.
    ^script
```

Create a short active interval

Add a method so that "as an active interval, I know how to set myself up as a short active interval."

ActiveInterval methodsFor: 'demo'

shortActiveInterval
```
    "Make me a two-minute interval for today"
```

```
startTime := Time now.
endTime := Time now addTime: (Time fromSeconds: 120).
self forToday
```

Add a corresponding script instance method, to connect a script with a the short active interval:

```
Script methodsFor: 'demo'
```

demoShortTimePeriod
```
self connectToActiveInterval: ActiveInterval new
shortInterval
```

Put together the script demo instance method

Add this method:

```
Script methodsFor: 'demo'
```

startDemo
```
self demoShortTimePeriod.
self run.
Screen default ringBell.
Transcript show: 'Happy trails.'
```

Put together the script demo class method

Add this method, so you can tell the script class to start a demo:

```
Script class methodsFor: 'demos'
```

demo
```
| lanes script |
lanes := Lane fourLaneDemo.
script := Script fourLaneDemo: lanes.
script startDemo
```

Try it out

You've done the work.
Now try it out.
Ready? Set? Go!

```
Script demo
```

Look! There on the transcript... you should see something like the following:

Lane B. I'm open.
Lane D. I'm open.
Lane A. I'm closing my crossing lanes in 3 seconds.
Lane C. I'm closing my crossing lanes in 0 seconds.
Lane A. I'm adjusting to 25 for 0 seconds.
Lane C. I'm adjusting to 25 for 6 seconds.
Lane B. I'm closing my crossing lanes in 3 seconds.
Lane D. I'm closing my crossing lanes in 0 seconds.
Lane B. I'm adjusting to 35 for 0 seconds.
Lane D. I'm adjusting to 35 for 6 seconds.
Lane A. I'm closing my crossing lanes in 3 seconds.
Lane C. I'm closing my crossing lanes in 0 seconds.

OOP—PROBLEM DOMAIN COMPONENT: C++

Choose the order in which you'll define your classes. Use the "backward through the script" principle: lane, step, active interval, and script.

The Lane Class

About declaring constructors with default arguments

Declare a basic constructor.

```
Lane();
```

Next, declare some constructors for convenience, ones that allow for a way to set an initial value for name, default rate, or both:

```
Lane(String a_name);
Lane(float a_max_flow_rate);
Lane(float a_max_flow_rate, String a_name);
```

Rather than declare all four constructors, you can take a short cut. Declare just two constructors with some default arguments.

```
Lane(float a_max_rate);
Lane(String a_name = "", float a_max_rate = 0.0);
```

When you call a constructor that has default arguments, it uses a default value for each missing argument.

Here are all the different ways you can create a lane using those two constructors:

```
Lane my_lane(35.0);        // No defaults
Lane my_lane;              // Defaults for a_name and
                           // a_max_rate.
```

```
Lane my_lane("Lane A", 35.0);   // No defaults
Lane my_lane("Lane A");         // Defaults for a_max_rate.
```

Be careful about how you declare a constructor using default arguments. Here's the catch: you can't have an argument *without* a default appearing in the argument list after an argument *with* a default:

```
Lane(String a_name = "", float max_rate);
     // No way! Not allowed
```

So, put arguments with defaults in the back of the argument list, like so:

```
Lane(float max_rate, String a_name = "");    // Fine!
```

About declaring other member functions with default arguments

You can use default arguments in any member function. For example, consider the four adjust flow rate services in the OOD model:

> adjust flow rate
> adjust flow rate only when requested
> adjust flow rate to max
> adjust flow rate to max only when requested

Using default arguments, write just one member function to handle all four services:

```
Boolean adjust_flow_rate(int transition_duration,
    int duration,
    float desired_flow_rate = MAX_FLOW_RATE,
    Boolean only_when_requested = false);
```

This one member function takes care of all four options. For example:

```
// Adjust flow rate.
adjust_flow_rate(a_transition_duration, a_duration,
      a_desired_rate);

// Adjust flow rate only when requested.
adjust_flow_rate(a_transition_duration, a_duration,
        a_desired_rate, only_when_requested_flag);
// Adjust flow rate to max.
adjust_flow_rate(a_transition_duration, a_duration);
```

```
// Adjust flow rate to max only when requested.
adjust_flow_rate(a_transition_duration, a_duration,
     MAX_FLOW_RATE, only_when_requested_flag);
```

With this "one member does it all" approach, you must define and use a flag (a symbolic constant, "MAX_FLOW_RATE") to tell a lane object to adjust to its own maximum flow rate. And that means that other objects must know about the flag in order to tell a lane to adjust its flow rate to maximum. Yuck!

A better way? Use two member functions, instead:

```
Boolean adjust_flow_rate(float desired_flow_rate,
     int transition_duration,
     int duration,
     Boolean only_when_requested = false);

Boolean adjust_flow_rate_to_max(int transition_duration,
     int duration,
     Boolean only_when_requested = false);
```

About the lane list

For implementing the crossing lanes collection, use an ordered list parameterized over lane pointers. Declare a "lane list" as a synonym for this parameterized list.

```
// Forward reference
class Lane;

typedef Ordered_List<Lane*> Lane_List;
```

Declare the class

Using the OOA/OOD model, declare the lane class:

```
class Lane {
public:

    // Constructors/destructors
    Lane(float max_rate);
    Lane(String a_name = "", float max_rate = 0.0);
    ~Lane() { }

    // Implementors
    // Rate adjustment
    Boolean adjust_flow_rate(float desired_flow_rate,
```

```
        int transition_duration,
        int duration,
        Boolean only_when_requested = false);
    Boolean adjust_flow_rate_to_max(int transition_duration,
        int duration,
        Boolean only_when_requested = false);

    void cut_flow_rate_in_half();

    // Safety precautions
    void close_crossing_lanes(int transition_duration);

// Accessors
    float get_current_flow_rate()
        { return current_flow_rate; }
    void set_current_flow_rate(float new_value)
        { current_flow_rate = new_value; }

    float get_max_flow_rate() { return max_flow_rate; }
    void set_max_flow_rate(float new_value)
        { max_flow_rate = new_value; }

    Lane_List& get_crossing_lanes()
            { return crossing_lanes; }

    void connect_to_crossing_lane(Lane& new_lane);
    Boolean disconnect_with_crossing_lane(Lane& aLane);

    Boolean get_requested() { return requested; }
    void set_requested(Boolean new_value)
        { requested = new_value; }

    String get_name(){ return name; }
    void set_name(String new_name){ name = new_name; }
private:

    // Data members
    float current_flow_rate;
    float max_flow_rate;
    Lane_List& crossing_lanes;
    Boolean requested;

    String name;
};
```

Wow! That's a mouthful!

Define the constructor member functions

The constructors seem a bit too large for inline definition. So define them here, instead:

```
Lane::Lane(float max_rate)
{
   current_flow_rate = 0.0;
   max_flow_rate = max_rate;
   requested = false;
}

Lane::Lane(String a_name, float max_rate)
{
   current_flow_rate = 0.0;
   max_flow_rate = max_rate;
   requested = false;
   name = a_name;
}
```

Add the insertion operator

Declare and define the overloaded insertion operator, making it easy for a lane to print itself. Make it a friend of the lane class; then it can access the data members directly.

Declare it:

```
// Overloaded operators
friend ostream& operator<< (ostream& os, Lane& a_Lane);
```

And define it:

```
ostream& operator<< (ostream& os, Lane& a_lane)
{
   os << endl
      << "Current flow rate:  " << a_lane.current_flow_rate
      << endl
      << "Max flow rate:  " << a_lane.max_flow_rate
      << endl
      << "Requested:  " << a_lane.requested
      << endl;
   return os;
}
```

Define the "adjust flow rate" member functions

"I'm a lane. I adjust my flow rate." Here's how:

> adjust flow rate (desired flow rate, transition duration,
> duration, only when requested).
> If I'm told to run only when requested, and I'm not,
> I'm done.
> Tell each of my crossing lanes to close itself over the
> transition duration.
> Set my flow to the desired flow rate,
> using whichever is less:
> the desired flow rate
> my maximum flow rate.
> Wait for the duration.

The closing member functions

With a synchronous architecture, you can't just tell each cross-ing lane to go do its thing and let you know when it is done. But you *can* step each crossing lane down to its close.

Here, close the crossing lanes by closing halfway, waiting half of the transition duration, closing the rest of the way, and waiting for the rest of the transition duration.

```
void Lane::close_crossing_lanes(int transition_duration)
{
    Lane* next_lane;
    cout << name << ". " << "I'm closing my crossing lanes
            in " << transition_duration << " seconds." << endl;
    crossing_lanes.reset();

    while (!crossing_lanes.end_of_list())
        {
        next_lane = crossing_lanes.current();
        next_lane->cut_flow_rate_in_half();
        crossing_lanes++; }
    this->wait(transition_duration / 2);
    crossing_lanes.reset();
    while (!crossing_lanes.end_of_list())
        {
        next_lane = crossing_lanes.current();
        next_lane->close();
        crossing_lanes++; }
    this->wait(transition_duration / 2);
}
```

```
void Lane::cut_flow_rate_in_half()
{
   current_flow_rate /= 2.0;
}
```

Add the open and close member functions.
Declare them.

```
// Rate adjustment
void open();
void close();
```

And define them.

```
void Lane::open()
{
   cout << endl << name << endl << "I'm open." << endl;

   current_flow_rate = max_flow_rate;

}
void Lane::close()
{
   cout << endl << name << endl <<
         "I'm closed." << endl;

   current_flow_rate = 0;
}
```

The "min" member function

C++ does not include a min (or max) member function as a part of the language itself. You could use a macro, but you don't get type checking; that's just not recommended in C++. A better solution: use a template and define a member function with a parameterized type.

Define it inline:

```
template<class Type>
inline Type min(Type magnitude1, Type magnitude2)
{
   return(magnitude1 < magnitude2 ? magnitude1 :
         magnitude2)
}
```

Great. This will work for any type that can be compared using the operator, "<."

Also, notice the shorthand notation for if-then-else.[4]

The wait member function

Add a wait member function. Use the delay library function[5]; it expects milliseconds, so multiply the duration (in seconds) by 1,000. Declare it; define it inline:

```
void wait(int duration_in_seconds)
   { delay(duration_in_seconds * 1000); }
```

The "adjust flow rate" member function itself

Define the "adjust flow rate" member function.

```
Boolean Lane::adjust_flow_rate(float desired_rate,
            int transition_duration,
            int duration,
            Boolean only_when_requested)
{
   if (only_when_requested && (!this->get_requested()))
      return false;

   this->close_crossing_lanes(transition_duration);
   current_flow_rate = min(desired_rate, max_flow_rate);
   this->wait(duration);
   return true;
}
```

Here's the adjust rate to max member function.

```
Boolean Lane::adjust_flow_rate_to_max
            (int transition_duration,
            int duration,
            Boolean only_when_requested)
{
   return (this->adjust_flow_rate(max_flow_rate,
            transition_duration,
            duration,
            only_when_requested));
}
```

---

[4]The statement: `conditional-test ? result1 : result2` means if the conditional test is true (non-zero) the statement evaluates to result1 else result2.

[5]Some C++ libraries contain a sleep function. The sleep function expects seconds (rather than milliseconds).

Run the code

Declare a "print flow change" member function in the class declaration:

```
// Demo
void print_flow_change(float desired_flow_rate, int
        duration);
```

And then define it:

```
void Lane::print_flow_change(float desired_flow_rate, int
        duration)
{
    cout << endl << name << ".  " << "I'm adjusting to "
        << desired_flow_rate
        << " for " << duration
        << " seconds."
        << endl;
}
```

Next, use it in the adjust flow rate member function:

```
Boolean Lane::adjust_flow_rate(float desired_flow_rate,
            int transition_duration,
            int duration,
            Boolean only_when_requested)
{
if (only_when_requested && (!this->get_requested()))
    return false;

this->close_crossing_lanes(transition_duration);
current_flow_rate = min(desired_flow_rate, max_flow_rate);
this->print_flow_change(current_flow_rate, duration);
this->wait(duration);
return true;
}
```

Now try it out:

```
int main ()
{
    Lane lane_A("Lane A", 25);
    lane_A.adjust_flow_rate_to_max(2, 5);

    cout << endl << "Happy trails." << endl;

    return 0;
}
```

On the console you'll see something like this:

Lane A. I'm adjusting to 25 for 5 seconds.

Happy trails.

Define the "simulate lane requests" member functions

Use a random-number generator—with values between 0 and 100—to simulate a lane request.

Add an inline private member function to set it up:

```
private:
    // Simulating
    int next_random_number() { return random(100); }
```

Declare member functions to handle requests. And define two of them inline.

```
    // Lane requests
    void clear_requests() { requested = false; }
    void request() { requested = true; }
    void get_any_waiting_requests();
```

Define the "get any waiting requests" member function:

```
void Lane::get_any_waiting_requests()
{
    if (this->next_random_number() > 50)
        this->request();
}
```

Run the code

Write a main program that counts the number of times a lane looks for requests before it gets one.

```
int main ()
{
    Lane lane_A;
    int message_count = 0;

    while (!lane_A.get_requested())
        {
        message_count++;
        lane_A.get_any_waiting_requests();
        }
    cout << "I checked " << message_count <<
        " times until the lane was requested.";
```

```
    cout << endl << "Happy trails." << endl;
    return 0;
}
```

And on the console you should see something like this:

I checked 2 times until the lane was requested.

Happy trails.

You've finished the lane class! Whew! Keep up the good work.

The Step Class

Declare the class

Using the OOA/OOD model, declare the step class:

```
class Step {
public:

    // Constructors/destructors
    Step();
    Step(float flow_rate, int transition_duration,
        int step_duration, Boolean request_flag = false);
    ~Step() { }

    // Implementors
    void run();

    // Accessors
    int get_transition_duration()
        { return transition_duration; }
    void set_transition_duration(int new_value)
        { transition_duration = new_value; }

    int get_duration() { return duration; }
    void set_duration(int new_value) { duration =
            new_value; }

    float get_desired_flow_rate() { return
            desired_flow_rate; }
    void set_desired_flow_rate(float new_value);

    Boolean get_only_when_requested()
        { return only_when_requested; }
    void set_only_when_requested(Boolean new_value)
        { only_when_requested = new_value; }

    Lane& get_lane() { return *a_lane; }
```

```
void connect_to_lane(Lane& new_lane) { a_lane = &new_lane; }
```

```
private:
```

```
    // Data members
    int transition_duration;
    int duration;
    float desired_flow_rate;
    Boolean only_when_requested;
    Lane* a_lane;
    static float flow_rate_maximum;
};
```

Define the constructor member functions

The constructors seem a bit too large for inline definition. So define them here:

```
Step::Step()
{
    transition_duration = 0;
    duration = 0;
    desired_flow_rate = 0.0;
    only_when_requested = false;
}

Step::Step(float flow_rate, int a_transition_duration,
        int step_duration, Boolean request_flag)
{
    transition_duration = a_transition_duration;
    duration = step_duration;
    desired_flow_rate = flow_rate;
    only_when_requested = request_flag;
}
```

Add the insertion operator

Declare and define the overloaded insertion operator, making it easy for a step to print itself.

Declare it:

```
    // Overloaded operators
    friend ostream& operator<< (ostream& os, Step& a_step);
```

And define it:

```
ostream& operator<< (ostream& os, Step& a_step)
{
```

```
        os << "Transition duration:   "
           << a_step.transition_duration
           << endl
           << "Duration:   " << a_step.duration
           << endl
           << "Desired flow rate:   "
           << a_step.desired_flow_rate
           << endl
           << "Requested:   " << a_step.only_when_requested
           << endl
           << "Lane:   " << *a_step.a_lane
           << endl;
        return os;
    }
```

Define the run member functions

"I'm a step. I run myself." Here's how:

> If my desired flow rate is "maximum," then I tell my lane
> to adjust to its maximum flow rate
> else
> I tell my lane to adjust to my desired flow rate.

The "maximum flow rate" member functions

Add a data member representing the maximum allowable flow rate. Make it static so the value will be the same for all steps.

Declare the member in the step class:

```
    static float flow_rate_maximum;
```

Then define it outside of the class:

```
    float Step::flow_rate_maximum = 65.0;
```

Keep this value private. Add a public member function to set the desired flow rate to the maximum.

Declare it:

```
    void set_desired_flow_rate_to_max();
```

Define it:

```
    void Step::set_desired_flow_rate_to_max()
    {
        desired_flow_rate = flow_rate_maximum;
    }
```

Add a member function that tests for the maximum flow rate. First, declare it:

```
// Testing
Boolean desired_flow_rate_is_max();
```

Next, define it:

```
Boolean Step::desired_flow_rate_is_max()
{
   if (desired_flow_rate == flow_rate_maximum)
     return true;
   else
     return false;
}
```

The "run" member function itself

Define "run":

```
void Step::run()
{
   if (this->desired_flow_rate_is_max())
      a_lane->adjust_flow_rate_to_max(transition_duration,
            duration,
            only_when_requested);
   else
      a_lane->adjust_flow_rate(desired_flow_rate,
            transition_duration,
            duration,
            only_when_requested);
}
```

Run the code

Make a lane. Make a step for that lane. Run the step.

```
int main ()
{
   Lane lane_A("Lane A", 25);
   Step a_step(35, 2, 5);
   a_step.connect_to_lane(lane_A);
   a_step.run();
   cout << endl << "Happy trails." << endl;

   return 0;
}
```

And on your computer screen you should see something like this:

Lane A. I'm adjusting to 25 for 5 seconds.

Happy trails.

The lane knows its own maximum flow rate and enforces it. Nice work.

The Active Interval Class

Time out for time

An active interval knows about times and dates.

Use the date and time classes provided on the source diskette included with this book.

When referring to days of the week, use the enumeration defined in the date class file:

```
enum Weekday { sun, mon, tue, wed, thu, fri, sat };
```

Declare a weekday list as another name for an ordered list parameterized over weekdays.

```
typedef Ordered_List<Weekday> Weekday_List;
```

Declare the class

Using the OOA/OOD model, declare the active interval class:

```
class Active_Interval {
public:

    // Constructors/destructors
    Active_Interval();
    Active_Interval(int day_index1, int day_index2,
            int step);
    ~Active_Interval() { }

    // Implementors
    Boolean check_if_active_now();

    // Accessors
    Weekday_List& get_weekdays() { return days_of_the_week; }

    Time get_start_time() { return start_time; }
    void set_start_time(Time new_value)
                { start_time = new_value; }

    Time get_end_time() { return end_time; }
```

```
void set_end_time(Time new_value) { end_time =
    new_value; }

private:

    // Data members
    Weekday_List days_of_the_week;
    Time start_time;
    Time end_time;
};
```

Define the constructor member functions

```
Active_Interval::Active_Interval()
{
    Date today;
    days_of_the_week.add(today.day_of_week());
    end_time = start_time.add_time(0, 2, 0);
}

Active_Interval::Active_Interval(int day_index1,
        int day_index2, int step)
{
    for (int i = day_index1; i <= day_index2; i += step)
            days_of_the_week.add( (Weekday) i);
    end_time = start_time.add_time(0, 2, 0);
}
```

Add the insertion operator

Declare and define the insertion operator, making it easy for an active interval to print itself.

Declare it:

```
// Overloaded operators
friend ostream& operator<< (ostream& os,
        Active_Interval& an_active_interval);
```

And define it:

```
ostream& operator<< (ostream& os, Active_Interval&
        an_active_interval)
{
    os << endl << "Start Time:    "
        << an_active_interval.start_time << endl;
    os << "End Time:    " << an_active_interval.end_time
        << endl;
    return os;
}
```

Define the "check if active now" member functions

"I'm an active interval. I check myself to see if I'm active now."

I'm active if
(days of the week includes today's day of the week)
and
(start time < now < end time)
otherwise I'm inactive.

The "contains day of week" and "contains day" member functions

Add two supporting member functions to help an active interval check itself:

I need to check if I'm active on a particular
day of the week.

I need to check if I'm active on a particular date.

Here they are:

```
// Testing
Boolean contains_day_of_the_week(int weekday_index);
Boolean contains_date(Time a_time);
```

Define "contains day of the week":

```
Boolean Active_Interval::contains_day_of_the_week
  (Weekday a_weekday)
{
  return (days_of_the_week.includes(a_weekday));
}
```

Define "contains date" using "contains day of the week":

```
Boolean Active_Interval::contains_date(Date a_date)
{
  return (this->contains_day_of_the_week
    (a_date.day_of_week()));
}
```

The "before time" and "after time" member functions

First, declare two supporting member functions:

```
// Comparing
Boolean after_time(Time a_time);
Boolean before_time(Time a_time);
```

and define them:

```
Boolean Active_Interval::after_time(Time a_time)
{
   return (start_time > a_time);
}

Boolean Active_Interval::before_time(Time a_time)
{
   return (end_time < a_time);
}
```

The "contains time" member function

Now define the "contains time" member function:

```
// Testing
Boolean contains_time(Time a_time);

Boolean Active_Interval::contains_time(Time a_time)
{
   Boolean is_before_time =
          (this->before_time(time_of_day));
   Boolean is_after_time =
          (this->after_time(time_of_day));

   return (!is_before_time && !is_after_time);
}
```

The "check if active now" member function itself

Using the supporting member functions, now define the "check if active now" member function itself.

```
Boolean Active_Interval::check_if_active_now()
{
   Time current_time;   // Default constructor
                        // initializes to now.
   Date current_date;   // Default constructor
                        // initializes to today.

   Boolean contains_date =
        (this->contains_date(current_date));
   Boolean contains_time =
        (this->contains_time(current_time));
   return (contains_date && contains_time);
}
```

Run the code

Set up a demo.

Create an active interval for today and now.
Set its end time for 2 minutes after the start time.
Ask if it's active.
Next, increase the start and end time by 2 minutes each.
Ask the active interval if it's active.

Here is the main program:

```cpp
int main ()
{
    cout << "Active intervals" << endl << endl;

    Time start_time;    // Default constructors
                        // use current time.
    Time end_time;
    Active_Interval now_interval;

    // Add zero hours, two minutes, and zero seconds.
    end_time = start_time.add_time(0, 2, 0);

    now_interval.set_start_time(start_time);
    now_interval.set_end_time(end_time);

    cout << now_interval;
    if (now_interval.check_if_active_now())
            cout << "Yes, I'm active now." << endl << endl;
    else
            cout << "No, I'm not active now." << endl << endl;

    now_interval.set_start_time(end_time);
    now_interval.set_end_time(end_time.add_time(0, 2, 0));

    cout << now_interval;
    if (now_interval.check_if_active_now())
            cout << "Yes, I'm active now." << endl << endl;
    else
            cout << "No, I'm not active now." << endl << endl;

    cout << "Happy trails." << endl;

    return 0;
}
```

On the console, you should see something like this (assuming a correct time of 15:28):

Active intervals

Start Time: 15:28:55
End Time: 15:30:55

Yes, I'm active now.

Start Time: 15:30:55
End Time: 15:32:55

No, I'm not active now.

Happy trails.

The Script Class

Declare the class

Then, using the OOA/OOD model, declare the script class:

Use parameterized ordered lists for the connections between a script and its active intervals and steps. Declare names for the different types of lists:

```
typedef Ordered_List<Step*> Step_List;
typedef Ordered_List<Active_Interval*>
    Active_Interval_List;

class Script {
public:

  // Constructors/destructors
  Script() { step_index = 0; };
  ~Script(){ };

// Implementors
  // Running
  void run();

  // Accessors
  Active_Interval_List& get_active_intervals()
    { return active_intervals; }
  void connect_to_active_interval
    (Active_Interval& new_interval);

  Step_List& get_steps() { return steps; }
  void connect_to_step(Step& a_step);

  int get_step_index() { return step_index; }
  void set_step_index(int new_value)
    { step_index = new_value; }
```

```
private:

   // Data members
   Active_Interval_List active_intervals;
   Step_List steps;
   int step_index;
};
```

Define the run member functions

"I'm a script. I run myself. And I keep doing this same old thing."

look for an active interval that's active now
get the next step
run the next step
increment the step index

The "check if active now" member function

Declare it.

```
// Testing
Boolean check_if_active_now();
```

And define it.

```
Boolean Script::check_if_active_now()
{
   Active_Interval* an_active_interval;
   active_intervals.reset();
   while(!active_intervals.end_of_list())
      {
      an_active_interval = active_intervals.current();
      if (an_active_interval->check_if_active_now());
         return true;
      active_intervals++;
      }
   return false;
}
```

The "get the next step" member function

Declare it:

```
// Stepping
Step* get_next_step();
```

And define it:

```
Step* Script::get_next_step()
{
   return steps.item_at(step_index);
}
```

The "run the next step" member function

Declare the member functions which run the next step or run a specific step:

```
// Running
void run_next_step();
void run_step(Step* a_step);
```

Define them:

```
void Script::run_next_step()
{
   if (steps.size < 0)
      cout << "Sorry, no steps in current script" << endl;
   else
      this->run_step(this->get_next_step());
}

void Script::run_step(Step* a_step)
{
   a_step->run();
   this->increment_number_of_steps();
}
```

The "increment step index" member function

Declare it.

```
// Stepping
void increment_number_of_steps();
```

And define it, using a wraparound on the step index:

```
void Script::increment_number_or_steps()
{
   if (step_index == steps.size()- 1)
      step_index = 0;
   else
      step_index++;
}
```

The "run" member function itself

You've built all the supporting member functions.
Now define the run member function itself:

```
void Script::run()
{
    while (this->check_if_active_now())
        this->run_next_step();
}
```

Run the code

Create two lanes. Set their maximum flow rate values. Connect
them so they cross each other. Open one lane.

Set up two steps. Give each one a desired flow rate equal to the
maximum flow rate. Connect one step to one lane, connect the other
step to the other lane.

Create a script. Connect a script to a step. Tell the script to run
the next step. And again, tell the script to run the next step.

```
int main ()
{
    Lane lane_A("Lane A", 25);
    Lane lane_B("Lane B", 35);

    lane_A.connect_to_crossing_lane(lane_B);
    lane_B.connect_to_crossing_lane(lane_A);
    lane_B.open();

    Step step_A(0, 2, 4);
    Step step_B(0, 3, 6);

    step_A.set_desired_flow_rate_to_max();
    step_B.set_desired_flow_rate_to_max();

    step_A.connect_to_lane(lane_A);
    step_B.connect_to_lane(lane_B);

    Script a_script;
    a_script.connect_to_steps(step_A);
    a_script.connect_to_steps(step_B);

    a_script.run_next_step();
    a_script.run_next_step();
    cout << endl << "Happy trails." << endl;

    return 0;
}
```

On the console, you should see something like this:

Lane B.　I'm open.
Lane A.　I'm closing my crossing lanes in 3 seconds.
Lane A.　I'm adjusting to 25 for 4 seconds.
Lane B.　I'm closing my crossing lanes in 2 seconds.
Lane B.　I'm adjusting to 35 for 6 seconds.

Happy trails.

Run the Code—Another Four Lane Demo

Here's the plan:

> the script demo setup member function:
> 　create the lanes
> 　create the steps
> 　create the script
> 　tell the script object to start its demo
> the script demo member function:
> 　create a short active interval
> 　tell myself to run
> 　ring a bell when I'm done

Create the lanes

About lists and arrays

You've already seen how useful the parameterized ordered list is, but sometimes it's more than you need. If you have a collection with a fixed number of elements, you don't need a list that can grow dynamically. An array will do, and it comes with a lot less overhead.

The source diskette that comes with this book includes a parameterized array collection class. Here's the declaration:

```
template<class Item_Type>
class Array_Collection {

public:

   Array_Collection ();
   Array_Collection(int size);
   ~Array_Collection() { delete[] item_array; }

   void add(const Item_Type& new_item);
   void add_at(const Item_Type& new_item, int location);

   Item_Type& operator[] (int subscript);
   int size() { return array_size; }
```

```
    int tally() { return number_of_ items; }

    void reset() { position = 0; }

    int operator++ ();          // Prefix increment
    int operator++ (int);       // Postfix increment
private:

    int number_of_items;
    int array_size;
    int position;
    Item_Type* item_array;
};
```

The chief advantage of the array collection over an ordinary array is that it knows its own size and the number of items it contains. This makes iterating over the elements much simpler.

Consider an example of how to use the array collection class:

```
// Make an integer array of size 5.
Array_Collection<int> int_array(5);

int_array.add(1);          // Put 1 in next available location.
int_array.add(2);
int_array.add_at(3, 2); // Put 3 at location 2.

// Print the number of elements (3) in the array collection.
cout << "Array tally: " << my_array.tally() << endl;

// Iterate over the array collection using the operator++.
// The array returns the location of the next item,
// or -1 when the end of the items is reached.
while ((location = ++my_array) != -1)
   cout << my_array[location];
```

Nice, eh?

Use the array collection in the four lane demo. Declare a lane array to be another name for an array collection of lane pointers:

```
typedef Array_Collection<Lane*> Lane_Array;
```

Add this member function to the lane class.
Declare it:

```
// Demo
void four_lane_demo(Lane_Array& a_lane_array);
```

And define it:

```
void Lane::four_lane_demo(Lane_Array& a_lane_array)
{
```

```
Lane* lane_A = new Lane("Lane A", 25);
Lane* lane_B = new Lane("Lane B", 35);
Lane* lane_C = new Lane("Lane C", 45);
Lane* lane_D = new Lane("Lane D", 55);
lane_B->open();
lane_D->open();
lane_A->connect_to_crossing_lane(*lane_B);
lane_A->connect_to_crossing_lane(*lane_D);
lane_C->connect_to_crossing_lane(*lane_B);
lane_C->connect_to_crossing_lane(*lane_D);
lane_B->connect_to_crossing_lane(*lane_A);
lane_B->connect_to_crossing_lane(*lane_C);
lane_D->connect_to_crossing_lane(*lane_A);
lane_D->connect_to_crossing_lane(*lane_C);
a_lane_array.add(lane_A);
a_lane_array.add(lane_B);
a_lane_array.add(lane_C);
a_lane_array.add(lane_D);
}
```

Create the steps

Declare step array to be another name for an array collection of step pointers:

```
typedef Array_Collection<Step*> Step_Array;
```

Add a member function to the step class, one that creates a pair of steps and lanes.
Declare it:

```
// Demo
void demo_steps(Step_Array& step_array, Lane* lane1,
        Lane* lane2);
```

Declare and define two supporting member functions:

```
int demo_step_duration() { return 6; }
int demo_transition_duration() { return 3; }
```

Now define the "demo steps" member function:

```
void Step::demo_steps(Step_Array& step_array,
        Lane* lane1, Lane* lane2)
{
    Step* step1 = new Step(25,
        this->demo_transition_duration(),
        0);
```

```
step1->connect_to_lane(*lane1);
step_array.add(step1);
step1->set_desired_flow_rate_to_max();
Step* step2 = new Step(35,
     0,
     this->demo_step_duration()
     );
step2->connect_to_lane(*lane2);
step_array.add(step2);
step2->set_desired_flow_rate_to_max();
}
```

Create the script

Add a member function to the script class.
Declare it:

```
// Demo
void four_lane_demo(Lane_Array& a_lane_array);
```

Define it. The input for the function is an array of pointers to lanes. It creates two steps for two lanes at a time—A and C, then B and D.

```
void Script::four_lane_demo(Lane_Array& a_lane_array)
{
  Step* demo_step;
  Lane* lane_A = a_lane_array[0];
  Lane* lane_C = a_lane_array[2];
  Step_Array steps_AC(2);

  demo_step->demo_steps(steps_AC, lane_A, lane_C);
  this->connect_to_steps(*steps_AC[0]);
  this->connect_to_steps(*steps_AC[1]);
  Lane* lane_B = a_lane_array[1];
  Lane* lane_D = a_lane_array[3];
  Step_Array steps_BD(2);

  demo_step->demo_steps(steps_BD, lane_B, lane_D);
  this->connect_to_steps(*steps_BD[0]);
  this->connect_to_steps(*steps_BD[1]);
}
```

Create a short active interval

Add a member function to the script class. For the demo, a script needs to create a short active interval for its use.

Declare the member function.

```
// Demo
void demo_short_active_interval();
```

Define the member function. "I create an active interval, beginning now and ending 2 minutes from now."

```
void Script::demo_short_active_interval()
{
    Active_Interval* now_interval = new Active_Interval();
    Time start_time = now_interval->get_start_time();
    Time end_time = start_time.add_time(0, 2, 0);

    now_interval->set_end_time(end_time);
    this->connect_to_active_interval(*now_interval);
}
```

Put together the main script demo

Declare the "start demo" member function:

```
// Demo
void start_demo();
```

Define it. "I create an active interval and run."

```
void Script::start_demo()
{
    this->demo_short_active_interval();
    this->run();
}
```

Tell the script to start its demo

Finally, declare the member function that sets up and kicks off the whole demo.

```
// Demo
void demo();
```

Define it:

```
void Script::demo()
{
    Lane_Array a_lane_array(4);
    Lane demo_lane;

    // Create the lanes.
```

```
demo_lane.four_lane_demo(a_lane_array);

// Create the steps and connect them to
// this script.
this->four_lane_demo(a_lane_array);

// Start the demo.
this->start_demo();
}
```

Try it out

You've done it! Try it out!

```
int main ()
{
    // Create a demo script.
    Script demo_Script;

    // Run the demo.
    demo_Script.demo();

    cout << endl << "Happy trails." << endl;

    return 0;
}
```

On the console, you should see something like this:

Traffic flow

Lane B. I'm open.
Lane D. I'm open.
Lane A. I'm closing my crossing lanes in 3 seconds.
Lane C. I'm closing my crossing lanes in 0 seconds.
Lane A. I'm adjusting to 25 for 0 seconds.
Lane C. I'm adjusting to 25 for 6 seconds.
Lane B. I'm closing my crossing lanes in 3 seconds.
Lane D. I'm closing my crossing lanes in 0 seconds.
Lane B. I'm adjusting to 35 for 0 seconds.
Lane D. I'm adjusting to 35 for 6 seconds.
Lane A. I'm closing my crossing lanes in 3 seconds.
Lane C. I'm closing my crossing lanes in 0 seconds.

Happy trails.

Way to go!

OOD—HUMAN INTERACTION COMPONENT

Identify the problem domain objects that need some interaction with a person.

> Lane
> > A person needs to know what my flow rate is.

That's it.

Design a Layout; Design the Human Interaction Component

Design a layout—lane

After long hours and extensive studies, your boss comes up with a bright idea—the ultimate display layout for a lane flow rate (Figure 4–33).

Figure 4–33: A display layout for lane flow rate.

Design the human interaction component

> It's time to play "Name that Object."[6]
> What's the display layout called? "I'm a traffic light."
> What does it do? "I display the current flow rate for a lane."
> No! Look at it a bit more carefully.
> "I'm a view container."
> Yes!

Hold it! You've already built a model-value view container, a reusable design component (Figure 4–34). It has display boxes and buttons. Maybe, just maybe, you'll be able use it here.

---

[6]And now here's your host, Object Coad.

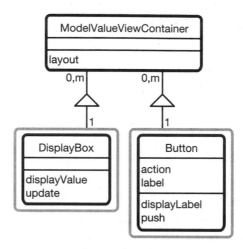

Figure 4–34: A model-value view container: a reusable design component.

You could use display boxes. One box could show a current flow rate; the other could display a maximum flow rate.

But you're looking for a different way to display a model value. With a different kind of box.

A light box!

What does a light box know? It knows its color and its shape (Figure 4–35).

Figure 4–35: "As a light box, I know things."

What does a light box do? "I display my value" (Figure 4–36).

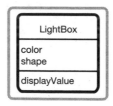

Figure 4–36: "As a light box, I know things and I do things."

But how does a light box know when to be on or off? Different light boxes might use different criteria. For example:

A "go" light box is on when current flow rate = max flow rate
A "caution" light box is on when
    0 < current flow rate < max flow rate
And a "stop" light box is on when current flow = 0

How do you capture these differences?

One approach. Add a specialization class for every new rule. But this would go on forever! Recall the "perpetual employment" principle: adding a class with endless specializations is not effective, but it can keep you perpetually employed.

An alternate approach. Let each light box know its own display rule (Figure 4-37). In this way, you get a much more concise design. And something that is much easier to reuse as is.

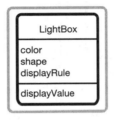

Figure 4–37: What a light box knows and does—adding a display rule.

Add a light box class to your model-value view container, making your reusable design component even more valuable (Figure 4–38).

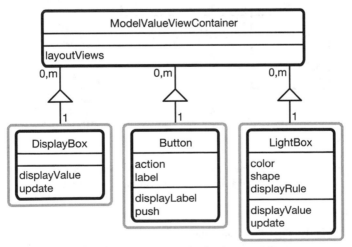

Figure 4–38: A model-value view container: a reusable design component—improved.

OOP—HUMAN INTERACTION COMPONENT: SMALLTALK

It's time to build the human interaction component in Smalltalk.

The human interaction component for the traffic flow system looks like this (Figure 4–39):

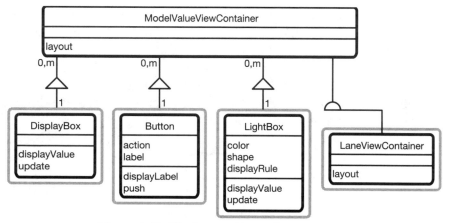

Figure 4–39: The human interaction component.

And the interaction between the human interaction component and the problem domain component looks like this (Figure 4–40):

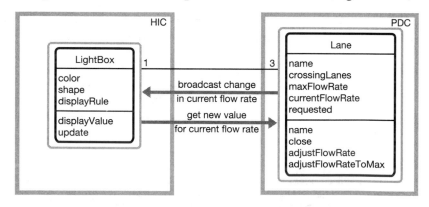

Figure 4–40: The interaction between the human interaction component and the problem domain component.

Here's the plan:

> Build the light box class.
> Add methods to the model-value view container class.
> Build the lane view container class.

The Light Box Class

Add a class and its instance variables

Add the light box class as a subclass (specialization) of the view class. Why? So the light box class inherits what it needs to know and do to respond to model change broadcasts.

```
View subclass: #LightBox
    instanceVariableNames: 'color shape displayRule '
    classVariableNames: ''
    poolDictionaries: ''
    category: 'Traffic Flow Views'
```

Add initialization

LightBox methodsFor: 'initialize-release'

initialize
```
color := ColorValue black.
displayRule := [:m | true].
self beCircle: 20@20 radius: 15
```

Note that "as a light box, I tell myself to set my shape and size."

Add attribute accessors

A view needs accessors, just like a model. But a view doesn't need a statement to support change broadcasting (a model does).[7]

Go ahead and define the accessors for a light box. Include accessors for color, shape, and display rule.

To set color and rule with one method, as a matter of convenience since you might often want to set them both at the same time, include something like the following:

LightBox methodsFor: 'accessing'

```
color: colorValue displayRule: displayRuleBlock
    self color: colorValue.
    self displayRule: displayRuleBlock
```

To set the shape for a light box, write methods for some common shapes. Use these methods to hide the details of how a light box shape is implemented.

LightBox methodsFor: 'shapes'

---

[7]Actually, you can build a view on a view. And then the underlying view would need statements to support change broadcasting.

```
beCircle: center radius: radius
    shape := Circle center: center radius: radius

beRectangle: origin corner: corner
    shape := Rectangle origin: origin corner: corner

beSquare: origin length: sideLength
    | corner |
    corner := origin x + sideLength @ (origin y +
        sideLength).
    self beRectangle: origin corner: corner

bePolygon: vertices
    shape := Polyline vertices: vertices
```

Add connection accessors

A light box is connected to its model. The connection accessors are inherited from the view class.

You do not need to add connection accessors.

Add object creation

Here, you don't need to add a service to create a new object and tell it to initialize itself. Why? Because you don't need it to do any more than its inherited behavior.

Add display and update methods

"I'm a light box."
"I display a value. I update myself when my model changes."

> display value
>> display myself on my surface
>>> choose a color
>>>> check if I'm on
>>>> if I'm on, use my color, else use a color that
>>>>> will erase my shape
>>> display my shape with a color
> update
>> display value

Strategy: build the supporting methods, and then the overall methods that you need.

About display rules

The light box needs a display rule, one that it can use to know whether it's on or off.

The display rule variable holds a few lines of code, in a "block." For example, it could hold something like this:

```
[:lane | lane currentFlowRate = lane maxFlowRate]
```

This block takes one argument. And the block returns a result—in this case, true or false.

Tell a block to execute itself by sending it the message "value:."

```
[:lane | lane currentFlowRate = lane maxFlowRate]
        value: aLane
```

The "check if on" method

The light box is connected to a lane. "I'm a light box. I'm 'on' if my display rule is true for my model (lane)."

```
LightBox methodsFor: 'testing'
```

checkIfOn
```
    "Execute my rule for my model"

    ^displayRule value: model
```

So far, so good.

The "display color" method

You need a method to determine display color.

"If someone asks me what my display color is, my answer when I'm 'on' is my color."

```
    ^self color
```

"But my answer when I'm off is just the background color of my display surface."

```
    ^self graphicsContext medium backgroundColor
```

Every visual component knows about its "graphics context." The graphics context knows about and takes care of things like color, font, and line width.

Putting this together in one method:

```
LightBox methodsFor: 'displaying'
```

displayColor
```
    self checkIfOn
      ifTrue: [^self color]
      ifFalse: [^self graphicsContext medium
             backgroundColor]
```

The "display on" methods

Here's how a light box displays its shape:
"I tell the graphics context what color to use for drawing."

```
graphicsContext paint: displayColor
```

"I tell my shape to display itself, filled in, on the graphics context."

```
shape displayFilledOn: graphicsContext
```

Note that geometric shapes, such as rectangles, circles, and polygons, know how to draw themselves.

Add a method for displaying a light box.

```
LightBox methodsFor: 'displaying'
```

displayOn: graphicsContext **color:** displayColor
    graphicsContext paint: displayColor.
    shape displayFilledOn: graphicsContext

Each visual component class must implement a "displayOn:" method. That's the method that its window invokes.

Each visual component often is told to display itself on a graphics context. How often? At least each time its window opens, refreshes, or gets uncovered.

Consider how a light box responds to a "displayOn:" message. "I display myself using my color."

```
LightBox methodsFor: 'displaying'
```

displayOn: graphicsContext
    self displayOn: graphicsContext color: self displayColor

The "display value" method itself

"I display a value. Here's how: I tell myself to display on my graphics context."

```
LightBox methodsFor: 'displaying'
```

displayValue
    self displayOn: self graphicsContext

The update method itself

A lane is a specialization of model; a light box is a specialization of view.

A model object broadcasts to its dependents that some aspect of the model has changed. In this case, you can use:

```
self changed: #currentFlowRate
```

The built-in broadcast system takes care of sending each dependent object a corresponding update message:

```
dependent update: #currentFlowRate
```

Every object understands an update message. The default is a no-op. You can define what response you want by extending the update method.

"I'm a light box. I update myself when my model changes." Here's how:

```
LightBox methodsFor: 'updating'
```

update: aspectChanged
   "My model has changed.
   Update my display"

   self displayValue

You've done it. You've built a light box.

Run the code

```
| window container light laneA rule |
window := ScheduledWindow new.
container := ModelValueViewContainer new.

light := LightBox new.
rule := [:lane | lane currentFlowRate = lane maxFlowRate].

light displayRule: rule.
light color: ColorValue blue.

laneA := Lane new.
laneA maxFlowRate: 25.
laneA open.
light model: laneA.
container addView: light in: (container constraintFrame:
        0 @ 0 corner: 1 @ 1).
window component: container.
laneA inspect.
window open
```

You should see something like this (Figure 4–41):

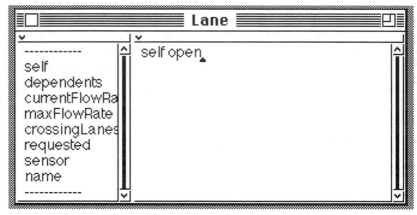

Figure 4–41: A light box and an inspector for a lane.

Inside the inspector for the lane, you can tell the lane to open and close:

```
self close.
self open
```

"As a lane, when I change my current flow rate, I broadcast that I've changed":

```
self changed: #currentFlowRate
```

In response, "as a light box, when I'm told that a 'current flow rate' change has occurred, I'll get the value, invoke my rule, and update my display."

Great. You're just about ready to build the lane view container and make some real traffic lights!

But first, you need to revisit and add something to a familiar class: the model-value view container class.

Adding Light Boxes to the Model-Value View Container Class

"I'm a model-value view container. I know how to build views that display or interact with a value in a model."

A model-value view container consists of some number of display boxes, buttons—and now, light boxes, too.

ModelValueViewContainer methodsFor: 'view creation'

makeLightBoxFor: lane **color:** colorValue **rule:** ruleBlock
| lightBox |
lightBox := LightBox new.
lightBox color: colorValue displayRule: ruleBlock.
lightBox model: lane.
^lightBox

makeLightBoxFor: lane **color:** colorValue **rule:** ruleBlock
        shape: geometricShape
| lightBox |
lightBox := self
        makeLightBoxFor: lane
        color: colorValue
        rule: ruleBlock.
lightBox shape: geometricShape.
^lightBox

Why two methods? To make it easier to use:

The "you make it so easy to use me" principle. When you define what an object does, "anticipate the ways that I might be used; and make it easy to use me."

The first method is simpler to use—no shape need be specified by a sender. A sender can then settle for the default shape. Or a sender can tell light box to set its own shape with one of its defined shape methods.

The second method allows for other shapes beyond those so easily set with the shape methods.

The Lane View Container Class

Now you can subclass (specialize) a model-value view container, adding a class for the specific kind of container you want: a lane view container.

Add a class and its instance variables

```
ModelValueViewContainer subclass: #LaneViewContainer
    instanceVariableNames: ''
    classVariableNames: ''
    poolDictionaries: ''
    category: 'Traffic Flow Views'
```

Add methods to build a vertical light

"As a lane view container, I build a vertical light for a lane":

> build a vertical light for a lane
> > make a light box (go light, caution light, stop light)
> > > set color (go color, caution color, stop color)
> > > set rules (go light rule, caution light rule, stop light rule)
> > lay out the views
> > > set up the constraint frames
> > > arrange the boxes in their constraint frames

The color methods

Here are some helpful methods for knowing what color to send to a light box:

LaneViewContainer methodsFor: 'colors'

goColor
```
^ColorValue green
```

cautionColor
```
^ColorValue yellow
```

stopColor
```
^ColorValue red
```

The rule methods

Here are some helpful methods for establishing what rule to send to a light box:

LaneViewContainer methodsFor: 'private-rules'

goLightRule
```
^[:lane | lane currentFlowRate = lane maxFlowRate]
```

cautionLightRule
```
^[:lane | 0 < lane currentFlowRate
        and: [lane currentFlowRate < lane maxFlowRate]]
```

```
stopLightRule
    ^[:lane | lane currentFlowRate = 0]
```

The "make light box" method

Next, make a light box.

"Here's how I make a light box. I get help from the methods defined in model-value view container, my 'super'."

LaneViewContainer methodsFor: 'view creation'

```
makeLaneLightBox: lane color: colorValue rule: ruleBlock
    | lightBox aShape |
    aShape := Circle center: 20 @ 20 radius: 15.
    lightBox := super
            makeLightBoxFor: lane
            color: colorValue
            rule: ruleBlock
            shape: aShape.
    ^lightBox
```

The "build a light" methods

"This is how I build a go light."

LaneViewContainer methodsFor: 'build views'

```
buildGoLightFor: lane
    ^self makeLaneLightBox: lane
        color: self goColor
        rule: self goLightRule
```

Following this pattern, go ahead and add the methods for building a caution light and a stop light.

The view layout methods

"I use these default constraint frames for arranging the vertical light."

LaneViewContainer methodsFor: 'private-layout'

```
topArea
    ^self constraintFrame: 0 @ 0  corner: 1 @ (1/3)
```

```
verticalMiddleArea
    ^self constraintFrame: 0 @ 1/3  corner: 1 @ (2/3)
```

```
bottomArea
    ^self constraintFrame: 0 @ 2/3  corner: 1 @ 1
```

"I arrange the light boxes in a vertical column or horizontal row."

LaneViewContainer methodsFor: 'view layout'

```
verticalLightFor: lane
    | redLight yellowLight greenLight |

    redLight := self buildStopLightFor: lane.
    yellowLight := self buildCautionLightFor: lane.
    greenLight := self buildGoLightFor: lane.

    self addView: redLight in: self topArea.
    self addView: yellowLight in: self verticalMiddleArea.
    self addView: greenLight in: self bottomArea
```

The window opening methods

"I create a window for myself; and I tell it to open itself on the screen."

LaneViewContainer methodsFor: 'window opening'

```
openOn: lane
    self openVerticalLightOn: lane at: 50 @ 50 label:
            'Traffic Lane'

openVerticalLightOn: lane at: screenPoint
        label: windowLabel
    | window |
    self verticalLightFor: lane.
    window := ScheduledWindow new.
    window component: self.
    window minimumSize: 50 @ 150.
    window label: windowLabel.
    window openDisplayAt: screenPoint
```

That's it. Ready for a trial run?

Run the Code

Run a one lane demo

This opens a three-light traffic light:

```
| laneA |
laneA := Lane new maxFlowRate: 25.
LaneViewContainer new openOn: laneA.
laneA inspect
```

You should see something like Figure 4–42:

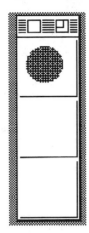

Figure 4–42: A single-lane traffic light.

Use the inspector on the lane to adjust the current flow rate; observe what happens each time. Try

```
self open
```

then

```
self cutFlowRateInHalf
```

and finally

```
self close
```

The light boxes turn on and off as the lane's rate changes.

Adding better human interaction to the four lane demo

Add the human interaction component to the four lane demo that you worked out earlier in this chapter.

Add a button to send the script a start demo message.

```
Script class methodsFor: 'demo'

demoStarterFor: script
   | window composite button frame |
   window := ScheduledWindow new.
   composite := ModelValueViewContainer new.
   button := composite
         makeButton: 'Start demo'
         on: script
         for: #startDemo.
```

```
frame := composite constraintFrame: 0 @ 0 corner: 1 @ 1.
composite addView: button in: frame.
window label: 'Flow'.
window component: composite.
window minimumSize: 120 @ 20.
window open
```

Next, add a method to create a traffic light for each lane:

Script class methodsFor: 'demos'

demoFor: script **and:** lanes
```
    | screenPoint |
    self demoStarterFor: script.
    screenPoint := 20 @ 50.
    lanes
        do:
            [:lane |
            LaneViewContainer new
                openVerticalLightOn: lane
                at: screenPoint
                label: 'Lane'.
            screenPoint := screenPoint + (75 @ 0)]
```

Finally, modify the demo method in the script class:

Script class methodsFor: 'demos'

demo
```
    | lanes script |
    lanes := Lane fourLaneDemo.
    script := self fourLaneDemo: lanes.
    self demoFor: script and: lanes
```

And you're ready to go.

Running a four lane demo

Run it (Figure 4–43).

```
Script demo
```

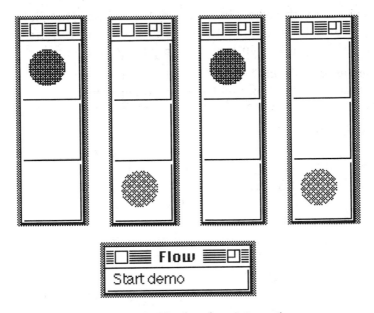

Figure 4–43: The four-lane intersection.

Wow! You've come a long way.
Congratulations!

OOP—HUMAN INTERACTION COMPONENT: C++

It's time to build the human interaction component in C++.

But before you start, spend some time thinking about how you want your display to look.

What's important in the traffic flow human interface?

Color. Each light box needs to display its current color. For example,

            Lane A Red
            Lane B Green
            Lane C Red
            Lane D Green

When? You could do it once, after each step. Who? The script. How? At the end of a step, the script could tell each light box to update itself.

Ugh!

That approach seriously weakens the relationship between the light box and its lane, since they can't coordinate their activities without a third (mother-in-law) object getting involved.

The "mother-in-law" principle. Keep each human interaction object and its corresponding problem domain object loosely coupled. Don't let a mother-in-law move in to manage their affairs.

The alternative?

> I'm a lane.
>> When I change my current flow rate,
>>> I notify each of my views,
>>>> telling it to update its display.

> I'm a light box.
>> Someone tells me to update my display.
>> I tell my container to arrange me.

> I'm a lane view container.
>> Someone tells me to arrange that part on the screen.
>> I arrange that part on the screen.

That's much better.

The human interaction component for the traffic flow system looks like this (Figure 4–44):

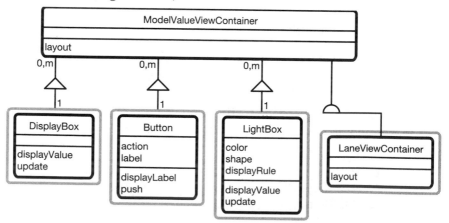

Figure 4–44: The human interaction component.

And the interaction between the human interaction component and the problem domain component looks like this (Figure 4–45):

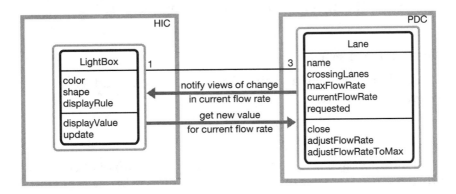

Figure 4–45: The interaction between the human interaction component and the problem domain component.

About Implementing a Display Rule

How should you refer to and invoke the display rule that a light box uses to determine if it is visible?

You can express a display rule as a member function. Then just let a light box keep a pointer to that member function. And let it use that pointer to invoke the member function.

A pointer to a member function is a derived type in C++. For this application, use something like this:

```
typedef Boolean (Lane_View_Container::*Rule)(Lane*
        traffic_lane);
```

Since you've not yet defined the lane view container class, you need to add a forward reference:

```
// Forward reference
class Lane_View_Container;

typedef Boolean (Lane_View_Container::*Rule)(Lane*
        traffic_lane);
```

This makes the name "Rule" a synonym type for

a pointer to an member function of Lane_View_Container
...taking a Lane* argument
...and returning a Boolean

Whew! That's a mouthful.

Declare the light box display rule using the Rule type:

```
Rule display_rule;
```

Adding color and shape

For light box color and shape, you could just go ahead and define two enumerated types:

```
enum Color { red, yellow, green };
enum Shape { circle, rectangle, square, triangle };
```

This approach falls short when you need to display color names and shape names. Then you need to supply mappings between each enumerated type value and a corresponding string name. Keeping such mappings in order is a real pain.

A much simpler approach: introduce a display color class and a display shape class.

The Display Color Class

I'm a display color.
I have a name.
When someone tells me to do so, I set my name to a specified color.

Declare the display color class:

```
class Display_Color {
public:

    // Constructors/destructors
    Display_Color() { be_background(); }
    Display_Color(String color_name) { name = color_name; }
    ~Display_Color();

    //Implementors
    void be_red() { name = "Red"; }
    void be_blue() { name = "Blue"; }
    void be_green() { name = "Green"; }
    void be_yellow() { name = "Yellow"; }
    void be_white() { name = "White"; }
    void be_black() { name = "Black"; }
    void be_background() { name = " "; }

    // Accessors
    String get_name() { return name; }
    void set_name(String color_name) { name = color_name; }
```

```
     // Overloaded operators
     friend ostream& operator<< (ostream& os,
                     Display_Color& display_color);
     Boolean operator== (Display_Color& display_color);

   private:

     String name;
   };
```

Most of the member functions are defined inline.

What remains?

Write out any display color name by using the insertion operator. Define it this way:

```
ostream& operator<< (ostream& os, Display_Color&
     display_color)
{
  os << display_color.name;
  return os;
}
```

Compare display colors by using the equivalence operator. Define it this way:

```
Boolean Display_Color::operator== (Display_Color&
     display_color)
{
  return (name == display_color.get_name());
}
```

The Display Shape Class

> I'm a display shape.
>   I have a name.
>   When someone tells me to do so,
>   I set my name to a specified shape.

Declare and define a display shape class, too. Follow the same approach that you used for defining the display color class.

The Light Box Class

> I'm a light box.
>   I know my color, shape, and display rule.
>   When my display rule is satisfied:
>   I display my color.
>   I display my shape.

I know about a lane.
I know about a lane view container.

Declare the class

```
// Forward reference
class Lane_View_Container;

typedef Boolean (Lane_View_Container::*Rule)(Lane*
    traffic_lane);

class Light_Box {
public:

  // Constructors/destructors
  Light_Box();
  Light_Box(Display_Color color_value,
      Display_Shape geometric_shape,
      Rule light_display_rule);
  ~Light_Box() {}

  // Implementors

  // Displaying
  void display_value();
  void update_display();

  // Testing
  Boolean check_if_on();

  // Accessors
  Display_Color get_color() { return color; }
  void set_color(Display_Color new_value)
      { color = new_value; }

  Display_Shape get_shape() { return shape; }
  void set_shape(Display_Shape new_value)
      { shape = new_value; }

  void set_location(int new_location) { location =
          new_location; }
  int get_location() { return location; }

  Rule get_display_rule() { return display_rule; }
  void set_display_rule(Rule new_value)
      { display_rule = new_value; }
```

```
Lane& get_lane() { return *lane; }
void connect_to_lane(Lane& new_value) { lane =
        &new_value; }

Lane_View_Container& get_lane_view_container()
    { return *lane_view_container; }
void connect_to_lane_view_container(Lane_View_Container&
        new_value)
        { lane_view_container = &new_value; }

private:

    // Data members
    Display_Color color;
    Display_Shape shape;
    int location;
    Rule display_rule;
    Lane* lane;
    Lane_View_Container* lane_view_container;
};
```

Define the constructor member functions

```
Light_Box::Light_Box()
{
    color = Display_Color("Red");
    shape = Display_Shape("Circle");
    location = 0;
}

Light_Box::Light_Box(Display_Color color_value,
        Display_Shape geometric_shape,
        Rule light_display_rule)
{
    color = color_value;
    shape = geometric_shape;
    display_rule = light_display_rule;
    location = 0;
}
```

Define the "display value" member functions

In the first person:

> I'm a light box.
>> I display my value.
>> I update myself when my model changes.

Here's the plan:

> display value
> > get color
> > > check if I'm on
> > > if I'm on, I display my shape and color
> >
> > update my display

The "check if on" member function

How does a light box know if it's on?

> I'm a light box.
> > To find out if I should be on or off,
> > > I execute my display rule,
> > > using my lane as an argument.

Build it:

```
Boolean Light_Box::check_if_on()
{
   // Invoke the pointer to member function stored in
   // the display_rule data member.
   Boolean result =
         (lane_view_container->*display_rule)(*lane);
   return result;
}
```

The "display value" member function itself

Add the member function to display the light box at its location:

Lane A   Green Circle
Lane D   Yellow Circle
Lane B   Red Circle
              <--- location ->
              <----------------- location ->
              <- location->

You can control the location of the cout output like this:

```
cout.width(15);
```

This creates a 15 character field width. Any string or numeric output will use at least 15 characters. Extra spaces if needed are padded on the left side, making the text right-justified.

Now define the member function.

```
void Light_Box::display_value()
{
   if (!this->check_if_on())
     return;
   else
     {
     cout.width(location);
     String display = color.get_name() + String(" ")
          + shape.get_name();
     cout << display;
     cout.width(0);
     }
}
```

An "on" light box with a red color and square shape displays something like this:

> Red Square

An "off" light box just displays a blank line.

Define the "update display" member function

Here's what the light box does at this point:

> I'm a light box.
> > Someone tells me to update my display.
> > I tell my container to arrange me.

And here's the code:

```
void Light_Box::update_display()
{
   lane_view_container->
     display_components();
}
```

You've done it. You've built a light box.

Try it out.

Trying out the light box is a wee bit tricky. Its display rule is a pointer to a lane view container member function, but you haven't defined that class yet.

Don't let that stop you. Just create a simple lane view container class and use it for your demo. It only needs two member functions, one that serves as a light box rule and another that is called when a light box updates its display.

```
class Lane_View_Container
{
public:
  Lane_View_Container() { }
  ~Lane_View_Container() { }

  Boolean is_open(Lane& a_lane)
     { return (a_lane.get_current_flow_rate() > 0); }
  void display_components(){}
};
```

In your test program, do these steps:
- Create a light box whose display rule is the member function, is_open.
- Connect the light box to a lane and to a lane view container.
- Open the lane.
- Tell the light box to display its value (the light box uses its display rule to determine its state).
- Close the lane.
- Tell the light box to display itself (again, the light box uses its rule to determine its state).

```
int main ()
{
  Display_Shape a_shape;
  Display_Color a_color;
  a_shape.be_circle();
  a_color.be_green();

  Rule open_rule = &Lane_View_Container::is_open;

  Lane lane_A("Lane A", 35);
  Lane_View_Container a_lane_view_container;
  Light_Box a_light_box(a_color, a_shape, open_rule);

  a_light_box.connect_to_lane(lane_A);
  a_light_box.connect_to_lane_view_container
          (a_lane_view_container);

  lane_A.open();
  cout << endl << endl
       << "Light box display when lane A is open: ";
  a_light_box.display_value();
  lane_A.close();
  cout << endl << endl
```

```
                << "Light box display when lane A is closed: "
                << endl;
           a_light_box.display_value();

           cout << endl << "Happy trails." << endl;

           return 0;
        }
```

On your console you should see something like this:

Lane A. I'm open.
Light box display when lane A is open: Green Circle
Lane A. I'm closed.
Light box display when lane A is closed:

Happy trails.

Connecting a Light Box to a Lane

What does a lane do with its light boxes?

I'm a lane.
　　When I change my current flow rate,
　　　　I notify each of my views,
　　　　telling it to update its display.

First, add a data member to the lane class, to hold a lane's view(s):

```
           typedef Ordered_List<Light_Box*> Light_Box_List;

           // Data members for human interaction component
           Light_Box_List traffic_lights;
```

Add the corresponding accessors.

```
           // For the human interaction component
           Light_Box_List& get_traffic_lights() { return
                  traffic_lights; }
           void connect_to_traffic_light(Light_Box& a_light_box)
           { traffic_lights.add(&a_light_box); }
```

Declare the change mechanism, so a lane can notify its views.

```
           // View interaction
           void notify_views();
           void change_current_flow_rate(float new_rate);
```

To keep the container (display light) and part (display box) interaction simple for this example, assume that a lane has just one display light. Then, since all the lane's light boxes are in the same container, the lane only needs to notify one light box. That light box will notify its container. And the container will tell *each* of its light boxes to update.

```
void Lane::notify_views()
{
   if (traffic_lights.is_empty())
      return;
   Light_Box* first_light = traffic_lights.item_at(0);
   first_light->update_display();
}
```

Continue!

"When I change my current flow rate, I notify each of my views."

```
void Lane::change_current_flow_rate(float new_rate)
{
   // Only notify if the new rate is different
   if (current_flow_rate != new_rate)
      {
      current_flow_rate = new_rate;
      this->notify_views();
      };
}
```

When does a lane change its flow rate, anyway?

"I change my rate when I adjust my flow rate, cut my rate in half, open or close myself."

So, in each case just use this new "change current flow rate" member function.

```
Boolean Lane::adjust_flow_rate(float desired_rate,
                   int transition_duration,
                   int duration,
                   Boolean only_when_requested)
{
   float new_rate;
   if (only_when_requested && (!this->get_requested()))
      return false;
   this->close_crossing_lanes(transition_duration);
   new_rate = min(desired_rate, max_flow_rate);
   this->change_current_flow_rate(new_rate);
   this->wait(duration);
   return true;
}
```

```
void Lane::cut_flow_rate_in_half()
{
    this->change_current_flow_rate(current_flow_rate / 2.0);
}

void Lane::close()
{
    this->change_current_flow_rate(0);
}

void Lane::open
{
    this->change_current_flow_rate(max_flow_rate);
}
```

The Lane View Container Class

Now it's time to build a lane view container class.

> I'm a lane view container.
>> I hold light boxes for a lane.
>> When someone tells me to arrange him on the screen,
>>> I arrange that part on the screen.

Declare the class

```
class Lane_View_Container {
public:

    // Constructors/destructors
    Lane_View_Container () { }
    ~Lane_View_Container () { }

    // Implementors
    // Build views
    Light_Box& build_stop_light(Lane& traffic_lane);
    Light_Box& build_caution_light(Lane& traffic_lane);
    Light_Box& build_go_light(Lane& traffic_lane);

    // Make views
    Light_Box& make_light_box(Lane& traffic_lane,
            Display_Color color_value,
            int location,
            Rule a_rule);

    // Opening
    void open_light(Lane& traffic_lane, String lane_label);

    // Colors
    Display_Color get_stop_color() { return stop_color; }
```

```
    Display_Color get_caution_color()
            { return caution_color; }
    Display_Color get_go_color() { return go_color; }

    // Shapes
    Display_Shape get_light_box_shape()
            { return light_box_shape; }

    // Rules
    Boolean stop_light_rule(Lane& traffic_lane);
    Boolean caution_light_rule(Lane& traffic_lane);
    Boolean go_light_rule(Lane& traffic_lane);

    // Layout
    void display_components();
    void add_view(Light_Box& light_box);
    int stop_location();
    int caution_location();
    int go_location();

    // Accessors
    String get_label() { return label; }
    void set_label(String new_label) { label = new_label; }

    // Demo

private:

    // Data members
    Light_Box_List components;
    String label;
    static Display_Color stop_color;
    static Display_Color caution_color;
    static Display_Color go_color;
    static Display_Shape light_box_shape;
};
```

Define the static member initialization

```
// Initialization of static members
Display_Color Lane_View_Container::stop_color
                ("Red");
Display_Color Lane_View_Container::caution_color
                ("Yellow");
Display_Color Lane_View_Container::go_color
                ("Green");
Display_Shape Lane_View_Container::light_box_shape
                ("Circle");
```

Define the "make light box" member functions

A lane view container makes light boxes.

Color. The stop, caution, and go colors are defined in static members, something each object in the class knows. The corresponding accessors are defined inline.

Rules. How do you set up the rules? Here's how:

```
Boolean Lane_View_Container::stop_light_rule(Lane&
        traffic_lane)
{
   return (traffic_lane.get_current_flow_rate() == 0);
}

Boolean Lane_View_Container::caution_light_rule(Lane&
        traffic_lane)
{
   return ((0 < traffic_lane.get_current_flow_rate()) &&
      (traffic_lane.get_current_flow_rate()
        < traffic_lane.get_max_flow_rate()));
}

Boolean Lane_View_Container::go_light_rule(Lane&
        traffic_lane)
{
   return (traffic_lane.get_current_flow_rate() ==
        traffic_lane.get_max_flow_rate());
}
```

The lane view container lays out the light boxes in a horizontal row (Figure 4–46):

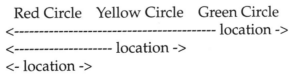

Figure 4–46: The lane view container layout.

Add member functions to compute locations for the different light boxes. A light box location is determined by the number of characters (shape + color) and the location of the light boxes before it in the row. Also add a spacing constant to each location to put a fixed margin between the light boxes.

Define the member functions.

```
int Lane_View_Container::stop_location()
{
   int location;

   location = stop_color.get_name().size()
      + 1
      + light_box_shape.get_name().size()
      + 5
}

int Lane_View_Container::caution_location()
{
   int location;

   location = caution_color.get_name().size()
      + 1
      + light_box_shape.get_name().size()
      + 5
      + this->stop_location();
   return location;
}

int Lane_View_Container::go_location()
{
   int location;

   location = go_color.get_name().size()
      + 1
      + light_box_shape.get_name().size()
      + 5
      + this->caution_location();
   return location;
}
```

Make a light box by invoking the light box class constructor. *Tell* it the specific color, shape, rule, and container that it needs to do the job right.

```
Light_Box& Lane_View_Container::make_light_box (
      Lane& traffic_lane, Display_Color color_value,
      int location, Rule a_rule)
{
   Light_Box* light_box = new Light_Box(color_value,
               light_box_shape,
               a_rule);

   light_box->connect_to_lane(traffic_lane);
   light_box->set_location(location);
```

```
        light_box->connect_to_lane_view_container(*this);
        return *light_box;
    }
```

Build a go light, caution light, or stop light using the same basic pattern. For example, this is how to build a go light:

```
Light_Box& Lane_View_Container::build_go_light(Lane&
        traffic_lane)
{
    return (this->make_light_box(traffic_lane,
            this->get_go_color(),
            this->go_location(),
            &Lane_View_Container::go_light_rule));
}
```

Define the "display components" member functions

Add each light box to the container's components list. The order in which they are added determines the order in which they are displayed.

```
void Lane_View_Container::add_view(Light_Box& light_box)
{
    components.add(&light_box);
}
```

Next, build a light.

```
void Lane_View_Container::open_light(Lane& traffic_lane,
        String lane_name)
{
    // Build the light boxes.
    Light_Box& stop_light =
            this->build_stop_light(traffic_lane);
    Light_Box& caution_light =
            this->build_caution_light(traffic_lane);
    Light_Box& go_light =
            this->build_go_light(traffic_lane);

    // Arrange them inside of me.
    this->add_view(stop_light);
    this->add_view(caution_light);
    this->add_view(go_light);

    this->set_label(lane_name);

    // Arrange the light boxes for the lane.
    traffic_lane.connect_to_traffic_light(stop_light);
```

```
    traffic_lane.connect_to_traffic_light(caution_light);
    traffic_lane.connect_to_traffic_light(go_light);
}
```

Finally, display the components of a light.

```
void Lane_View_Container::display_components()
{
    Light_Box* light_box_component;
    cout << label;
    while (!components.end_of_list())
    {
        light_box_component = components.current();
        light_box_component->display_value();
        components++;
    }
    components.reset();
    cout << endl;
}
```

That's it.

Run the Code

Add the light boxes to your script demo. This means creating a lane view container for every lane in the demo. Add the necessary statements to your script demo member function.

```
void Script::demo()
{
    Lane_Array a_lane_array(4);
    Lane demo_lane;
    Lane_View_Container* a_lane_view_container;

    demo_lane.four_lane_demo(a_lane_array);
    this->four_lane_demo(a_lane_array);

    a_lane_view_container = new Lane_View_Container;
    a_lane_view_container->open_light(*a_lane_array[0],
            "Lane A");

    a_lane_view_container = new Lane_View_Container;
    a_lane_view_container->open_light(*a_lane_array[1],
            "Lane B");

    a_lane_view_container = new Lane_View_Container;
    a_lane_view_container->open_light(*a_lane_array[2],
            "Lane C");
```

```
    a_lane_view_container = new Lane_View_Container;
    a_lane_view_container->open_light(*a_lane_array[3],
            "Lane D");

    this->start_demo();
}
```

Great. Now write your test program.

```
int main ()
{
    // Create a script.
    Script traffic_script;

    // Run the demo, creating and displaying a traffic light
    // view.
    traffic_script.demo();

    cout << endl << "Happy trails." << endl;

    return 0;
}
```

The script begins with lanes A and C opening, but first they must close lanes B and D. As lanes B and D cut their flow rate in half, they notify their light boxes. When the caution light boxes come on the others go off. When lanes B and D turn off, the stop light boxes come on.

Here goes!

Lane B		Yellow Circle	
Lane D		Yellow Circle	
Lane B	Red Circle		
Lane D	Red Circle		
Lane A			Green Circle
Lane C			Green Circle

Happy trails.

Wow! Take a bow, chum.

SUMMARY

In this chapter, you learned and applied:

OOA and OOD
- Identifying and applying system purpose
- Applying the targeted analogy strategy

- Improving your model with scenario scripts
- Working with object interactions to explore what an object needs to do

OOP (Smalltalk)

- Generating random numbers
- Working with dates and times
- Writing timed simulations using delay objects
- Creating graphics objects
- Working with shapes, colors, and graphics context
- Implementing state-dependent rules (using blocks)
- Adding methods to display a view
- Adding methods to respond to model broadcasts

OOP (C++)

- Using default arguments in member functions
- Writing parameterized functions
- Generating random numbers
- Working with dates and times
- Implementing state-dependent rules (using pointers to member functions)
- Building human interaction classes that respond to notify messages

You also learned and applied these principles:

The "dig yourself a large enough whole" principle. Whenever you name the "whole" in a whole-part structure, use a name that is applicable (large enough to apply) across the variety of collections that you may need to support.

The "pay attention to the man behind the curtains" principle. Look past the current human interaction wizardry—and get to the underlying problem domain.

The "25 words or less" principle. Always, always, always begin by asking "What's the purpose of the system, in 25 words or less?" Put that purpose on a decorative poster! And use the purpose of the system to guide your every move.

The "targeted analogy" principle. When the true underlying problem domain is unclear, look for analogous systems that exist to achieve a similar purpose. Learn from the parallels between the systems.

The "my oh my" principle. Every service name should make perfect sense when the words "I" or "me" or "my" or "myself" are added alongside the verb in the service name. If not, change the service or change the class name so that it does make sense.

The "I'd rather do it to myself" principle. If an object in an OOA/OOD model acts on something not yet in the model, replace the object in the model with one that acts on itself. And let the new object do the action on itself.

The "analogy to class to metaphor" principle. Find a targeted analogy. Identify core classes. Identify which problem domain class and targeted analogy class are metaphors for each other. Add what you learned from the targeted analogy to your OOA/OOD model.

The "I'll be back" principle. If I'm a problem domain class, don't throw me away just because you think you can smash me in with another class. I'm probably needed. I'll be back.

The "interaction then action" principle. Examine needed object interactions. And add the corresponding actions.

The "don't butt into someone else's business" principle. As an object, I don't butt into another object's business, sending it a message to peek at its values and then another message to get the real work done. Instead, I just send one message, telling the object what I want it to do (let it check its own status).

The "I get by with a little help from my friends" principle. Methods that get help from little methods that do one thing, and one thing well, facilitate reuse.

The "you make it so easy to use me" principle. When you define what an object does, "anticipate the ways that I might be used; and make it easy to use me."

The "mother-in-law" principle. Keep each human interaction object and its corresponding problem domain object loosely coupled. Don't let a mother-in-law move in to manage their affairs.

Enjoy!

Epilogue

Congratulations! You've come a long way, and accomplished a lot. Take a deep bow. You've earned it.

But don't rest on your laurels for too long. You are an object; take responsibility for your own behavior! It's time to realize that you must USE IT or LOSE IT!

OBJECT THINKING

Watch your language

How you *talk* about your software affects how you think about it. So clean up your language!

Watch out when you hear someone say things like this:

> "This coordinates/handles/controls/manages..."
> "Save a few lines of code by factoring out and inheriting..."
> "The object decides what to do based on the type of that other object..."
> "Just get its value and do something with it."

Walk that walk; talk that talk.

Not *"object speak"*	*"Object speak"*
How can it do ___ to that object?	I am a ___. I know how to ___myself.
What are the functions in the system?	What are the objects in the system?
It decides what to do based on the type of object.	I am a ___ object. I know about these kinds of objects. I send them the ___ message.
Get its ___ and do ___ with it.	I am a ___ object. I know my ___ , and use it to ___myself.

Say it with pictures

Use diagrams to help you conceive, refine, and communicate an effective object-oriented architecture.

Apply the principles

Practice vital object-oriented problem-solving techniques, including domain-based architecting, personification, concurrent development, and targeted analogies.

Keep applying the principles (see the appendixes for a complete list).

Continue learning—an exciting adventure

Apply object-oriented programming. Do it. And continue reading. Here are some recommendations.

For C++, read:

Advanced C++: Programming Styles and Idioms, James O. Coplien. Addison-Wesley, 1992.

For Smalltalk, take a look at:

Inside Smalltalk, Volume I, Wilf R. LaLonde and John R. Pugh. Prentice Hall, 1990.

Also for Smalltalk, spend some time "reading the literature." Use the Smalltalk browsers to browse code, reading for insight from the practical application of object-oriented programming.

For Eiffel, be sure to read:

Eiffel: The Language, Bertrand Meyer, Prentice Hall, 1992.

For Objective-C, check out:

Object-Oriented Programming: An Evolutionary Approach, Second Edition, Brad Cox, Addison-Wesley, 1992.

For CLOS, see:

Object-Oriented Programming in Common LISP: A Programmer's Guide to CLOS, Sonya E. Keene, Addison-Wesley, 1989.

For working with objects in other programming languages, read:

Object-Oriented Reuse, Concurrency and Distribution: an Ada-based Approach, Colin Atkinson, ACM Press, 1992.

Object-Oriented Software Construction, Bertrand Meyer, Prentice Hall, 1988. (This book includes a chapter on how to apply objects in a variety of languages.)

Object-Oriented Programming with the X Window System Toolkits, Jerry D. Smith, John Wiley & Sons, 1991.

And stay in touch! Your insights, comments, and suggestions are appreciated. And we may publish additional solutions... including those in a variety of OOPLs; to get information on these additional goodies, just send a note to Object International, Inc., 3202 W. Anderson Lane, 208-724, Austin, Texas 78757-1022 USA.

Just do it

An old Chinese proverb says:

> When you hear something, you will forget it.
> When you see something, you will remember it.
> But not until you do something, will you understand it.

Enjoy!

Appendixes

The OOP book includes these three guides:

     A. Concise Practical Language Summaries

     B. OOA and OOD Notation

     C. OOP Principles

The purpose? To help you take what you learn in this book and put it into practice.

Enjoy.

Appendix A

Practical Language Summaries

This appendix presents practical language summaries, helpful in day-to-day OOP.

The Smalltalk guide spans the complete language syntax *and* the most frequently used classes.

The C++ guide spans the object-oriented features of the language syntax and the input-output classes (since these are the only classes included in the C++ language as of this writing).

A PRACTICAL SUMMARY: SMALLTALK

This practical summary presents the following key topics:

Literal constants	Conditional statements
Message expressions	Iteration statements
Parsing rules	Defining classes
Variable syntax	Defining methods
Statement syntax	Magnitude classes
Binary messages	Collection classes
Blocks	Stream classes

Literals

Literals are objects that can be denoted by literal expressions.

Number literal	
27	A number literal is denoted by numeric digits.
-27	A preceding minus indicates a negative number.
3/2	Create a fraction as the result of integer division.
0.75	Floats must include a zero before the decimal point.

Number literal *(cont.)*

8r25	Use different bases by prefixing the number with the base and the letter, r.
16rFF	For bases greater than ten, use capital letters for digits greater than 9.
1234e-3	1.234 in exponential notation
-254.3d2	-25430.0 in double precision

Character literal

$A	A character literal consists of a dollar sign, $, followed by an ASCII character.
$a	Lower-case characters are distinguished from upper-case.
$1	Numeric characters are fine.
$^	Non-alphanumeric characters are okay, too.

String literal

'hello, earth'	A string literal is a character sequence enclosed in single quotes.
'I''m a count'	A single quote within a string must be preceded by a single quote.

Symbol literal

#value	A symbol literal is a character sequence preceded by a number sign, #.
#Integer	A symbol is used to uniquely name something, such as a class.
#'a string'	Each symbol has its own unique character sequence. No two symbols can have the same character sequence.

Symbol literal *(cont.)*

`#'7^'`	Use single quotes for symbol names with special characters.

Byte literal

`#[0 11 255]`	A byte array literal is enclosed in square brackets and preceded by a number sign, #.
	Its elements must be integers, from 0 to 255.

Array literal

`#(12.5 2r11 'hello' $Z)`	An array literal is enclosed in parentheses and preceded by a number sign, #.
`#(#(1 2 3) 4 5 #[6 7])`	Its elements are separated by spaces.
	Its elements can be any literal, including other literal arrays.

Special literals

`true`	The true literal refers to the sole object of the boolean class, True.
`false`	The false literal refers to the sole object of the boolean class, False.
`nil`	The nil literal refers to the sole object of the UndefinedObject class.
	The nil object is used as the null value.
	The names true, false, and nil are reserved.

Message Expressions

The basic unit of Smalltalk syntax is the message expression.

```
<object> <methodName>
    <arguments>
```

Method name corresponds to a method which is either implemented by an object's class or inherited from one of its superclasses. The object on the left hand side of the message expression is the receiver of the message.

Every method returns an object. The default returned is the object itself.

```
<methodName>
    <arguments>
```

A message is a message expression without a receiver.

Send a unary message to an object.

```
john goToStore
```

A unary message is a message with no arguments.

A method name begins with lower-case letters, by convention.
A method name with more than one word uses capital letters to separate the words, also by convention.

Send a binary message to an object.

```
7 + 2
```

A binary message is a message with special character(s) and one argument. Arithmetic operations and relational comparisons are invoked with binary messages.

Arguments are untyped.

The method name of this binary message is a special character, +.

Send a keyword message to
an object.

`john goToStore: 'WallyMart'`   A keyword message is a message
with one or more arguments.

`goToStore:` is a keyword (an
argument descriptor). An argument
must always follow a keyword.
Here, the string, `'WallyMart'` is the
argument.

Send a keyword message
with two arguments to
an object.

`john goToStore: 'WallyMart'`   Each additional argument requires
`    for: 'bread'`   an additional keyword.
The corresponding method name is
formed by concatenating all the
keywords.
Here, the corresponding method is
`goToStore:for:`.

Send a keyword message
with three arguments to
an object.

`john goStore: 'WallyMart'`   A message (and the name of its
`    for: 'bread'`   corresponding method) may have
`    and: 'milk'`   any number of keywords.

Parsing Rules

Parsing rules determine the
order of evaluation when there is
more than one message expression
in a statement.

Parse expressions in parentheses
before nonparenthesized
expressions.

`12 + (3 * 7) + 6`	Evaluates to 39
`12 + 3 * 7 + 6`	Evaluates to 111

Parse unary messages left to right.

`Date today weekday`	Send the message `today`, to the Date class. The result is a date object. Send the message, `weekday`, to that object.
`(Date today) weekday`	Equivalent to the above.

Parse binary messages left to right.

`12 + 3 * 7 + 6`	Evaluates to 111
`((12 + 3) * 7) + 6`	Equivalent to the above.

Parse unary messages before binary messages.

`12 + 3 negated`	Evaluates to 9
`12 + (3 negated)`	Equivalent to the above.

Parse binary messages before keyword messages.

`orderedCollection add:` `    3 + 5`	Tell the ordered collection to add 8 to itself.
`orderedCollection add:` `    (3 + 5)`	Equivalent to the above.

Use parentheses to separate keyword messages.

`count value:` `(orderedCollection at: 1)`	Send the count object a `value:` message with argument, `(orderedCollection at: 1)`.
`count value:` `orderedCollection at: 1`	Send the count a `value:at:` message with arguments `orderedCollection` and `1`.

Use a semicolon to cascade messages to the same object.

```
orderedCollection
    add: $a; add: 'four'
```

Send the orderedCollection object the `add:` message with argument, `$a`, followed by the `add:` message with argument, `four`.

Variable Syntax

Define a temporary (local) variable, anInteger.

```
| anInteger |
```

A temporary variable name begins with a lower-case letter, by convention.

One or more temporary variables are defined between vertical bars, `| |`.

A temporary variable must be defined before it is used.

Assign a value to a temporary variable, anInteger.

```
| anInteger |
anInteger := 6
```

A temporary variable must be defined before all statements with the same scope. Most often, it is defined at the beginning of a method (although it may be defined elsewhere, instead).

The assignment operator is `:=` . It must be preceded by a space.

Define a global variable.

```
GlobalInteger := 123
```

A global variable name must begin with an upper-case letter.

A global variable lasts for the lifetime of the system, unless explicitly removed.

```
Smalltalk removeKey:
    #GlobalInteger
```

Remove the `#GlobalInteger` global variable.

Statement Syntax

The statement separator is
a period, "." .

```
| integer1 integer2 |
integer1 := 1.
integer2 := integer1 + 10.
integer1 := integer2 + 12
```

Don't use a separator after a
temporary variable declaration.
Use a separator to separate one
statement from the next.
Don't use a separator after the last
statement.

Assignment statements can
be chained.

```
|integer1 integer2 integer3|
integer1 := integer2 := 1.

integer3 := integer1 + 10.
integer2 := integer1 := -10
```

Assign `integer1` and `integer2` the
value 1.
Assign `integer3` the value 11.
Assign `integer1` and `integer2` the
value -10. The value of `integer3`
remains 11.

Binary Messages

A binary message is a message
with special character(s) and
one argument.

```
12 + 8
(3/4) <= 0.86
```

A binary message has a
receiver and one argument.

```
12 + 8
```

The receiver is 12; the message is
`+ 8`; the argument is `8`.

Binary messages may be user
defined.

Arithmetic binary messages

+ *(add)*	The corresponding method is defined in specializations of ArithmeticValue.
5 + 1	Evaluates to 6
(5@6) + 1	Evaluates to 6@6
(5@6) + (1@4)	Evaluates to 6@10
3/2 + (5/2)	Evaluates to integer, 4 (Fraction arithmetic returns reduced fractions or integers.)

- *(subtract)*	The corresponding method is defined in specializations of ArithmeticValue and Set.
0.45 - 1.05	Evaluates to -0.60
3/4 - 1	Evaluates to -1/4
setA - setB	Evaluates to a set with all elements in setA not in setB

* *(multiply)*	The corresponding method is defined in specializations of ArithmeticValue.
3.0 * (16/5)	Evaluates to 9.6
6@3 * (2@3)	Evaluates to 12@9
3/2 * (2/3)	Evaluates to integer, 1

/ *(divide)*	The corresponding method is defined in specializations of ArithmeticValue.
3 / 4	Evaluates to fraction, 3/4
3 / 4.0	Evaluates to 0.75
6@12 / 2	Evaluates to 3@6

** *(raised to)*	The corresponding method is defined in specializations of Number.
3 ** 3	Evaluates to 27
3 ** 0.5	Evaluates to 1.73205

// *(integer division)*	The corresponding method is defined in the Point class and in specializations of Number.
3 // 4	Evaluates to 0 (integer quotient of division)
11.0 // 4	Evaluates to 2
11@5 // (2@4)	Evaluates to 5@1

\\ *(modulo)*	The corresponding method is defined in the Point class and in specializations of Number.
3 \\ 4	Evaluates to 3 (remainder of division)
11.0 \\ 4	Evaluates to 3.0
11@5 \\ (2@4)	Evaluates to 1@1

Comparison binary messages

< *(less than)*	The corresponding method is defined in the specializations of Magnitude and CharacterArray.
6 < 7	Evaluates to true
2@4 < (11@5)	Evaluates to true
2@6 < (11@5)	Evaluates to false
$a < $b	Evaluates to true
$a < $A	Evaluates to false
$A < $a	Evaluates to true
'abc' < 'abd'	Evaluates to true
dateA < dateB	true if dateA precedes dateB
timeA < timeB	true if timeA is earlier than timeB

<= *(less than or equal)*	The corresponding method is defined in the specializations of Magnitude and CharacterArray.
`'ABC' <= 'abc'`	Evaluates to true
`3/4 <= 0.75`	Evaluates to true

> *(greater than)* **>= *(greater than or equal)***	The corresponding method is defined in specializations of Magnitude and CharacterArray.
`5 > (4 + 1)`	Evaluates to false
`5 >= (4 + 1)`	Evaluates to true

= *(equality)*	The corresponding method is defined for all classes. Two objects are equal if they are structurally identical.
`3 = 3.0`	Evaluates to true

`| x y |`
 `x := #(1 2 3).`
 `y := #(1 2 3).`
 `x = y`
	
	Evaluates to true

== *(equivalence)*	The corresponding method is defined for all classes. Two variables that hold an object are equivalent if they hold the same object.
`3 == 3.0`	Evaluates to false

`| x y |`
 `x := #(1 2 3).`
 `y := x.`
 `x == y.`
 `y := #(1 2 3).`
 `x == y`
	
	Evaluates to true
	
	Evaluates to false

~= (not equal) **~~ (not equivalent)**	The corresponding methods are defined for all classes.
`3 ~= 3.0`	Evaluates to false
`3 ~~ 3.0`	Evaluates to true

~= (not equal) **~~ (not equivalent) (cont)**	
`| x y z |`	
`x := #(1 2 3).`	
`y := #(1 2 3).`	
`z := #(3 2 1).`	
`x ~= y.`	Evaluates to false
`x ~~ y.`	Evaluates to true
`x ~= z.`	Evaluates to true
`x := z.`	
`x ~~ z.`	Evaluates to false

Logical binary messages	
& (logical AND)	The corresponding method is defined for Boolean classes.
`(5 < 6) & (12 > 3)`	Evaluates to true

| (logical OR)	The corresponding method is defined for Boolean classes.
`(5 > 6)	(12 > 3)`	Evaluates to true

Other binary messages	
, (concatenate)	The corresponding method is defined in specializations of SequenecableCollection.
`#(1 2 3) , #(4 5 6)`	Creates new array #(1 2 3 4 5 6)
`'a b c', ' ', 'd e f'`	Concatenates three strings to create new string, 'a b c d e f'

@ *(form point)*	The corresponding method is defined in specializations of Number.
`6 @ 7`	Creates a point with x-coordintate = 6 and y-coordinate = 7

-> *(associate)*	The corresponding method is defined for all classes.
`'name'->'Barney'`	Creates an association with key, 'name' and value, 'Barney'

Blocks

The evaluation of a sequence of statements can be deferred by placing them within a block.

A block is enclosed in square brackets, [ ] .

| ```
| integer1 integer2 aBlock|
aBlock := [integer1 := 1.
   integer2 := integer1 + 1]
``` | Create a block containing two statements. At this point, the temporary variables `integer1` and `integer2` still have undefined values. The statements inside the block are not evaluated until the block is told to execute itself. |
|---|---|

A block statement that does not use parameters is executed when it receives the message, `value`.

| ```
| integer1 integer2 aBlock|
aBlock := [integer1 := 1.
   integer2 := integer1 + 1].
aBlock value
``` | Create a block that does not require parameters. Tell the block to execute its statements. The block executes itself. Now temporary variables `integer1` and `integer2` have values 1 and 2, respectively. |
|---|---|

A block may have parameters.
You must declare each
parameter at the beginning of
a block.

``
| integer1 integer2 aBlock|
aBlock := [:number |
   integer1 := number.
   integer2 := integer1 + 1].
``
	Create a block that requires one parameter.
	Each block parameter declaration begins with a colon, : .
	Don't use the colon when referring to the parameter within the body of the block.

``` aBlock value: 3 ```	Tell the block to execute itself, using the number 3 as the value for its parameter.

A block may have up to 255
parameters.

``` aBlock value: 6 ```	Execute a block with one parameter.
``` aBlock value: 6 value: 7 ```	Execute a block with two parameters.
``` aBlock value: 6 value: 7 value: 8 ```	Execute a block with three parameters.

``
aBlock
   valueWithArguments:
   #(6 7 8 9)
``
	Execute a block with more than three parameters. Parameter values are placed within an array.

A block may include temporary
variables.

`` | integer1 aBlock| aBlock := [:number | 	doubled | doubled := number * 2]. integer1 := aBlock value: 3 ```	Create a block with one temporary variable.

Conditional Statements

A branch in flow of control occurs as a result of conditional messages sent to boolean objects.

A conditional statement has three parts:

<conditional test>
<conditional selector>
<conditional block>

A conditional test is a message expression that returns a boolean object.

```
name == 'Barney'
type ~= #integer
number >= 99
file isReadable
```

A conditional test may be any message expression that returns a boolean object.

A conditional selector is a keyword selector understood by boolean objects.

```
ifTrue:
ifTrue:ifFalse:
ifFalse:
ifFalse:ifTrue:
```

A conditional block is any block.

Define a conditional statement that executes a conditional block only if the conditional test returns true.

```
(number > 99)
    ifTrue: [Transcript show:
            'yes']
```

If the boolean object returned from the conditional test is true, it will execute the block. If the boolean object is false, it will ignore the block.

Define a conditional statement
that executes only if the test
returns false.

(number > 99)
  ifFalse: [Transcript
  show: 'no']
	If the boolean object returned from the conditional test is false, it will execute the block. If the boolean object is true, it will ignore the block.

Define a conditional statement
that executes different blocks,
depending upon the result of
the conditional test.

number > 99
  ifTrue: [Transcript
  show: 'yes']
  ifFalse: [Transcript
  show: 'no']
	Parentheses about the conditional test are optional when the conditional test does not include a keyword message.

A conditional test may consist
of compound boolean
statements.

(number > 99 or:
  [number < 25])
  ifTrue: [Transcript show:
  'yes']
  ifFalse: [Transcript
  show:'no']
	Parentheses about the conditional test are necessary because of the keyword or:. The short-circuit or: operator does not evaluate its second test if the first is true. Note that the second test itself must be expressed as a block.

Iteration Statements

An iteration statement repeatedly
executes a block of statements.

Conditional iteration

```
[number < 100] whileTrue:
   [number := number + 1]
```

While number < 100, increment number.

Number iteration

```
100 timesRepeat:
   [number := number + 1]
```

Increment number 100 times.

```
1 to: 15 do:
   [:index | number :=
   number + index]
```

Add the numbers between 1 and 15, inclusive to number.

```
1 to: 15 by: 2 do:
   [:index | number :=
   number + index]
```

Add the odd numbers between 1 and 15, inclusive to number.

Collection iteration

```
#(1 2 3) do:
   [:each | number :=
   number + each]
```

The array evaluates the block for each of the array's elements.

```
collectionA select:
   [:each | each <= 10]
```

The collection returns a new collection containing all of its elements that satisfy (return true) the conditional test in the block.

```
collectionA reject:
   [:each | each <= 10]
```

The collection returns a new collection containing all of its elements that do not satisfy the conditional test in the block.

```
#(1 2 3) collect:
   [:each | each + 1]
```

The array returns a new array, containing the results of evaluating the block for each of the array's elements.

```
collectionA detect:
   [:each | each = 3]
```

The collection returns the first element that satisfies the block; return an error if no element satisfies the block.

```
collectionA
   detect: [:each | each = 3]
   ifNone: [nil]
```

Same as above but returns nil if no element satisfies the block.

Defining Classes

Define a sensor class.

| ```
Model subclass: #Sensor
instanceVariableNames: ''
classVariableNames: ''
poolDictionaries: ''
category: 'Sensors'
``` | A class name begins with an upper-case letter, by convention. Sensor is a subclass of Model. The superclass of sensor is Model; a class may have only one superclass. Sensor is in the class category, Sensors. Use a class category to group classes together, notably those classes for a major design component. |

Add the address and value instance variables to the sensor class.

| ```
Model subclass: #Sensor
instanceVariableNames:
  'address value '
classVariableNames: ''
poolDictionaries: ''
category: 'Sensors'
``` | An instance variable name begins with a lower-case letter, by convention. An instance variable is inaccessible to other objects except through accessor methods. However, an instance variable is inherited by subclasses.<br>An instance variable is initially equal to 'nil'.<br>An instance variable is untyped. |

Add a DefaultStatus class variable to the sensor class.

| ```
Model subclass: #Sensor
instanceVariableNames:
  'address value '
classVariableNames:
  'DefaultStatus'
poolDictionaries: ''
category: 'Sensors'
``` | A class variable name begins with an upper-case letter.<br>A class variable is accessible by each object in the corresponding class. |
```

Add a pool variable, StatusCodes, to the sensor class.

```
Model subclass: #Sensor
instanceVariableNames:
  'address value '
classVariableNames:
  'DefaultStatus'
poolDictionaries:
  'StatusCodes'
category: 'Sensors'
```

A pool variable name begins with upper-case letters, by convention. A pool variable is accessible by each object in a set of classes that declares the pool. These classes can access the variables stored in the pool variable's dictionary.

Define critical sensor as a subclass of sensor.

```
Sensor subclass: #CriticalSensor
instanceVariableNames: 'tolerance '
classVariableNames: ''
poolDictionaries: ''
category: 'Sensors'
```

Defining Methods

Smalltalk has two kinds of methods, class methods and instance methods.

The one class method you'll use most often is new.

Define a class method that creates a new sensor object with a given value.

`new: initialValue` `"Make a new sensor object` `with value = initialValue"` `	newOne |` `newOne := self new.` `newOne value: initialValue.` `^newOne`	The method name is `new:` . The parameter is `initialValue`. A comment is enclosed in double quotes. The special variable `self` refers to the executor of the method; here, it's the sensor class. The expression after the caret, `^`, is returned by the method. The default return value is the object itself. A class method is inherited by the specializations of the class.

Define an instance method that sets the value instance variable for a sensor object.

`value: newValue`
`  value := newValue.`
`  changed: #value`
	An instance method may access an object's instance variables, including inherited ones.
	Assign `newValue` to the instance variable, `value`.
	Tell the dependents that the value has changed. The special variable `self` refers to the executor of the method; here, it's the sensor object.

Define an instance method that sets the value instance variable for a critical sensor.

`value: newValue`
`  super value: newValue.`
`  value > tolerance`
`    ifTrue: [^false]`
`    ifFalse: [^true]`
	This instance method overrides the inherited method of the same name. Call the inherited method by using the special variable, `super`. Note that more than one return statement is allowed if each one is on a different branch of control.

Define an instance method that sets
the tolerance and value instance
variables for a critical sensor.

`tolerance: newTol value:`
`newValue`
  `self tolerance: newTol.`
  `self value: newValue`
	The method name is `tolerance:value:`. The method parameters are `newTol` and `newValue`.
	
	Note: By using this style (rather than assigning the values directly), you localize the actual value change to just one method. In case you need to broadcast such a change, such localization is very helpful.

Magnitude Classes

Magnitude comparison operators

```
>
<=
>=
max:
min:
between:and:
```

Magnitude subclasses

Character

comparison operators
```
<
=
```

conversion
```
asLowercase
asUppercase
asInteger
```

tests
```
isAlphabetic
isDigit
```

---

tests (cont.)
```
isLowercase
isSeparator
isAlphaNumeric
isLetter
isUppercase
```

Date

comparison operators
```
<
=
```

conversion
```
asSeconds
asDays
```

arithmetic functions
```
addDays:
subtractDate:
subtractDays:
previous:
```

utilities
```
day
monthName
weekday
dayOfMonth
monthIndex
year
```

Time

comparison operators
```
<
=
```

conversion
```
asSeconds
```

---

arithmetic functions
```
addTime:
subtractTime:
```

---

utilities
```
hours
seconds
minutes
```

ArithmeticValue

binary operators
```
*
-
<
+
/
=
```

---

unary operators
```
abs
negated
squared
reciprocal
```

---

tests
```
isZero
negative
sign
positive
```

ArithmeticValue subclasses

Point

mathematical functions
```
dotProduct:
normal
dist:
transpose
```

coordinate transformations
```
r
scaleBy:
theta
translateBy:
```

Number

binary operators
```
//
@
\\
```

mathematical functions
```
sin
cos
tan
log
exp
raisedTo:
rem:
arcSin
arcCos
arcTan
ln
sqrt
quo:
```

tests
```
odd
even
```

truncation and conversion
```
ceiling
rounded
asDouble
asInteger
floor
truncated
asFloat
```

Number subclasses

Integer

mathematical functions

gcd:	Greatest common divisor
lcm:	Lowest common multiple
factorial	

LimitedPrecisionReal

truncation and conversion

degreesToRadians
radiansToDegrees
integerPart
fractionPart

Fraction

fraction utilities and conversion

numerator
denominator
asRational

Integer subclasses

SmallInteger

comparison operators

~=

LargeNegativeInteger
LargePositiveInteger

comparison operators

~=

LimitedPrecisionReal subclasses

Float

comparison operators

~=

Double

comparison operators
```
~=
```

Collection Classes

Collection

testing
```
size
isEmpty
includes:
occurencesOf:
```

adding and removing
```
add:
addAll:
remove:
remove:ifAbsent:
removeAll:
```

iterating
```
collect:
detect:
reject:
do:
detect:ifNone:
select:
```

converting
```
asBag
asSet
asArray
asOrderedCollection
asSortedCollection
asSortedCollection:
```

Collection subclasses

Bag

A bag is an unordered collection of unique elements. A bag remembers how many times it's been told to add each element.

```
| bag |
bag := Bag new.
bag add: $a; add: 7; bag add: $a.
bag occurrencesOf: $a                 Returns 2
```

Set

A set is an unordered collection of unique elements. When told to add an element it already has, it does nothing about it.

```
| set |
set := Set new.
set add: $a; add: 7; set add: $a.
set occurrencesOf: $a                 Returns 1
```

SequenceableCollection

accessing

```
first
last
replaceAll:with:
replaceFrom:to:with:
atAllPut:
```

copying and conversion

```
concatenation,
copyFrom:to:
copyWith:
copyWithout:
readStream
writeStream
```

iteration
```
findFirst:
reverse
with:do:
findLast:
reverseDo:
```

Set subclasses

Dictionary

A dictionary is a set of associations. Use a dictionary to store values with keys.

```
|dictionary|
dictionary := Dictionary new.
dictionary at: #myKey put: 'Barney Rubble'
```

SequenceableCollection subclasses

OrderedCollection

An ordered collection remembers the order in which its elements were added. An ordered collection adds elements at its end.

```
| orderedCollection |
orderedCollection :=
    OrderedCollection new.
orderedCollection add: $a; add: 7.
orderedCollection addFirst: $z.
orderedCollection at: 1.            Returns $z
orderedCollection last              Returns 7
```

ArrayedCollection

An arrayed collection does not implement the `add:` message. Use a subclass, `Array`, when the size of a collection is fixed.

```
| array |
array := Array new: 3.
array at: 1 put: 'red'.
array at: 2 put: 'yellow.
array at: 3 put: 'green'
```

OrderedCollection subclasses

SortedCollection

A sorted collection has an associated sort block. When it's told to add an element, a sorted collection uses its sort block to order its elements.

```
| sortedCollection |
sortedCollection := SortedCollection
sortedCollection sortBlock:            Set the sort block
  [:elem1 :elem2 | elem1 >= elem2].    to order largest
sortedCollection add: 1; add: 7.       elements first.
sortedCollection add: 12; add: -3.
sortedCollection at: 1.                Returns 12
sortedCollection last                  Returns -3
```

Stream Classes

Use a stream to read from a collection, write to a collection, or both.

Stream

reading and writing
```
skipThrough:
through:
upTo:
upToEnd
next
nextPut:
nextPutAll:
```

contents checking
```
atEnd
flush
contents
```

character writing
```
cr
crtab
tab
```

---

character writing (cont.)

```
space
crtab:
tab:
```

Stream subclasses

ReadStream

Use a read stream to read from a collection. If you try to write to a read stream, that read stream produces an error.

```| readStream |```
```readStream :=```
```ReadStream```
``` on: 'Home, home```
``` on the range...'.```
	Create a read stream on a collection of characters (a string).

```readStream upTo: $,.```	'Home'
```readStream next.```	space
```readStream next.```	$h
```readStream through: $t.```	'ome on t'
```readStream readPosition```	15

WriteStream

Use a write stream to write to a collection. If you try to read from a write stream, that write stream produces an error.

```| writeStream |```
```writeStream :=```
```WriteStream```
``` on: (String new: 100).```
	Create a write stream on a collection of characters (a string).

```writeStream nextPutAll:``` ``` 'Home,'.```	Write a collection of characters.
```writeStream nextPut:``` ``` Character space.```	Write one character.
```writeStream nextPutAll:``` ``` 'home on'.```	
```writeStream nextPut:``` ``` Character space.```	
```writeStream nextPutAll:``` ``` 'the range...'.```	
```writeStream writePosition```	26

ExternalReadStream

Use an external read stream to read from a file.

```
| readStream bag filename |
filename := (Filename
  named: 'tagfile').
readStream := filename
  readStream.
bag := Bag new.
[readStream atEnd]
  whileFalse: [bag add:
  readStream next].
readStream close.
^bag contents
```

External streams are normally created by creating a `filename` object. Open an external read stream on the file.

Read one character; add it to a bag; continue until you read the end of the file.

Return a dictionary; its keys are the characters found in the file; its values are the number of occurrences of the corresponding characters found in the file.

ExternalWriteStream
ExternalReadWriteStream
ExternalReadAppendStream

Use an external write stream to create, append, or overwrite a file.
Use an external read write stream to create, read, or overwrite a file.
Use an external read append stream to read and append to a file.

```
| writeStream readStream
  filename |
filename := Filename named:
  'newOne'.
writeStream := filename
  writeStream.
writeStream nextPutAll:
  'Home,'.
writeStream nextPut:
  Character space.
writeStream close.
readStream := filename
  readStream.
```

Open the file for writing.

Write a string to the file.

Write one character.

Close the file.
Open the file for reading.

```Transcript cr; show: readStream upToEnd.```	Print the contents of the file on the transcript.
```readStream close.```	Close the file.
```writeStream := filename readAppendStream.```	Open the file for reading and appending.
```writeStream nextPutAll: 'home on the range'.```	Append the string.
```Transcript cr; show: writeStream upToEnd.```	Print the contents of the file on the transcript.
```writeStream close```	Close the file.

A PRACTICAL SUMMARY: C++

This practical summary presents the following key topics:

Classes
Constructors and destructors
New and delete
Derived classes
Member functions
Virtual functions
Overloading functions
Working with objects
Templates
User–defined type conversions
Scope
Streams

Classes

```class Sensor {```	Declare a new class Sensor.
``` float raw_data;```	Private access by default.
```public:```	Public means generally accessible.
``` Sensor();```	A constructor has the same name as the class and no return type.
``` Sensor(int addr);```	
``` ~Sensor();```	A destructor has the same name as the class, prefixed by ~. The ~, C's complement operator, is meant to suggest that the complement of a constructor is a destructor.
``` virtual void monitor();```	Virtual functions allow derived classes to provide member functions that override base class member functions.[1]
``` virtual void read_state();```	
```protected:```	Protected means accessible only to members of derived (specialized) classes.

[1]Even when invoked for a derived class object accessed through a pointer or reference to a base class object.

```
    char* model;
    int address;
    float value;
private:                          It's okay to repeat access controls.
    static char* object_type;     A static member exists as just one
                                  copy; it's shared by every object of
                                  the class.
    friend class Reader;          Allow members of Reader access to
                                  non-public members of Sensor.
};
```

```
class Critical_Sensor
    : public Sensor {              Critical_Sensor is a derived class
                                   (specialization) of Sensor.
public:
    Critical_Sensor();
    Critical_Sensor(float tol);
    ~Critical_Sensor();
    void monitor();                Redefine the monitor function.
protected:
    float tolerance;               Add a data member.
};
```

```
union Swap_Sensor {               Declare a new type Swap_Sensor
                                   with all of its members with
                                   public accessibility.

    Critical_Sensor sensor_1;
    Sensor sensor_2;               Storage is shared between a
                                   Critical_Sensor and Sensor.

    Swap_Sensor
      (Critical_Sensor s)
      {sensor_1 = s;}              Initialize as a critical sensor.
    Swap_Sensor
      (Sensor s)
      {sensor_2 = s;}              Initialize as a sensor.
} my_swappable;                    Declare this object as an object of
                                   the shared storage class
                                   Swap_Sensor.
```

Constructors and Destructors

Constructors:

```
Sensor::Sensor() {...}
```
The default constructor has no arguments.

```
Sensor::Sensor(int a=0) {...}
```
Arguments can have defaults.

Initialization Lists:

```
Critical_Sensor::(float t):Sensor(0) {...}
```
The order of initialization is base class(es) first, then the members, in order of declaration within class, regardless of the order in the list

Destructors:

```
Sensor::~Sensor() {...}
```
A destructor has no arguments and no return type; only one destructor is allowed for a class.

Union Initialization:

```
Swap_Sensor my_sensor = Critical_Sensor;
```
Define an object of the union Swap_Sensor, initialized by Critical_Sensor().

```
Swap_Sensor your_sensor = Sensor;
```
Define an object of the union Swap_Sensor, initialized by Sensor().

New and Delete

The new and delete operators manage the free memory (heap memory). The new operator allocates memory and the delete operator reclaims memory.

```
new <type-specifier>
new <(address)type-specifier>
```

```
new <type-specifier[array-size]...>
new <type-specifier(initializer)>
new <(address)type-specifier(initializer)>

delete <pointer>
delete[] <array>
```

The new operator returns a pointer whose type is a pointer to the type specifier. The delete operator must be given a pointer that was returned from a new operation.

`int* i_ptr = new int;`	Allocate storage for an integer and assign `i_ptr` the pointer to that storage location.
`char* str = new char[30];`	Allocate storage for an array of characters and assign `str` the pointer to that location.
`Sensor* snsr_1 = new Sensor;`	Allocate storage for a Sensor and assign `snsr_1` the pointer to that storage location.
`delete str,`	Delete the array of characters.
`delete snsr_1;`	Delete the object and call the Sensor's destructor Sensor::~Sensor().

Derived Classes

Base classes do not inherit anything.
```
class Sensor {...};
```

A derived class (specialization) inherits from a single base class.
```
class Critical_Sensor : public Sensor {...};
```

A derived class (specialization) inherits from multiple base classes.
```
class IR_Sensor : public Sensor, private IR {...};
```

When a base class is public, the public and protected members of that base class become public and protected members of its derived classes.

When a base class is private, the public and protected members of a base class become private members of its derived classes.

Member Functions

Member function declarations within a class declaration follow this format:

```
class Sensor {...void set_model(char*);...};
```

The function set_model takes a char* as an argument and returns nothing.

Short member function definitions may appear inline within a class definition.

```
class Sensor {...void read_state(){raw_data =
    port[address];}...};
```

Most member function definitions occur outside the class definition, using this format:

```
void Critical_Sensor::monitor(){...}
```

Virtual Functions

Nonvirtual member functions are ordinary C-like functions. You cannot use them polymorphically. However, you can redeclare nonvirtual member functions with the same or different interfaces in derived classes (see the section on Overloading).

A virtual member function uses the keyword "virtual" in its function declaration.

```
class Sensor {...virtual void monitor();...}
```

The virtual member function monitor has no arguments and returns nothing. Classes derived from Sensor may elect to redefine the monitor function. All redeclarations in derived classes must have the same interface, although the use of the keyword virtual is optional. You can use virtual functions polymorphically.

A pure virtual member function declares the function but not an implementation. A pseudo-definition of = 0 marks it as "pure."

```
class Sensor {...virtual void read_state() = 0;...}
```

A derived class (derived from Sensor) then needs to implement the read function. You cannot create objects of a class that contains one or more pure virtual functions.

Overloading Functions

You can overload function names. That is, you can use the same name for multiple functions, as long as each function's argument list is different (unique).

An argument list is unique if the number of parameters, the types of the parameters, or both are different.

```
initialize(int);
initialize(double);
initialize(char);
initialize(char*);
initialize(int, int);
```

You don't need an exact argument type match when you call an overloaded function. The compiler will use type conversion in an attempt to find the unique match. It will apply standard type conversions first, then user-defined type conversions.

You also can use function overloading to overload operators.

```
int String::operator<(String&)
String operator+(String&, String&)
```

Working with Objects

See the Classes section for the declaration of the classes used in the following examples.

`Sensor my_sensor;`	Define a Sensor object and name it `my_sensor`.
`Sensor your_sensor(44);`	Define a Sensor object and invoke the constructor Sensor::Sensor(int); `your_sensor` has address 44.
`my_sensor.monitor();`	Invoke the member function "monitor" for `my_sensor`.

Working with Pointers

`Critical_Sensor a_sensor;`	Define a critical sensor object and name it `a_sensor`.
`Sensor* s_ptr;`	Define a pointer to a sensor.
`s_ptr = &a_sensor;`	Assign the address of the object `a_sensor` to the pointer `s_ptr`.
`s_ptr->read_state();`	Invoke the `Sensor::read_state()` member function for the object pointed to by `s_ptr`.
`s_ptr->monitor();`	Invoke `Critical_Sensor::monitor()` member function. Since this is a virtual member, the type of object pointed to by `s_ptr` is examined to select the function to invoke.
`Sensor* zone[10];`	Define an array of pointers to sensors and name it `zone`.
`zone[0] = s_ptr;`	Assign `s_ptr` to the first location in `zone`.
`zone[0]->monitor();`	Invoke the member function "monitor" for the first sensor pointer in the array, `zone`.

Working with References

`Critical_Sensor a_sensor;`	Define a critical sensor object and name it `a_sensor`.
`Sensor& s_ref = a_sensor`	Define a reference to a sensor and initialize it to `a_sensor`. References must be initialized when they are defined.
`s_ref.read_state();`	Invoke the `Sensor::read_state()` member function for the object named by `s_ref`.
`s_ref.monitor();`	Invoke `Critical_Sensor::monitor()` member using the virtual function mechanism for references.

Templates

Templates add support for parameterized types.
Example 1—an array with a parameterized type:

`template <class Some_Type>`	Declare a template with parameterized type called `Some_Type`.
`class Array {`	Declare a new template class.
`public:`	
`  Array(int the_size)`	
`    {size = the_size;`	
`    array =`	The constructor creates a new array
`      new Some_Type[size];}`	of type `Some_Type`.
`  ~Array() {delete[] array;}`	The destructor deletes the array of type `Some_Type`. Destructors for the
`  Some_Type& operator[]`	array elements will be invoked, too.
`    (int index)`	Overload the `[]` operator. The return
`    {return array[index];}`	value is a reference to `Some_Type`.
`protected:`	
`  int size;`	Size of the array
`  Some_Type* array;`	An array of type `Some_Type`.
`};`	
`Array<int> int_array(10);`	Create an array class with size 10 and int as the parameterized type.
`Array<double> dbl_array(30);`	Create an array class with size 30 and double as the parameterized type.
`int_array[5] = 987;`	Assignments
`dbl_array[23] = 453.44;`	
`int my_int = int_array[5];`	

Example 2—a comparator with a parameterized type:

`template <class Some_Type>`	Declare a template with a parameterized type, called `Some_Type`.

`Some_Type`
`minimum(Some_Type y,`
`Some_Type z) {`
`    return y < z ? y : z;`
`}`
	Return the minimum value.

`int min; double dmin;`	
`min = minimum(10,20);`	
`dmin = minimum(23.5,55.3);`	

User-Defined Type Conversions

You can convert objects from one type to another by using single-argument constructors or by overloading the conversion operators.

`class Boolean {` `public:`	Declare the Boolean class.
`    Boolean(int bool = 0)` `        {boolean = bool != 0;}`	This single-argument constructor converts an integer value into a Boolean object.
`    operator int()` `        {return boolean != 0;}`	This conversion operator converts a Boolean into an integer.

`private:`
`    int boolean;`
`};`	

`Boolean my_flag, working;`	Define some Boolean objects.
`int bitmap = int(my_flag);`	Convert a Boolean object into an integer.
`int status = 10;`	Define an integer.
`working = status;`	Convert an integer into a Boolean object.

Scope

In addition to the normal C scoping rules for file, local, and function, C++ includes scoping rules for classes.

Every class declares the names of members that are contained with the scope of that class.

A member is always within the scope of the other members in the same class. An accessible member which is outside of scope requires its class name and the scope resolution operator (::).

Streams

Input/output facilities are not defined in the C++ language. However, standard libraries are implemented in C++ for input/output.

The iostream class provides bidirectional input/output. The output operation is performed by the insertion operator ("<<"). The input operation is performed by the extraction operator (">>").

The standard streams are:	
cin	Standard input stream
cout	Standard output stream
cerr	Standard error stream
clog	Buffered cerr

Examples:	
`#include <iostream.h>`	Include the iostream library header file.
`cout << "Hello World";`	Send a string to the standard output stream.

`int age;`
`cout << "Your age:" << endl;`
`cin >> age;`
	Ask for someone's age.
	Extract the integer and put it into an age variable.

The strstream library extends the iostream functionality for in-memory character formatting:

`#include <iostream.h>`	Include the `iostream` library header file.
`#include <strstream.h>`	Include the `strstream` library header file.
`char in_str[256];`	Declare a character array for reading.
`char out_str[256];`	Declare a character array for writing.
`istrstream istrm(in_str);`	Create a new input stream for reading, using the characters from `in_str`.
`ostrstream ostrm;`	Create a new output stream for writing.
`strstream iostrm;`	Create a new stream for both reading and writing.

The `fstream` library extends the `iostream` functionality for file formatting:

`#include <iostream.h>`	Include the `iostream` library header file.
`#include <fstream.h>`	Include the `fstream` library header file.
`FILE* in_file("infile","r");`	Open `infile` for reading.
`FILE* out_file ("outfile","w");`	Open `outfile` for writing.
`ifstream infstrm(in_file);`	Create an input file stream named `infstrm`, using the file descriptor `in_file`.
`fstream fstrm;`	Create an input/output file stream without opening a file.
`fstrm.open("myfile" ,ios::out);`	Open the `myfile` file for output and connect it to the `fstrm` file stream.
`fstrm.close();`	Close the `fstrm` file stream.

Appendix B

OOA and OOD Notation

This is a "class-&-object" symbol. It represents a class and one or more objects in that class. The heavy, inner rounded rectangle represents a class. The lighter, outer rounded rectangle represents one or more objects in that class.

Attributes are listed in the center section. Attributes describe what an object knows.

This is a "class" symbol. It represents a class that has no objects; only its specializations may have objects.

Services are listed in the lower section. Services describe what an object does.

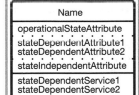

Additional attribute and service subsections... especially suitable for real-time systems.

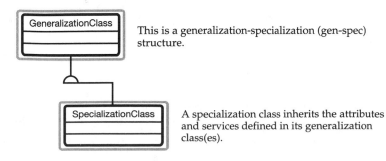

This is a generalization-specialization (gen-spec) structure.

A specialization class inherits the attributes and services defined in its generalization class(es).

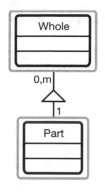

This is a whole-part structure.

The range or limit markings appear next to an object that needs to know about another object. In this example, a whole object may know about some number of part objects, and a part object knows about its corresponding whole object.

The "triple dot" notation is an ellipsis. An ellipsis indicates that some portion of a model is currently collapsed, hidden from view.

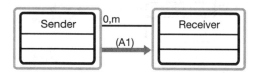

The solid connecting line is an object connection. The range or limit markings appear next to an object that needs to know about another object. In this example, a sender object may know about some number of receiver objects.

The patterned (dashed) arrow is a message. An optional message label consists of a scenario letter and message number (or it may consist of a name or description). In this example, a sender object sends a message to a receiver object; the receiver returns a response to the sender; the message is used in Scenario A, message 1.

This shaded box is a subject. A subject has a name and a reference tag (in this case, a number). A subject may be fully collapsed (as shown), partially expanded (listing its classes), or fully expanded (revealing its part of the model). Subjects guide a reader into major portions of a model.

HIC. Human Interaction Component

This shaded box is a design component. A design component has a name and a special reference tag (PDC, HIC, DMC, TMC). A design component may be fully collapsed (as shown), partially expanded (listing its classes), or fully expanded (revealing its part of the model). This box may be collapsed (shown here), partially expanded (listing its classes), or fully expanded (showing its part of the model).

Figure B-1: OOA and OOD notation summary.

Appendix C

OOP Principles

You've successfully applied a number of principles in this book. Here they are, chapter by chapter, in their order of appearance:

Principles from Chapter 1, The Count

The "I'm alive!" principle. Objects can be better understood by thinking about them and talking about them in the first person—"I know my own _____ and I can _____ myself."

The "read it again, Sam" principle. Read your model aloud. Do your words make sense? Do they really? If what you say doesn't make sense, don't blame it on object-oriented thinking (a lame excuse, indeed!). Instead, revise the model to better reflect what you want them to say.

The "-er-er" principle. Challenge any class name that ends in "-er." If it has no parts, change the name of the class to what each object is managing. If it has parts, put as much work in the parts that the parts know enough to do themselves.

The "amount of object think" principle.
Low	Functions—applying functional decomposition rather than an object-oriented partitioning across much of a system
Medium	Managers and data encapsulators—putting all the work in the manager, leaving its subordinates with very little to do
High	Objects at work—putting each action in the object that knows enough to directly carry it out

The "continuum of representation" principle. Use a single underlying representation, from problem domain to OOA to OOD to OOP.

The "one model" principle. Use a single model for classes, objects, and other constructs—across OOA, OOD, and OOP. (Multiple model approaches have floundered ever since first introduced in the 1970s.)

The "simplicity, brevity, and clarity" principle. OOA, OOD, and OOP notations and strategies find strength in simplicity, brevity, and clarity. What's needed is just enough notation (1) to communicate well and (2) to accelerate frequent, tangible results.

The "simpler specializations first" principle. For a class, systematically explore potential specializations, from ones that are simpler and easier understood to ones that are more complex.

The "perpetual employment" principle. Adding a class with endless specializations is not effective, but it can keep you perpetually employed.

The "what's the same; what's different" principle. For two or more specialization classes, ask what's the same? what's different? For differences in presentation, use a service. For differences in attributes and services, apply generalization-specialization.

The "do as I say, not as I do" principle. Use a generalization class to establish a convention that its specializations, both now and in the future, must follow, even when the generalization does no more than define the convention itself.

The "don't touch the whiskey" principle. Don't rapidly respond to management's "WHISKEY" cry: "Why in the H— Isn't Someone 'Koding' Everything Yet?"

The "no big bang" principle. Never, never, never write all the code at once. No big bang event will suddenly make it work correctly.

The "good politics" principle. Implement capabilities beginning with the ones that are most valued by the client, followed by lesser capabilities, in descending order.

The "success breeds success" principle. Implement capabilities that are easier. Demonstrate success. Then build on that experience to help you with more challenging capabilities.

The "tiny step" principle. Choose a very tiny first step. Get it working. Then add more very tiny steps.

The "strut your stuff" principle. Implement a rudimentary version of the human interaction class(es) early, so others can appreciate what you are accomplishing.

The "concurrent development" principle. Apply a concurrent activity development process: with your team, concurrently apply OOA, OOD, and OOP. Why? To improve your understanding of what is needed. To reduce risk. To deliver frequent, tangible results. To get working products to the international marketplace sooner.

The "smaller is better" principle. Put together a small team of up to 12 participants. Include people with special ability—in problem domain knowledge, in OOA, in OOD (human interaction, task management, data management), and in OOP. With larger projects, put together a number of loosely coupled teams.

The "I do it all; I'm the best at ..." principle. As a team member, you may have special ability in the problem domain, in OOA, in OOD, or in OOP. Get busy doing what you do best. And contribute in each of the other areas, too.

The "OOA on OOD" principle. To design an OOD human interaction component, task management component, or data management component, apply OOA strategies upon the respective specialized design area.

The "name a window by what it holds" principle. Name a window by what it holds, rather than by a project-specific, limiting name.

The "separation of concerns" principle. Keep problem domain classes, human interaction classes, task management classes, and data management classes distinct. Why? To facilitate change and reuse, by making it easier to add or change classes in one component without severely impacting the others.

The "I find. I show. I change." principle. For each human interaction object, define what it takes to do this: "I *find* the information that I need to find; I *show* the information that I need to show; and I *change* the information that I need to change."

The "communication then presentation" principle. Design how human interaction objects communicate with problem domain objects. Then incrementally refine the presentation of the results.

The "throw out the middle man" principle. Throw out objects that do nothing more than take a request and pass it on to another object.

The "selecting GUI classes" principle. For each OOD human interaction class, look in the available GUI class libraries—and consider the purpose of each class. Go for (1) an exact match, (2) a generalization you can specialize, (3) a part of what you need, or (4) something more than what you need.

The "discuss the design, not the designer" principle. Discuss the design and how to make it better. Don't tear down the designer; all of us make mistakes; unkind words are of no profit.

The "conservation of architecture" principle. Whenever possible, preserve the shape of the OOD architecture when programming it in an OOPL. Even if some of the classes have very few responsibilities, you'll benefit—the same class architecture will still apply when you add or change capabilities in the future.

The "strip search" principle. Take a compound name and strip out each partial name. Examine each partial name, and see if it might be (1) the name for another class, one that you need, or (2) something that is unnecessarily limiting.

Principles from Chapter 2, The Vending Machine

The "pay up" principle. Pay me now. Or pay much, much more later.

The "haste makes waste" principle. Haste makes waste, even with objects.

The "hacker's paradise" principle. No matter what the language, the universal cry for hackers is "I just code it up." Systems built this way are truly a hacker's paradise.

The "change, change, change, change, change" principle. Use a simple set of pictures to architect a system. Use a medium that you can inexpensively change again and again, encouraging and supporting creativity and innovation. Simple, flexible notation is essential.

The "emotionally attached" principle. Architect with OOA and OOD. Look for innovative ideas and apply them early in your work (while the project is young and your emotional investment in a particular solution is not as great). A warning sign? Rejecting new ideas with the words "after all, I've already built this much and it runs just fine." Such emotional attachment can be very counterproductive to finding new, breakthrough ideas on how to best architect a system.

The "perpetual employment" principle. Years ago, assembly language programmers learned that obscure coding resulted in perpetual employment. By shortcutting past OOA and OOD, you can do the same; the code will be so obscure and so brittle that you'll be sorely needed, forevermore.

The "Frankenstein" principle. Be careful what you hack up one night in the lab; the result may follow you for years to come.

The "variety pack" principle. Consider a series of human interaction alternatives, from simple to futuristic. If you are already familiar with just one or two approaches, work through a family of possibilities.

The "it's my name; generalize it" principle. Take all or part of a class name. Generalize it into a new name. If both names imply identical system responsibilities, then just use the more general name (encourage wider reuse). However, if the names imply different system responsibilities, use both classes in your model (increase the problem domain partitioning of system responsibilities).

The "service with a smile" principle. As an object, I know things and I do things, all for the direct or indirect benefit of someone who uses the system.

The "select ain't my job, it's your job" principle. As a problem domain object, let me set you straight: "select" services aren't my job; it's a human interaction object's job.

The "me, myself, and I" principle. Think about an object in the first person. Talk about an object in the first person. Write about an object in the first person. Put yourself in the midst of the architecture. "I'm a _____ object; I know my _____ ; and here's what I do: _____." Keep "it, its, and itself" to a minimum.

The "don't expect me to do all the work" principle. Don't just ask another object for its value(s), and then work on it yourself. Tell the object to do the work for you, giving you a more meaningful result.

The "more than just a data hider" principle. If an object acts as just a data hider when an object sends it a message, check if it can do something more. Even if the work is modest, you may find a way to improve both distribution of responsibility, and encapsulation, partitioned by problem domain classes.

The "good politics" principle. Design and code the capabilities that will most impress your customer (or perhaps your boss).

The "nice threads" principle. Design and code the capabilities that support a major thread of execution (a major scenario script).

The "backward through the script" principle. When programming methods to implement the OOD services, work backward through the script. Why? This strategy lets you start small, try it, and test it; then you can add pieces that can invoke the methods you've already programmed.

The "great code is readable code" principle. Great code is readable. By you. By other members of the team. And by those who will read your work in the future.

Principles from Chapter 3, Sales, Sales, Sales

The "person, place, thing" principle. Find initial classes by listing potential classes of objects—objects which may be a person, place, or thing.

The "high-speed breadth" principle. Push person, place, and thing. Go wild, identifying many, many classes.

The "high-speed depth" principle. Apply generalization–specialization and whole–part to each class. New generalizations, specializations, wholes, and parts add depth to your OOA model.

The "heart and soul" principle. Make an extensive list of classes in a problem domain. Then select a small number of classes . . . ones that together represent the heart and soul, the core of the problem domain under consideration. Do OOA and OOD on these first. Build them. Demonstrate working results. Then go for more.

The "behavior across a collection" principle. Let a collection do just the work that applies across a collection. Push work down into each part.

The "mail dominance" principle. Design small, domain-based human interaction containers that communicate and coordinate via mailboxes. Why? Better distribution of responsibility. And increased likelihood of reuse.

The "let the domain classes be your guide" principle. Let the problem domain classes guide you in organizing the classes in each design component.

Principles from Chapter 4, Go With the Flow

The "dig yourself a large enough whole" principle. Whenever you name the "whole" in a whole-part structure, use a name that is applicable (large enough to apply) across the variety of collections that you may need to support.

The "pay attention to the man behind the curtains" principle. Look past the current human interaction wizardry—and get to the underlying problem domain.

The "25 words or less" principle. Always, always, always begin by asking "What's the purpose of the system, in 25 words or less?" Put that purpose on a decorative poster! And use the purpose of the system to guide your every move.

The "targeted analogy" principle. When the true underlying problem domain is unclear, look for analogous systems that exist to achieve a similar purpose. Learn from the parallels between the systems.

The "my oh my" principle. Every service name should make perfect sense when the words "I" or "me" or "my" or "myself" are added alongside the verb in the service name. If not, change the service or change the class name so that it does make sense.

The "I'd rather do it to myself" principle. If an object in an OOA/OOD model acts on something not yet in the model, replace the object in the model with one that acts on itself. And let the new object do the action on itself.

The "analogy to class to metaphor" principle. Find a targeted analogy. Identify core classes. Identify which problem domain class and targeted analogy class are metaphors for each other. Add what you learned from the targeted analogy to your OOA/OOD model.

The "I'll be back" principle. If I'm a problem domain class, don't throw me away just because you think you can smash me in with another class. I'm probably needed. I'll be back.

The "interaction then action" principle. Examine needed`object interactions. And add the corresponding actions.

The "don't butt into someone else's business" principle. As an object, I don't butt into another object's business, sending it a message to peek at its values and then another message to get the real work done. Instead, I just send one message, telling the object what I want it to do (let it check its own status).

The "I get by with a little help from my friends" principle. Methods that get help from little methods that do one thing, and one thing well, facilitate reuse.

The "you make it so easy to use me" principle. When you define what an object does, "anticipate the ways that I might be used; and make it easy to use me."

The "mother-in-law" principle. Keep each human interaction object and its corresponding problem domain object loosely coupled. Don't let a mother-in-law move in to manage their affairs.

Bibliography

PRIMARY BIBLIOGRAPHY

Here, you'll find the books and the articles that helped—really helped—the authors develop and write this book.

Object-Oriented Programming Languages

[Coplien] Coplien, James. *Advanced C++: Programming Styles and Idioms*. Addison-Wesley, Reading, Mass., 1992.

[Ellis and Stroustrup] Ellis, Margaret A., and Stroustrup, Bjarne, *The Annotated C++ Reference Manual*. Addison-Wesley, Reading, Mass., 1990.

[Goldberg-2] Goldberg, Adele, and Robson, David, *Smalltalk-80: The Language*. Addison-Wesley, Reading, Mass., 1989.

[LaLonde and Pugh] LaLonde, Wilf R., and Pugh, John R., *Inside Smalltalk, Volume 1*. Prentice Hall, Englewood Cliffs, NJ., 1988.

[Lippman] Lippman, Stanley, *C++ Primer*, 2nd Ed. Addison-Wesley, Reading, Mass., 1991.

[Stroustrup] Stroustrup, Bjarne, *The C++ Programming Language*, 2nd Ed. Addison-Wesley, Reading, Mass., 1991.

Object-Oriented Architectures

[Goldberg-1] Goldberg, Adele, "Information Models, Views, and Controllers." *Dr. Dobb's Journal*, July 1990.

[Johnson] Johnson, Ralph, and Wirfs-Brock, Rebecca, "Object Oriented Frameworks." Tutorial notes. ACM OOPSLA, 1991.

[Leibs] Leibs, David, and Rubin, Kenneth, "Reimplementing Model View-Controller." *The Smalltalk Report*, March/April 1992.

Architecture

[Alexander] Alexander, Christopher, *The Timeless Way of Building*. Oxford University Press, New York, 1979.

ADDITIONAL OOP PUBLICATIONS

These are some additional OOP publications that the authors used and benefited from.

[Atkinson] Atkinson, Colin, *Object-Oriented Reuse, Concurrency, and Distribution*. Addison-Wesley, Reading, Mass., 1991.

[Barkakati] Barkakati, Naba, *The Waite Group's Turbo C++ Bible*. Howard W. Sams, Indianapolis, 1990.

[Budd] Budd, Timothy, *An Introduction to Object Oriented Programming*. Addison-Wesley, Reading, Mass., 1991.

[Cox] Cox, Brad, *Object-Oriented Programming: An Evolutionary Approach*, 2nd Ed., Addison-Wesley, Reading, Mass., 1992.

[Digitalk] Digitalk, *Smalltalk/V Windows Object-Oriented Programming Systems*, Digitalk, Inc., 1991.

[Eckel] Eckel, Bruce, *Using* C++. McGraw-Hill, New York, 1989.

[Goldberg-3] Goldberg, Adele, *Smalltalk—80: The Interactive Programming Environment*. Addison-Wesley, Reading, Mass., 1985.

[Goldberg-4] Goldberg, Adele, *Smalltalk—80: The Language And Its Implementation*. Addison-Wesley, Reading, Mass., 1983.

[Hansen] Hansen, Tony, *The C++ Answer Book*. Addison-Wesley, Reading, Mass., 1990.

[Harbison] Harbison, Samuel, and Steele, Guy, *C: A Reference Manual*. 3rd Ed. Prentice Hall, Englewood Cliffs, N.J., 1991.

[Keene] Keene, Sonya E., *Object-Oriented Programming in Common LISP*. Addison-Wesley, Reading, Mass., 1989.

[Linton] Linton, M., Calder, P.R., and Vlissides, J.M., *Interviews: A C++ Graphical Interface Toolkit*. Stanford University, Stanford, California, 1987.

[Meyer-1] Meyer, Bertrand, *Object-Oriented Software Construction*. Prentice Hall, Englewood Cliffs, N.J., 1988.

[Meyer-2] Meyer, Bertrand, *Eiffel: The Language*. Prentice Hall, Englewood Cliffs, N.J., 1988.

[Smith] Smith, Jerry D., *Object-Oriented Programming with the X Window System Toolkits*. Wiley & Sons, 1991.

[Sphar] Sphar, Chuck, *Object-Oriented Programming Power*. Microsoft Press, 1991.

[Stevens] Stevens, Al, *Teach Yourself C++*, 2nd Ed., MIS Press, 1991.

COMPANION PUBLICATIONS

[Coad-1] Coad, Peter, "Object-Oriented Patterns." *Communications of the ACM*, September 1992.

[Coad-2] Coad, Peter, and Yourdon, Edward, *Object-Oriented Analysis*, 2nd Ed. Prentice Hall, Englewood Cliffs, N.J., 1991.

[Coad-3] Coad, Peter, and Yourdon, Edward, *Object-Oriented Design*. Prentice Hall, Englewood Cliffs, N.J., 1991.

Index

Dear Object Enthusiast,

Hi, I'm Peter Coad. My team and I would like to continue serving you. So we've developed a number of ways to help out, going beyond what we can deliver within the pages of this book.

Get valuable follow-up with The Coad Letter®—free. I want to do more than just "write another book." That's why I write The Coad Letter, packed with the latest in practical object-oriented tips and strategies. As a reader of this book, you qualify for a free one-year subscription. (Why am I doing this? Because sooner or later you may need some help with object-oriented development...and if I continue to deliver the best in practical, up-to-the-minute, and helpful object-oriented insights, you might consider my company when you're ready for education, tools, and consulting.)

Experience a new OOA & OOD to OOP tool—called ObjecTool™. Key features include a complete, multi-faceted model; five selectable layers; full multi-platform support (Windows, Unix, Mac, and OS/2); support for larger models; reusable requirements and design templates; customizable strategy cards; model critiques; scalable postscript printing; and C++ and Smalltalk code generation.

Motivate others to get into objects—with The Object Game®. The Object Game—with its lively video, game boards, game pieces, whistles, and game ball—is a wild, entertaining, and thoroughly captivating experience. It helps people gain first-hand experience with "object think." Use The Object Game to help your team, your boss, and your customers get a qualitative understanding of what object-oriented development is really all about.

Experience innovative, thought-provoking, hands-on object training. At these exclusive events, you'll gain accelerated understanding of how to more effectively put objects to work on your project. How? You'll work with new advances in object-oriented development; you'll benefit from amplified learning using multi-intelligence engagement (it's highly effective...and fun, too); and you'll experience object technology for yourself, producing actual project results. Most importantly, you'll learn how to more effectively "object think"—and feel the satisfaction and confidence that comes from successfully applying object technology. "The course was great. Exceeded my expectations." D. Sena

Yes! Please send me:

___**The Coad Letter**—a free one-year subscription. I prefer:
   ___a paper edition (limited availability outside the US)
   ___an e-mail edition (available worldwide)

___**ObjecTool spec sheet**—with details on automated support for OOA & OOD to OOP

___**The Object Game**—$45 each. Send it now...so I can help others get moving with object-oriented development (add $8 shipping; overnight in the US, air mail elsewhere) ___ VHS ___ PAL

ObjecTool
"OOA & OOD to OOP"

___**Object training info**—tell me more about your "learn by doing" events.

All products come with a 30-day no-hassle money-back guarantee.
Prices and specific product offerings are subject to change without notice.

name   _____

title   _____

company   _____

home / work address (circle one): _____

The Object Game
"Fun & effective"

city _____ state/prov _____ postal code _____ country _____

phone _____ fax _____ e-mail _____

visa/mc/amex _____ exp date _____

signature _____

Object International, Inc.
Education - Tools - Consulting
7301 Burnet Road, Suite 102-259
Austin TX 78757-1022 USA

1-800-OOA-2-OOP (662-2667)
1-512-795-0202
1-512-795-0332 fax
object@acm.org

BUSINESS REPLY MAIL
FIRST-CLASS MAIL   PERMIT NO. 7135   AUSTIN TX

POSTAGE WILL BE PAID BY ADDRESSEE

OBJECT INTERNATIONAL, INC.
7301 BURNET RD STE 102-259
AUSTIN TX   78757-9974